Tecumseh's Bones

McGill-Queen's Native and Northern Series
Bruce G. Trigger, Editor

TECUMSEH'S

B O N E S

GUY ST-DENIS

McGILL-QUEEN'S UNIVERSITY PRESS   Montreal & Kingston • London • Ithaca

© McGill-Queen's University Press 2005

ISBN 0-7735-2843-1

Legal deposit second quarter 2005
Bibliothèque nationale du Québec

Printed in Canada on acid-free paper that is 100% ancient forest free
(100% post-consumer recycled), processed chlorine free.

This book has been published with the help of a grant from the Canadian Federation for the Humanities and Social Sciences, through the Aid to Scholarly Publications Programme, using funds provided by the Social Sciences and Humanities Research Council of Canada.

McGill-Queen's University Press acknowledges the support of the Canada Council for the Arts for our publishing program. We also acknowledge the financial support of the Government of Canada through the Book Publishing Industry Development Program (BPIDP) for our publishing activities.

Library and Archives Canada Cataloguing in Publication

St-Denis, Guy, 1960–
Tecumseh's bones / Guy St-Denis.

(McGill-Queen's native and northern series; 47)
Includes bibliographical references and index.
ISBN 0-7735-2843-1

1. Tecumseh, 1768?–1813—Death and burial. 2. Thames River (Ont.),
Battle of, 1813. I. Title. II. Series.

E99.S35T35 2005   971.03'4'092   C2004-906609-9

Designed and typeset by studio oneonone in 10/13 Sabon

For
John Dal Castledine
1927–1999
A native of Dunderdin, Western Australia

CONTENTS

Illustrations

Preface

My first encounter with the mystery of Tecumseh's bones was in the summer of 1972. I was eleven years old that summer, which was the same summer my father decided our family would be better off in the country. We soon found ourselves living in an old farmhouse out in the middle of nowhere, and surrounded by an agrarian landscape I repeatedly disparaged as being completely "dull and boring." It was quite a predicament, but I managed to cope by seeking out anything that offered the slightest semblance of interest. Much to my surprise, this quiet corner of southwestern Ontario soon began to reveal its fair share of curiosities. There were, among other things, a forest-shrouded "Indian" reserve, a murky meandering river, and – most intriguing of all – a ranch-style house.

Clad with imitation peeled logs and stained a reddish hue, this ranch-style house looked for all the world like a ranger's station in a national park ... except that there was no such park for miles around. It was a profound mystery and one that continued to deepen, until a well-intentioned grown-up ruined everything with an unsolicited explanation. The ranch-style house, as it turned out, was not a misplaced ranger's station, but rather a museum – although not a real museum like Madame Tussaud's. Quite the contrary. Our local repository was dedicated to the "dull and boring" history of a long-vanished church mission. With this revelation, I promptly redirected my energies to other curiosities. I had an abrupt change of heart, however, when a visiting cousin recalled the many treasures he had seen displayed just beyond the museum's faux log facade. Of course, all this talk of treasure could mean only one thing. Pirates! There certainly was nothing "dull and boring" about pirates. It was a point I reiterated until my parents finally agreed to a tour of the Fairfield Museum.

A kindly old gentleman met us at the front door, and there delivered what must have been an oft-repeated introduction. Founded in 1792 by the Moravians (a Protestant sect adhering to Hussite doctrines), Fairfield was later burned to the ground by the Americans during the War of 1812. The determined Moravians returned, rebuilt on the other side of the river, and ministered to their Native converts until 1903, when they transferred responsibility for the mission to the Methodist Church of Canada. In 1925, the Methodists joined forces with the Presbyterian and Congregational denominations to form the United Church of Canada. This merger explained the presence of the old gentleman, who suddenly and deliberately revealed that he was a retired minister. We were in for a sermon.

As the curator launched into a painfully detailed recital of the Moravian saga, I slowly edged my way back along a display case. Much to my disappointment, there were none of the much-anticipated treasures. All I found was a handful of charred artifacts from an everyday existence on the frontier. I decided it was time to leave. But in turning for the door, I was stopped in my tracks by a fierce-looking "Indian" – which was really nothing more than a wooden bust capped by a feather headdress. "That's Tecumseh," the curator called out. "There's a monument to him just down the road ..." I fixed my gaze upon "Tecumseh," desperately hoping to avoid further notice. The curator, however, mistook my attempt to ignore him with a spellbound fascination for what he had to say. Speaking from across the room, he explained that Tecumseh was the Shawnee leader of a powerful "Indian" confederacy who opposed American encroachment upon tribal lands. He continued with the great chief's war record, including his alliance with the British during the War of 1812. Then came the part about Tecumseh's premonition of his own death on a nearby battlefield in 1813, and that was when I heard the magic words: "*His body was never found.*"

I wheeled around and focused my attention on the curator who, somewhat taken aback, went on to tell us all about the mystery of Tecumseh's bones. Native tradition held that a band of loyal warriors returned to the battlefield under the cover of darkness and carried Tecumseh's body deep into the woods for a clandestine burial. After camouflaging the grave, they swore an oath of secrecy and then went their separate ways. I had a grand time conjuring up mental images of the lugubrious scene, but the daydream was shattered when my father asked if anyone knew where Tecumseh was buried. Pointing in the direction of Moraviantown, the curator replied – in a suitably melodramatic tone – that it was a secret "no white man can ever know."

Before we left the museum, my father bought me a book on the Moravians, a toy tomahawk, and a model birchbark canoe. I never read the book, I broke the tomahawk, and I have no idea what became of the canoe. But somehow the story of Tecumseh's secret burial managed to survive my careless childhood. Years later, as I searched for ancestors among the columns of old newspapers, the occasional article about Tecumseh's grave would momentarily reawaken my earlier fascination. Invariably, however, each and every one of these accounts was dismissed as the fanciful product of an overactive imagination. It was easy to ignore disparate tidbits of historical romance, until they began to appear everywhere my research led me. Eventually, I decided to investigate. After the better part of a decade, I finally began to understand the origin and evolution of the mystery in all its many aspects.

Following the War of 1812, most Upper Canadians in the western regions of the province believed that Tecumseh had been buried near the battlefield, and that his grave was well known to the Natives. This was the extent of their interest in the great chief's sepulchre. Then, in the mid-1830s, their curiosity was aroused by politicians in the United States who began to argue over the identity of Tecumseh's killer in order to win votes. During the presidential campaign of 1840, one of William Henry Harrison's more zealous supporters attempted to dig up Tecumseh's bones for a political rally. This "Yankee fellow" must have thought it a fitting gesture, since Harrison commanded the American forces at the Battle of the Thames, in which contest Tecumseh was killed. But to the citizens of a British garrison town known as Amherstburg, it was a despicable outrage and one they decided to avenge in the most patriotic terms possible. Impressed by plans to reconstruct the recently desecrated monument honouring Sir Isaac Brock, whose memory likewise suffered abuse from across the border, the leading gentlemen of Amherstburg likewise proposed a monument to Tecumseh. While none of them thought it necessary to acquire the great chief's bones in order to achieve their lofty goal, they soon realized that calls for a mere cenotaph would never be answered by generous donations. The endeavour failed, but Amherstburg's example inspired subsequent monument drives. It also served as a valuable lesson. Success was contingent upon a level of financial support that only the government could provide. And the discovery of Tecumseh's bones came to be regarded as the most effective means by which to secure this support.

The Natives of what is now southwestern Ontario reacted to the ghoulish fascination of their white neighbours by instituting a long tradition of secrecy and deception. Nor were they alone in shaping the mystery of Tecumseh's bones. Every now and then, some white devotee of Tecumseh would come forward to give a self-serving slant on the Native version of events. This intertwining of Native and white fabrications produced a mass of conflicting variations on Tecumseh's burial, which effectively and continually discouraged any serious attempt to unlock the secret. In 1985, however, John Sugden provided a valuable synopsis of the mystery in *Tecumseh's Last Stand*. My own investigation followed several years later, and was soon characterized by a determined effort to trace the mystery's many strands back to their respective sources. During this involved process, I was obliged to consider the motives of the many contributors to the saga – both Native and white alike. It was only then that I was able to begin piecing together the fate that befell Tecumseh's bones.

Tecumseh's Bones

Introduction

A SUDDEN BLARE OF BUGLES resounded through the open wood, and in the moment it took the British general to ask for an explanation the unnerving calls were repeated a second time. "That is the advance, Sir," his brigade-major tersely observed, "for the bugle is nearer."[1] Major-General Henry Procter reacted by hastily leading his steed toward the front line of his defence. After a few steps, he heard the third call of the bugles and the first sporadic shots from the muskets of lurking American snipers. "Damn that gun," Procter cursed, "why does it not fire?"[2] His brigade-major galloped off to investigate the cannon's silence, only to meet the gun crew in full flight. Turning his mount, the subordinate arrived back at Procter's side just as the American cavalry charged. A volley from the general's regiment slowed but did not stop the enemy advance, and with hordes of screaming mounted Kentucky riflemen bearing down upon them, the British regulars in the front line began to turn and run. "For shame men!" "For shame 41st!" "What are you running away for?" "Why do you not form?"[3] It was no use; the general's protests fell on deaf ears.

The Battle of the Thames, or the Battle of Moraviantown as it is also known, was a humiliating defeat for the Forty-first Regiment of Foot. It was also the finishing stroke in a series of misfortunes that plagued the British army in the western sector of Upper Canada over the course of 1813. At the outset of the War of 1812, daring attacks on Michilimackinac and Detroit secured the colony's extended frontier border from the threat of American invasion. The man responsible for these bold initiatives was Major-General Isaac Brock, whose boldness subsequently cost him his life at the Battle of Queenston Heights, near Niagara Falls, in October of 1812.[4] Brock's replacement as military commander of Upper Canada was Major-General Roger Hale Sheaffe, a good but cautious officer who thought it prudent to bolster defences in the central and eastern regions of the colony. Sir George Prevost, the governor-in-chief and military commander of British North America, was of a similar mind. Prevost further naively believed that Native warriors could be relied upon to combat the Americans in the west, with little or no assistance.[5] This latter strategy made it especially difficult for the officer charged with the defence of the remote western regions to retain the Crown's Native alliances. Fortunately for then Colonel Henry Procter, Tecumseh had already cast his lot with the British.[6]

For several years prior to the war, Tecumseh – the charismatic warrior chief of the Shawnee Nation – had been organizing a Native confederacy with the express purpose of resisting American encroachment south of the Great Lakes. By 1811, Governor William Henry Harrison of the Indiana Territory considered the threat posed by this confederacy to be so menacing that he took military action against it.[7] When the United States subsequently declared war on Great Britain in June of 1812, Tecumseh seized the opportunity to employ the British in his own struggle against the Americans. He was well aware that without the added strength of British arms, his loose confederacy stood little chance of halting the American appropriation of Native territories – and that the Shawnee would be among the first to lose their lands to the likes of Harrison.[8] His fears were allayed in August of 1812, when a combined British and Native force captured Detroit. With this victory, the confederacy was effectively consolidated under Tecumseh's control. But in order to maintain Native support, the great chief required additional victories. Brock's boldness, he believed, promised many more to come.

After Brock's untimely death, however, the British high command in the Canadas assumed a very reserved approach to the war in the western sector and, despite the threat posed by Harrison's massing of a large invasion force, Procter was left to fend largely for himself. Accordingly, when an advance party of the American army moved within range of Fort Malden at Amherstburg in mid-January of 1813, Procter took action to both appease the Natives and deal the enemy a decisive blow. Although Tecumseh had long since taken his leave, Procter mobilized a combined British and Native expedition, marched it to the River Raisin in the southeastern Michigan Territory, and there defeated the Americans.[9] Later, in April, he and Tecumseh launched a siege of Fort Meigs, on the Maumee River in northwestern Ohio, where the main body of the American invasion force was commanded by Tecumseh's old adversary, Major-General William Henry Harrison.

Despite heavy losses, the Americans remained undefeated in their fort.[10] Procter and Tecumseh were forced to withdraw, but they returned the following summer for another try. Unable to breach the walls of Fort Meigs, or to lure an absent Harrison back to its defence, Procter turned his attention to Fort Stephenson on the nearby Sandusky River. While Tecumseh guarded against a possible counter-attack from Fort Meigs, Procter ordered an ill-fated assault.[11] This time it was the British who suffered heavy losses, after which Procter was forced to retreat. Having failed to destroy Fort Meigs, the American supply line remained intact and Procter's situation at Fort Malden soon became precarious. Lacking reinforcements, provisions, and ordnance, Procter's problems were further compounded by Native allies who were becoming increasingly disillusioned. His only hope was the successful outcome of an impending contest for naval superiority on Lake Erie.

On 9 September 1813, a British flotilla, which had been hurriedly constructed at Amherstburg, sailed out into Lake Erie to engage an approaching American squadron. The next day, after a fierce battle off Put-in-Bay in the Bass Islands, the American Commodore Oliver Hazard Perry forced the surrender of his British counterpart, Commodore Robert Heriot Barclay. When news of the defeat reached Procter, he secretly ordered the evacuation of Fort Malden.[12] American control of Lake Erie not only compromised his own supply lines, it also left him vulnerable to attack. Procter concluded that his only course of action was to fall back to Chatham, about 104 kilometres inland from Amherstburg.[13] It was a sound decision, but the coy manner in which the order was executed cost him considerable Native confidence. Only when Procter promised that he would make a stand on the lower Thames River was Tecumseh able to avert the mass exodus of his warriors.[14]

On 23 September, the British abandoned Fort Malden and marched north to Sandwich (now part of Windsor). Four days later, as the Americans invaded Amherstburg, Procter's forces began a slow retreat toward Chatham. After two days of hard slogging along a bad road made worse by heavy rains, the British arrived at Louis Trudelle's farm on 29 September. They were then approximately eight kilometres beyond the mouth of the Thames, and still some twenty-one kilometres from Chatham.[15] Procter later blamed the straggling families of his Native allies for the delay in reaching Chatham.[16] Arguably, he could not allow Tecumseh and his followers to form the impression that their families were being deserted. However, Procter himself raised this very suspicion when he raced past them as they approached Trudelle's. It was no less disconcerting for his own rank and file. Although the secretive general was only going as far as Chatham in order to inspect its potential for defence, the sight of his carriage speeding off into the distance could hardly have been an inspiring sight.[17]

At Trudelle's farm, Procter stopped long enough to leave instructions for Lieutenant-Colonel Augustus Warburton to make camp there. The regiment remained at Trudelle's until the morning of 1 October, when reports of American vessels at the mouth of the Thames prompted an evacuation to Matthew Dolsen's farm, about five kilometres below Chatham.[18] Word was sent to Procter, who then hastened back to his army and, late in the evening of the same day, ordered an ensign to investigate the American advance.[19] After conducting some reconnaissance of his own, Procter satisfied himself that the reports of an American invasion fleet were unfounded. Once again he took leave of his army, so he could finish reviewing the place where he planned to make his stand against the Americans ... which was no longer Chatham. Procter had opted in favour of the Moravian mission at Fairfield, or Moraviantown as it was also known, located thirty-two kilometres above Chatham – and where his wife and family happened to be safely ensconced.[20] During Procter's lengthy absence, Warburton received disturbing news late in the morning of 3 October. The ensign sent down river had been captured by Harrison's advance guard.[21]

Warburton prepared for battle, but Tecumseh and a number of other chiefs withdrew to Chatham where they expected to find Procter ready and waiting to repulse the Americans. Instead, they discovered the place deserted and unfortified. Interpreting this negligence as deceit, the Natives began to abandon the British in large numbers.[22] In the meantime, Warburton decided to follow his allies to Chatham and, upon his arrival, found Tecumseh desperately attempting to check the dispersal of his confederates. Tecumseh's best efforts were of no avail, and soon only he and some 500 of his followers were left.[23] Later that evening, the remaining chiefs of the confederacy grudgingly agreed to make a stand with Procter, who they were led to believe was fortifying the Moravian mission at Fairfield. When Warburton learned that the Natives were planning to join Procter, he decided to follow their lead for a second time.[24] The next morning, 4 October, as the British regulars and Native non-combatants began their march, Tecumseh and his warriors waited in ambush for Harrison's soldiers. The Americans, however, had been alerted to the threat. Proceeding cautiously, they suffered only light casualties during the ensuing skirmish.[25]

News of Harrison's rapid pursuit reached Procter in Fairfield earlier that same morning of 4 October, and obliged the general to rejoin his soldiers. He accompanied them as far as Lemuel Sherman's farm, near modern Thamesville. Then, inexplicably, he returned to Fairfield.[26] The regiment resumed its march early in the morning of 5 October, but as the regulars came within three kilometres of Fairfield their flitting general suddenly reappeared and ordered them to form for battle. Procter, alarmed by news that Harrison had captured his supply-laden gunboats, was convinced the Americans would soon overtake him.[27]

A six-pounder cannon was quickly positioned on the Longwoods Road, while the British regulars were formed into a line extending some 230 metres to the right of the river, and through an open wood toward a small swamp. When Tecumseh expressed concern about American snipers, Procter thinned out the formation by ordering a second, or reserve, line. Tecumseh's warriors extended the front of this line, which arched forward from behind the small swamp and along the edge of a larger, much longer swamp.[28] Stationed in their impromptu positions, enduring the occasional gale-force shower of cold rain, the British and Natives waited for the Americans ... waited, and then waited some more. After about three hours, Harrison and his army finally arrived and prepared for battle.[29] By then, the British soldiers were utterly demoralized. Their dissatisfaction with Procter's indecision was detected by at least one officer, who heard his men grumble that they did not like "doing neither one thing nor the other."[30]

Procter's miscalculation cost him an orderly evacuation to Fairfield, where provisions awaited the arrival of his men, and where artillery was poised to check the American advance. Instead, Procter let his soldiers idle away, one hour after another, without so much as an abatis of felled trees to protect them.[31] It was a costly waste of time, as even this most basic of defences could have altered the outcome of the battle. Initially, Harrison planned to use his cavalry in conjunction with an infantry charge against the Natives on his left. But the intervening small swamp made that tactic unfeasible. Then came news of the loose British formation, and a change in strategy. Instead of sending his poorly disciplined militia infantry to do battle with the well-trained British regulars, Harrison decided to pierce their open lines with a cavalry charge. The militia would be left to prevent any outflanking manoeuvre attempted by Tecumseh and his warriors. It was a daring plan of attack, and one that proved the soundness of Harrison's judgment.[32]

The offensive began with a line of snipers, who quietly made their way within range of the British lines and took their deadly toll. Then, as a small force of American regulars advanced on the solitary cannon, four columns of mounted Kentuckians suddenly charged. The six-pounder never fired a shot, and a volley of gunfire from the British infantry only momentarily slowed the onslaught. The front line was rapidly breached. As his soldiers began to retreat, Procter rode up and tried to shame them into making a stand.[33] His urgings had no effect, although some of his officers at the reserve line managed to halt the fleeing regulars long enough that they "turned half round and fired."[34] This haphazard response had little effect on the mounted Kentuckians, who were soon outflanking the reserve line. Unnerved by this manoeuvre, the rest of the British regiment began to scatter.[35]

Procter reacted to this awful sight by reeling his horse around and making a dash for the Longwoods Road. Finding the way blocked by a throng of his own panic-stricken men, the general became disoriented and did not seem to hear his brigade-major propose an alternate route through the woods. In desperation, the subordinate rode off shouting, "This way, General, this way!"[36] Roused from his trance, Procter spurred his horse in the direction of safety – but he soon had second thoughts. Mindful of his allies farther down the line, Procter halted and asked, "Do you not think we can join the Indians?" The brigade-major, in glancing around, exclaimed, "Look there, Sir, there are the mounted men betwixt you and them!"[37] The American cavalry had gotten in the way and Procter, satisfied that he had done the full extent of his duty, made good his escape.

Unaware that the British lines had collapsed, Tecumseh and his warriors engaged in a fierce hand-to-hand combat with a contingent of the American cavalry. Although the Natives thought their position would deter such a charge, the resourceful Kentuckians had discovered a byway through the small swamp as they prepared to attack the British. Soon after the American snipers opened the assault, Tecumseh and his closest followers heard the sound of cavalry thundering toward them. Leading the charge were twenty riders known as the "forlorn hope," who suffered the full effect of a Native fusillade.[38] Two additional columns followed close behind, but the swampy terrain forced the cavalry to dismount and engage the Natives in a melee-style of warfare. Tecumseh led the Native advance and soon received a mortal wound.[39] Dispirited at the sight of their leader's death, Tecumseh's closest followers fled back through the large swamp and into the forest.[40] Farther along the line, where Tecumseh's fate went unnoticed, the Natives surged forward and drove the American militia back a considerable distance.[41] Harrison's intervention with a timely reinforcement then compelled these warriors to retreat upon Tecumseh's position, where they discovered the great misfortune that had befallen them. Defeated, yet still defiant, the last of Tecumseh's legions exchanged a "spasmodic" gunfire as they disappeared among the trees.[42]

Harrison's victory was complete. The British were vanquished and their Native allies were dispersed. Yet the defeat was not as disastrous for the British as it first appeared. They still retained their Native alliances, the American hold on western Upper Canada was tenuous at best, and the loss of Tecumseh actually worked in their favour. No longer bound by expensive frontier offensives in order to earn the support of his Native confederacy, the British were free to redirect precious resources toward strategic eastern campaigns.[43] The same held true for the Americans, once they satisfied themselves that Tecumseh and the threat he posed had in fact been eliminated.

Despite credible reports from several captured British officers, Harrison refrained from announcing the great chief's fate.[44] The mutilations inflicted upon the Native dead by vengeful Kentuckians, compounded by Harrison's own lack of familiarity with his arch-enemy's features, left considerable doubt in his mind as to the identity of the swollen corpse he viewed the day after the battle.[45] Much of his skepticism stemmed from reports of Tecumseh's death only a week earlier, which had proven false. Harrison was not about to risk another resurrection, so he prudently omitted any reference to Tecumseh in his dispatch to the American secretary of war.[46] Eventually, Tecumseh's death was confirmed. But Harrison's reluctance to point out Tecumseh's body gave rise to the story of a secret burial, and, in time, to a seemingly impenetrable mystery involving his bones.

Shaping the Mystery

ON A JUNE DAY IN 1840, a "Yankee fellow" by the name of Thomas Moores travelled up the Canadian Thames to the village of Chatham. His appearance in Stephen Probett's British Hotel excited little notice.[1] Many Americans stopped there to refresh themselves as they traversed the shortcut that Upper Canada provided between the states of Michigan and New York. This particular American, however, was not merely passing through.

Expressing a determination to visit the battlefield where his countrymen defeated the British and Natives in 1813, Moores solicited Probett's services as a guide.[2] Although Probett had only a vague knowledge of the battlefield, he was not about to be denied an easy profit. He readily agreed to the proposition, and then suggested that Moores employ the services of yet another guide.

Probett had Henry N. Smith in mind.[3] In addition to keeping a tavern, Smith carried the Royal Mail up and down the Thames Valley. He would know better than anyone where the battlefield was located. Moores proved amenable to having the extra guide, and soon he and Probett were on their way to Smith's Tavern, which was only a short distance upstream at Louisville. Finding Smith able and willing to help, the trio set out for the battlefield. Once there, Moores promptly chopped down two trees in order to fashion flagpoles out of them. His search for souvenirs then turned ghoulish when he happened upon some nearby graves. Convinced that Tecumseh was within easy reach, Moores violated several of these burials.[4] Gathering up the resulting jumble of skeletal bits and pieces, he hastened back to Detroit boasting that he had discovered Tecumseh's bones.

The inspiration behind this disgraceful affair was the American presidential election of 1840, in which William Henry Harrison and Martin Van Buren vied for the highest office in the United States. Harrison was nominated to lead the Whig Party, which had organized against the presidential power-mongering of Van Buren's predecessor, the Democrat Andrew Jackson.[5] In a raucous campaign characterized by passion, prejudice, and patriotism, the Whig Party promoted a home-spun image of Harrison. The "Log Cabin-Hard Cider" campaign appealed to the common man, and during a massive rally at Perrysburg, Ohio, on 11 June 1840, the Whigs exploited Harrison's reputation as an old Indian fighter.[6] This folksy convention recalled his defence of Fort Meigs in May of 1813, and ultimate triumph over Tecumseh at the Battle of the Thames in October of that same year. Moores, the vandalizing Yankee fellow, was one of Harrison's more avid supporters and, in anticipation of this "monster meeting," he had decided to honour his candidate by assembling some artifacts from the battlefield where Tecumseh was killed.[7]

Moores must have thought it a novel promotion, but Harrison's campaign was not the first to exploit Tecumseh's memory. In 1837, a Kentucky Democrat named Richard M. Johnson had capitalized on his reputation as Tecumseh's killer to win the vice-presidency of the United States.[8] Nor was Johnson the only claimant for this gruesome distinction. The uncertainty surrounding Tecumseh's death and the lure of public office had steadily increased the number of Tecumseh slayers over the years.[9] Yet Johnson remained the most likely candidate, and in the end he also proved the most honest.[10] On one occasion during Johnson's retirement, the oft-repeated question concerning the great chief's demise prompted a straightforward answer from the exasperated old man: "They say I killed him; how could I tell? I was in too much of a hurry, when he was advancing upon me, to ask him his name, or inquire after the health of his family. I fired as quick as convenient, and he fell. If it had been TECUMSEH or the PROPHET, it would have been all the same."[11]

In Upper Canada, where there was no political gain to be had from Tecumseh's death, the great chief's memory – while revered – attracted far less attention. This situation soon changed as news of the Yankee fellow's vandalism made the rounds early in the summer of 1840. The reaction was one of indignation, a feeling intensified by the report that one of his guides was also an ensign in the provincial militia.[12] After suggesting an investigation, which did not proceed, the editor of the *Montreal Gazette* dismissed the likelihood that Tecumseh was among those exhumed, as "no one present at the disgraceful outrage on the sanctuary of the dead could point out the grave of that gallant and lamented warrior."[13] The editor had a point. Not even John

Richardson, who fought with the British at the Battle of the Thames, could draw on his recollections of 5 October 1813 to locate the place of Tecumseh's last stand.[14] In April of 1840, about two months before the Yankee fellow paid his visit to the battlefield, Richardson travelled overland from Montreal to Sandwich. In approaching the vicinity of the battlefield, he made a determined effort to discover the grave, "which was said to contain the bones of the well-known but unfortunate Tecumseh."[15] Richardson, however, failed to find even the battlefield, for the simple reason that the "wood bore so monotonous a resemblance."[16]

At the time of Richardson's nostalgic search, it was widely believed that Tecumseh was buried near the battlefield and that his grave was conspicuously marked by a wooden post. In 1830, James B. Gardiner, an American Indian agent from Ohio, visited the grave and described the post as hewn, "three inches square and five feet long" with "faint traces of Indian [characters]," which had been drawn using red paint.[17] The claim that this was Tecumseh's grave appeared to be substantiated by the Natives themselves, who related that his body had been taken into the nearby forest for burial.[18] Harrison's reticence in making a positive identification of his arch-enemy's corpse allowed the Natives considerable benefit of the doubt.[19] And the curiously inscribed post lying beside a low mound certainly gave the impression of a grave.[20] This "humble hillock," as Gardiner called it, was located just beyond the northeastern edge of the battlefield, which helped to convince him that it was in fact Tecumseh's grave. "In the feeling of the moment," Gardiner felt compelled to take pen in hand and honour Tecumseh with a poem.[21] Unfortunately for the well-intentioned Indian agent from Ohio, his musings were misspent on a surveyor's stake.

Earlier, in February of 1821, the surveyor general of Upper Canada instructed Mahlon Burwell to lay out the Township of Zone. Several months later, as Burwell ran the baseline of his survey in an easterly direction toward the Thames River, he found himself in the vicinity of the battlefield.[22] After quickly recording in his notebook that "about here is the Battle Ground," Burwell proceeded midway through the sixth concession to a point near the Longwoods Road and within a short distance of the river.[23] There he planted a "centre Picket" in order to mark the middle of the concession.[24] This was one of five large survey stakes he placed at intervals along the baseline of his survey (now the Base Line Road). Although Burwell's notes make no mention of any mounds, his pickets might very well have crowned earthen bases.[25] Moreover, the position of the picket nearest the Longwoods Road corresponds with the location of the curious hewn post that Gardiner beheld in 1830.[26] Undoubtedly, this post was one of Burwell's elaborate survey stakes. Still, Gardiner did not just assume that the survey stake was a burial post; he had good reason to believe it marked Tecumseh's grave.

Unlike John Richardson, Gardiner had a guide in the person of a local settler named Thomas Shaw. According to Daniel R. Dunihue, who was Gardiner's nephew and travelling companion, Shaw was known to have been "on the battle-ground immediately afterward, *plundering the dead!*"[27] It was an abhorrent form of credential, but one that convinced Gardiner and Dunihue of Shaw's qualification to conduct them around the battlefield. After viewing a number of sunken graves, and pointing out the scenes of engagement, Shaw led his American tourists a short distance up the Longwoods Road to what he claimed was Tecumseh's grave. There, Gardiner and Dunihue examined a large mound which was "still 10 or 12 inches above the surrounding level of the earth."[28] The post, which was discovered lying alongside, was formerly "capped by a handsome Indian ornament," or so Shaw claimed.[29] But despite Shaw's authority in the matter, it seems unlikely that the Natives would go to all the trouble of marking Tecumseh's grave in such a conspicuous fashion if, according to their own tradition, he was given a secret burial.[30] Shaw, one can easily imagine, perhaps told his paying customers whatever he thought they wanted to hear.[31]

The newspaper account of this tour confirmed the widespread belief that Tecumseh was buried near the battlefield and that his grave could be located. It also inspired Moores in his attempt to appropriate Tecumseh's bones. Interestingly enough, however, this Yankee fellow's mischief was not considered just cause for the construction of a monument over Tecumseh's grave.

Almost a year after Moores's vandalism, in April of 1841, an anonymous admirer of Tecumseh suggested the erection of a monument to perpetuate his fame. Making comparisons with Napoleon, recalling past glories from the War of 1812, and goading his readers' British pride, Tecumseh's secret admirer managed to drive home his point.[32] In late June of 1841, a subscription drive was launched in Amherstburg – an old garrison town with many War of 1812 associations.[33] But Amherstburg's surge of patriotism was not so much a response to the Yankee fellow's attempted violation of Tecumseh's grave as it was a reaction to an outrage committed upon the tomb of another War of 1812 hero.

Early in the morning of 17 April 1840, an explosion reverberated through the small village of Queenston, near Niagara Falls. Upon investigation, the monument erected to Sir Isaac Brock on the heights above the village was found to be damaged beyond repair.[34] The name Benjamin Lett was soon bandied about as the villain behind the dastardly deed. Lett was a known conspirator in "most, if not all the outrages committed on this [the Niagara] frontier."[35] In the end, however, the Grand Jury of the Niagara District Assizes was unable to assign guilt.[36] But there was no mistaking the real culprit. It was America.

In Upper Canada, where border tensions during the Rebellions of 1837 left the population with a lingering siege mentality, the destruction of Brock's Monument was viewed as symbolic of American hostility toward everything British.[37] In June of 1840, while commenting on Harrison's presidential campaign at Perrysburg, the editor of the *Toronto Patriot* expressed what must have been the prevailing attitude of his countrymen:

We of Canada care but little who *presides* over the people of the United States; the policy of that people – for the people are the Government – towards England and her North American Colonies will remain unchanged; the same unmitigated hostility towards British Institutions, the same piratical plunderings and burnings will continue, and whether it be Van Buren who humbugs, or Harrison who blusters, the same deceptive trickery towards Britain and the British will be practised; so that as regards the effect of Presidential *changes*, we have nothing to hope for, indeed nothing much to care about.[38]

But even as the editor resigned himself and his readers to more of the same abuse, a reaction to the perceived aggression of the United States was beginning to mount. It came in the form of a consensus that Brock's Monument must be rebuilt, which was followed soon after by plans for a public show of support on Queenston Heights at the end of July 1840. As news of the monument's proposed reconstruction spread, resentment toward the United States heightened, prompting "John Bull" of Toronto to defiantly suggest "that a strong Martello Tower be erected in the place of the column, on which shall be mounted two ninety-eight pounders, to carry hollow shot, the effect and uses of which it is unnecessary for me to enlarge on."[39] Fortunately, cooler heads prevailed and, on 30 July upward of 10,000 people assembled around the base of the shattered monument, where they listened to one prominent speaker after another deliver stirring accounts of Brock's gallantry. The event struck a patriotic chord and generated a high degree of enthusiasm.[40] In essence, it was Upper Canada's response to Perrysburg.

The effect of the demonstration at Queenston was most profoundly felt in Amherstburg, where a group of civic-minded men perceived that they had their own abused hero to vindicate. Although Tecumseh had no monument to blast apart, the Yankee fellow's clumsy attempts to defile his grave produced the same degree of outrage. Amidst growing fears of annexation by the burgeoning republic to the south, Upper Canadians in the western region of the province reacted with patriotic enthusiasm when it was announced in June of 1841 that Amherstburg would raise a monument to Tecumseh.[41] Of course, the members of the newly-organized Tecumseh Monument Committee refused to admit the degree to which their fear of America had motivated them. Instead, one supporter of the proposed monument attributed their sudden interest in Tecumseh to an oversight: "we cannot but experience a degree of mortification that we have forgotten to pay that tribute of respect to the memory of the noble Indian warrior, who was Brock's friend and companion in arms."[42] The committee members, however, congratulated themselves for their initiative in erecting a monument to an untutored Indian. As they deigned to observe, Tecumseh's "sterling worth and noble conduct" entitled his memory to their "lasting gratitude."[43]

The "noble savage" stereotype, so typical in mid–nineteenth century North America, was echoed and exemplified by the editor of the *Chatham Journal*. That gentleman was convinced Tecumseh had been denied "a niche in the temple of fame" because he was a Native, which was all the more reason to honour his "civilized" qualities.

When we behold him an untutored savage, – roaming the [boundless] forests of his native land, free, unrestrained, no salutary law to check the rising dictates of his fierce nature, *self* the ruling principle of his race; and see a soul bursting from beneath a cloud of intellectual darkness, swelling under the most exalted feelings of benevolence and patriotism, rallying around him his warlike brethren, to join the standard of

British freedom, and nobly offering up his life, in the glorious struggle of Canadian independence, – he claims the admiration and homage of every true British heart.[44]

To the genteel classes of white society, Tecumseh epitomized the noblest of savages, and one who deserved a monument fit for a white hero. While race had been a factor in denying Tecumseh a monument in the first place, since it had not occurred to Upper Canadians that such an honour was appropriate for a Native, racism in the form of the noble savage myth was then vigorously employed to make amends.

In order to advance their monumental cause, the members of the Tecumseh Monument Committee had to raise money. Accordingly, they launched a subscription drive, and through newspaper coverage hoped to entice funding from other locales. Drawing moral support for the project proved an easy task; securing pledges of financial support was a different matter. As the editor of the *Chatham Journal* complained: "A very good lesson in human nature may be learned by any one desirous of studying that *curious* book, and that is simply by carrying round a subscription list. The patriotism of some totally evaporates at the sight, and in fond remembrance of their *pockets*, they forget they have 'a country.'"[45]

News of the subscription drive spread eastward across the province and even into New York State, where the editor of the *Buffalo Patriot* observed that "Col. JOHNSON ought to give liberally, for no man living owes so much to TECUMSEH."[46] This cynicism was a sign of things to come. As the summer of 1841 wore on, it became painfully obvious to the Tecumseh Monument Committee that the degree of support it had anticipated was not going to materialize. Small sums were promised occasionally, particularly from British officers in garrison towns, but the population at large proved parsimonious almost to the point of giving new meaning to the word. Much of this caution stemmed from the lingering effects of the Panic of 1837, a severe downturn in the trans-Atlantic economy which lasted for several years.[47] As late as November of 1841, the editor of the *Gazette* in London, Canada West (formerly Upper Canada), was sorely disappointed when he tried to coax his tight-fisted readers by reporting the subscription of £15 by officers stationed at St John's, in far-off Newfoundland. In despair, he asked, "Will nothing be done here?"[48] His ploy had no effect. Nor were prospects any more promising elsewhere in the Canadas, except in Montreal.[49] The citizens of the mercantile capital of British North

America took a great interest in the Tecumseh Monument, which translated into generous subscriptions ... and the establishment of a branch committee. Back in Amherstburg, the editor of the *Western Herald* lauded Montreal's participation in the project as "an example, most creditable to themselves, which we should be most happy to see followed by every city, town and village throughout the province."[50]

Despite this heartening development, the pace of the monument drive faltered as the topic became increasingly hackneyed. In September of 1841, a meeting was held at Chatham in support of the project, but several representatives from Sandwich and Amherstburg were soon at odds with their hosts. As Peter Paul Lacroix recalled, "differences of opinion as to the site and of the nature of the monument, caused as cold water in the matter."[51]

Lacroix, who was a surveyor of highways, was also the tireless promoter of a new line of road between Windsor and Chatham. In 1840, he named the road in honour of Tecumseh, as a "useful Monument to the memory of that late Indian Hero."[52] A year later, when he saw the subscription drive beginning to wane, Lacroix decided to make a pitch for the pledges: "I ... suggested the propriety of requesting the [Tecumseh monument] sympathizers of Montreal to allow their contributions to be applied on that road, which is laid out upon the very ground which the late Indian warrior and his party retreated through Chatham, [where] he crossed the Thames for the last time. No monument can be more to the public's observation than this road, being as much travelled by foreigners to and from the city of Detroit as any road in Canada."[53] The utilitarian beauty of Lacroix's logic was lost on those desiring an "ostensible" monument. But happily for Lacroix, his beloved Tecumseh Road was eventually improved at the expense of the newly-established Board of Works.[54]

After the divisive meeting in Chatham, the Tecumseh Monument Committee persevered with its original plan. Near the end of November 1841, a meeting was held to resume efforts for the erection of the monument in Amherstburg.[55] Determined to succeed, the committee decided to focus its fundraising campaign on the various British regiments stationed in the Canadas, which were considered duty-bound to pledge their support. After two regiments were successfully solicited, the editor of the *Brantford Courier* optimistically predicted, "Of course every Regiment will do the same, in which case the spirited Committee may, as they propose, commence the erection of the monument early in the ensuing spring."[56] The editor was sadly mistaken.

While some regiments contributed generously, and most sympathized, it was presumptuous to think that the British army in the Canadas would foot the bill for a monument to Tecumseh. By the spring of 1842, the subscription drive had ground to a halt.

With this disappointment, the monument was forgotten until September of 1846, when the editor of the *Toronto Herald* published an open letter enquiring about the state of affairs. Once again, Lacroix, the surveyor, insinuated himself in the matter by arguing that Chatham "should be preferred to Amherstburg, where the travelling public never will have the opportunity to view the monument."[57] Lacroix's outspoken support for Chatham, where he lived, belied an interest in having the head of his road graced with a monument commemorating its namesake. The citizens of Amherstburg could not be swayed, however, and neither could the Montreal committee, which continued to collect money on Amherstburg's behalf. After all, these subscriptions were specifically earmarked for the benefit of the Tecumseh Monument Committee in Amherstburg – not Lacroix's pet project in Chatham.[58]

By 1848, however, the Montreal committee began to lose patience, and in March of that year decided to go ahead with plans of its own. The driving force behind this bold action was James Holmes, the treasurer of the Montreal committee.[59] Holmes was an ardent advocate in favour of a monument honouring Tecumseh, and he derived much of his enthusiasm for the project from his brother. During the War of 1812, Benjamin Holmes, subsequently a prominent Montreal businessman and member of Parliament, served as ensign in the Canadian Light Dragoons under Procter's command.[60] He also happened to be the same ensign who was captured during the American advance up the Thames River in October of 1813.[61] Inspired by his brother's participation in the events leading up to Tecumseh's death, James Holmes was determined to pay tribute to the great chief ... and in Montreal if at all possible.

Writing to Major-General Charles Gore, the military commander of the Montreal district, Holmes acquainted him with the history of the monument scheme and alluded to the money "lodged in the Savings' Bank at Interest." Holmes then observed that "if this sum can be increased a trifle more, an Obelisk some forty feet in height, similar to that which honors the memory of Wolfe & Montcalm at Quebec, can be erected – and it is conceived such a memorial would do honor to the Dead, and to the Britons who erected it."[62] As Gore braced himself for a funding request, Holmes instead simply asked for permission to construct the proposed monument on the western or upper portion of Île Sainte-Hélène, where he was convinced it "would command the notice of all who descend or ascend the St Lawrence, & be in full view from the City."[63] Having sufficiently argued his case for a monument to Tecumseh on Île Sainte-Hélène, Holmes then raised the issue of a possible donation from the garrison of Montreal – which Gore had been expecting all along. Yet, in closing his letter, Holmes emphasized that money was a secondary consideration: "Even if I do not obtain another subscription," he informed Gore, "it shall be put up, but if the means at command be larger, the monument will be more sightly & commanding."[64]

Holmes's determination to secure a plot of land for Tecumseh's monument on Île Sainte-Hélène was more complicated than he anticipated. The final decision, he soon discovered, did not rest with Gore, but rather with the Master-General of Ordnance – who first required a feasibility report from the Inspector General of Fortifications. In advising Gore of this requirement, Colonel William Holloway of the Royal Engineers acknowledged that technically it might be possible to accommodate Holmes, since only a small parcel of land was required.[65] But, even if the proposed monument did not interfere with the island's defensive capabilities, he was convinced the Master-General of the Board of Ordnance would object to the public's right to approach it. Much to Holloway's surprise, the reply that arrived in June of 1848 granted the request.[66]

Despite this favourable decision, Holmes let the matter drop and a monument to Tecumseh was never raised on Île Sainte-Hélène.[67] His passion for the project fell victim to a highly contentious political issue, and his brother's involvement in it. Along with many other English-speaking businessmen in Montreal, Benjamin Holmes had become disenchanted with Canada's imperial connections. Britain's abolition of preferential duties on Canadian lumber and wheat, intended to promote free trade, actually intensified the onset of another crushing economic depression toward the end of 1847.[68] To make matters worse, responsible government (a form of limited self-governance) was granted to Britain's North American colonies in 1846.[69] Fears of political domination by the largely French Canadian population of Canada East (or Quebec) drove many of the English merchant classes, both Reformers and Tories alike, to desperate measures in order to preserve their financial and political status. The result was the Annexation Association of Montreal, which was established in 1849.[70] Of the many outspoken proponents of union with the United States, one of the most prominent was Benjamin Holmes.[71] Disillusioned by this treasonous behaviour, James lost interest in his brother's military exploits and abandoned his plans to raise a monument to Tecumseh at Montreal.[72]

The initiative shown by James Holmes, coupled with the knowledge that a substantial amount of money was accruing interest in a Montreal bank vault, had a reinvigorating effect on the Tecumseh Monument Committee.[73] In April of 1849, the editor of the *Amherstburg Courier* commended the renewed patriotism of his fellow townsmen: "Truly, we stand in need of some record to recall to our minds the enthusiastic loyalty that was *once* manifested to the British Government, and the love and devotion that the people of Canada *once* felt for British institutions. Is not the present an appropriate time to mark our gratitude for being still under British rule[?]"[74]

Apparently it was not, given the Tecumseh Monument Committee's failure to attract the necessary capital. Although the estimated cost of the Tecumseh Monument is unknown, the committee appears to have desired something comparable to the monument planned for Sir Isaac Brock, which ultimately cost – all told – just under £12,000.[75]

Ironically, while the reconstruction of Brock's Monument aroused the patriotism of Upper Canadians and in turn prompted Amherstburg's plans for a monument to Tecumseh, the attention commanded by the former precluded any possibility of the latter. With barely enough money to lavish on one hero, let alone two, the subscription drive for the new Brock Monument served as extremely hard competition. Delays in constructing the Brock Monument also gave rise to concerns of fiscal mismanagement, and the Tecumseh Monument Committee began to feel the effect of an increasingly wary public very soon after it organized in June of 1841. In August of that year, several prominent gentlemen from Niagara (now Niagara-on-the-Lake) stipulated that the pledges they canvassed for Tecumseh's monument should not be expected immediately, "as the case of General Brock's monument furnishes good reason for many persons to say that they will not contribute until something is commenced to show that the expectations of the Committee and Secretaries at Amherstburgh are sanguine [or likely to succeed]."[76] This dilemma persisted and proved a major factor in the failure of the Tecumseh Monument Committee in 1849.

Several years later, in 1853, construction finally began on Sir Isaac Brock's new shrine on Queenston Heights.[77] After three years spent erecting the monument, and another three years devoted to landscaping the grounds around its base, the magnificent column rising fifty-six metres was at last dedicated in 1859.[78] Not once during the ceremony was anything said about a possible monument for Tecumseh. Yet the glaring imbalance in the way British Canadians honoured their heroes was impossible to ignore, and eventually Brock's commanding monument would once again inspire action on Tecumseh's behalf.

Benson J. Lossing's portrait of Tecumseh, which he published in 1869, was based on a much earlier sketch made by a fur trader named Pierre Le Dru. Lossing was an accomplished artist, and thus his treatment of Tecumseh's facial features is likely a faithful copy of Le Dru's original work. Lossing, however, is known to have taken liberty with the chief's attire. Tecumseh might have worn a British brigadier-general's coat on occasion, but he never held the rank of a commissioned officer in the British army. *Pictorial Field-Book of the War of 1812*

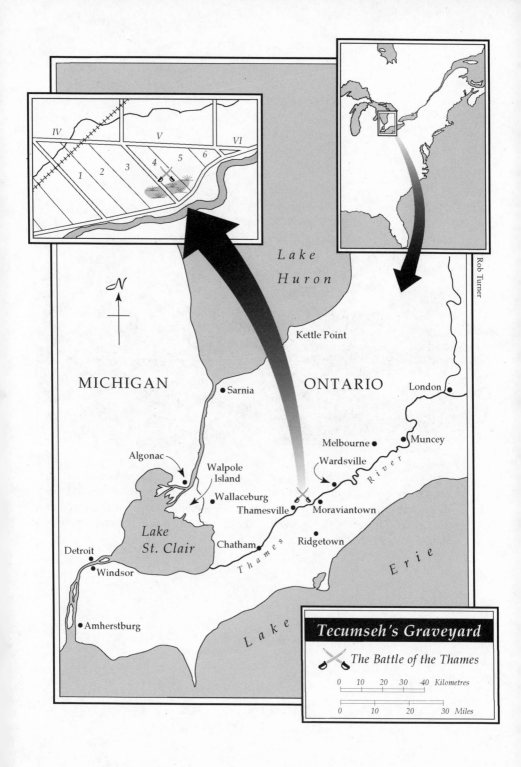

Rob Turner

IV V VI
1 2 3 4 5 6

N

Lake Huron

MICHIGAN   ONTARIO

Kettle Point

London

Sarnia

Melbourne   Muncey

Algonac   Wardsville

Walpole Island

Wallaceburg   *River*

Thamesville   Moraviantown

Lake St. Clair

Detroit   Chatham   Ridgetown

Windsor   *Thames*   *Erie*

Amherstburg   *Lake*

Tecumseh's Graveyard

The Battle of the Thames

0   10   20   30   40 Kilometres

0   10   20   30 Miles

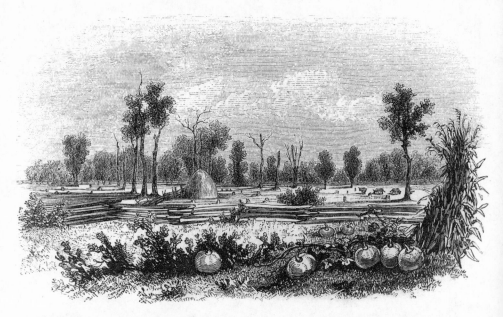

This view of the battlefield was drawn by Benson J. Lossing in 1860, and depicts the early stages of its transformation from forest to farm. Lossing made this sketch from roughly the Native position, looking in a southerly direction toward the Thames River (marked in the distance by a line of trees). *Pictorial Field-Book of the War of 1812*

By the time this sketch was made, circa 1883, all traces of the battlefield had disappeared. The Longwoods Road had also been rerouted to the riverbank – probably to avoid swampy terrain. Highway improvements over the last 120 years have gradually moved the road back to nearly its original route. *Picturesque Canada*

The site of the Battle of the Thames would be difficult to ascertain without the nearby Tecumseh Monument. This picture, taken in the autumn of 2002, looks across the Longwoods Road in a southwesterly direction toward lot 4, Gore of Zone Township. Courtesy Guy St-Denis

A Patriotic Fiasco

IN 1869, SEVERAL OLD GENTLEMEN of Toronto decided it was high time to organize a historical society. Dubbing themselves the York Pioneers, they set about preserving their recollections of earlier days in and around the provincial capital.[1] These nostalgic seniors were pleasantly surprised when their mission statement met with wide popular appeal. Their meetings were well-attended, and at the end of the first year one of the Pioneers decided to expand the society's range of operations by suggesting an excursion to Brock's Monument. Towering high atop Queenston Heights, the majestic column was unquestionably the most appropriate backdrop for a program dedicated to the "Hero of Upper Canada" – as Sir Isaac Brock was often described. The idea was heartily endorsed, and it was no coincidence that the date chosen was the fifty-eighth anniversary of Brock's capture of Detroit in 1812.[2]

On 16 August 1870, the Pioneers, along with some 200 friends and relatives, boarded a steamboat and set out across Lake Ontario for Queenston on the Niagara River. There, upon the heights and in the shadow of Brock's Monument, they enjoyed picnic lunches followed by an afternoon of speeches idolizing their hero.[3] The outing proved so successful that the Pioneers planned another trip to Queenston Heights. At the end of July 1871, the Pioneers returned to Brock's monument, accompanied by several hundred representatives from similar societies across southwestern Ontario.[4]

Having sung Brock's praises the year before, the Pioneers turned to Tecumseh for patriotic inspiration. It was a logical enough progression, and one that focused considerable attention on the regrettable fact that Tecumseh had no towering monument to honour him ... or to picnic around. This sad state of affairs seriously perturbed one of the Pioneers, a millstone manufacturer from Toronto by the name of Richard H. Oates, who took it upon himself to rectify the injustice.[5] In a rousing speech extolling Tecumseh, Oates acquainted his audience with the great chief's exploits – which also served to set the stage for the next speaker. In answer to his name, Joseph T. Kerby, a newspaper editor from Niagara (now Niagara-on-the-Lake), stepped up and abruptly resolved that a special committee be formed to raise funds for an obelisk to "mark the spot where the brave Shawnee chief Tecumseh fell defending, with the British, the soil of Canada."[6] Amid great cheering, the resolution was easily carried. Bolstered by this overwhelming show of support, the York Pioneers' Tecumseh Monument Fund Committee optimistically arranged to lay the corner stone in June of 1872. As members of the committee soon realized, however, loud cheers were easier to garner than hard cash.[7]

Little had changed since the monument drives of the 1840s, and the people of Ontario certainly were no more inclined to fund a monument to Tecumseh than their forebears had been thirty years earlier. Much of this reluctance had to do with the proposed site of the monument, which had already been decided in favour of the distant and relatively remote site of the battlefield. By the end of June 1872, having failed to accomplish anything at the battlefield, the committee members decided that Queenston Heights was a better location for Tecumseh's monument.[8] The laying of the cornerstone was optimistically rescheduled to take place in August of 1873. But when only a small fraction of the estimated $20,000 required to build a "desirable" monument was raised, the Pioneers gave up on the idea of an obelisk for Tecumseh.[9]

Oates, however, remained hopeful and soon began to consider another means by which to commemorate Tecumseh. It was the United Canadian Association. Established in 1872, the United Canadian Association was an amalgamation of historical and patriotic organizations which shared a common goal of fostering a greater sense of Canadian nationalism.[10] Hero-worship was one of the principle methods employed by the United Canadians in pursuing their goal, and, as such, Richard Oates was convinced that Tecumseh would one day meet with their approval.[11]

After a lapse of several years, in June of 1876, Oates suddenly decided to enlist the United Canadians on Tecumseh's behalf. Having been elected their president the year before, Oates was in a perfect position to promote a monument to Tecumseh.[12] However, when he called a special meeting of the United Canadians, it quickly became clear that a monument was not the issue. It was Tecumseh himself. As his astonished colleagues listened, Oates expressed his determination to seek out Tecumseh's bones and arrange for their burial next to those of Brock on Queenston Heights. It was an extraordinary proposal, and yet Oates was convinced that he could find Tecumseh's grave. Fatefully, he persuaded his fellow United Canadians to approve an expedition.[13]

On the same day that America celebrated a century of nationhood, Richard Oates, the millstone manufacturer, Solomon J.J. Brown, a farmer, and George A. Clement, a bookseller, boarded a westbound train of the Canada Southern Railway (now the Michigan Central) at Niagara.[14] When the train pulled into Hagersville, Oates and his party were joined by George H.M. Johnson, chief of the Six Nations Reserve near Brantford. It was a crucial rendezvous, given that Johnson carried a map to Tecumseh's grave.[15] This curious little chart, drawn as it was on the last page of an old pocket diary, was the source of Oates's confidence. According to Johnson, it was based on the eyewitness account of Ockawandah, a deceased Shawnee elder who once lived on the Six Nations Reserve. Ockawandah claimed to have fought at the Battle of the Thames, after which he and two other warriors retrieved Tecumseh's body and secretly buried it. Although Ockawandah lived out his days among the Mohawk of the Six Nations, he reputedly made occasional visits to Tecumseh's grave. For this reason, despite the passage of almost half a century, he was able to provide the necessary co-ordinates in order for Johnson to map the location of Tecumseh's grave.[16]

Johnson's map might have been dismissed, had it not been for the corroboration of a station master at Onondaga on the Grand Trunk Railway (now the Canadian National). During his own tour of the battlefield, which he made some years earlier, A.J. Nelles made enquiries regarding Tecumseh's burial. An old man in the neighbourhood directed him to a grave, which had been pointed out to him by a Shawnee elder. Timothy Snake of the Moraviantown Reserve was well known for his own claims to have been present at Tecumseh's burial – claims he frequently recounted before his death in 1869.[17] Nelles made a sketch of the grave's location, which he subsequently turned over to the United Canadians for comparison with Johnson's map. When the two maps were found to agree with one another, Ockawandah's story was considered substantiated. All the United Canadians had to do was follow Johnson's map and, where a line extending due west from a log house on the battlefield intersected the boundary of the next lot, Tecumseh's grave would be found.[18] It was a golden opportunity, and Oates was determined not to let it slip away.

At Highgate, the nearest station to Moraviantown on the Canada

Southern, the United Canadians left the train and proceeded to the vicinity of the battlefield. Over the next two days, they conducted an investigation consisting largely of interviews with local farmers and Natives.[19] Late in the afternoon of 6 July, the United Canadians finally began the archaeological phase of their expedition.[20] There was just one problem. The log house was nowhere to be found. The determined United Canadians, however, soon learned that the house was formerly situated on the farm of William Watts, and with some diligent searching they managed to trace its outline in the soil.[21] Wasting no time, they paced their way into the late day sun until they came to a snake fence on the lot line. Oates later reported that "on reaching the spot marked on the diagram and examining it[,] we discovered what appeared to be the outline of a grave which had evidently been hastily filled in, as the earth had sunk about eight inches."[22] This depression seemed to bear out what Ockawandah had said about the burial, and how the warriors "had been obliged to inter Tecumseh in a hurry; and that, so as to prevent the discovery of the grave by the enemy[,] they had studiously avoided making any mound; but had rather carefully smoothed the ground so as to make it appear uniform with the surrounding earth."[23]

The United Canadians immediately began to dig. At a depth of about seventy-six centimetres, they came upon a scalping knife and the flint lock mechanism of a musket – items which Ockawandah claimed would identify Tecumseh's grave.[24] After carefully excavating a bit deeper, they discovered a partially decayed bone, "which appeared to be a thigh-bone."[25] By this point, the United Canadians were absolutely convinced that they stood on the edge of Tecumseh's grave and any bones, short of a mastodon's, would have been hailed as those of the great chief. Although Oates and his United Canadians were eager to complete the exhumation, they were forced to quit and make plans to finish the job at a later date. It had become too dark.[26] It had also become uncomfortably warm.

In the two days leading up to their dig, the United Canadians had managed to inflame passions in much of the surrounding countryside. While the Natives of Moraviantown favoured the idea of removing Tecumseh's bones to Brock's Monument, their white neighbours were decidedly opposed to the suggestion, and even threatened to forcibly prevent it. Oates dismissed the uproar as the product of "local jealousies."[27] The editor of the *Chatham Planet* probably came closer to the truth. In defence of the jealous locals, he asserted that they were just as willing to support the United Canadians in their search for

Tecumseh's grave as anyone else. At the same time, however, they saw no reason why the "shaft that is to perpetuate for ages to come his good name, his great fame, and his self-sacrificing valour" should not be at the site of his "last and bravest exploit."[28] It did not matter that the United Canadians had already established there was insufficient funds for a monument to Tecumseh. Their logic that his remains should be placed under Brock's Monument, rather than left hidden without honours, had absolutely no effect. The jealous locals were not about to relinquish what they saw as their best chance for some future monument.

These "local jealousies" were a great nuisance to Oates. He was especially annoyed that they had prevented him from fully excavating the grave he was sure belonged to Tecumseh. But Oates did not intend to be put off for long, and he had little patience for anyone who interfered with his plans. Nor did John Ross Robertson, the editor of the Toronto *Telegram*, who empathized that it was

only when it became known that outsiders valued these remains that the people of Bothwell and neighbourhood awoke to the fact that they possessed a treasure which was worth preserving and keeping in honoured memory. Had the proposition to erect a monument to Tecumseh emanated from the neighbourhood of the slaughter of the fifth October, it would have been universally admitted that the fittest site for such a monument would have been either the field whereon he fell or the spot where his remains were committed to their rest. But in view of the inappreciation and inaction displayed by the malcontents, it will be universally allowed that they have forfeited all claims to the pretensions they now at the eleventh hour so strenuously put forward.[29]

Emboldened by this and similar support, the United Canadians made plans to complete the exhumation. But before they could set out for the battlefield, they first had to neutralize the local opposition. The approach they chose was influenced by the favourable reception they had received from the Natives of Moraviantown, which led Oates and his colleagues to believe that they could expect the same treatment from the Grand General Indian Council of Ontario.[30] The United Canadians thought a Native vote of approval would grant them full authority to retrieve Tecumseh's bones. It was an appealing concept, and the United Canadians must have thought it a happy coincidence when they learned that the next meeting of the Grand Council would soon convene on the Saugeen Reserve.[31]

The United Canadians had just enough time to make the trip and present their case. As Oates predicted, the assembled chiefs and delegates responded favourably to the request but, before they could grant the United Canadians' wish, the Natives in turn had to seek the approval of the governor-general of Canada.[32] As a matter of routine, the Department of Indian Affairs interceded and replied that the petition of the Grand Council would be taken into consideration "upon the Department being informed of the whereabouts of the late Chief's remains."[33] Oates was unwilling to divulge this information, and rather than waste more time, he decided to circumvent the Department of Indian Affairs by seeking the opinion of the attorney general for Ontario.

Oliver Mowat saw no legal reason why the United Canadians should not proceed with their plans. Disregarding the jurisdiction of the Department of Indian Affairs, Mowat gave Oates permission to bury Tecumseh's bones at Brock's Monument.[34] Soon after, on 15 July 1876, the public was served notice when an unidentified correspondent to the Toronto *Mail*, possibly Oates himself, confidently predicted that "the different towns in the west which have been claiming the right to have the ashes of Tecumseh, and professing a desire to erect a monument to him, will respect the wish expressed in the resolution [of the Grand Council], and join in the demonstration in removing his ashes alongside those of Brock, if we find the grave, and of that I have very little doubt."[35] What the United Canadians failed to recognize, however, was that flaunting their authority in such a flagrant manner did not command respect; it invited disaster.

On 29 August 1876, almost two months after their initial expedition, the United Canadians finally set out to complete the exhumation. The same gentlemen agreed to venture back to the battlefield, but before they got there, Oates parted company in order to go and investigate another lead.[36] The next day, Oates's colleagues proceeded without him and made short work of unearthing "the skull and the greater portion of the skeleton."[37] They failed to find some of the smallest bones, which they concluded must have moldered away. It appeared reasonable that some of Tecumseh's bones would be missing, given the "length of time which has elapsed since the Chief was interred; and from the fact that the bones were so near the surface that the action of the frost and water would reach them."[38] In any case, the earlier recovery of the scalping knife and gun mechanism far outweighed the importance of a few missing bones. Moreover, one of the leg bones showed signs of a fracture, which seemed to agree with an observation made by Chief Johnson's aged father that Tecumseh was "a little lame in the right leg."[39]

Hoping to avoid a confrontation with jealous locals, the United Canadians quickly gathered up the earthly remains of their hero and beat a hasty retreat. But before they got very far, they were met by a Native from Moraviantown, one William Logan, who casually enquired about the nature of their business.[40] Unable to contain themselves, the United Canadians triumphantly announced their great discovery. Logan was unimpressed and countered by insisting that a scalping knife and gun would have to be found in order to positively establish Tecumseh's identity.[41] When Solomon Brown eagerly replied that they had found the very items Logan described, the Native placed both his hands on Brown's shoulders and exclaimed: "Then you have found Tecumseh, and need make no further search."[42]

Chief Frederick Jacobs of Moraviantown, who along with Oates and another gentleman arrived just in time to witness this dramatic exchange, piped up in agreement with Logan's assessment. Claiming that his father had told him the same story about Tecumseh's burial, Jacobs assured the United Canadians that there was "no occasion for searching further."[43] Jacobs even offered to certify that the bones were those of Tecumseh, presumably in his capacity as chief of Moraviantown. But the United Canadians politely declined and continued on their merry way to Ridgetown. The next morning, Oates and his colleagues boarded a Canada Southern train for Niagara – with their precious cargo in tow.[44]

Newspapers across Ontario were quick to publish news of the discovery, and just as quick to cast doubts about it. The first swipe came from the editor of the Toronto *Mail*:

Mr Oates and his party will not think us unkind for pointing out the probability that the letters *W R* on the scalping knife, which is the chief witness to the identity of the remains, do not stand for *William Rex*, and, therefore, do not go to show that the weapon was one of William the Third's presents to the Indians. *Gul. R* or *Guliel R* for *Gulielmus Rex* would be orthodox enough, but WR for *William Rex* would lead one to believe irreverently that His Most Gracious Majesty had studied his Latin in the bogs by the Boyne, where *Capricornus William* is "classical" for "billy-goat."[45]

Actually, the cipher of William III does consist of the letters "WR."[46] It was a minor point, but the *Mail*'s lighthearted charge of incompetence was still a slap against the United Canadians – and one that stung their pride. It would not be the last, nor would it be the most painful.

While the majority of editorials regarding the discovery were limited to opinion pieces, the St Thomas *Canadian Home Journal* went so far as to send a reporter to Ridgetown in order to investigate the story. One of the people interviewed was Dr Jacob Smith, who assured the reporter that the bones were those of some other victim of the Battle of the Thames. According to Smith,

both Mr Watts and Mr Dixon [*sic*] frequently turned up human remains in ploughing over the battle field, and I know that their custom was to re-inter such remains in some spot where they would not likely be disturbed again. The skeleton dug up I understand was found in an angle of the fence dividing Watts' and Dixon's farms, just where the thickest of the fight took place. I would not indeed be surprised to hear of bones being found beneath any square foot of that locality; but it also occurs to me as very probable that the remains exhumed on Wednesday had been re-interred by Mr Watts.[47]

Watts, however, never claimed responsibility for the grave. Nor did Smith give due consideration to the possibility that the grave just might have been left undisturbed from the time of the battle, having been protected from the farmer's plough by the fence allowance. More troubling than Smith's lack of objectivity was his lack of familiarity. He never spoke with the United Canadians, and when the reporter asked if he had seen the bones he had to reply: "No, I regret to say that I did not. I was ill – hardly able to get about – and though my boys told me that evening that they had the bones of the great chief down at Benton's hotel, I thought it was only some straggling showman who had a skeleton to exhibit. I didn't know till the next morning that the remains were Tecumseh's."[48] Despite Smith's incapacitation, he was certain that the bones were not those of Tecumseh.

Surprised by the sudden change in editorial attitude toward them, Oates and the other United Canadians decided it was best to remain aloof, at least until they had a chance to explain themselves to Mowat. But a "Clergyman" from Thamesville soon forced them to break their silence. In a scathing letter to the Toronto *Mail*, the Clergyman accused the United Canadians, or the "Tecumseh Resurrection Party" as he called them, of having desecrated the grave of a Christian missionary. This damning charge, as bad as it was for the United Canadians, was exacerbated by the Clergyman's claim that the missionary's bones were then made a gift to one of their "chums."[49]

The ire-raising incident related by the Clergyman had taken place during the United Canadians' second trip to Tecumseh's grave. Upon their arrival at the Great Western Railway station in Thamesville, in the evening of 29 August 1876, Oates and his team had been greeted by Dr William J. Graham, a member of their association from nearby Bothwell. Leaving his colleagues to make their way to a hotel for the night, Oates climbed into Graham's buggy and drove off – the president of the United Canadian Association had a very disturbing report to investigate. That night, at the Marcus Hotel in Bothwell, Oates listened with rapt attention to what the proprietor had to say about Tecumseh's burial. According to Robert Marcus, "the grave was on Chief Jacobs' farm, on rising ground back off the road."[50] But the real surprise came when Marcus identified his informant as Timothy Snake – the same Shawnee elder who had pointed out Tecumseh's grave on the Watts farm for the benefit of Nelles, the Grand Trunk station master. Troubled by the news of this second grave, and unable to question the deceased Snake about it, Oates had decided that an inspection was in order.[51]

The next morning, 30 August, Oates and Graham drove back down the Longwoods Road toward Thamesville. At the Jacobs farm, located two kilometres east of the Watts homestead, they found the chief and asked him what he thought of Snake's story that Tecumseh was buried on his property. Chief Jacobs had his doubts, although he did recall an old Native burial ground that was probably the place Marcus described. Leading the way, Jacobs conducted his guests to a small grove in the middle of a field. The shaded graves, however, were not pagan. They were Christian. Unbeknownst to them, the three men stood in "Hutberg," the Moravian mission cemetery. Consecrated in 1792, this small plot of land served as the last resting place of both the Fairfield missionaries and their Native converts.[52] Had Oates been aware of this fact, he might have exercised more restraint when he caught sight of a "singular" mound. It was "of conical shape, about eight feet in diameter at the base and four feet high."[53] It was also a mystery. When Jacobs was unable to satisfy his visitors' curiosity regarding the occupant of this particular grave, Oates asked for permission to excavate it ... even though Ockawandah's story stressed that Tecumseh's warriors "studiously avoided making any mound" when they buried their great chief.[54]

Jacobs was quick to grant the request, but Oates – possibly taken aback by the rapid pace of negotiations – decided that he should first consult with his colleagues. All three men then drove off to the Watts farm, where they arrived just in time to witness Logan's affirmation that Tecumseh's bones had been discovered. When the other United Canadians heard about the "singular" mound, they agreed that it was prudent to ensure that Tecumseh had but one final resting place.

Travelling to the Jacobs farm, the United Canadians gathered around the mound and opened it: "the first thing found in the centre was a half pint tin cup, and about three feet below the base we struck what appeared to be a hollow log, and which proved afterwards to be a coffin, made of two halves of a basswood log which had now fallen in by decay. The bones in this primitive coffin were found in good preservation, and the remains were to all appearances those of a white man."[55] Doubting that a brave Shawnee war chief would have been laid to rest in a coffin with nothing more martial to accompany him than an old tin cup, the United Canadians concluded that Tecumseh was not buried under the mound – or anywhere else on the Jacobs farm. Having reached this consensus, they should have insisted on restoring the grave. Instead, they stood idly by as Jacobs made a gift of the bones to Dr Graham.[56] It proved to be a serious lapse in judgment.

Oates answered the Clergyman's charges with an explanation, hoping against hope that it would quell the rising controversy. Unfortunately, the haughty tone of his letter did nothing to strengthen his weak defence. While he was willing to concede that "the remains were to all appearances those of a white man," he refused to admit that the bones might have belonged to a Moravian missionary.[57] No one, he argued, knew where the missionary was buried, and that included Chief Jacobs. Incredibly, Oates then went on to blame persons unknown – and presumably the Moravians themselves – for having misplaced the missionary's tombstone. "One thing is certain," he observed, "had the parties who sent or brought over the tombstone placed it in its right place, and that place this singular mound, we should not have molested it."[58] To the Clergyman's call for the return of the bones, Oates replied: "We were for replacing the bones, but Chief Jacobs gave them to Dr Graham in my presence, and as the chief was the owner of the soil, we concluded that he could do as he liked in the matter."[59]

Native graves warranted little, if any, respect in nineteenth-century Ontario. Consequently, any such grave, whether pagan or Christian, was fair game to the United Canadians in their obsessive pursuit of Tecumseh. Victorian society, however, did not tolerate the same lax attitude toward white burials. To exhume Tecumseh's skeleton in order to provide it with an honorific burial was viewed as a commendable act. But to dig up the grave of a Moravian missionary and dispose of his bones like some kind of chattel property was considered an outrage.[60]

The Hutberg incident cost the United Canadians what little remained of their editorial support. Even the *Nation*, which represented the views of the nationalistic Canada First Movement, and had been a staunch defender of the like-minded United Canadians, found the violation of a Christian burial inexcusable.[61] Kindred spirit aside, the *Nation*'s editor had no choice but to conclude that "patriotic ardour may go too far in this direction, and it will be well if research is not prosecuted at the expense of shocked feelings and violated graves. It appears to be a fact, from almost incontestable evidence, that the burial place of Tecumseh is unknown, and is likely to continue so."[62]

Public opinion continued to turn against the United Canadians, just as it had against the Yankee fellow who violated the Native graves in 1840. But whereas Moores's misguided zeal did not backfire on the American Whig Party, the grave robbing antics of Oates and his colleagues caused irreparable damage to the "Tecumseh Resurrection Party."

Soon after the Clergyman's letter made its appearance, Attorney General Mowat requested a meeting with Oates.[63] Mowat could not have been pleased. The embarrassment caused him by the dispute over the authenticity of the bones was bad enough, but thanks to the United Canadians the attorney general of Ontario had become an unwitting accessory to grave robbery.[64] The alleged violation of the Moravian burial posed a serious threat to the government of the province, especially since it just so happened that Mowat was also the Liberal premier of Ontario. During his long tenure from 1872 to 1896, Mowat acted as his own attorney general.[65] It was a perfectly acceptable arrangement, and although Mowat had assented to the request of the United Canadians in his capacity as attorney general, it was Mowat the premier who would be held accountable for their mischief.[66]

Mowat moved quickly to neutralize the scandal. First, he requested that Oates provide him with a report on the discovery. Then he arranged for an independent investigation.[67] The person Mowat asked to scrutinize the findings of the United Canadians was Daniel Wilson, a professor of English literature and history at the University of Toronto, whose many interests included the developing fields of ethnology and archaeology.[68] It was a shrewd choice. Mowat was well aware that the judgment of the eminently qualified Wilson would be incontestable and therefore final. The United Canadians would likely be discredited in the process, but that was none of Mowat's concern.

Wilson rose to the challenge, and after communicating with Oates it became clear to him that the skeleton was missing more than just a few of the smaller bones. Most notably absent was the lower jaw. Wilson found it "difficult to conceive of the removal of the skull, along with other bones, from the original place of interment of an undisturbed skeleton, without finding the under jaw *in situ.*"[69] As a result, he resigned himself to the necessity of a personal examination of the grave site.

With Oates acting as his guide, Wilson set out for the battlefield on 19 September 1876. He began his fieldwork by taking precise measurements from the road to the grave, and from the site of the log house to the grave. He then prepared to search for the missing bones, but Oates informed him that Dr Graham had already performed that task. Wilson summoned the physician's attendance, and when Graham arrived he was able to convince the professor that the grave had been "thoroughly ransacked."[70] Just to be sure, Wilson dug a trench to see if any additional bones might turn up. Instead of digging near the grave, which his measurement placed at eighty-four rods (422 metres) from the road, Wilson opted for a spot at less than half that distance.[71] Wilson claimed to undertake this exercise in order to test the accuracy of Ockawandah's information. But the estimate of forty rods (201 metres) originated with Oates, which explains why the professor found nothing more than the stained soil of a former swamp.[72]

Wilson soon finished his examination of the grave site, but before he returned to Toronto he decided to do some ransacking of his own. Fascinated with Native skull sizes and shapes, Wilson was always looking for new specimens to add to his collection.[73] While he had no expectations on this occasion, he did hope to find at least one cranial souvenir from the battlefield.[74] Sure enough, the owner of the adjacent farm presented him with a skull.[75] Yet, Wilson was disappointed. Despite its obvious Native origin, he had not found the skull himself *in situ,* and so it did not suit him. The cemetery on the Jacobs farm was tempting enough, but the controversy involving the United Canadians forced Wilson to look elsewhere. When he enquired if there were any Native burial grounds in the district, he was directed to a location on the Sydenham River near Florence, some sixteen kilometres northwest of the battlefield.[76]

Wilson was soon on his way, and upon his arrival he found the burial ground relatively secluded, which allowed him to excavate without recrimination. Once again, Wilson dug a trench. This time he found a complete skeleton of an "Indian chief" in an undisturbed condition, which the professor packed up and carried off with him.[77] He later justified this exhumation on the need for anatomical comparison: "As I was still under the belief that a nearly perfect skeleton had been found lying undisturbed in the place of its original interment, I thought it desirable to obtain some other Indian skulls from the vicinity, in the hope that they might aid me in deciding on the characteristics of the supposed skull of the Shawnee chief."[78] As it transpired, the skeleton was not used in the investigation. But Wilson kept it anyway, in hopes of having it "articulated, and placed in the University [of Toronto] Museum."[79]

After Wilson and Oates returned to Toronto, the box containing the bones discovered by the United Canadians was brought over from Niagara. On 25 September, the contents were subjected to the scrutiny of Wilson and several other learned gentlemen.[80] Almost immediately, they confirmed what Wilson had known all along: that a large number of the major bones were missing.[81] Although Wilson had not bothered to search the grave himself, he assured the investigating team that the bones had not been overlooked. And, since a skeleton found *in situ* should have been complete or nearly so, it was unanimously agreed that the grave must have been disturbed at some point. As the team examined the individual bones in detail, they found that a number of them were not male or even human.[82] Furthermore, it was obvious from variations in the colour and condition that the bones represented a number of different burials. The investigators were forced to conclude that none of the bones were those of Tecumseh.[83]

Although convinced of their findings, Wilson and his colleagues felt obligated to consider the last shred of evidence supporting the United Canadians' claim. But in looking for signs of a healed fracture on one of the leg bones, the investigators could discern nothing more than "the strongly defined point of attachment of the muscle on the tibia of a man of muscular development."[84] The bones were discredited, and yet Wilson's penchant for collecting Native remains probably resulted in at least some of them having been preserved in his collection – in which case they likely went up in flames during the fire that destroyed Toronto's University College in 1890.[85]

In his report, Wilson admonished the United Canadians for having left their excavation unfinished for nearly two months. Their dereliction had allowed more than ample time for an exchange of bones, which was undertaken to convince the United Canadians that they "need make no further search."[86] Wilson considered it regrettable that they had not secured "the services of some person possessed of sufficient knowledge of anatomy to have pointed out to them at the first the obvious deficiencies in their discovery."[87] Yet, while Wilson was critical of the methods employed by the United Canadians, he tried to be as gentle as possible. Having undertaken similar excavations himself, he could sympathize with them.

The next day, 26 September 1876, Wilson submitted his report to Attorney General and/or Premier Mowat. This time Mowat could not have been displeased. The findings, as far as he was concerned, closed the matter in a manner that was not unfavourable to his government. Soon after, the report was released to the public.[88] Unfortunately for Oates and the United Canadians, Wilson's magnanimity was not shared by the press.[89] The *Canadian Home Journal* in St Thomas gloated with particular unkindness under a headline that must have caused the United Canadians much grief:

THE BONES OF TECUMSEH

Prof. Daniel Wilson's Report – The Bones
shown to belong to a Man, a Woman, a
Child, a Deer and a Dog![90]

Like many other newspapers, the *Canadian Home Journal* reprinted Wilson's report without much analysis ... except to smugly observe that "the conclusions of Prof. Wilson agree pretty closely in the main with the conjectures of Dr Smith."[91] Because Oates was president of the United Canadians, as well as the leader of the expedition to find Tecumseh's grave, he was singled out for the lion's share of editorial abuse. The Toronto *Mail* was particularly unkind:

Mr R.H. OATES and his friends of the United Canadian Association need not be amazed, therefore, at their discovery of the remains of TECUMSEH being received with "loud laughter and ironical cheers," especially from the western end of the Province. These sixty odd years past, white men and Indians on the Thames have sought in vain for the bones of the great Shawnee, and now the green-eyed monster [jealousy] consumes them for that Mr OATES has been enabled to walk straight to the spot and dig up the hallowed dust with as much dignity and *savoir faire* as a hungry Irishman displays in disembowelling a hill of potatoes.[92]

This contempt for Oates was unfortunate, as he had only the best of intentions for both Tecumseh and Canada. Despite this humiliation, however, the old gentleman remained an esteemed colleague of both the United Canadians and the York Pioneers.[93]

Just as Mowat blamed the United Canadians for his embarrassment, they in turn blamed the Natives of Moraviantown for their own. There is little doubt that Jacobs and Logan deceived the United Canadians. It does not necessarily follow, however, that they acted out of malevolence. Through no fault of their own, the Natives of Moraviantown found themselves in a cultural predicament. While they were honoured that the United Canadians wished to bury Tecumseh next to Brock, they were not willing to give up the bones they had some reason to believe constituted his skeleton. The solution they chose was influenced by their esteem for the United Canadians, and a desire to avoid overtly offensive behaviour. Instead of an outright refusal and the possibility of a direct confrontation, they preferred to give the impression of assent. Had the United Canadians persisted with the exhumation during their first visit, the Natives might have been forced into a more militant stance. Conveniently enough, as it turned out, the jealous locals relieved them from having to appear belligerent: by not finishing the job, the United Canadians accommodated the Natives with ample time to secretly switch the bones. This solution was really quite charitable. The unsuspecting United Canadians got the relics they required in order to pay homage to Tecumseh, while the Natives preserved the sanctity of his purported burial.[94] What the Natives could not have foreseen, however, was Wilson's scrutiny.

While the United Canadians blamed the Natives for having perpetrated a base trick against them, the Natives harboured no resentment in return ... except toward Chief Johnson, who had provided the map to Tecumseh's grave. After the Native ploy was revealed, he was severely criticized by an "Indian of Moraviantown." Interestingly, Johnson was not directly accused of having betrayed the secret of Tecumseh's grave. Such an admission would have suggested that Tecumseh's grave had in fact been found, and might have trained unwanted attention on the whereabouts of its original occupant. Rather, Johnson was blamed for having misled the United Canadians – and for personal gain, no less. "Chief Johnston [sic] knows that the dead can't speak," the Indian explained, "and therefore would have a chance of turning a penny, because he did not come here for nothing, nor did he come through patriotism."[95] The Indian went on to accuse Johnson of having planted the knife and the gun mechanism so that they would be discovered along with the bones, which he claimed were those from the Moravian missionary's grave.

Johnson's character was much maligned by the Indian, whose indignation was no doubt shared by many other Natives of Moraviantown. Obviously, they were upset that Johnson was willing to betray Tecumseh's grave to the whites. Yet, if a railway station master could learn where Tecumseh was supposedly buried, then it must have been a pretty loosely-guarded secret. What probably angered the Natives more than anything else was the manner of Johnson's betrayal. He had acted as badly as his white associates, which was completely out of character with the behaviour expected of a visiting Native of chiefly rank. Granted, Johnson should have known how to conduct himself in a society that emphasized respect for the dead and non-interference in the affairs of others; however, he was by no means the unscrupulous opportunist the Moraviantown Indian alleged. In fact, he was well known in the Six Nations community and the surrounding white society as a highly principled man.[96] He also had a reputation as a hopeless romantic "who thrived on adventure and pageantry, high-flown words, heroic deeds, lavish ceremonies, and the symbols of power and importance."[97] As such, he fatefully ignored the sensibilities of his fellow Natives for the sake of a noble white deed.

The Natives of Moraviantown probably felt regret over the embarrassment they caused the United Canadians, but they were not about to accept responsibility for it. They had switched the bones, true enough, but it was not their intention to publicly belittle the United Canadians by then pointing out the deception. That dubious distinction went to Archibald Blue, the editor of the St Thomas *Canadian Home Journal*. From the first news of the United Canadians' discovery, he was convinced they were "mistaken."[98] Most editors were content to merely express their opinion regarding the authenticity of the bones, but Blue actively promoted the views of the highly critical Dr Smith. As Blue commented in a letter to a friend, "Oates cannot easily dispose of the Dr's objections."[99] He was right. Smith possessed a seemingly incontestable knowledge of the battlefield, and none of his remarks could be construed as partisan. Blue appeared to be just as disinterested, but such was not the case.

Unfortunately for the United Canadians, their discovery happened to coincide with Blue's promotion to editor of the *Canadian Home Journal*.[100] New to his job and eager to make an impression with his readers, Blue was able to devote as much coverage to a particular story as he saw fit. And Blue had a personal interest in the story that Tecumseh's bones had been discovered. Having grown up near Moraviantown, he was well aware of the many contradictory claims regarding the great chief's burial – claims which convinced him, and many other people in southwestern Ontario, that Tecumseh's bones could never be found.[101]

In 1876, Richard H. Oates led an expedition to discover Tecumseh's grave. Oates and his fellow United Canadians planned to reinter Tecumseh under Brock's Monument on Queenston Heights. *York Pioneer Annual Report*, 1910

George H.M. Johnson was a hereditary chief of the Six Nations Reserve. He accompanied the United Canadians to Moraviantown with a map purporting to show the location of Tecumseh's grave. *Magazine of American History*, 1885

Dr Jacob Smith of Ridgetown was convinced that the bones unearthed by the United Canadians were not those of Tecumseh, but of someone else killed at the Battle of the Thames. *Illustrated Historical Atlas of the County of Kent, Ontario*

Daniel Wilson was a professor of English and history, whose interest in ethnology and archaeology qualified him to investigate the discovery made by the United Canadians. He concluded that the mixed lot of bones was not Tecumseh's skeleton, "for it is nobody's!" Toronto *Globe*, 3 March 1876

Timothy Snake was a Shawnee who lived among the Delaware of
Moraviantown. He achieved local prominence with claims that he
knew where Tecumseh was buried. Courtesy Moravian Archives,
Bethlehem, Pennsylvania

3

Racists and Revisionists

As FAR AS PROFESSOR WILSON was concerned, the case was closed. The bones unearthed by the United Canadians did not belong to Tecumseh, and he had no interest in pursuing the skeleton carried away by the Natives. In his estimation, it was just one more loose end in an ever expanding mystery. Yet, despite the obviously limited range of the professor's investigation, no one was brave enough to question the scope of his report. Wilson was one of the leading Canadian academics of his time, and therefore his findings were incontrovertible. Everyone who had become embroiled in the United Canadians' botched exhumation accepted his decision as final – even the jealous locals, who took advantage of the situation to garner support for a monument on the battlefield where Tecumseh had made his last stand.

In mid-January of 1877, the citizens of east Kent County met, appropriately enough, in the Tecumseh schoolhouse near the site of the battlefield. During a very spirited discussion, they considered plans to construct a marble column adorned with "a concise description of the life and actions of this immortal son of the forest."[1] Confidently, they anticipated that provincial funding would allow them to bring their project to fruition the following summer. All they needed was someone to approach the government on their behalf. They chose Dr William J. Graham of Bothwell to represent them.[2] This was the same Dr Graham who was severely criticized for his part in exhuming the grave in the Moravian mission cemetery. Surprisingly, the much-maligned physician agreed to participate in the monument scheme. But before Graham could attempt to redeem his good name, however, he was forced to wait out another controversy involving Tecumseh.

On 26 January 1877, an anonymous letter was published in the *St Thomas Journal* under the provocative headline: "A MONUMENT TO A SAVAGE."[3] The author, who identified himself only as "J.S." of

Ridgetown, could not have been more blunt: "Sir, I observe that there is a proposition to build a monument to Tecumseh. Will the proposers tell us why? Will they give us a record of his noble deeds, of great and magnanimous acts, some traits of real greatness deserving of the honor of national gratitude in monumental display? Have the proposers ever for one moment reflected upon the proposition?"[4] No, they had not. To most Canadians in 1877, Tecumseh was the personification of the noble savage, and a national hero as well. There had never been the slightest doubt that he deserved a monument. The author of the letter might just as well have taken exception with God.

Perhaps sensing the challenge facing him, J.S. immediately followed up by citing the barbarity of Native warfare. After relating a long list of horrors, and an assortment of graphic details, J.S. finally made his point: "If being a thoroughly pagan savage, a first class butcher of his enemies of the white race in peace or in war, in ambush or the battle-field, or of prisoners taken in honorable warfare, deserves a monu-ment, by all means erect one to Tecumseh!"[5] This J.S. certainly had a negative impression of the great chief. The only other person known to hold such strong opinions about Tecumseh was Dr Jacob Smith, who had the same initials as J.S., and also hailed from Ridgetown.[6] It was no coincidence. Not content with having refuted the identity of the bones discovered by the United Canadians, Smith was determined to block the Tecumseh monument proposal. Whereas his earlier objec-tions appeared to be based on a desire for historical accuracy, Smith was actually motivated by a racist disposition. He did not like Natives, and his contempt extended all the way back to Tecumseh. Smith soon discovered, however, that aspersions cast upon Tecumseh's character would not stand unchallenged. With the fledgling Dominion of Cana-da approaching its first decade of Confederation, English-speaking Ontarians were imbued with the idea of cultivating a national senti-ment. Smith could not have chosen a worse time to vilify one of their greatest heroes.

The first response came from "Autos" of Tyrconnel, in east Elgin County, who skilfully undermined Smith's racist contention. "Had the writer [Smith] opposed the erection of a memorial on the grounds that all war is a relic of barbarism, and those who engage in it undeserving of the honor of having their names and actions inscribed in imperish-able marble, I could appreciate his arguments and sympathize with his opposition to the matter in question."[7] But it did not appear to Autos that J.S. objected to "monuments erected to perpetuate the memory of men who have fallen, bravely battling for all that men hold dear," such as Major-General Isaac Brock, whose "lofty shaft" a grateful country "upreared on the consecrated rock at Queenston."[8] There was no question that Brock was worthy of a towering monument for his gallantry during the War of 1812, and Autos had ample evidence to suggest that Tecumseh was just as deserving.

Launching into a spirited defence of Tecumseh's good name, Autos argued that he was a remarkable man who had risen instinctively above the passions of his race. "He despised plunder; he abjured the use of spirits. His prowess in the field was only equalled by his eloquence in council. With the skill of a statesman he reconciled all interests, and united all minds in a crusade against the cruel and implacable foes of his tribe and race."[9] Autos continued his redemption of Tecumseh by observing that the "universal testimony of all who were competent to give an opinion, and who have left it on record is, that judged by an enlightened standard, he was one of nature's noblemen."[10] This distinction was sufficient to absolve him of the brutality associated with Native warfare.

Autos then employed a tit-for-tat approach in which he argued that the Americans were just as brutal as their Native enemies, "as witness Custer's butchery of a tribe during the civil war who had put themselves under his protection at his own request, and then at dead of night let loose his 'hell-hounds' upon them."[11] Actually, the incident Autos referred to was the Sand Creek Massacre in Colorado, which occurred in the southwestern Colorado Territory in November of 1864 when a large force of Colorado cavalry attacked a village of Cheyenne who were friendly to the United States.[12] Although General George A. Custer had had nothing to do with this slaughter, the fact that he and his cavalry suffered the same fate at the Battle of the Little Bighorn in June of 1876 probably accounts for much of Smith's opposition to a monument for Tecumseh. Smith, who was a racist to begin with, was obviously upset over the severity of the Native victory and reacted by taking his anger out on Tecumseh.

Wisely, most readers of the St Thomas Journal kept their distance from this escalating newsprint fray. Yet, both Autos and Smith did manage to attract their respective supporters. "J.A.W." from Port Burwell sided with Autos and expressed much the same sentiments.[13] But when "E.D.H." from Rodney came to the defence of Dr Smith, he made good use of the opportunity to vent his own extreme hatred:

There is not a single attribute of the Indian character that is noble. On the contrary, his character is made up of everything that is despicable. He is cruel and bloodthirsty; he is treacherous; he is a coward and won't fight fair;

he will lie like a thief, for he is a thief; he is as lazy as a white dog, and as dirty as a hog. This is the real Indian character, and if the history of the race does not bear me out in that description I am ready to fall down and worship Tecumseh as a hero and the deliverer of our country, and give $5 towards his monument besides.[14]

Confidently did E.D.H. defame every unoffending Native in southwestern Ontario and elsewhere in the Americas. After all, it was a white man's debate in a white man's world. Much to his surprise, however, it was a Native who came forward to contest his abusive rhetoric.

Oronhyatekha, an educated Mohawk from the Six Nations Reserve near Brantford and a practicing physician in London, Ontario, was not about to suffer the abuse of some small-town racist.[15] "*The gentleman*," as Oronhyatekha condescendingly presumed in responding to the *St Thomas Journal*, "very properly writes under a *nom de plume*; but notwithstanding he does not honor the world with his name, yet I suppose he is a *gentleman*, and I know further he is a *white man*, for the most degraded *savage* (sic) would be unable to use such *gentlemanly* expressions as 'liar,' 'thief,' 'lazy as a white dog,' 'dirty as a hog,' and other elegant and choice phrases in speaking of a fellow man."[16] Oronhyatekha countered these aspersions by citing Lewis Henry Morgan and Henry Rowe Schoolcraft, both prominent American ethnologists of the time, as well as Lucy Stone, an activist in the American women's rights movement, all of whom concurred "that there were many traits in Indian character worthy of admiration." It was then that Oronhyatekha turned the table on the racist from Rodney: "If, now, the Indian is a 'coward,' 'thief,' and 'liar,' it only proves that they are capable of learning to do these things from *white gentlemen* of the ilk of 'E.D.H.'"[17]

Oronhyatekha continued by addressing the question of Native warfare. Citing Wendell Phillips, the prominent American abolitionist and reformer, he blamed the United States for Native uprisings on its western frontier.[18] The Americans, having broken every treaty negotiated with Native people, while refusing to recognize Native rights, had brought retribution upon themselves. With Phillips as his authority in the matter, Oronhyatekha had no intention of making excuses for the brutality of Native warfare, and he delighted in reminding E.D.H. of Brock's ruse in taking Detroit by playing on General William Hull's fear of a massacre. E.D.H. might have counter-argued that this admission proved his point, and that Tecumseh's warriors were actually as "cruel and bloodthirsty" as alleged. But the contradiction went unnoticed. Oronhyatekha concluded his letter with one last swipe. In what at first seemed to be a conciliatory tone, he conceded that the Native race was "not what they once were ... *brave, just* and *honest*," but he then sarcastically added "my only wonder is that having been in more or less constant intercourse with *white gentlemen* like 'E.D.H.' for a century or so, they are not ten times worse than they are."[19]

In Oronhyatekha, E.D.H. had met his match. Prudently, the racist shied away from sparring with such a well-versed Native. Nonetheless, although subdued and sullen, E.D.H. was by no means repentant. In one last letter to the *St Thomas Journal*, he justified his remarks by claiming that he referred only "to the savage, and not the civilized Indians."[20] He further acknowledged that "there are always exceptions to every rule," and he grudgingly held up Oronhyatekha's accomplishments as a notable example of what Natives could achieve if they directed their energies "in the right channels, instead of vainly struggling against the onward and irresistible march of civilization."[21] E.D.H. would have gladly supported the monument proposal, had Tecumseh done as much as Oronhyatekha "for the amelioration of mankind." Instead, he considered such a commemoration to be the height of folly, declaring that Tecumseh was "an implacable enemy of our race, and who, if his mad schemes had been successful, would have swept the hated palefaces – our forefathers included – into the sea."[22]

Actually, Tecumseh's "mad schemes" were entirely consistent with British policy. After the American Revolution, John Graves Simcoe, the lieutenant-governor of Upper Canada (now Ontario) had promoted the idea of a Native homeland to buffer the territorial ambitions of the United States.[23] Admittedly, it was one of history's finer points, and one that escaped the notice of both debaters. In any case, the Native doctor was satisfied – both by his obvious victory over E.D.H., and also the racist's flattering remarks. It was Oronhyatekha's weakness; he craved recognition.

Although Oronhyatekha was proud of his Mohawk heritage, his one great ambition was to make a name for himself in white society. That opportunity presented itself in 1878, when he managed to gain membership in the all-white ranks of the London, Ontario, branch of the Independent Order of Foresters. This American-based fraternal organization provided Oronhyatekha with the ladder to his success. Soon after his enrollment, he was elected high chief ranger of the Ontario High Court and, until the time of his death in 1907, Oronhyatekha's sound management combined with an aggressive marketing strategy transformed the nearly bankrupt Independent Order of Foresters into the largest and most solvent fraternal institution in the world.[24] Curiously, he never used his influence among the upper echelons of Canadian society for the construction of a monument to Tecumseh.[25] But if nothing else, Oronhyatekha had put a stop to the racist remarks of E.D.H. Dr Smith, however, was not so easily deterred.

By focusing his attention on pagan "savages" as opposed to Christian Natives, Smith managed to circumvent the same stinging censure that E.D.H. had unwittingly brought upon himself. Emphasizing this distinction allowed Smith to continue with his argument that Tecumseh was undeserving of a monument. Ignoring the many accounts of Tecumseh's humanity, Smith implicated him in every instance of Native brutality during the War of 1812. As leader of the Native forces, Tecumseh was ultimately responsible for the savagery committed under his command. Therefore, he deserved no monument from the descendants of his Canadian allies, and "to boast of our alliance with such a savage is a disgrace to Christianity."[26] The image of Tecumseh as an avowed enemy of God would have been a powerful argument against any proposal to build a monument to him, except that Smith inadvertently neutralized much of its effect when he tried to portray William Henry Harrison as "a lover of peace."[27] The controversy over Tecumseh's proposed monument gradually subsided, and early in March the letters to the St Thomas Journal ceased.[28]

Having observed that the tempest had blown itself out, Dr Graham optimistically proceeded with his plans to raise funds for the Tecumseh monument by organizing a troupe of Native singers from the Moraviantown Reserve.[29] Graham was convinced that the proceeds generated from theatre tours in North America and Europe would enable the Natives to construct their own monument to Tecumseh, and in such a way as to avoid every form of criticism and controversy.[30] Toward the end of May 1877, the first of these Native concerts was held in Bothwell. It proved a success and Graham, encouraged by the report that "great enthusiasm prevails over the movement," decided to take his Native singers to Detroit.[31] After the first American performance, however, Graham's hopes of raising $20,000 vanished. The Americans had little interest in seeing "real live Indians" imported from Canada, as they had plenty of their own.[32] Embarrassed, once again, Graham abandoned his troupe and sulked home in disgrace.

Fortunately for the stranded and cash-strapped Native singers, a man calling himself "Professor Flanders" came to their rescue. With their return to the Canadian side of the Detroit River, Flanders managed to get them back to Moraviantown by organizing a series of concerts along the way.[33] These performances proved quite popular with

Canadian audiences, who, unlike their American cousins, had a greater appreciation for the troupe's goal in honouring Tecumseh with a monument.[34] Among those who rose to the occasion were the abused United Canadians, who called for a subscription drive in support of the project. But it was too late. Ironically enough, if Graham had set out for Toronto instead of Detroit, he probably could have taken in enough receipts to pay for his singers' passage to England and perhaps on to Europe ... where exotic performances were a paying proposition.[35] Graham might very well have returned with enough money to build Tecumseh his monument. Instead, the well-meaning but unfortunate doctor exiled himself and the monument scheme was abandoned.[36]

For years afterwards, the occasional newspaper article on Tecumseh would prompt appeals to commemorate his memory – but no one dared to follow Dr Graham down the gauntlet of controversy to almost certain humiliation. Eventually, however, the temptation got the better of an old carpenter who fancied himself a writer. Thomas Gowman lived in Melbourne, a small village on the Longwoods Road located forty-three kilometres northwest of the battlefield, and it was there in the early 1890s that he began to toy with the idea of writing a biography of Tecumseh.[37] Gowman considered himself an authority on the topic, a notion he based on stories he remembered from his youth. Years earlier, in 1834, his family settled on a farm near Louisville, a village on the route of Procter's retreat up the Thames River.[38] There, young Thomas was introduced to Tecumseh's exploits by neighbours who claimed first-hand knowledge of the events culminating in the Battle of the Thames. Enthralled, the boy developed what would prove to be a lifelong interest in Tecumseh – and a sizeable hatred for the Shawnee.

In 1876, during the excitement caused by the reputed discovery of Tecumseh's grave, a then middle-aged Gowman was outraged when the *London Advertiser* credited Jacob Pheasant, a Shawnee elder from Moraviantown, with the story of Tecumseh's secret burial.[39] Dashing off a rather disjointed letter in response, Gowman attacked Pheasant's character by falsely implicating him in the Yankee fellow's vandalism in 1840. According to Gowman, Pheasant and another Native, Timothy Snake, were hired to point out Tecumseh's grave.[40] Gowman, however, dismissed the possibility that Pheasant possessed any knowledge of Tecumseh's burial, basing his rejection on the evidence of a scarlet sash. Gowman emphasized the importance of this sash by insisting that Tecumseh wore it into battle, presumably as a belt, and that the Americans fully expected to identify his body based on this ostentatious accessory. They were ultimately disappointed, and as Gowman observed, "if the Americans could not find the body, how could these ... Shawnee braves find it after night; and if they did find it, what did they do with the sash?"[41] Gowman's fixation with the red sash may have verged on being obsessive, but it did serve a purpose. It eliminated Pheasant and Snake as expert witnesses. Just for good measure, Gowman stereotyped all Shawnee as opportunists eagerly awaiting any chance to point out Tecumseh's grave for "a pint of whiskey or fifty cents."[42]

In concluding his letter, Gowman promised a correct version of Tecumseh's death and burial. On 25 September 1876, the same day that Wilson and his colleagues ruled out the bones discovered by the United Canadians, the *London Advertiser* published Gowman's submission as front-page news. The old carpenter began by acknowledging that his information was based largely on a story of one Duncan Holmes.[43] Gowman, however, was evasive and simply described Holmes as "the only white man that ever professed to know where Tecumseh was buried."[44] With this brief introduction out of the way, Gowman continued with Holmes's animated recollections.

Holmes, as Gowman related, was "about two rods" (ten metres) from Tecumseh when he was killed. After a desperate struggle to retrieve their chief's body, Holmes and a companion by the name of Washaway disappeared into "a cloud of dust and smoke."[45] They "laid the body behind a log and ran back to help in the fight, but it was no use; the Indians couldn't hear the voice of Tecumseh any more, and they were scattering like skeert chickens."[46]

In making good their own escape, Holmes and Washaway carried Tecumseh's body into the forest. After travelling a considerable distance, they stopped to rest beside an oak tree that had split and fallen against an adjacent maple. The spectacle inspired the idea of burying Tecumseh beneath the toppled tree. Holmes recalled that he went to the river for two paddles, and that

Washaway made a sort of digger while I was gone. We had a pretty hard time getting through the first foot, and our tomahawks got dull cutting roots, but after that we got on better, and dug about three feet altogether. I brought some elm bark from an old wigwam, and laid [it] in the bottom. We then laid in the body, covered it with bark, and filled in the earth. There is a small tomahawk, a tomahawk-smoke-pipe, a scalping knife and war club buried with him, and his silk sash is around his body. As we stood on each side of the grave we joined hands, [and] he (Washaway) swore by his Kishamanite [or Great Spirit], I, by my God, never to show the grave to anyone, white or Indian. Two days after that we visited the grave, and found the wolves had been digging at it a little, so we procured axes, and falling a small basswood against the maple we managed to fall the maple back into the split oak. This completely hid the grave from view, and prevented the wolves from digging. So Tecumseh's bones will not be found.[47]

Holmes's account of Tecumseh's burial is one of the more fantastic contributions, and it is also one of the most problematic. Apart from the raising of a cloud of dust on a wet and rainy day, his impromptu trip to the river where he just happened to find a couple of paddles to serve as shovels, and the conveniently located wigwam that provided the elm bark lining for the grave, there is the array of accoutrement supposedly placed in Tecumseh's grave ... which Holmes and Washaway would have had to stop and collect while Tecumseh's other warriors scattered like "skeert" chickens. Equally difficult to comprehend is the method by which they camouflaged Tecumseh's grave. It seems questionable that a maple straining forward under the weight of a riven oak could be felled backwards.

Shrewdly, Gowman added a disclaimer: "I now wish that I could say Holmes was a man of truth, but I cannot; his veracity was always doubted."[48] Perhaps for this reason, no one, not even Dr Smith in Ridgetown, questioned Gowman's honesty.[49] More likely, however, it was the old carpenter's assertion that Tecumseh's bones "will not be found" that shielded him from a barrage of criticism.[50] After all, this observation was completely in line with public opinion. There was also another factor working in Gowman's favour. His greatest potential detractors were dead.

It was just as well that Pheasant and Snake had been laid in their graves, given the abuse Gowman heaped upon their reputations.[51] His low opinion of them, however, was not universally shared. At the time of Snake's death in 1869, the Moravians hailed him as "the best 'Moravian' in the tribe," the "only whole souled one," and "the best friend of the mission."[52] The Moravians even went so far as to honour Snake with a fine marble tombstone, inscribed with the acknowledgment that he was a *RELATIVE OF TECUMSEH.*"[53] As for Snake's claim to have fought beside Tecumseh at the Battle of the Thames, the Moravians were pleased to observe that he "did not like to speak of these things," as he had "learned to put away fighting, & follow the Prince of Peace."[54] With the death in July 1872 of "Captain" Jacob Pheasant, so nicknamed for his participation in the Battle of the

Thames, the Moravian Church lost another valued communicant.[55] While he could not boast family ties with Tecumseh, Pheasant did receive one of the much-coveted medals which were distributed in commemoration of the taking of Detroit in 1812.[56] Whether or not Gowman was aware of the high standing enjoyed by these Shawnee among the Moravian missionaries, he steadfastly refused to give their stories about Tecumseh's secret burial the slightest credence ... even though the account he ascribed to Duncan Holmes was essentially the same as those of the Natives. Perhaps if Gowman had interacted with these Natives to the same degree as James Dickson had, he might have been more inclined to give them the benefit of his doubt.

Dickson, the farmer who presented Wilson with the skull in 1876, owned one of the farms which had been surveyed over the battlefield. Having taken possession of his property in 1846, Dickson soon began to clear it of the wilderness.[57] Eventually, he discovered the carvings of "an eagle, a horse, a turtle, &c. on some large black walnut trees immediately to the north of the Morass" (presumably the small swamp of the battlefield).[58] Dickson gave little thought to these blazed trees as they fell one after another under the repeated blows of his axe. But when Pheasant and Snake "remonstrated," an intrigued Dickson questioned them about the significance of the carvings. Neither Shawnee was willing to divulge their secret, and so Dickson continued with his determined program of deforestation.

After Snake's death in 1869, Pheasant became somewhat more indulgent and revealed that the carvings marked the place where Tecumseh fell. When Pheasant began to make allusions to Tecumseh's burial, the farmer listened intently, but the old Native refused to disclose the location.[59] As Dickson discovered, Pheasant could be quite talkative when the topic was Tecumseh's last resting place – but only to a point.

Gowman fully believed that both Pheasant and Snake played their reputed authority in the matter of Tecumseh's grave for all it was worth. If so, this practice undoubtedly would have undermined their credibility. Most of their white neighbours, however, did accept the basic premise that Tecumseh's body was hastily concealed to prevent its mutilation by the enemy.[60] Yet, by their very willingness to discuss Tecumseh's burial, no matter how obliquely, both Pheasant and Snake had encouraged white variations on the sequence of events.

Thomas Gowman proved himself to be particularly accomplished in this regard. Drawing on both Native and white stories alike, he produced a folksy narrative of Tecumseh's burial and then assigned authorship of it to Duncan Holmes. It was a very dishonest approach, and one made more so by the fact that Holmes was more imagined than real.

Prominent among the earliest settlers of the Thames Valley was Hugh Holmes, who took up land near the modern village of Kent Bridge in the mid-1790s. Holmes was the progenitor of a large family of four sons and three daughters.[61] Although none of his sons was named Duncan, one of them had been christened Daniel. This Daniel Holmes served in the Kent Militia throughout the War of 1812, and he must have had many thrilling stories to tell about his experiences.[62] However, it is unlikely that he had any personal knowledge of Tecumseh's death, as Procter did not deploy the militia at the Battle of the Thames.[63] Still, Daniel did see action in another local engagement. In March of 1814, he was wounded at the Battle of the Longwoods, a skirmish that took place east of modern Wardsville, Ontario. The injury he received, besides rendering him lame, appears to have caused his early demise in about 1822.[64]

Since the Gowmans did not arrive in the Thames Valley until 1834, young Thomas probably heard Daniel Holmes's wartime exploits second-hand, and from the same neighbours who told him their stories about Tecumseh. Holmes became larger than life, and when Gowman needed a character for his book, a character who could be credited with an intimate knowledge of Tecumseh's death and burial, he chose Daniel Holmes – whose first name he disguised ever so slightly. It did not matter that Holmes was not with Tecumseh in his last moments; Gowman could improvise by drawing on the many stories that circulated regarding the great chief's death and burial.[65] Among the most colourful were the reminiscences of a curious character known variously as "Indian" or "Trader" Johnson, who not only claimed to have helped bury Tecumseh, but also counted himself as one of the great chief's boyhood friends.[66]

Joseph Johnson arrived in what is now Howard Township, on the south bank of the lower Thames River in 1794. By 1826, he had removed to the Sydenham River in Dawn Township near present-day Florence, Ontario, where he shared his story of Tecumseh's burial with his new neighbours.[67] In time, Johnson's narrative became a staple of local folklore, and eventually it began to make its way into the press – although never as a first-hand account.[68] One such occasion was in 1883, when an anonymous contributor to the *Chatham Planet* took offence with an "American version" of Tecumseh's death in the then recently-published *Picturesque Canada*. Rather than giving Colonel

Richard M. Johnson credit for Tecumseh's death, as the "American version" related, the *Planet's* contributor promoted Joseph Johnson's claim that Tecumseh was killed by a stray bullet while he sat wounded a short distance from the action.[69] According to the Johnson tradition, Tecumseh continued to cheer on his warriors. But when his voice suddenly ceased to be heard, "consternation immediately seized the ranks of the Indians, and they fled in all directions."[70] In the midst of this deadly pandemonium, Tecumseh's corpse "was carried off the field by his faithful body guard, and buried, an oath being taken over the grave, never to reveal the whereabouts, for fear the Americans might dig him up, if the spot were known."[71] Joseph Johnson was credited with having been "one of the six who formed Tecumseh's body guard, and who helped to bury him."[72]

Although Gowman did not make use of the stray-bullet version of Tecumseh's death, the old carpenter's fanciful tale of Tecumseh's secret burial was inspired by the Johnson tradition – and it is no wonder that he was not willing to admit it.[73] After all, even Gowman must have considered Johnson's claims a bit far-fetched. That a white man living in the Thames Valley in October of 1813, having settled there years earlier, should suddenly find himself reunited with a Native he recognized from his youth in a distant land – and not just any Native, but the great Tecumseh himself – must have seemed extremely doubtful. There is evidence, however, to support the sheer coincidence of it all. In May of 1796, more than seventeen years prior to the Battle of the Thames, Joseph Johnson had requested a grant of Crown land. In his petition, Johnson describes how he was "taken Prisoner by the Indians on the Frontiers of Maryland about Seven years ago [*circa* 1789]," and how these same Natives, "after killing my father & mother brought me & my Sisters into Captivity, where we experienced all the Cruelty that was possible for Savages to inflict."[74]

Johnson's claim to have been a Native captive was well known, but the better part of a century would pass before his story involving Tecumseh was corroborated by an eyewitness. In April of 1882, eighty-six years after Johnson submitted his land petition, Dr Tecumseh K. Holmes of Chatham received an intriguing letter from an American historian who was collecting information for a book on Tecumseh. In the course of his research, Lyman C. Draper had discovered that Dr Holmes's aged father possessed a clear recollection of Tecumseh.[75] With this lead, Draper wrote to the doctor requesting whatever information his father might be able to provide. Abraham Holmes, who happened to be Daniel Holmes's younger brother, was only too willing to help. He recalled seeing hordes of Natives passing his father's farm the day before the battle, and how "it soon was known that Tecumseh was retreating before General Harrison."[76] Being a curious sixteen-year-old, Abraham had set off for Arnold's Mill, opposite modern Kent Bridge, where he hoped to catch a glimpse of the great chief. He was not disappointed. Upon his arrival, young Abraham found Tecumseh conversing in the "Indian tongue" with none other than Joseph Johnson.[77]

It would seem that there is some validity to the claims that Johnson knew Tecumseh. However, familiarity alone does not prove that Johnson fought with the Natives at the Battle of the Thames or that he had anything to do with Tecumseh's burial.[78] Abraham Holmes certainly never bothered to publicly advance Johnson's claim to this honour, although he did believe that Tecumseh's body "was taken by his friends ... and buried."[79]

Gowman was equally silent, which is not surprising. He had already cited the imaginary Duncan Holmes as his source, and that part of Johnson's story dealing with Tecumseh's secret burial was perhaps too reminiscent of those told by Pheasant and Snake – the two Natives he despised.[80] Gowman's hostility, however, was not merely hateful; it was also useful. As Gowman discovered in September of 1876, his vehement reaction to the *London Advertiser* for giving Jacob Pheasant credit for the story of Tecumseh's burial provided a convenient means of having his own material published. It was a simple enough formula: first, dispute the source of information; second, provide an alternative and arguably more reliable source. By the autumn of 1893, an aging Gowman was anxious to get a portion of his manuscript into the columns of some local newspaper and possibly noticed by a publisher. His only problem was in finding a pretext for presenting his story to the public. A nearby Native reserve soon offered a viable solution.

Toward the end of October 1893, the fall fair of the Oneida Reserve in Delaware Township, located some twenty-four kilometres southwest of London, was reported in the London *Free Press*.[81] The item was a fairly standard listing of the prizes awarded for various competitions, yet Gowman did not get far down the column before his eyes met an offending passage. In a rage, and writing under the pseudonym of Peter Pancrees, Gowman accused the author of "a few very absurd statements," and in particular one claiming that the "Oneida, Muncey, Chippewa, Mohawk and [certain] other Canadian Indians" did not represent individual tribes, but "belong to one, the Iroquois or Six Nations."[82] Although Gowman was right, in so much as the Muncey were really Delaware and the Chippewa were Ojibwa, he was not particularly kind in the way he pointed out the mistake. In a very rude manner, he brought forward a number of confusing linguistic examples to argue his case. At the end of his rambling letter, and for no apparent reason, he abruptly vowed to submit a piece on Tecumseh.

Gowman got right to work, satisfied that he had successfully repeated the same stunt he first used in 1876. Within a few days, however, he discovered a response in the *Free Press* from the person responsible for the report on the Oneida Fall Fair. Defensively, the correspondent claimed to have merely stated that the names of the "cantons of the Six Nation Indians (or Iroquois) had been given to several localities, viz.: – Mohawk, Oneida, Onondago, Cayuga, Seneca, Tuscarora, &c."[83] Miffed and insulted, the unidentified correspondent reacted by trying to dismiss Peter Pancrees as someone who "must 'read with his eyes and understand with his elbows.'"[84] Gowman simply brushed the objection aside as he busied himself in copying excerpts from his *magnum opus*.

The opening installments, which Gowman alias Peter Pancrees offered to the *Free Press* readership in late November and early December, as "A GOOD INJUN STORY," began by challenging the widely held belief that Tecumseh was a Shawnee.[85] In an outrageous attempt to revise history, Gowman claimed that Tecumseh was really the son of an Aztec ruler. With all the flair of a compulsive liar, Gowman further portrayed Tecumseh as having been abducted by a party of Cree from Saskatchewan during one of their aborted trading missions to the south. That the Aztecs were an ancient race of people whose empire no longer existed by Tecumseh's time was a minor point, and one Gowman conveniently chose to overlook. The old carpenter was bent on reinventing his hero, with his determination based largely on his low opinion of Jacob Pheasant and Timothy Snake. Since these Natives were both Shawnee, Gowman refused to accept that such a remarkable warrior as Tecumseh could have sprung from their midst. To Gowman's peculiar way of thinking, Tecumseh's martial achievements were more in line with the Aztec culture, as he considered southern Native peoples superior to those of northern regions.[86] When these incredible claims failed to produce the slightest reaction, Gowman confidently prepared to give the readers of the *Free Press* more of the same.

On 30 December 1893, Gowman presented the account of Tecumseh's death and burial according to Duncan Holmes, alias Joseph Johnson.[87] Except for a few minor modifications, one of which was

Holmes's Native name of Waubishkink, it was the same story Gowman sent to the *London Advertiser* back in 1876.[88] And, as in the case of his first submission, no one raised the question of honesty. Gowman must have wondered why he had gone to all the trouble of using a pseudonym. Perhaps it had something to do with an unfortunate perjury indictment dating from 1860.[89] Whatever Gowman's reason, he seemed destined once again to have the last word on Tecumseh's burial. The complacent old man had no way of knowing that a challenger was waiting in the wings.

At the end of January 1894, the opening installment of a rival Tecumseh serial suddenly appeared in the *Free Press*.[90] The author was Nelles F. Timothy, or Toma Pa-meh-laut, a Delaware from the Caradoc Reserve.[91] With neither snideness, nor the slightest suggestion of confrontation, Timothy launched into his own version of Tecumseh's life and times – which ran completely counter to that provided by Peter Pancrees. Although Timothy gave no explanation for his contribution, it probably had something to do with Gowman's unprovoked attack upon the correspondent who had submitted the report on the Oneida Fall Fair. Very likely, the correspondent and Nelles F. Timothy were one and the same person. Gowman either failed to make the connection, or chose to ignore it. Whatever the case, Timothy was allowed to continue with a standard account of Tecumseh's Shawnee origins, to which he added the forceful contradiction: "Never was he a prisoner."[92] But this was not the worst of it. Gowman must have been mortified when he discovered Timothy's statement that Pheasant, Snake, and the rest of the burial party were all Delaware – a northern tribe that was no better than the Shawnee.[93] It was more than the poor old revisionist could stand.

Donning his Native persona once again, Gowman dashed off a another letter to the *Free Press*. Expressing little surprise at the challenge, Uncle Pete Pancrees, as he had also taken to calling himself, claimed that he fully expected a Delaware would disagree with him.[94] The battle in which Tecumseh lost his life was fought near the Moravian mission to the Delaware Natives, and so they naturally "laid claim to Tecumseh as being one of their tribe."[95] It also explained how Pheasant and Snake came to be regarded as Delaware, when in fact they were both Shawnee. Gowman's logic was sound enough, but rather than debating Timothy in a concise manner, he confused the issue with irrelevant arguments, ineffectual analogies, pious biblical quotes, and some very unseemly remarks. Gowman did make one point perfectly clear: "what Mr Timothy says about the Delaware warriors burying

Tecumseh is too sickening to read."[96] Knowing that Timothy would point to Pheasant and Snake as authorities on Tecumseh's burial, Gowman tried his best to defame their reputations by accusing them of having sold the great chief's bones a "good many times."[97] The attempted sabotage had no effect.

Timothy, quite unperturbed, carried on with his next installment, which appeared early in February of 1894. In it, he promised his readers that he would "keep closely to historical facts recorded by some of the English generals, colonels, and captains" who were intimately acquainted with Tecumseh, and also those war chiefs who "were present at the taking of Detroit, and at the Battle of Moravian Town on the Thames."[98] True to his word, Timothy based some of his research on British Captain John B. Glegg's observations of Tecumseh, which were found in an old book on the life of Sir Isaac Brock.[99] However, Timothy did not give his source. He was even less forthcoming when it came to the dialogue he used in portraying the meeting of Tecumseh and Harrison at Vincennes, Indiana Territory, in August of 1810. It certainly was not of Glegg's making, but rather originated with a patriotic Canadian poet and playwright by the name of Charles Mair, who, in 1886, published his epic *Tecumseh: A Drama*.[100] Mair's intellectual ownership was of no concern to Timothy. It was more important for him to command Pete Pancrees's attention by demanding: "I am on the platform; sit down, please. Order."[101]

In his next segment, Timothy continued to plagiarize Mair's highly romanticized exchange between Tecumseh and Harrison.[102] But Gowman soon caught up with him. On 24 February 1894, Pete Pancrees imposed upon the *Free Press* for what proved to be the last time. In a desperate bid to discredit Timothy, Gowman pronounced the speeches of Tecumseh and Harrison to be a fraud: "[they] are worded so much in the same strain that they are evidently the outcome of one prolific brain."[103] Gowman was convinced that Timothy was inventing most of his information, just as he himself had done. Of course, Gowman could hardly argue this point too strenuously.

In an effort to undermine his Native antagonist, Gowman tried to find fault with the source of Timothy's information regarding Tecumseh. But Timothy's misleading reference to Glegg's "minute accounts" confounded Gowman, who laboured under the misconception that Glegg was responsible for having transcribed the lofty oratory between Tecumseh and Harrison. The old carpenter was at a loss. Yet, he was desperate to discredit Timothy's serial, and so a criticism of some kind had to be found. In a bold move, Gowman asserted that Tecumseh could not have made the speeches, as he "did not open his mouth at that council, from the very fact that he was not there."[104] As Gowman elaborated, the Shawnee warrior was at that time off enjoying an extended visit to Arnold's Mill, on the Thames River, in Upper Canada.[105] Considering the weakness (if not the absurdity) of his challenge, Gowman quickly turned to Waubishkink's narrative of events following the Battle of the Thames, but not before taking a parting shot at his Native nemesis. Childishly, Gowman ridiculed Timothy's Native name of Toma Pa-meh-laut. "If Mr Tome-ass-fau-me-lout has the platform, he is welcome to keep it; the planks are too rotten to suit me."[106] While Gowman was eager to proceed with more of what he freely admitted were "yarns," the *Free Press* did not share his enthusiasm. Nothing more of Gowman's manuscript was seen in the London daily.

Timothy, in the meantime, had continued by paraphrasing Mair's depiction of the Battle of the Thames, which included a highly romantic version of Tecumseh's dying words spoken in the presence of several warriors: "Brothers, I am shot. Bear my body hence. Give no alarm, lest our poor braves lose courage. Make haste; I have not long to live. Yet hear my words, bury me in the deep and densest forest, and let no white man know where I am laid. Promise this, my warriors."[107] In Mair's original version, Tecumseh had spoken his dying words to a Delaware chief, which Timothy must have thought a particularly appropriate choice for having the great chief's last wishes respected. After all, Timothy had already laid claim to the secret of Tecumseh's burial on behalf of the Delaware nation. Having finished with Tecumseh, Timothy turned his attention to a spirited defence of Timothy Snake, who he insisted had steadfastly refused white bribes to reveal Tecumseh's grave. Having thus far maintained the moral high ground, Timothy was able to convincingly observe that "Pete Pancrees' miserable whiskey would never do."[108]

Thinking the contest over, Timothy soon found himself confronted with a copy of Gowman's final submission to the *Free Press*. Unaware that this was Pete Pancrees's last word on the subject, and unable to restrain himself further, Timothy responded to the insults by fighting fire with fire. Starting off with the muddled account of Tecumseh's meeting with Harrison, he berated "Mr Pete Pan-grease" for his ignorance of "that memorable meeting of the two great warriors."[109] Timothy then pounced on Gowman's own admission that he was "just telling yarns," and in the process managed to sidestep Gowman's accusations of fraud regarding the speeches of Tecumseh and Harrison. Expanding on the theme of yarns, Timothy exposed what he believed was a hidden agenda to deprive the Delaware of their relationship to Tecumseh. If Pete Pancrees really intended to "hang" the Delaware with his yarns, as Timothy put it, he would first have to contend with the vaguely familiar argument that his yarns were "too rotten" and "would not hang a fly."[110] Gowman, however, having been shunned by the *Free Press*, had no choice but to endure Timothy's judgment that Tecumseh was "a Lenni Lennepi [or Delaware] after all."[111]

With his disgust hidden behind his disguise, Thomas Gowman made no further attempts to publish his manuscript and a few years later, in May of 1898, he died.[112] Thanks to a Native with an axe to grind, Gowman did not have the last word on Tecumseh's burial, and his contributions to the London *Free Press* were soon forgotten. His papers were preserved, however, and in the 1920s they were donated to the Archives of Ontario, where they continue to perplex hapless Tecumseh scholars to this day. Yet, had Gowman pursued the oral traditions of his childhood with greater honesty, he might have made a valuable contribution to the literature on Tecumseh. Unfortunately for him, he delighted a little too much in "just telling yarns."

Confusing the Issue

As THE DEBATE IN THE LONDON *Free Press* drew to an end, Nelles F. Timothy tauntingly enquired of his antagonist: "which is your right name of the two, Pete Pancrees, or Wau-pis-skunk?"[1] Timothy was convinced that Waubishkink's narrative was just another one of the yarns told by Pete Pancrees. Timothy's jab, however, did not have the desired effect, and Thomas Gowman never betrayed his true identity or that of Waubishkink, alias Duncan Holmes, alias Joseph Johnson. Shielded by Gowman's penchant for pseudonyms, Johnson continued to be regarded as a reliable source of information regarding Tecumseh's burial. This was especially true in the lower Thames Valley, the neighbourhood of Gowman's youth. With the turn of the twentieth century, however, Johnson came under heavy attack.

In August of 1901, George W. Sulman announced his determination to have a monument honouring Tecumseh erected in Chatham, Ontario.[2] Impressed by the Joseph Brant monument in Brantford, Sulman thought his city should have something similar for Tecumseh – if for no better reason than the fact that Chatham was located on the route of the British and Native retreat.[3] Sulman was sure of success. Not only was he the mayor of Chatham, he had the full support of an active Chatham-based literary society known as the Macaulay Club, and – most importantly – Thaddeus Arnold was on side.[4]

This gentleman was known to possess important information about Tecumseh, which he derived from researching his family's history. In the later 1790s, as Arnold discovered, his grandfather had established a grist mill on the south bank of the Thames River, nearly opposite present-day Kent Bridge. It was there, in October of 1813, that Tecumseh performed the good deed for which he was immortalized in the pages of the Arnold family history. After the British had retreated upriver, Tecumseh lingered to guard against the destruction of Arnold's Mill by marauding Natives.[5] This humane act ensured that Arnold and his neighbours would not starve for want of flour. One of these neighbours, it turned out, was Joseph Johnson – and it was the Arnold family's low opinion of him that made Thaddeus Arnold such an asset to Chatham.

As a child, young Thaddeus would listen intently as his father talked about their family's encounter with the famous Tecumseh. "I remember well a number of times," the younger Arnold recalled, "when out hunting with my father, that he would, while sitting down to rest, repeat to me the many oft-told incidents that he had gathered in reference to that memorable man, Tecumseh, and the manner of his death."[6] Years later, in 1901, Arnold put his research to good use by writing an article on Tecumseh's death and burial. While pride in his family's association with the great chief appeared to be the inspiration behind this piece, Arnold was also motivated by a desire to dispute Johnson's most outspoken supporter: William K. Merrifield.[7] Drawing heavily upon his father's recollections, Arnold presented a scathing description of Johnson's character: "My father always stated that Joe Johnston [sic] was not a trader, neither was he a warrior, and [he] was not with the Indians at Chatham; nor was he with Tecumseh the night before the battle; in short, [he] was not at the Battle of the Thames; nor was he ever associated with Tecumseh in any of his undertakings; that he possessed none of the characteristics of a warrior, in fact [he] was unfitted in every way for any martial achievement."[8] This negative assessment was well received in Chatham, where it was touted in order to diminish the importance of the battlefield as a potential site for Tecumseh's monument.

Although Johnson still had a good number of champions – as well as descendants – living in and around Chatham, no one came to his defence.[9] Even Merrifield kept his distance, ignoring Arnold's obvious attempt to bait him. As one of the founding members of the Macaulay Club, Merrifield probably restrained himself for the sake of Chatham's monument scheme.[10] If so, his self-control did nothing to facilitate the project. In March of 1902, the *Chatham Planet* wryly observed that a "close search in Tecumseh Park after the thaw failed to discover that monument to Tecumseh, which the Macaulay Club proposed erecting last year."[11] The Macaulays had accomplished nothing, except an expedition to the site of Arnold's Mills. But in looking for "remembrances of Tecumseh," they quickly extracted all the pertinent local traditions and soon found themselves compensating with recollections of a prolific hickory nut tree, a Native murder, a tree-felling accident, and a good rat story.[12] For this reason, despite generous newspaper coverage of their quest, the Macaulays were unable to sustain interest in their monument scheme. Six years would pass before Tecumseh once again became newsworthy.

In June of 1907, the London Conference of the Methodist Church assembled at Goderich, Ontario. Foremost among the topics of debate was the liquor licensing laws, especially as they pertained to unscrupulous hotel keepers. Morally satisfied that an "honest effort" was being made in controlling the illicit liquor trade, the delegates "warmly commended" the provincial government's strict enforcement of the law. But one minister, unable to resist playing devil's advocate, wondered how well the law was being enforced with regard to "giving liquor to Indians."[13] This question touched a nerve with Albert Tobias, the lay delegate from the Moraviantown Reserve. "Whisky has almost depleted our people," he declared in a trembling voice, "but it has not been given to them by hotelkeepers so much as by low white men."[14] Tobias saw no solution to the problem, as the natives could not be forced to disclose the names of their suppliers. To illustrate his point, Tobias told the audience how white men had long tried to "ferret out the grave of Tecumseh," but their attempts to reveal this native secret proved equally futile. Tobias was "listened to with deep attention and warmly applauded by the members of the conference," who then promptly turned their attention to the "nonsensical delusion" of Christian Science.[15] But the matter of Tecumseh's grave did not end there.

The proceedings of the Methodist conference were duly reported in the London *Free Press*, and before long the remark about Tecumseh's grave was widely circulated. In Hamilton, the editor of the *Hamilton Spectator* was sufficiently intrigued to ask: "Is there not some tradition among the natives of the Moravian settlement which might be properly revealed at this late day, touching [upon] the resting place of Tecumseh?"[16] One of his readers thought there might be, and helpfully responded with extracts from Thaddeus Arnold's article.[17] This development caught the attention of the *Chatham Planet*'s editor, who, anticipating a revival of interest in Tecumseh, reprinted the article just as it appeared in the *Hamilton Spectator*. This in turn attracted Merrifield's attention early in August.[18] Unfettered by Chatham's bid for a monument, Merrifield jumped at the chance to defend Johnson's participation in Tecumseh's secret burial. Although Arnold's low opinion of Joseph Johnson was omitted from the reprint, Merrifield still had good reason to respond.[19] By doing so, he could introduce a new version of Johnson's story.

In Merrifield's adaptation, when Tecumseh's death became apparent to his bodyguards, which was almost immediately, they reacted by throwing his body "between two logs, and, rallying the rest of the Indians, fought with such fury that they again drove back the Yankees. But when the Indians realized that their great chieftain was dead they began to disperse. It was now getting late in the afternoon, and the bodyguard carried the remains far into the night to a stream which they dammed up, and then dug his grave and buried him in the channel. They then tore away the dam, making the place look as natural as possible."[20] This burial in a streambed was a new take on an old story, and one that did not originate with Joseph Johnson. Neither was it gleaned from a Native elder. The source was a Harwich Township schoolgirl.

In 1889, Abigail Smith entered a Canada-wide literary contest sponsored by the Montreal *Witness*.[21] Abigail chose to submit a story about Tecumseh, which she told through the exploits of a United Empire Loyalist from Montreal by the name of Joseph Brenton. Abigail's story begins in 1808, when Brenton led a large party of men to explore the country bordering several of the Great Lakes. Somewhere in the region of a lesser body of water know as Lake St Clair, Brenton became separated from his expedition. It was then that he experienced a chance meeting with Tecumseh, and the ensuing "friendship so strangely begun, grew into a love that was almost brotherly."[22] Eventually, Brenton and Tecumseh parted company, only to be reunited during Procter's retreat in October of 1813 ... and with a predictable sequence of events. Not only did Brenton fight alongside Tecumseh at the Battle of the Thames, he also assisted with his friend's burial in a streambed. Abigail described the scene in the following terms: "At midnight six Indian Chiefs and a white man might be seen carrying the body of the beloved Tecumseh to its place of burial. It was laid on the bank of a rushing stream while the seven set to work to dam the torrent. This done, a grave was dug in the bed of the stream, the Chieftain buried, the dam broke, and the waters rolled over Tecumseh."[23]

Abigail's entry won her the provincial literary prize for Ontario, along with a fair degree of fame. Her story was published in the Montreal *Witness*, reprinted in the *Chatham Planet*, and also featured in an anthology of the contest's best contributions.[24] With this success, Abigail had achieved all she ever intended: a prize-winning essay. And she owed it all to a vivid imagination, which explains why no record can be found of Brenton's survey or of Brenton himself.[25]

When a correspondent to the *Witness* questioned whether the story was "history or fiction," a defensive Abigail claimed to have "followed the account given by an old Delaware chief, named Jewel Snake, who died some fifteen years ago."[26] Actually, the young lady meant Timothy Snake, the Shawnee elder from Moraviantown. Unfortunately for Abigail, there is no evidence to suggest that she obtained the story regarding Tecumseh's streambed burial from Snake. It would seem more plausible that she took liberties with Joseph Johnson's claim to have helped bury Tecumseh. Yet, by citing a Native elder, who conveniently enough was dead, she managed to avoid further potentially embarrassing enquiries – which was absolutely necessary if she hoped to retain her prize. The contest rules stipulated that all stories submitted had to be true, and so Abigail could ill-afford to have her veracity questioned.[27]

Apart from its romantic appeal, there was little to recommend Abigail's story. This, however, did not prevent her contribution from fundamentally altering the mystery. Before Miss Smith took up her pen, Tecumseh's body had only ever been buried near, or under, a toppled tree. There was never any mention of a streambed.[28] But after her essay was published, no one – other than the naysaying correspondent to the *Witness* – questioned the likelihood of such an impressive feat of engineering. Merrifield, for one, fully accepted Abigail's variation. Much, if not all, of his confidence stemmed from the posthumous verification of George Laird, who was credited with having had a first-hand knowledge of the secret burial. Although Laird died in 1879, a daughter-in-law perpetuated his recollections of the event. As Sarah Ann Laird recalled almost twenty years later, her husband's father

always claimed that the grave of Tecumseh would never be found. He said that after Tecumseh was killed the Indians carried him to a large tree near the bank of the river on the side of a deep ravine at the foot of which a little stream trickled into the Thames. They then dispersed till night fell as the Americans were hot on their trail. At night a chosen band, amongst whom was Mr Laird, stole back and buried Tecumseh temporarily beneath the waters of the streamlet at the bottom of the ravine. They first dammed the water back and then after the burial let it flow again.[29]

Despite the questionable participation of yet another white man in Tecumseh's burial party, Mrs Laird's version of the streambed burial meshed quite nicely with Abigail Smith's story. But Mrs Laird was hardly a reliable source of information.

At the same time she repeated her father-in-law's exploits, Mrs

Laird also recalled an article that claimed Tecumseh had been assassinated by a drummer boy.[30] "I have often thought," she scattily conjectured, "that it must have been George Laird who shot Tecumseh. He was a drummer boy to Tecumseh's force. I can hardly tell what makes me think so. One thing is that my father-in-law, although he would state that he knew who did it and saw it done, would never say who fired the shot. Little things that I remember him saying have given me this impression."[31] Mrs Laird was quite mistaken. Her father-in-law was not Tecumseh's drummer boy. He was a private in the Kent Militia.[32] Merrifield knew that Tecumseh had no need of a drummer boy, but it was a minor discrepancy and one that did not compromise Mrs Laird's credibility. Merrifield simply corrected her by referring to George Laird as having been "a drummer boy in Proctor's army" as opposed to "a drummer boy to Tecumseh's force."[33] Yet, there remains a fundamental problem with Mrs Laird's information. Her stories about Tecumseh's burial did not originate with George Laird.

In 1829, Laird purchased land in Dawn Township, not far from what is now the village of Florence, and within a short distance of Joseph Johnson.[34] These aging militiamen must have shared many interesting stories about the War of 1812, which Laird no doubt did his best to perpetuate. And Sarah Ann Laird would have heard her father-in-law recite his and Johnson's experiences on numerous occasions, although it appears she had only a passing interest in them. It is easy to imagine that Mrs Laird's indifference caused her to confuse the exploits of Joseph Johnson with those of her father-in-law, resulting in the misconception that George Laird was a member of Tecumseh's burial party. Slightly more difficult to speculate is the inspiration behind Mrs Laird's elaborations on the streambed burial, until it is revealed that her son was a printer at the *Chatham Planet* – the same newspaper that reprinted Abigail Smith's essay from the Montreal *Witness* in November of 1889.[35] Clearly, Mrs Laird's assertions are flawed and there is no evidence to suggest that George Laird ever claimed to have helped bury Tecumseh. But Mrs Laird might have thought her father-in-law said as much, just as she thought he admitted to having assassinated Tecumseh.[36]

When Merrifield responded to the *Chatham Planet*'s reprinting of excerpts from Arnold's article in August of 1907, he incorporated the streambed burial as though it were part of Johnson's original story.[37] Moreover, he used the evidence of Joseph Brenton and George Laird to corroborate Johnson's story. These accounts, of course, agreed with each other, which led Merrifield to conclude that here are stories from three different men who were actual participants in the battle, and happened to be in the vicinity when Tecumseh died. It [appears] to me that those stories are about as accurate as could be expected under circumstances like theirs – the remnants of a beaten army whose chief, being dead, had to look out for their own lives in the midst of a wilderness. And it seems to me that the man [Joseph] Johnson, who had long been a member of Tecumseh's fighting force, and of his body guard, would be the most apt to remember the exact occurrences on that occasion.[38]

No one questioned Merrifield as to his sources, and Merrifield did not concern himself further with Tecumseh. However, by having responded to the *Hamilton Spectator*'s call for information regarding Tecumseh's burial, Merrifield likely inspired the next attempt to raise a monument to the great chief.

In October of 1907, a widow from Morpeth, in Kent County's Howard Township, tried to renew interest in the idea of a monument by addressing a letter about it to the *Chatham Planet*. Augusta D. Richardson singled out several prominent men she thought might form a suitable committee to oversee a fundraising drive for a statue of the great chief in Chatham's Tecumseh Park. Confidently, she predicted "substantial donations" from all levels of government, not to mention the generous support of the business community.[39]

In waiting and watching, it became embarrassingly apparent to Mrs Richardson that her appeal had failed. Far from giving up, however, she took it upon herself to excite interest in Tecumseh's death and burial at the national level. In a January 1908 issue of the Toronto *Globe*, she published a short article under the crafty title: "WAS COLONEL JOHNSON THE SLAYER OF TECUMSEH?"[40] Mrs Richardson already knew the answer and, after giving Richard M. Johnson due credit, she went on to describe a chance meeting she had some years earlier with a Native elder named Gottlieb Tobias.[41] When she casually asked if he knew where Tecumseh was buried, the astonished old man replied:

Tecumseh! Tecumseh! Nobody know where he buried. Some say old burying ground here [Moraviantown]; some say Turin; some say near T'emsville; some say in a hollow log under the river; but nobody know now. They was a man once, Timothy Snake, used to live in Moraviantown. He knew. He was Tecumseh's sister's child – a what you call um? Yah. Nephew. But he dead now. No, he never tell. The Government offer him heaps of money to tell where Tecumseh was buried, but he wouldn't. Lots of um want to know, but he – what you call super – super – yah! superstitious (for this word was also beyond him and he had to prompted). He afeard Tecumseh's spirit would 'witch him if he tell, and he'd die right away. So he never tell.⁴²

Being a devout Christian, Mrs Richardson could well accept the excuse that Snake had been spiritually constrained from revealing Tecumseh's grave. As for the exaggerated version of Abigail Smith's streambed burial, which conflicted with the old story of Tecumseh's burial under the toppled tree, Mrs Richardson simply combined the two stories – just as Merrifield had done.

Tecumseh's grave in the base of a tree, she proposed, was merely a temporary measure to keep the wolves at bay. Then, as if for effect, she threw in a story about a fire that raced through the forest within a few years of Tecumseh's burial, destroying all traces of the battlefield.⁴³ Mrs Richardson could only ponder the consequence: "Did this fire consume the remains of the brave Tecumseh? Or were they 'buried in darkness at dead of night' under the sullen, muddy Thames, which had been deflected from its channel for the purpose?"⁴⁴ Despite her best efforts, Mrs Richardson's prodding failed to rally the *Globe*'s readers. But her article did eventually draw a response. Unfortunately for the well-intentioned widow, it was not the positive rejoinder she expected.

In April of 1908, an old Canadian expatriate living in California soundly repudiated Mrs Richardson's remarks concerning the great chief's fate. "Colonel Johnson did not kill Tecumseh," Albert Greenwood declared.⁴⁵ Furthermore, and although Mrs Richardson had not even raised the issue of Tecumseh's mutilated corpse, Greenwood contended that no Kentuckian ever "laid a finger on it."⁴⁶ The old man was no less adamant in contradicting Mrs Richardson's attempted reconciliation of the several variations describing the burial of Tecumseh's body: "It was not consumed by fire, or buried in the river," and the "locality was not 'unknown,' nor is it unknown to-day."⁴⁷

Greenwood was insistent that Tecumseh's grave had been kept a secret in order to foil American trophy hunters. Yet, the Canadian government supposedly always knew "what was done with the chief's body, and that whenever they were ready to treat his memory as they had treated that of his peer, Gen. Brock, the grave would be promptly pointed out to them."⁴⁸ But, as Greenwood added, he was never approached by anyone during his half century of residence in the vicinity of the battlefield, except mere curiosity seekers. "A few more years," he lamented, "and it may be vain to seek, as it is extremely doubtful if a man living, beside myself, can prove that he has kept the right trail by pointing out the grave."⁴⁹ Along with this revelation, Greenwood announced that he was prepared to convince the most skeptical that "I know just whereof I speak."[50] No one – including Mrs Richardson – bothered to take up this ambiguous challenge.[51] However, as the one hundredth anniversary of Tecumseh's death loomed, Greenwood would prove increasingly difficult to ignore.

Early in February of 1909, Samuel Stevely, the mayor of London, Ontario, received a curious letter from an "Iroquois girl" living in New York City. Like Mrs Richardson before her, Evelyn Johnson suggested a subscription drive to raise the funds necessary to construct a monument to Tecumseh. But unlike Mrs Richardson, Miss Johnson was willing to commit to her scheme with the promise of a twenty-five dollar donation. An impressed Mayor Stevely thought this was "a great idea," and that London was the city "to have the monument."[52] But, just as Stevely mistook Miss Johnson for a girl, when she was in fact a middle-aged spinster, he also assumed that she intended London to be the future site of the monument.[53] Actually, all she wanted was Stevely's help in raising the matter with the Canadian Club, a patriotic organization with a branch in London that was about to convene. Although Miss Johnson really preferred the battlefield as the site of the proposed monument, Mayor Stevely's enthusiasm prompted her to endorse London. Soon after, she dutifully wrote out a cheque to the Tecumseh Monument Fund.[54]

Much of Miss Johnson's interest in seeing a monument erected to Tecumseh originated from within her own family. Her father was Chief George H.M. Johnson from the Six Nations Reserve – the same Chief Johnson who had participated in the United Canadians' bungled search for Tecumseh's grave over thirty years earlier. And Pauline Johnson, the famous Canadian poetess who popularized Native themes, was her sister.[55] Like her esteemed father and her celebrated sister, Evelyn Johnson wanted to make a name for herself. A monument to Tecumseh would be her claim to fame.

In spite of her generous donation, Miss Johnson was unable to generate much interest in her proposal – except in a village near the battlefield. The citizens of Thamesville were infuriated by her support of London's sudden grab for the monument.[56] Horrified that she might have inadvertently caused a schism in her grand scheme, Miss Johnson penned a letter to the London *Free Press* in July of 1909, and diplomatically left the question of the site of Tecumseh's monument to be settled "by wise heads and loyal Canadian hearts."[57] Hoping to quash any further threat of partisanship, she concluded with a "strong personal and patriotic appeal to the U.E. Loyalists, the Imperial Daughters of the Empire, the historical societies, the Canadian clubs, the Indians, and all loyal Canadians, to eliminate personal and municipal hopes and [supposed] rights, and all get to work for the glory of Canada and the Empire in 1912, and, laying aside all personal feeling, all animosity, all bitterness, work and give to memorialize one of Canada's most valiant heroes, Great Britain's ally, who gave his life."[58] Far from uniting Canadians in a magnificent show of patriotism, Miss Johnson's letter sparked the most divisive reaction in the quest for a monument to Tecumseh since the United Canadians' fiasco of 1876.

Disregarding Miss Johnson's appeal, the London *Free Press* alerted its readers to the fact that Tecumseh's "body was never seen again" and "no man can tell where it was laid," suggesting that London, Ontario, was just as good a place for his monument as anywhere else.[59] This opinion drew another heated response from Albert Greenwood. Writing from his new home in Hillsborough, New Hampshire, in mid-August of 1909, Greenwood repeated his earlier claims that he alone knew the secret burial place of Tecumseh, which he would consent to point out only if arrangements were made to build the monument where the great chief fell – which certainly was not London. In closing his letter, Greenwood boldly asserted that "Tecumseh's grave has always been known, and is known now."[60] It was a remark intended to entice interest and inquiry, but once again Greenwood was ignored. Finally, in December of 1909, he relented somewhat and offered to assist Chatham with the benefit of his knowledge.

Greenwood considered Chatham an acceptable compromise. For one thing, Chatham was the place where Tecumseh had expected to make a stand against the Americans. It was also the seat of Kent County – the county in which the great chief had "slept so long."[61] For these reasons, questionable though they were, Greenwood was willing to break solidarity with the "old scout" who had participated in the secret burial, and later defied a curious governor-general of Canada by refusing to give up the secret unless a monument was built where Tecumseh was killed.[62] In giving this vague clue as to his informant, Greenwood hoped to attract attention. And he did, much to his chagrin.

Several months later, in April of 1910, the Wallaceburg Board of Trade devoted the better part of its regular meeting to the surprising news that the community it represented held the strongest claim to Tecumseh's monument. Wallaceburg, a thriving village located twenty-six kilometres north of Chatham, had never been known for any association with Tecumseh. Nevertheless, the board of trade's president,

Thomas B. Dundas, enthusiastically embraced the idea, and fully expected that government funding would be made available. By way of some background, Dundas explained how a local farmer had alerted the board of trade to Wallaceburg's right in the matter. With his next breath, Dundas proclaimed that "the monument could be located in no better place than in Wallaceburg, that we never get anything if we don't ask for it, and we have been accustomed to get what we go after."[63] He then introduced the man responsible for raising the issue: Matthew Fisher.

Upon hearing his name, an elderly gentleman rose and addressed the assembly. After recounting Tecumseh's life and times, Fisher revealed that Tecumseh's "remains were taken from the original burial place near the battlefield and buried not far from Wallaceburg."[64] The source of Fisher's information was an uncle who got the story directly from the Native who had retrieved Tecumseh's bones. Being careful not to betray the identity of this elder, other than to say that he was Tecumseh's aide-de-camp, Fisher continued by describing the circumstances surrounding the removal of Tecumseh's bones.[65] After his death at the Battle of the Thames, Tecumseh was buried in the forest thereabouts and

behind an oak log, with two other chiefs. The old aide-de-camp made the pilgrimage every year to his dead chief's grave, and performed certain rites. About 1864 or 1865, the farm was being cleared up, the oak log removed, and the old man worried about it, fearing the bones would be plowed up. What he did he afterwards told Uncle John Fisher, who afterwards divulged the secret as I now give it to you. The aide-de-camp removed the bones of Tecumseh in a bag, brought them home with him, and buried them in his own burial-ground. There he placed a stake and a British ensign that wore away to shreds.[66]

Fisher also explained that the aide-de-camp made his home on St Anne's Island, one of several delta tracts at the mouth of the St Clair River known collectively as the Walpole Island Reserve.[67] Fisher went on to volunteer that his family's farm was directly across the Chenal Ecarté (or River Snye) from St Anne's Island, as if to suggest how his uncle had become aware of the aide-de-camp's secret.[68] Proximity alone, however, could not have secured Native trust, but John Fisher did have an advantage over most, if not all, of his white neighbours. His mother was Shawnee.[69] Curiously, Matthew Fisher did not care to elaborate on this aspect of his family history, even though a Shawnee connection would have made a strong case for the aide-de-camp's indulgence toward his uncle.

After Fisher took his seat, the members of the board of trade enthusiastically appointed a committee to investigate the burial in order to make their case for a monument.[70] The local newspaper, the *Wallaceburg News*, did its part for the old hometown by printing a long report of the meeting, which soon found its way to Albert Greenwood in far-off New Hampshire.[71]

Greenwood immediately objected to the proceedings in Wallaceburg, but once again his protest was characterized by veiled references to his sources, which did nothing to strengthen his argument against Fisher's revelation. Yet, neither did it stop him from impugning the aide-de-camp's character with some exaggerated statistics. "There were about 6,000 [men] at that battle," Greenwood asserted.[72] But only "three knew what became of Tecumseh's body, and that Walpole Indian was not one of them."[73] He continued to discredit Fisher's source by stating "there has never been produced a shred of evidence that any one of these three ever pointed out that grave to any man."[74] Greenwood concluded by reiterating his support for Chatham, and offering to meet with its duly authorized monument committee once it received the necessary funds. Unfortunately for Greenwood, his attempt to force Chatham into compliance simply hastened a reaction by Fisher.

In mid-May of 1910, Fisher addressed a letter to the *Wallaceburg News* in which he made a "clean breast of the whole affair."[75] He began by revealing that his wife and Greenwood were cousins, and that they had corresponded with one another on a regular basis. From one of Greenwood's missives, written in January of 1910, Fisher learned that his wife's cousin expected to be called to Ontario in order to point out Tecumseh's grave. Then, in February, Fisher received news of Greenwood's offer to assist Chatham in securing a monument to Tecumseh. It was soon after, coincidentally enough, that Fisher happened upon "an important discovery concerning Tecumseh's grave."[76] What Fisher failed to mention, however, is that it was no coincidence that he made this "important discovery" when he did, or that it involved a grave on St Anne's Island. Nor was it any great secret where Fisher's interests lay, especially when he told the Wallaceburg Board of Trade that "Wallaceburg men were just as smart as Chatham men."[77]

While the idea of favouring Wallaceburg with his new-found largesse appealed to Fisher, he had no wish to subject his wife's cousin to unnecessary embarrassment. For this reason, as Fisher confessed in making his "clean breast of the whole affair," he was willing to let

Greenwood take credit for pointing out Tecumseh's grave on St Anne's Island, thus avoiding the "unpleasant disclosures, which were sure to follow the building of a monument at Chatham."[78] Greenwood, however, did not appreciate Fisher's brand of conscientiousness. Only after Greenwood refused the olive branch, in February of 1910, did Fisher decide to take his case to the Wallaceburg Board of Trade. A few months later, he made his announcement regarding Tecumseh's burial on St Anne's Island – without revealing the identity of the Native aide-de-camp. Fisher was afraid that Greenwood would somehow twist the elder's story to deprive Wallaceburg of its chance to have Tecumseh's monument. Greenwood, however, had not been put off and attacked the aide-de-camp's story with all the assurance of a long familiarity. But he soon found himself hampered by his inability to put a name to the Native he so desperately tried to discredit. It was then that Fisher saw his opportunity to undermine Greenwood's authority in the matter, which began with his making a "clean breast of the whole affair."[79] But he would go one step further by unmasking the mysterious aide-de-camp.

In his letter to the *Wallaceburg News* in mid-May of 1910, Fisher agreed with Greenwood's assertion that Tecumseh's grave was known only to the men who buried him. Fisher expanded by adding that the grave had also been well guarded, and by no less a personage than Oshahwahnoo, a Chippewa chief of St Anne's Island and "aide-de-camp to Gen. [sic] Tecumseh, a man whom Mr Greenwood has never had the pleasure of meeting."[80] While Oshahwahnoo's role at the Battle of the Thames is now questioned, Fisher had no doubt that he fought alongside Tecumseh, that he was the Native equivalent of an aide-de-camp, or that he was directly involved in the secret burial – all of which convinced him that Tecumseh was buried on St Anne's Island.[81] Yet Fisher's attempt to impress the Canadian public had no effect. Oshahwahnoo's name, while it carried considerable weight on Walpole Island, unfortunately did not command much attention beyond the reserve – partly because he had been dead for almost forty years.[82] It soon became clear to Fisher that if he were to succeed in bestowing Tecumseh's monument upon his friends in Wallaceburg, he would have to find some other way to do it.

Three weeks later, on a damp and disagreeable day in early June of 1910, a small steam launch pulled away from its dock in Wallaceburg and chugged down the Sydenham River. On board, several members of the board of trade and their friends pressed together under the cover of tarps.[83] Before long, the launch passed out of the Sydenham River, which empties into the Chenal Ecarté, and made its way alongside St Anne's Island in the direction of the St Clair River. Waiting some distance down the riverbank were Matthew Fisher and a small group of his associates. A few Native men also participated, and were soon leading the way to a small cemetery. The procession ended at a grave which was prominently marked with a Canadian flag and a wooden cross.[84] After posing for their picture, one of the party began to dig beside Oshahwahnoo's burial mound. When nothing turned up, someone suggested they try digging at the head of the grave. Almost immediately, the spade struck a small coffin. Inside were the bones of a large man. It was Tecumseh, and there could be no doubt about it. The discovery of the grave validated Oshahwahnoo's story, and in turn verified the identity of the bones. The expedition was a success, and Matthew Fisher "was naturally jubilant as the find bore out his statements persistently made in spite of the skeptical ones."[85]

With the discovery of Tecumseh's bones, the members of the Wallaceburg Board of Trade suddenly found themselves at a loss to know exactly what to do with them. Their original intention was simply to photograph the skeleton and then return it to its grave. However, it now occurred to them that news of the discovery might lead to the grave being pilfered. Faced with this threat, they decided to ask the attending Natives for permission to borrow the bones in order to safeguard them. Before doing so, they quietly arranged that Dr George Mitchell of Wallaceburg should be appointed custodian. Not only was he qualified to examine the skeleton, he was also well known and highly respected on Walpole Island.[86]

The Natives reacted to the proposal by withdrawing some distance and debating amongst themselves. Grudgingly, they consented, on one condition: that the bones would be returned whenever they were requested. Dr Mitchell readily agreed to this provision, and soon the precious relics were en route to Wallaceburg.[87] They might just as well have remained on St Anne's Island.

5

Beyond the Exhumation

WORD OF THE DISCOVERY SPREAD quickly, and Dr Mitchell just as quickly became Wallaceburg's most popular citizen. On 3 June 1910, only a day after his return from St Anne's Island, the doctor went before the Wallaceburg Board of Trade. Speaking to a large and receptive audience, he confidently announced that the bones in his possession were those of Tecumseh.[1] It was quite a coup, but one that proved extremely short-lived. The very next day, Dr Mitchell had a surprise visit from Chief Joseph White of the Walpole Island Reserve. After a brief exchange of pleasantries, the chief abruptly demanded Tecumseh's return. Although it pained Smith to have to do so, he reluctantly complied. As he handed over the bones, little did he realize that there would be much more pain to come.[2]

Soon after the bones were repatriated, the first of many angry protests made its way into the press. Speaking on behalf of the Macaulay Club, Thomas Scullard from Chatham soundly denounced the exhumation. "Such action," he insisted, "degrades and insults the remains of a brave red man, who was the tried and trusted friend of our Government in a time of great need."[3] Scullard's reaction came as no surprise to the Wallaceburg Board of Trade, whose members were well-aware of Chatham's interest in having the Tecumseh monument. But before a suitable rebuttal could be agreed upon, the board found itself under attack from every quarter. Much to the dismay of Dr Mitchell and his colleagues, the significance of their discovery had been completely overshadowed by condemnations of the exhumation. As anger against Wallaceburg continued to mount, President Dundas of the board of trade was forced to make a public statement.

In a telephone interview with a reporter from the *Chatham News*, Dundas tried to blame the Natives for the unfortunate turn of events. "Upon the discovery of the bones," Dundas explained, "the Indians held a council and offered to allow Dr Mitchell to take the bones to Wallaceburg on the understanding that should he be called upon at any time to return them, he would do so."[4] It was a lame attempt to exonerate the board of trade. Fortunately for Dundas and his colleagues, the question of blame had already become a moot point. With news that the bones had been returned, the furor caused by the exhumation subsided just as quickly as it had flared up.[5] Still, without the skeleton, Wallaceburg's prospects for the Tecumseh monument were slim.

In order to salvage Wallaceburg's claim, and the reputation of its board of trade, Dundas had to produce evidence that the bones were really those of Tecumseh.[6] The best evidence, however, was the skeleton itself, which was as good as lost. In desperation, Dundas and his colleagues pinned their hopes on Norman Gurd, a lawyer from Sarnia who was writing a book on Tecumseh. Naively, they thought that Gurd would be willing to authentic the bones they no longer possessed, and based on little more than their success in having exhumed them in the first place.[7] Not surprisingly, Gurd refused to stake his reputation on their flimsy case. Without his collaboration, the Wallaceburg Board of Trade could do nothing more than wait for Albert Greenwood's denunciation.

Before news of the exhumation reached Greenwood, the London *Free Press* published a letter from Albert Tobias of the Moraviantown Reserve – the same Native who had made the moving remarks at the Methodist conference in Goderich three years earlier. Initially, Tobias ignored the reports of Tecumseh's burial on St Anne's Island, but his indignation was aroused when he learned that the Wallaceburg Board of Trade had actually gone out and dug up some bones, "the Lord knows of whom."[8] Emphatically, he contradicted the discovery: "They have not found nor will they ever find the grave of Tecumseh."[9] Then, referring to the story of Tecumseh's secret burial, Tobias advised Fisher and his friends to try their spades on the battleground where they might "perchance find some other Indian bones, but never the bones of Tecumseh."[10] Like Norman Gurd, Tobias was considered an expert on Tecumseh's burial for the simple fact that he was a Native – and therefore was assumed to be privy to the secret.[11] By repudiating the skeleton unearthed on St Anne's Island, Tobias confirmed a growing consensus which William R. Davies of the Thamesville *Herald* expressed in blunter terms: "There seems to be no doubt but that the Wallaceburg bones are a fake."[12]

Not only had Tobias raised suspicions regarding the discovery on St

Anne's Island, he had also inadvertently come out in support of Greenwood's argument that Tecumseh was buried somewhere in the vicinity of the battlefield. Greenwood's objections could never have carried the same weight, mainly because he was unwilling to reveal his source – and also because it was obvious that he knew next to nothing about Oshahwahnoo. These impediments would continue to hinder his ability to argue against Fisher's claim that Tecumseh's bones had been reburied on St Anne's Island.

Greenwood, who was as yet unaware of the letter from Tobias, could do nothing more than reiterate his authority, and repeat his offer of assistance, which he did in his usual harsh manner: "To a party authorized to build a monument where Tecumseh fell, or in Tecumseh Park, CHATHAM, I am ready to point out the spot where the Chief was buried ... NO OTHERS NEED APPLY. The man who guarded his grave till death went out without being accessory to its desecration, and the same can be done again."[13] When Greenwood finally received a copy of the Tobias letter, he could not have been more delighted. "If Tobias claims to know where the chief is buried," Greenwood announced in the Thamesville *Herald*, "that should be regarded as decisive."[14] Of course, Tobias made no such claim.[15] All he did was reject the validity of the St Anne's Island discovery.

The rest of 1910 passed quietly enough, with nothing particularly newsworthy to report about Tecumseh or his bones. But behind the scenes it was a different matter. In October, a farmer and former lake captain living near Wallaceburg decided to initiate a correspondence with Greenwood.[16] Natives, and more especially their artifacts, had long appealed to William Leonhardt. But the bones unearthed on St Anne's Island were of particular interest, as they recalled a strange occurrence from his younger days. Leonhardt remembered piloting a steamer around the "dark bend" of the Chenal Ecarté one evening, when a flame suddenly shot up from beyond the St Anne's Island shoreline. This phenomenon occurred several times, accompanied by chanting and the beating of a tom-tom. Leonhardt never forgot these strange sights and sounds, but it was not until 1910 that he realized the significance of his experience in the dark bend.[17]

With news of the discovery on St Anne's Island, Leonhardt became firmly convinced that Oshahwahnoo was responsible for the peculiar manifestations in the dark bend, and that he was performing pagan rites in honour of Tecumseh. Leonhardt decided to investigate the matter by writing to Greenwood, which he did in October of 1910.[18] The ever-cautious Greenwood was not about to give away any secrets, yet he did react favourably to the unexpected letter, mainly because Leonhardt's interest was of use to him. Greenwood needed someone in the vicinity of Wallaceburg to keep an eye on Fisher, and Leonhardt was perfectly situated to act as his spy.

In his reply to Leonhardt, Greenwood expressed his belief that the discovery of Tecumseh's bones on St Anne's Island was an invention designed to damage his credibility. After recounting his war of words with Fisher, Greenwood bitterly declared, "I do not care a rap whether the Canadian people ever know the truth concerning Tecumseh's grave."[19] Curiosity did, however, lead him to accept Leonhardt's offer to act on his behalf and attempt a viewing of the bones dug up on St Anne's Island. He was equally curious to know if Norman Gurd's biography of Tecumseh had been published, and casually observed that he was preparing his own manuscript on Tecumseh. In winding down his letter, Greenwood enticed Leonhardt with a vague offer to share the secret of Tecumseh's burial.[20] Leonhardt jumped at the opportunity to help set the record straight. But, try as he might, Leonhardt failed to get a look at the bones. Greenwood was not the least bit disappointed, and by mid-November of 1910 he managed to convince himself that Oshahwahnoo's reputed participation in Tecumseh's burial was nothing but a falsehood.[21]

Based on Fisher's estimate that Tecumseh's bones were removed to St Anne's Island in 1864, Greenwood calculated that Oshahwahnoo would have had to walk a total of ninety-six kilometres "at the frolicsome age of 94."[22] Ignoring the possibility that Fisher might have made a mistake in determining the year of Oshahwahnoo's trek, or that he himself might have been mistaken as to the chief's age, Greenwood concluded that the story was invented in exchange for whisky.[23] Leonhardt, however, was more inclined to give Oshahwahnoo the benefit of his doubt, suggesting that he might have secured a set of bones he honestly believed were those of Tecumseh – hinting that it was incumbent upon Greenwood to prove otherwise by pointing out Tecumseh's real grave.[24] But Greenwood was not to be baited, and simply dismissed Oshahwahnoo's story as impossible.[25] Certainly, the subtle art of persuasion was lost on Greenwood, and yet the self-centred old man was starting to come around to Leonhardt's way of thinking, namely, that it might be time to share his secret.

On 31 January 1911, Greenwood wrote a letter to Leonhardt in which he complained of illness and old age. The old man from New Hampshire was beginning to fear his own mortality, and he wanted to perpetuate something of the secret he held so dear. He admitted to having "much more to tell" about Tecumseh, but not to someone like Gurd who would garble his "knowledge, belief and sentiments."[26] Instead, Greenwood had decided that Leonhardt should be his confidant.[27] This honour, however, was not so much bestowed as it was sprung – and without warning. After writing at length about Tecumseh, Greenwood suddenly turned his attention to the "ignorant old frontiersman" who was the great chief's lifelong friend and the faithful guardian who watched over his grave for more than forty years. This was the "old scout" who Greenwood had earlier hinted was one of the participants in Tecumseh's secret burial, and his name was Joseph Johnson.[28] Leonhardt had never heard tell of Johnson, but it soon dawned on him that he had just been presented with the key to unlocking the mystery of Tecumseh's bones.

By way of a lengthy addendum, Greenwood recalled the first time he had encountered the mystery. It was in the autumn of 1851, and although he was only a boy, young Albert had listened with rapt attention as his father and another man exchanged stories about frontier times. What began with talk of hunting and Natives soon turned to Tecumseh. The man who conversed with Ira Greenwood claimed there was a white man who accompanied Tecumseh into battle. "That man," he continued, "is now living within a mile of this house and he knows what became of Tecumseh's body."[29] Ira Greenwood had no reason to doubt the word of George Laird, the same old militiaman whose daughter-in-law would later mistake him for one of Tecumseh's pallbearers. However, the senior Greenwood did take issue with the man whose identity he was sure Laird was about to reveal. "Yes," said Greenwood, "but Joe Johnson is such an infernal liar that no one pretends to believe a word he says."[30] Laird thought otherwise. In time, so did Albert Greenwood, who eventually accepted Johnson's story about Tecumseh's death and burial as the one authentic version, and the inspiration behind all later variations.

According to Laird, as paraphrased by Greenwood in his addendum, it was Tecumseh himself who had made provision for his burial. Prior to the battle, he had instructed Johnson to choose two trustworthy Shawnee for a special mission. Along with Johnson, these select Shawnee would form a bodyguard and, in the event of Tecumseh's death, it would be their duty to protect his corpse from falling into the hands of the enemy. Tecumseh suffered a gunshot wound to one of his thighs in the "first five minutes of the fight," whereupon Johnson immediately offered to remove him from danger.[31] Tecumseh refused, so Johnson "set him with his back to a tree where he continued to urge his men to fight."[32] Tecumseh's voice soon fell silent, and when Johnson looked over he saw the great chief's head resting on his chest. Realizing that Tecumseh was dead, Johnson seized him "by his hunting shirt and dragged the body some ten or fifteen feet directly toward the enemy, where a large oak tree was lying and the leaves were piled high. Digging away the leaves with his hands, he rolled the body against the log and covered it completely, hiding his rifle with him." It was only as a result of Native ingenuity that Johnson was able to carry out Tecumseh's last wishes in the thick of battle. "The moment that the chief's death was discovered was [also] the moment of Col. [Richard M. Johnson's] charge. If he and his mounted men were not cheated, Tecumseh's body must fall into the hands of the enemy. An Indian rushed out from [behind] his tree and threw his tomahawk at the Col[onel]. He could have done this and escaped; but he continued as if to use his knife. The Col[onel] fired a cavalry pistol directly in the Indian's face, and as he went down the nearby warriors shouted *'that is Tecumseh!'*"[33] The Americans, thinking the Native who attacked Colonel Johnson was Tecumseh, mutilated his dead body while the real object of their desire lay safely concealed nearby. Later, under the cover of darkness, Joseph Johnson and the two Shawnee retrieved Tecumseh's unmolested corpse and sequestered it some distance north of the battlefield. Although Greenwood stopped short of giving Leonhardt a description of the site, he later revealed that there was a fallen tree, an oak that "had been torn partly out by the roots," and in falling became lodged between two other trees.[34] Greenwood's second-hand recital of Johnson's story is nothing if not authoritative ... although it does bear an uncanny resemblance to the account of Captain William Caldwell junior.

As a member of the British Indian Department, Caldwell was one of the few white men known to have fought alongside the Natives at the Battle of the Thames.[35] In 1863, an elderly Caldwell informed the American historian Lyman C. Draper that Tecumseh was shot in the back at about the same time the British line was broken, and just prior to the American charge against the Natives.[36] As Caldwell related, Tecumseh began walking to the rear, but after a short distance he found himself so weak that he was unable to step over a large fallen oak tree. Instead, he tried to sit down in front of it, but in the process fell back and then rolled over dead.[37] This account was based on an earlier version dating from 1836, in which Caldwell gives himself credit for having tried to save Tecumseh. A then much younger Caldwell recalled that Tecumseh was watching the American advance when he suddenly "clapt his hand to his breast, and gave signs of agony."[38] Disregarding his own means of escape, Caldwell claimed to have yelled, *"Tecumseh mount my horse, and get out the way!"*[39] But the great chief "immediately drop't on a fallen tree and expired."[40]

While the Caldwell account does not exactly mirror Johnson's story, there are elements common to both which suggests something more than a coincidence. A wounded Tecumseh figures prominently, as does the presence of a fallen tree. There is also the shared theme of heroism on the parts of Johnson and Caldwell, as exhibited in their respective attempts to save Tecumseh's life. The only major difference involves the retrieval of Tecumseh's body, which Johnson accomplished but Caldwell did not even attempt. Given the similarities, it would appear that Johnson's story was an adaptation of Caldwell's account, and that Greenwood was responsible for it. Granted, the information Caldwell supplied to Draper was well beyond Greenwood's reach, as it was unpublished. But an earlier version of Caldwell's account did make its way into print, and quite possibly Greenwood's possession.[41] However, judgment against Greenwood must be tempered as there is convincing evidence to suggest that Johnson himself could have been responsible for incorporating the Caldwell account into his story. In February of 1822, Captain William Caldwell junior married Ruth Johnson – who happened to be Joseph Johnson's daughter.[42] This union exposed Johnson to his son-in-law's exploits, and probably coloured his own reminiscences. Such a melding of narratives about Tecumseh would have occurred well before Albert Greenwood's birth in 1845.[43] It seems unlikely, therefore, that Greenwood could have misappropriated the Caldwell account, although he certainly did compromise Joseph Johnson's story.

In continuing the addendum to his letter, Greenwood gave Leonhardt an intriguing account of how he had managed to pinpoint Tecumseh's grave. Johnson's wife supposedly left a "minute" description of the location, which was brought to Greenwood's attention. But Greenwood had ruled out a search because Mrs Johnson's information was "of such an ancient nature."[44] Curiosity, however, eventually got the better of him, knowing as he did that Johnson's son was living out his old age in Dresden, a village located twenty-four kilometres west of the battlefield. When Greenwood finally got around to visiting the old man, he was annoyed by what he heard. Joseph Johnson junior recalled that his father had offered to show him the grave, but he "cared nothing about the matter."[45] Still, Greenwood managed to uncover an important piece of evidence during the course of his conversation with the younger Johnson. This clue, which Greenwood was not willing to share, had allowed him to formulate an idea of the grave's position, as it also tied in with the detailed description provided by Johnson's wife.[46] The lead was significant enough that Greenwood had decided to put it to the test.

One August night in 1890, during the "full moon of the ripe corn," Greenwood went to the battlefield and took a seat on an oak stump. In this dark and shadowy setting, he proposed nothing less than to conjure up images from the past. "I will live this battle over," he thought to himself. "I will try to see every thing that was done here."[47] Then, like a dowser looking for water, Greenwood was up and leading himself to what he considered the most logical place for Tecumseh's burial. As he later recalled: "The ground compared favorably with the story of the old scout [Johnson], and the distance, direction and everything I could think of appeared as I thought it would if the story was true."[48] But the results of the exercise remained inconclusive, as Greenwood could find no evidence of a grave.

Some time later, Greenwood met up with an old man who had known the locale for over fifty years, and had cleared a good deal of the forest from it. When Greenwood asked him if he had encountered an uprooted oak wedged between two other trees, a look of astonishment came over the old man's face. Yes, he knew the very trees! Greenwood followed up by asking if anything had been found at the site, and the old man distinctly remembered unearthing a large skeleton he believed was that of a Native man.[49] Greenwood immediately assumed it was Tecumseh. But when he enquired if there were any peculiarities about the skeleton, the old man recalled a "fully knitted" thigh bone. It was not what Greenwood was hoping to hear. In Joseph Johnson's story, a gunshot wound to the thigh disabled Tecumseh at the outset of the battle, and so Greenwood expected Tecumseh's skeleton would be distinguished by a still broken femur.[50] The healed bone described by the old man indicated a much earlier trauma, and therefore someone other than Tecumseh. Greenwood was baffled by this quandary until several years later when he learned that Tecumseh had suffered a broken thigh during a hunting accident in his youth. Only then did he recognize the significance of the "fully knitted" thigh bone.[51]

Greenwood never told Leonhardt the name of the old man who had provided him with the evidence of Tecumseh's burial. Yet, he did venture to say that the skull was not with the rest of the skeleton after 1851, suggesting that it might have been the same cranial specimen James Dickson gave to Daniel Wilson in 1876. Greenwood, however, also admitted that the skull was housed a short distance away from the battlefield, and that it was still there as late as 1894.[52] In this case, it could not have been the skull Wilson took back to Toronto. Furthermore, Dickson happened upon six skeletons, whereas Greenwood's informant had found just one. If not Dickson, then the old man Greenwood had questioned was probably Abraham Culp, a farmer who lived beyond the northern fringe of the battlefield. Culp "used to tell that while ploughing one of his fields, about three-quarters of a mile from the spot where Tecumseh fell, he turned up a solitary skeleton."[53]

In light of this discovery, Culp's story appears to have been the one that verified the location of Tecumseh's secret burial. There was just one problem. Cornwall's Creek flowed through the Culp farm, and this watercourse had recently come to be associated with the story of Tecumseh's streambed burial. Greenwood, however, believed that Tecumseh's skeleton had already been found in a farmer's field. It was a serious complication, but not one that was directly linked to Abigail Smith. In June of 1910, several months before Greenwood began corresponding with Leonhardt, Alexander C. Sussex from nearby Bothwell claimed that Tecumseh was buried in a stretch of Cornwall's Creek that cut through the next farm to the west of Culp's. This farm was the property of Darby Featherston, another old man.[54] In backing up his story, Sussex identified Joseph Pheasant, a Native from Moraviantown, as the source of his information. Pheasant was supposed to have gotten his account from his father, Jacob Pheasant, who was well known for his claim to have been a member of Tecumseh's burial party. The younger Pheasant could not elaborate on Tecumseh's streambed burial, and it appears that he simply based his remarks on the story told by Abigail Smith. He was at least adamant that Tecumseh's "remains had never been tampered with from the day he was buried."[55]

Pheasant's disclosure was given space in the *Chatham Planet*, but nothing ever came of it. Sussex did not pursue the matter and, of course, neither did any of the citizens of Chatham, since they preferred to think that they should have the monument. Consequently, Pheasant's claim was quickly lost in the mass of confusion surrounding Tecumseh's burial.[56] This outcome worked in Greenwood's favour. However, the dilemma posed by the streambed burial remained, and so Greenwood was forced to rework Johnson's story. Greenwood must have had considerable difficulty in combining the stories of Abigail Smith and Joseph Johnson, which probably accounts for much of the secrecy surrounding the resulting composition. He needed time to try to explain how a farmer felling trees could have discovered Tecumseh's grave in the bed of a creek. And Norman Gurd offered a convenient excuse for Greenwood to delay his revelation. All Greenwood had to do was profess a mistrust of Gurd's motives, and this he did in his correspondence with Leonhardt.[57] To this end, Greenwood admitted having "had it out in the mail" with Gurd, which he elaborated upon in order to ensure that Leonhardt would not attempt to broker a reconciliation.[58] According to Greenwood, Gurd had claimed that he was authorized to write his book for use in Ontario schools and therefore thought he had a right to all information pertaining to Tecumseh's burial. Greenwood had bristled at this notion, and he convinced himself that Gurd would interpret any hesitation on his part as evidence that he knew nothing. This prospect, in turn, however, made Greenwood bristle all the more, so he defied Gurd by insisting that he would not "yield the secret to any but one provided with authority and funds to build a monument."[59]

Having thus alienated Gurd, it occurred to Greenwood that he might be accused of self-interest. Defensively, he denied any hope of reward or recognition, claiming instead that he was only trying to protect Tecumseh's grave from desecration.[60] But his abrasive manner had its usual repelling effect, and the correspondence between the two men became severely strained. With the failure of the "St Anne's affair" in 1910, Greenwood "rubbed it in good." Gurd "got hot" and made, as Greenwood recalled, "statements of an extremely offensive nature, declaring that he had rejected my claim to any knowledge of the subject. I replied, daring him to attack any statement I had made in the Ontario press. In his last, he wanted nothing more to do with me, and I replied reminding him that he had originated the correspondence and if dissatisfied it was not my fault as my offer did not include curiosity seekers."[61] As insulting as Greenwood proved he could be, his crowning stroke was yet to come. "I told him [further] that by the time the Chief had been dead a hundred years, his work would be of less value than a plugged nickel."[62]

Yet, Greenwood was still anxious to know what Gurd would have to say about Tecumseh's burial.[63] In desperation, he turned to his penpal. Writing to Leonhardt in February of 1911, Greenwood impatiently asked, "Why is the book not out?"[64] With this cue, Leonhardt obediently took advantage of the first opportunity to investigate. Soon after, during a business trip to Sarnia, he lingered in order to see a friend whose office happened to be in the same building as Gurd's firm.

Finding Gurd's door open, Leonhardt ventured in and asked if he was the same Gurd who was writing the book on Tecumseh. With Gurd's answer in the affirmative, Leonhardt shot right to the point: "Well, when will your book be on the market?"[65] Gurd, unperturbed by this brusque approach, answered that he expected the proofs any day, but that the printer was very slow.

Leonhardt then decided to make the most of the situation by subjecting the lawyer to an impromptu examination, from which he determined that Gurd had no definite information regarding either Tecumseh's death or his burial. In conveying this news to Greenwood, Leonhardt encouraged him to exploit this advantage by pre-empting Gurd and publishing his own book on Tecumseh.[66] Greenwood was not to be pushed, however. "The clouds must gather before it will rain," he replied.[67] Continuing with this meteorological metaphor, he observed, "You will find Gurd has a rain without clouds."[68] Even though Leonhardt had shown that Gurd was not the threat Greenwood made him out to be, the old man from New Hampshire was not prepared to admit as much. Greenwood was determined to wait out the lawyer's publisher, and all Leonhardt could do was play along.[69] Greenwood's penpal soon grew impatient, however.

At the end of March 1911, Leonhardt proposed a plan of action that would blast what little remained of Wallaceburg's claim to Tecumseh's bones. Emphasizing the "fully knitted" thigh bone, Leonhardt thought Greenwood should attack the St Anne's Island exhumation in the press. Once the matter had become sufficiently heated, Greenwood could lead a well-publicized expedition to the real grave, point out the healed bone as proof of Tecumseh's identity, and settle the question once and for all.[70] In a further attempt to motivate Greenwood, Leonhardt added that news of Tecumseh's broken thigh had reached Wallaceburg, and that Dr Mitchell and his colleagues were attempting to re-examine the bones confiscated by Chief White.[71] Unmoved, Greenwood answered Leonhardt by paraphrasing Napoleon: "When your opponents are making a mistake, give them plenty of time to make it."[72]

Not to be put off, Leonhardt undertook some discreet meddling on Greenwood's behalf. During a conversation with Secretary Smith of the Wallaceburg Board of Trade, Leonhardt managed to convincingly argue that any discovery of Tecumseh's grave would necessarily include evidence of a broken thigh bone. After a while, Smith had to admit that "so far as he could see there was no positive mark as to a poorly set bone."[73] Leonhardt considered Smith the "first pillar to fall," and he fully expected that Dr Mitchell would be the next in line. In writing Greenwood of his success, he predicted that the board of trade's monument scheme would soon be completely undermined. Greenwood expressed complete satisfaction when he learned of Leonhardt's intrigues.[74] He was confident that Wallaceburg could never come up with the broken thigh bone – so confident that he dabbled with a poem on the life of Tecumseh.[75] It soon became apparent, however, that the Wallaceburg Board of Trade was not ready to admit defeat.

In late May of 1911, Dr Mitchell gave the local press an affidavit he secured from an elderly lady who lived in Wallaceburg. In her testimony, Mrs Olive Hubble recalled a strange trip to St Anne's Island in the autumn of 1866. Along with two other young women, she had crossed the Chenal Écarté in search of wild plums. During the expedition, Miss Olive and one of her companions happened upon a nest of snakes, and instantly set off running through the woods. Emerging in a Native burial ground, they discovered an old man performing strange rites over one of the graves.[76] Boldly, Miss Olive struck up a conversation with the elder, who she later identified as Oshahwahnoo, and asked him who it was he honoured. "My general," he replied.[77] Not satisfied with this answer, the inquisitive young woman repeated her question, and this time Oshahwahnoo left no room for doubt. His "general" was no less than the great Tecumseh himself. This was evidence enough for Dr Mitchell, who was determined to salvage Wallaceburg's claim to the Tecumseh monument.[78] Unfortunately, Mrs Hubble's account proved ineffectual.

Not even Albert Greenwood felt sufficiently threatened to offer a protest.[79] No matter how compelling, the old lady's recollections could never outweigh the conclusive evidence of a broken thigh bone. However, it still remained to be seen whether or not Gurd would support Wallaceburg's monument aspirations. And there was no way for Greenwood to be sure of Gurd's intentions without first seeing a copy of his book. But Greenwood was in no rush. He was content to edit his poem, encourage Leonhardt's machinations, and find a way to integrate the streambed burial into Joseph Johnson's story.[80]

The void left by the collapse of the Wallaceburg scheme was quickly filled by Thamesville, where there was a renewed interest in honouring Tecumseh. Six years earlier, in November of 1905, Thamesville's citizens had assembled in order to consider their prospects of securing a monument to Tecumseh. Nothing came of the exercise until 1911, when a determined lawyer's wife decided to do something about it.[81] As Katherine B. Coutts reasoned, if Thamesville "could not have a big monument we might at least mark the battlefield, and having ascertained that $50.00 would pay for a respectable granite-boulder, [we] canvassed the village and soon secured the necessary sum."[82] In September of 1911, a boulder of grey granite commemorating both the Battle of the Thames and the death of Tecumseh was placed on the battlefield.[83] In April of 1912, however, Mrs Coutts had a change of heart, and made it abundantly clear that the boulder did not represent the full extent of Thamesville's efforts to pay tribute to Tecumseh. Rather, as she now insisted, it was a demonstration of Thamesville's commitment to secure something more impressive. Mrs Coutts used the monument to Sir Isaac Brock on Queenston Heights – located a short distance above the actual site of his death – as a precedent for the location of Tecumseh's monument, which she thought "should be set up in the town park at Thamesville, the municipality nearest the battlefield." The effect of "thus linking it with the scene of his death," she observed, "is greatly to increase its impressiveness."[84]

Albert Greenwood was quick to respond to Mrs Coutts's proposal. But rather than criticize it, as seemed to be his automatic reaction to ideas not of his own making, he offered Thamesville a full exposé of all the information he had about Tecumseh's burial.[85] Greenwood could just as easily have argued that if linking Tecumseh's monument to the scene of his death was such an important consideration, then the monument should be located on the battlefield as he had originally proposed. While he was at it, he might have added that although Brock's Monument did not mark the precise location of the general's death, it had at least been constructed on the battlefield where he was killed – and not in the nearest local municipality. Greenwood, however, was uncharacteristically restrained, and probably because he viewed Thamesville as an acceptable compromise for the location of Tecumseh's monument. It was only a short distance from the battlefield and, as he must have realized, perhaps as close to the actual site of Tecumseh's death as he could ever hope to see a monument constructed. In hastening to send off word of his approval, Greenwood forgot all about his mistrust of Gurd, which Leonhardt was given to believe was the reason why Greenwood kept Tecumseh's burial a secret. Of greater potential embarrassment to Greenwood, however, was his earlier offer to assist Chatham. Yet Greenwood's conscience must have been eased considerably by Chatham's apparent lack of interest in a monument for Tecumseh Park. The idea looked to have gone the way of Wallaceburg's claim and the dodo. But Chatham's enthusiasm for a monument was not quite extinct.

In March of 1912, three weeks before Mrs Coutts announced Thamesville's intention to have Tecumseh's monument, a "working woman" in Chatham made headlines by donating a dollar to establish a Tecumseh monument fund for that city.[86] The editor of the Chatham *Planet* responded with a subscription list and a promise to acknowledge everyone who likewise pledged their support – especially children, who were encouraged to make ten-cent donations. It soon became evident, however, that the youngsters of Chatham had no intention of allowing themselves to be exploited for the sake of a monument to Tecumseh, and so a group of interested adults assumed control of the project.[87] The resulting association, consisting of many prominent and politically well-placed citizens of Chatham, soon had a deputation before the Kent County Council, whose members were more than a little impressed when the cost of the monument was estimated at $30,000.[88] Obviously, the Chatham delegation had something rather more grandiose in mind than a fifty-dollar boulder. Despite the confident prediction that "the [federal] Government was prepared to make a grant of $10,000," the Tecumseh Monument Association of Chatham got nothing more concrete from the county council than its "cordial sympathy."[89] A subsequent attempt to appropriate money left over from the Old Boys Reunion met with greater success.

For five days in July of 1912, former residents of Chatham returned to renew old acquaintances in a festive celebration of their old home town.[90] The reunion proved a profitable exercise, and a number of visionaries, including the editor of the *Planet*, favoured the idea of transferring the event's $1,500 surplus to the Tecumseh Monument Association. In the end, this is exactly what the Chatham Old Boys decided to do with their profits.[91] Yet, as the members of the Tecumseh Monument Association came to realize, a far greater financial base would be required in order to gain the participation of either the provincial or federal governments. Subscription drives were proposed, but none of them managed to get beyond the planning stage before the grande dame of Thamesville took advantage of Chatham's tardiness.[92]

In March of 1913, Mrs Coutts was elected president of Thamesville's newly-formed Tecumseh Memorial Association. Her dedication to the project, along with encouraging assurances of support from both levels of government, resulted in a confident prediction: "It is now almost an absolute certainty that a monument will be erected to the Shawnee Chief Tecumseh in our town hall park."[93] An additional canvass of Thamesville had already defrayed the estimated $10,000 price tag of the monument, and subscriptions were being received from beyond the village as well.[94] Although the monument Mrs Coutts and her colleagues envisioned for Thamesville was considerably less-expensive than the one proposed for Chatham's Tecumseh Park, this economy did not make it any more popular in government circles. In May of 1913, Mrs Coutts and the Tecumseh Memorial Association were very disappointed to learn that no provision had been made for them in the estimated expenditures tabled by the federal finance minister – especially since $7,500 was allocated for the construction of a monument to Samuel de Champlain at Orillia.[95] At a meeting of the Tecumseh Memorial Association held soon after, Chatham was blamed for having compromised Thamesville's negotiations with the Dominion government by making a last minute bid of its own. "But we are still in the ring," a defiant Mrs Coutts declared, "and what is more, we are going to have that Tecumseh monument yet."[96] Mrs Coutts was just as obsessed with having revenge as she was with having the monument, and in September of 1913 she was found her opportunity to get even with Chatham.

More than a year earlier, in June of 1912, Chatham's Macaulay Club had volunteered to host the Ontario Historical Society's annual convention. The offer was quickly accepted, along with a pledge to secure the construction of a fitting monument to Tecumseh.[97] Convinced that they had an important ally in the Ontario Historical Society, the Chathamites prepared to lavish the full extent of their hospitality upon the visiting delegates – including a boat cruise to Amherstburg's various historic sites.[98] The still-fuming Mrs Coutts, however, had a little surprise in store for the interlopers. Soon after the Ontario Historical Society delegates arrived in Chatham, she offered to take them on a tour of the battlefield where Tecumseh was killed.[99] While only a few of the delegates were able to take advantage of the unexpected invitation, those who managed to go were suitably impressed with the reception Mrs Coutts had arranged for them.

Arriving at Thamesville by train, the delegates were driven to John McDowell's farm in newfangled automobiles. After viewing the Tecumseh boulder, the group visited the old church at Moraviantown, where they heard Albert Tobias deliver an eloquent recital of the story of Tecumseh's death and burial. Returning to Thamesville, the delegates were treated to a luncheon after which Mrs Coutts tried to win their support for Thamesville's monument drive.[100] Among the audience was John Dearness of London, then president of the Ontario Historical Society, who gave Mrs Coutts a hearty vote of thanks for her hospitality, but not a definite pledge of support.[101] It was another disappointment. Yet, by having commandeered the Ontario Historical Society, Mrs Coutts at least managed to frustrate Chatham's monument ambitions.

Although Mrs Coutts could not prevail upon the delegates from the Ontario Historical Society, she was relieved to learn that they were not prepared to endorse any particular place as the best location for Tecumseh's monument. When the position of the Ontario Historical Society became known in Chatham, that city's enthusiasm for the monument all but disappeared. However, a certain physician was determined to revive the project. Dr Tecumseh K. Holmes, whose father saw Tecumseh at Arnold's Mill during the British retreat in 1813, was convinced that if a substantial down payment on the monument could be raised locally it would compel assistance from both the federal and provincial governments. In September of 1913, he tried to launch another subscription drive.[102] But Chatham's rivalry with Thamesville had already sealed the venture's fate at the federal level, and if Dr Holmes thought his attempt would fare any better with Ontario's provincial parliament, he was sadly mistaken. As the Conservative premier, Sir James Whitney, told a lady who thought the province should provide $3,000 so that Amherstburg could honour Tecumseh, "no government would be justified in doing anything of the kind for the reason that by doing so it would encourage similar local applications from many different localities in the Province."[103]

Fortunately for Dr Holmes, he recognized the futility of his endeavour in time to avoid a similar embarrassment. It had become painfully apparent that the centenary of Tecumseh's death was not destined to be marked with the construction of a monument – not in Chatham, not in Thamesville, and certainly not anywhere else in Ontario. But, as Dr Holmes and the other disappointed monument seekers soon discovered, an expensive tribute of granite and bronze was not the only means by which to honour Tecumseh's memory.

According to Abigail Smith's prize-winning school essay, Tecumseh was buried in the bed of a stream in order to conceal his grave. *Chatham Tri-Weekly Planet*, 4 November 1889

Albert Greenwood claimed to have information regarding Tecumseh's grave, which he refused to share unless a monument to the great chief was constructed according to his terms. Courtesy Lambton Room, Lambton County Library

Oshahwahnoo, also known as John Nahdee, was credited with having sequestered Tecumseh's bones on St Anne's Island, near Wallaceburg, Ontario. Courtesy National Archives of Canada, c-8543

Prior to opening Tecumseh's reputed grave on St Anne's Island in 1910, the individuals participating in the exhumation posed for a photographer. Matthew Fisher stood fifth from the right, while Dr Mitchell was third from the left. Courtesy Mann Historical Files

Matthew Fisher countered
Greenwood by announcing that
Tecumseh's bones were buried
on St Anne's Island. Courtesy
Mann Historical Files

Charlatans, By and Large

AT THE END OF OCTOBER 1912, there had been a lull in the battle for Tecumseh's monument. It was a welcome relief, but the calm was soon shattered by a battle of another sort. Near Cedar Springs, a village located to the southwest of Chatham and not far from the Lake Erie shore, preparations had been made for a massive war game.[1] On the appointed day, the hinterlands of this normally quiet community were suddenly jarred by the repeated blasts of artillery, small gunfire, and the reverberating din of clashing armies.[2] The sham battle impressed its many spectators, and none more so than Edwin Beattie.[3] As the Indian agent for the Moraviantown Reserve, Beattie viewed the spectacle in terms of the approaching centenary of Tecumseh's death. Far from anticipating the arrival of that day, however, Beattie feared it would pass unnoticed amid all the squabbling over a monument.

The annual militia manoeuvres of 1912 gave Beattie an idea. Why not have the following year's exercises form the basis of a celebration in honour of Tecumseh? The participation of the militia would ensure that Tecumseh was not forgotten. Beattie had little trouble selling his idea to the militia brass. They were very receptive, and even agreed to accommodate the schedule of the Moraviantown fall fair when Beattie saw the opportunity to work that event into the program.[4] The date was set for 16 October 1913.

As the months leading up to that date passed, everything seemed to go according to plan. Early in September, however, Colonel W.E. Hodgins, the district commander, informed Beattie that limited militia funds might not be sufficient to cover the cost of transporting even so much as a couple of artillery guns. Beattie, however, was determined to have them for a salute, so he turned to the government of Ontario for financial assistance. Of course, the provincial government was still dominated by the Conservative administration of Sir James Whitney – the same premier who had turned down Amherstburg's request for a grant to honour Tecumseh. Fortunately for Beattie, his requirements did not involve a great deal of money. This and the fact that preparations for an impressive patriotic display had already been finalized, not to mention publicized, worked in Beattie's favour. Sir James and his cabinet could hardly say no.[5] Beattie would have his artillery.

The dawning of 16 October 1913 revealed an overcast sky, yet the threat of rain did not deter a tremendous crowd from gathering on John McDowell's farm. The Tecumseh boulder was the focal point, draped as it was in purple bunting and crowned with garlands of evergreen. Topping the decorations was a portrait of Tecumseh, which offered many people their first, albeit apocryphal, glimpse of the famous warrior. Just as eye-catching was a nearby platform crammed with dignitaries, including Dr Holmes and Mrs Coutts, who set aside their differences for the sake of Tecumseh.[6] At ten o'clock, music was faintly heard coming from the east. Gradually, the patriotic strains grew louder until the band of the Seventh Fusiliers burst onto the field followed by some five hundred militiamen in scarlet uniforms. After a thundering cheer from the spectators, the militia went through their manoeuvres and then formed themselves into rows opposite the platform. Silence greeted Edwin Beattie who, in his capacity as chairman of the occasion, stepped forward to give the first speech.[7]

None of the attending newspaper reporters gave Beattie credit for the event, possibly because the self-effacing Indian agent focused his remarks on Tecumseh rather than himself. Still, everyone present recognized their local Indian agent as the person responsible for the "Tecumseh Celebration."[8] Beattie finished off by introducing Dr Holmes. In addressing the audience, the doctor presented a brief outline of Tecumseh's life.[9] To anyone familiar with the great chief's biography, there was nothing particularly new in what Dr Holmes had to say. However, he did make one noteworthy, and rather surprising, statement when he admitted that Tecumseh's monument should be erected at Thamesville. "It was there," Holmes explained, that Tecumseh "spent his last hours and it was fitting that a remembrance should be made to him there, whatever people might do elsewhere."[10] This change of heart certainly placed Dr Holmes in good stead with the next speaker.

Mrs Coutts, after welcoming the spectators, read a telegram from Evelyn Johnson: "Canadians to-day honor themselves and Canada, in recognizing at last and in rendering a memorial to the great Tecumseh" who, along with his people, "gave the best of their blood and their homes and country, in defense of the Empire."[11] While Miss Johnson was somewhat off base, as there was no monument to unveil, her eulogistic remarks did suit the event – and Mrs Coutts as well.

With the surrender of Dr Holmes on the one hand, and the endorsement of Pauline Johnson's sister on the other, Mrs Coutts found it impossible to restrain herself. In a sudden gush of enthusiasm, and without the slightest consideration for Dr Holmes, she enthusiastically expressed her hope that the same audience would soon return to see Tecumseh's monument unveiled in Thamesville.[12] After Mrs Coutts had her say, Chairman Beattie made a clumsy attempt to assuage any hurt feelings. In acknowledging the fierce competition for the Tecumseh monument, Beattie impulsively suggested that several should be erected.[13] On this peculiar note, the opening ceremonies concluded and the militia marched up the Longwoods Road to a ford in the river. Crossing over a makeshift bridge of wagons and boards, they continued on into Moraviantown. A throng of spectators followed close behind, which kept the gate attendants at the fairgrounds busy collecting admission fees from over 8,000 people.[14]

After lunch, the program resumed with the booming reports of a solitary artillery piece. It turned out to be all Beattie could afford. Even so, Tecumseh's memory was suitably honoured with a fourteen-gun salute. Then came a trooping of the colours and assorted other manoeuvres, including a final march past and review. Next there was a curious Native ceremony conducted by Albert Tobias of Moraviantown. To the delight of the audience, Colonel Hodgins of the militia was made an honorary chief of the Delaware Nation and given the Native name of "Tooma pa me laut," or "Flying Wolf."[15] Had Thomas Gowman (alias Pete Pancrees) lived to see the day, he surely would have cringed upon hearing the name of his Native tormentor (Nelles F. Timothy). Colonel Hodgins, however, was blissfully unaware of the coincidence, and happily led off a new round of speeches. With the concluding remarks of the last speaker, the crowd gradually dispersed. The Tecumseh Celebration proved an unqualified success, and one that did not require the unveiling of a monument or the discovery of a grave.

Albert Greenwood would have been suitably impressed with the celebration had he been present. Instead, the old man chose to stay put in New Hampshire, annoyed that he had not been courted by the people of Canada. Greenwood tried to feign indifference as the day of the Tecumseh Celebration drew near, but in reality he seethed with anger knowing that he would be denied the recognition he desired. Ironically, Evelyn Johnson's telegram hailed Greenwood as the "only man who knows Tecumseh's grave," which the audience heartily applauded.[16] Greenwood, however, was convinced that his credibility in Canada had been irreparably damaged by Matthew Fisher. Based on this erroneous perception, Greenwood was determined to boycott the Tecumseh Celebration. But then came the eleventh hour.

Early in September of 1913, a month before the celebration, Greenwood had suddenly announced that Joseph Johnson was the source of his information regarding Tecumseh's burial.[17] Moreover, he used Gurd to get his message out. Although Gurd's *Story of Tecumseh* had been published early in 1912, Greenwood did not see a copy of it until a short time before he made his announcement.[18] And, despite Greenwood's paranoid mistrust of its author, he was hard-pressed to find anything objectionable about the book. There was nothing in it to indicate that Gurd adhered to Matthew Fisher's claim that Wallaceburg should have Tecumseh's monument. Nor were there any negative comments about Greenwood. As for Tecumseh's burial, Gurd's romantic and hazy description actually conformed to Greenwood's own views, except for one offending line: "The place of his interment, kept a secret by his devoted followers, no man other than they has ever known."[19] Whether or not Greenwood thought this passage was directed against him, he decided to treat it as a challenge. Greenwood was looking for an excuse to take Gurd to task, and a reason to offer-up Johnson's story of Tecumseh's burial. But Greenwood's attempt to blend Johnson's story with that of Abigail Smith resulted in a confusing description of Tecumseh's burial. "At the spot chosen," he began,

there was running water [presumably meaning a creek]. Above, and on the same bank, stood a hickory and a basswood tree close together. Below and on the same side an oak had been torn partly out by the roots and lodged between the first-mentioned trees, the body [trunk] of the oak having sent up sprouts along its entire length. The water [creek] was dammed above, and the [unspecified] obstructions remained below; then with their hands and knives, a shallow grave was made, and in it the body [of Tecumseh], stripped of everything that would aid in identification, was laid. When this was completed the obstructions were replaced below [which Greenwood indicates had remained in place], the dam [was] removed, and the falling rain obliterated every [remaining] mark made by the party.[20]

In this account, there is an allusion to a streambed burial. However, Greenwood does not actually specify that Tecumseh's grave was dug in a creek – much less Cornwall's Creek. His description could also be taken to mean that the burial was made in a bank alongside, and that the creek was dammed for a surge of water to wash away all signs of the shallow grave.[21] It would appear that Greenwood, having forced Johnson's story of Tecumseh's secret burial into line with that of Abigail Smith's streambed burial, anticipated trouble and decided to play it safe by being purposely vague.

As it transpired, Greenwood's revelation came too late to have any effect. Edwin Beattie's grand celebration had eliminated the need for a monument to commemorate the centenary of Tecumseh's death. Tecumseh's grave thus became irrelevant, as did everything that Albert Greenwood had to say about it. The bitter old man was ignored and when he finally went to his grave in 1929, he took the secret of Tecumseh's burial with him.[22] Given Greenwood's fascination with the spirit realm, both his secret and its loss are debatable. While it was never publicly revealed, Greenwood admitted to Leonhardt that he communicated with the dead on a regular basis.[23] On one occasion, he even claimed to have spoken with victims of the *Titanic*, who conveyed to him "all the sensations of drowning, and of the first consciousness they knew after the death struggle was over."[24] Greenwood was also convinced that Joseph Johnson conversed with Tecumseh, and that he had done so on the anniversary of the chief's death for some forty years. Johnson's "constancy and faithfulness in watching and waiting so many years is proof enough of it."[25]

Of course, Greenwood's self-professed ability to communicate with the dead raises an intriguing question: Why would he bother himself with Joseph Johnson's story in attempting to locate Tecumseh's grave, if he could just as easily have gotten directions from the great chief himself? After all, as Greenwood boasted, he and his wife had enough experience with spirit communication that they could talk with the departed soul of their choice at any time, day or night. "Sometimes," Greenwood had to admit, "we are told that the party is engaged."[26] Perhaps Tecumseh's line was always busy.

A year after Edwin Beattie's grand celebration, the militia units which had marched in honour of Tecumseh prepared to sail for Flanders. It was the autumn of 1914, and they were being sent to fight the very real battles of the First World War. Soon, hero worship in Canada focused on the many young soldiers who sacrificed themselves for king and country. Tecumseh was largely forgotten, but there was the occasional reminder of his own sacrifice a hundred years earlier.[27] The most dramatic example was the unearthing of a skeleton on John McDowell's farm in June of 1918.[28] In almost no time, Albert Greenwood cast his doubts and nothing more was heard of the skeleton.[29] Coincidentally, McDowell's discovery came to light during a far-fetched scheme to have the famous statue of the *Dying Tecumseh* transferred from Washington, D.C., to St Thomas, Ontario. American officials, however, resisted the suggestion and the venture gradually fizzled out in the summer of 1919.[30] Then, in 1921, improvements to the Long-woods Road at the battlefield promised to revive interest in commem-orating the site of Tecumseh's death.[31] Unfortunately, the proposal – which included a monument – did not proceed beyond the establish-ment of a small memorial park of redundant highway property.[32] Everyone, it seemed, had given up on the idea of a monument for Tecumseh. Even the determined Mrs Coutts found less stressful ways to occupy her time. Having been diagnosed with a weak heart in 1919, she limited her good work on Tecumseh's behalf to supervising sever-al enhancements to his boulder, and overseeing its relocation to the new park in 1924.[33] Nothing more was heard about Tecumseh or his monument ... until a couple of years later when there was surprising news out of London, Ontario.

In the middle of May 1926, the *London Advertiser* caused a sensa-tion by reporting that Tecumseh was buried near that city's fair-grounds.[34] Backing up this incredible claim was a recently published biography of Joseph Brant, in which it was revealed how London had come to be so honoured. According to the biographer's informant, Jasper Jones, who was an aged Native from the Six Nations Reserve, Tecumseh's body was retrieved from the battlefield under the cover of darkness. This undertaking was accomplished by Tecumseh's brother and his mother. After improvising a stretcher, they set out for the Mo-hawk Village on the Grand River near modern Brantford. At what is now London, eighty kilometres northeast of the battlefield, Tecumseh's mother became so fatigued that her surviving son decided to bury his brother in a field next to the road.[35] One hundred years later, in De-cember of 1913, this curious story was brought to the attention of Margaret Brown of Brantford, a one-time novelist who thought she might try her hand at writing a biography of Joseph Brant.[36] Initially, she was dubious of both Jasper and his story. But when a former war-den of Brant County vouched for Jasper's honesty, Mrs Brown threw caution to the wind. After all, the ex-warden was a breeder of Durham cattle and "men of this type," she observed, "are not easily deceived."[37]

Mrs Brown made her way to the Six Nations Reserve, and there she found Jasper living in a rough shack. But despite the squalid sur-roundings, Mrs Brown quickly became entranced – not only with what Jasper had to say, but with Jasper himself. "In the prime of life," she later fantasized,

he has been a strongly built well-made man, tall, lithe, sinewy, agile, daring, with something of the air of the gallant and the Imperial Knight about him.

Even in old age he carries himself erect, and displays much of the vitality of early manhood. He is quick, sharp and shrewd in thought and action, few shrewder men it would be difficult to find. He is kind and sensitive by nature, deferential and rather gentle in manner, but when roused to emotion or remembrance, he displays all the Shawnee fierceness and determination to do or die.[38]

The smitten Mrs Brown, thoroughly convinced of Jasper's integrity, was determined to push his claim. She wasted little time in asking John Dearness of London for his help and Dearness, who was president of the Ontario Historical Society, tried to be as accommodating as possible. Based on Jasper's description, Dearness thought that Tecumseh's grave might have been dug somewhere near the intersection of Queen's Avenue and English Street.[39] Dearness and other old residents remembered this area when it was covered by a thick pine wood. By 1913, however, the forest had been replaced by working class neighbourhoods. After considering all the changes to the landscape brought about by urbanization, Dearness was forced to conclude that "the quest seems hopeless."[40] Mrs Brown, however, did not share this opinion.

There might not be any trace of Tecumseh's grave in London, but Mrs Brown had no doubt that it was there. Surely, if anyone knew where Tecumseh was buried, it was Jasper Jones. After all, it was his father who had helped bury Tecumseh. Mrs Brown had such complete faith in Jasper that she fully accepted him as the son of the Shawnee Prophet. And when Jasper told her the Prophet had died in Lambton County, Ontario, in 1862, she believed that, too.[41] Despite the fact that she had been able to get a copy of Drake's *Life of Tecumseh*, which records the Prophet's death beyond the Mississippi River in the mid-1830s, Mrs Brown simply ignored the discrepancy. She preferred to believe Jasper, and diligently made a transcript of everything he told her about his father's life in Canada.[42] After the War of 1812, according to Mrs Brown's record, the Prophet sought refuge on the Six Nations Reserve and lived there under the assumed name of Simon Jones. Subsequently, he bought a farm in Moore Township, south of Sarnia, Ontario, which became his new home. Jasper remained at the Six Nations Reserve, and only twice made the long trek of 193 kilometres to his father's farm.[43] It was during his return from the second visit, in 1855, that his father shared the secret of Tecumseh's burial.

The main purpose of Jasper's trip was to help his father open a drain, and Jasper did not care to linger once the job was done. He was soon on his way home and, much to his surprise, his father tagged along. Nothing was said, and Jasper just assumed that his father had decided to take a trip to the Six Nations. As they approached London, however, Jasper's father let his real intention be known. He wanted to point out his brother's grave – the grave of Tecumseh. The two men walked on, skirting the northern edge of London, and eventually arriving at the Governor's Road, or Dundas Street, which runs east to the head of Lake Ontario. After having proceeded only a short distance, Jasper's father suddenly jumped a fence on the north side of the road and proceeded to a small pile of rocks. Tossing them aside, he exposed Tecumseh's tombstone, inscribed with the following lines: "Blessed is he that lays these bones. Cursed is he that removes these bones."[44]

Perhaps Mrs Brown was unfamiliar with Shakespeare's famous warning to posterity, which is remarkably like the epitaph Jasper found on Tecumseh's tombstone.[45] Or, perhaps the beguiled lady just refused to accept the possibility that her "Imperial Knight" could be lying through his teeth. Whatever the case, she was perfectly satisfied that Tecumseh had been buried in London, Ontario. Mrs Brown was not necessarily gullible, but she was known to embrace some pretty peculiar theories. Just as she could persuade herself that the Iroquois constituted the original Aryan race, she could just as easily acknowledge Jasper Jones as the son of the Shawnee Prophet.[46] And when Mrs Brown finally found a publisher for her biography of Joseph Brant, she still had complete faith in Jasper.[47] Unfortunately for her, there was not a shred of truth in what the old scoundrel had to say about the Prophet, or Tecumseh's burial for that matter.

In May of 1926, a short time after Mrs Brown's book made its appearance, the *London Advertiser* ran the story about Tecumseh's burial in London. A few days later, the same newspaper carried the disappointing news that a cursory search had proven "fruitless."[48] Still, this failure was thought to be of little consequence, and "if it is reasonably well established that this city is the great chieftain's burial place, it would seem fitting that some memorial to his memory should be erected during the coming centennial celebration."[49] Obviously, an event was being orchestrated, and it bore all the hallmarks of Arthur C. Carty.

In 1921, as a former reporter for both the *London Free Press* and the *London Advertiser*, Carty had decided to open a news and publicity service.[50] Among the many events he promoted, one of his more important commissions was the one hundredth anniversary of the founding of London, which was slated for 1926. It was while looking for interesting aspects of London's history that Carty happened upon Mrs Brown's *Life of Joseph Brant*, and the sensational scoop that Tecumseh was buried in London. Mrs Brown had also included the judgment of John Dearness, who thought it was hopeless to try to locate Tecumseh's grave. But Carty, who was about as scrupulous as any other sensation-seeking publicist of his era, suppressed this information in order to build interest in the story. A few days later, having perceived strong public support in London for a monument to Tecumseh, Carty began to promote its construction in association with the city's centennial celebration. He might have succeeded, had it not been for some meddlesome Natives.

Toward the end of the following June, McKenzie Nahdee of the Walpole Island Reserve announced his intention to lead an expedition to Tecumseh's grave, which he described as being "mebbe half-mile, mebbe ten miles" from the battlefield – but certainly nowhere near London.[51] Based on the stories of an ancestor by the name of Chief John Nahdee, who fought alongside Tecumseh and later helped to bury him, McKenzie was confident that he could locate Tecumseh's grave or come very close to it. McKenzie's sudden interest in locating Tecumseh's bones, so he claimed, was motivated by the Toronto *Globe*'s support for a monument to the great chief.[52] This support came in the form of publicity surrounding a renewed, but fleeting, attempt to place the monument at the battlefield, a promotion endorsed by Moraviantown.[53] What McKenzie chose not to disclose, however, was his determination to deprive London of its claim to Tecumseh's monument.

A week later, the Nahdees launched their expedition with a car ride through the countryside. It was a rare treat for McKenzie Nahdee, his elderly uncle, William Nahdee, and the uncle's middle-aged son, Willie.[54] Their destination was Tecumseh's boulder near Thamesville, where they planned to meet a newspaper reporter. The Nahdees made it to the boulder first, but eventually another car pulled up alongside – and out jumped Arthur C. Carty, whose arrival came as no surprise.[55]

Although the Nahdees had ruined one of Carty's more magnificent centennial promotions by disputing London's claim to Tecumseh's grave, the resourceful stringer still recognized a good story when he saw one. The expedition was really his idea, and having expended a considerable amount of time and effort in organizing it, Carty was anxious to get on with the tour. With McKenzie Nahdee acting as his navigator, Carty started driving back in the direction of London. On the heights above Wardsville, Ontario, and at a place where the old Longwoods Road had just recently been diverted away from the Thames River, McKenzie requested that Carty pull over. The view from this section of the new Number Two Highway appeared to correspond with old Nahdee family descriptions of the place where

Tecumseh was buried. There was the bend in the river that brought the stream right up to the road, and also the two requisite creeks which had cut deep ravines in the high bank.[56] William Nahdee, who with his son followed at some distance behind Carty, was similarly impressed with the lay of the land and likewise ordered his driver to stop. Although the two parties were out of sight of each other, they were not far apart. The inevitable reunion gave Carty reason to believe that the Nahdees might be on the right track. But he soon began to have his doubts.

As William Nahdee tried to get his bearings, his nephew impatiently suggested they consider a third creek a little farther to the east. "No," the old man snapped. "Two closest to the road."[57] Out of respect for his elder, McKenzie obediently surrendered the point. There was no doubt in William Nahdee's mind that he was standing in the same place he had visited many years earlier with his father. But apart from the two creeks, all the other landmarks had disappeared. Where he expected to see a wooded bank on the opposite side of the river, there was a pasture. He also remembered some rapids, which were nowhere to be seen. More disconcerting, however, was the absence of a log cabin and an old oak tree, both of which were required in order to triangulate the place of Tecumseh's burial. As William Nahdee muttered his frustration, the stump of a large old tree was found at the bottom of a ravine. With this timely discovery, he was able to continue with his search. As Carty watched, the old man

circumscribed a gradually diminishing area with a stout beech stake he used for climbing, and at length stood wistfully on the brink of the clay cliff crumbling even then in huge clods beneath his weight. He poled and dug and studied the [raw] clay face of the escarpment for traces of the old grave fill or other evidences of the burial place. Then he climbed down through the ravine smashing pieces from the gnarled old stump to satisfy himself that it had been an oak. For an hour or more the Indians combed through the smashed shale, coarse gravel and huge clamshells that cover the wide beach that spreads baking in the sun between the river and the foot of the cliff, except when the Thames is in flood. An old piece of horn was found but no bones and no evidence of the pipe and tomahawk which, according to the Naudee [sic] tradition, were buried with Tecumseh to identify his grave.[58]

Despite their failure to find a grave, the Nahdees refused to admit defeat. Instead, they left Carty with the impression that Tecumseh might have been buried farther up the sloping bank.[59] In any case, it was time for them to go.

After the Nahdees departed, a disappointed Carty tried to salvage what he could from the long and time-consuming trip. He went in search of the farmer who owned the property, and although David Walker was not at home, his wife was happy to entertain Carty's questions. The news of Tecumseh's burial had a startling effect on Mrs Walker. "Why, his monument is fifteen or twenty miles down the road at Thamesville," she exclaimed. "We never heard of such a thing."[60] Carty was not surprised, given that Tecumseh's burial was supposed to have been a secret. But at the very least, he thought Mrs Walker might be able to explain what had happened to the landmarks William Nahdee described. He was right. She confirmed that the southern bank of the Thames had once been wooded, and her daughter acknowledged that there was a rapids as recently as five or six years earlier. Mrs Walker could also point out what remained of the log cabin's foundation. As for the tree stump in the bottom of the ravine, she confirmed that it was all that remained of a magnificent oak her husband had cut down only a few years before – adding that the "stump just slid down the bank last spring."[61] Carty could not have been more delighted. Mrs Walker and her daughter had confirmed the Nahdee tradition for him. Bones or no bones, Carty still had a story.

The *Toronto Star* agreed, and published Carty's article under the headline: "STREAMS OF A CENTURY HAVE PROBABLY SWEPT TECUMSEH'S DUST AWAY."[62] Carty speculated that erosion, the same erosion that threatened to undermine the Longwoods Road, had already undermined Tecumseh's grave. "Tecumseh," he conjectured, "went down with the clay to be washed downstream past the battlefield where he met his death and through Chatham on to Lake St Clair."[63] It was a tidy explanation, and it allowed Carty to turn a non-event into a profitable exercise. In addition to the *Toronto Star*, the *London Advertiser* agreed to purchase the story. Carty even managed to get a reworked version published in the *London Centennial Review* – no doubt because he was one of its editors.[64] This last submission was rather a blatant appropriation of Wardsville's claim to Tecumseh's bones, but one that Carty easily justified. He simply commended London's centennial celebration for having stimulated the "awakening of interest in historic subjects," and the expedition in search of Tecumseh's grave.[65] Carty might have continued to exploit the story of Tecumseh's burial, had he not been distracted by the potential for an even more elaborate promotion. With the success of Lindbergh's famous trans-Atlantic flight in May of 1927, and the frenzy of publicity attending it, Carty wasted no time in arranging a similar aeronautic feat. Sadly, the London-to-London flight ended in disaster the following September.[66]

As for the Nahdees, their new-found celebrity proved as fleeting as Carty's passing interest in them. This rapid return to obscurity was the result of their failure to uncover Tecumseh's grave, which everyone assumed was the reason for the expedition in the first place – everyone except the Nahdees. Their primary objective had been to alert the world to the fact that Tecumseh's bones were not buried in London, and they did not need a skeleton to prove their point.[67] All they had to do was show Carty the general area where Tecumseh was buried. This they were able to accomplish by locating some of the landmarks described by their ancestor. Based on nothing more than the strength of their family history, the Nahdees had effectively ruled out London's claim to Tecumseh's grave. They could just as easily have eliminated Walpole Island's claim, had they noted that their ancestor, John Nahdee, was also known as Oshahwahnoo.[68] The resulting contradiction would have been obvious to anyone who remembered Matthew Fisher's claim that Oshahwahnoo had reinterred Tecumseh's bones on St Anne's Island, the delta tract contiguous to the Walpole Island Reserve. However, the Nahdees failed to mention Oshahwahnoo, and with this omission they lost their best chance to set the record straight.[69] It was an unfortunate oversight, and it was also intentional.

Just prior to their expedition, the Nahdees were challenged by a Native from the Kettle Point Reserve north of Sarnia, Ontario. By way of a letter to the *London Free Press*, Beattie Greenbird presented his family's account of Tecumseh's burial. In keeping with earlier stories, he explained how two nephews of Tecumseh had secretly buried their uncle to rest with "some article that will never get rotten" as proof of the great chief's identity. These nephews subsequently lived out the rest of their lives at Kettle Point, where they married and produced the progeny that guarded the secret of Tecumseh's burial from one generation to the next.[70] Greenbird was one of these descendants, which is why he disputed the Nahdees. However, he was not particularly bothered by the attempted discovery of Tecumseh's grave, as he himself had generously offered to share the secret with anyone at a week's notice.[71] Rather, it was the perceived theft of his family history that caused him so much upset.

It just so happened that one of the two nephews from Kettle Point who helped bury Tecumseh was Greenbird's great-grandfather, whose name – coincidentally enough – was also Oshahwahnoo.[72] While the Nahdees had studiously avoided making any reference to their ancestor's Native name, Greenbird's dispute with them suggests that he knew they claimed descent from Oshahwahnoo – his Oshahwahnoo.

What Greenbird appears not to have considered, however, is the pos-sibility that there might have been more than one elder by that name.[73] In fact, there were at least two. One was the Chippewa chief of St Anne's Island, who was also known as John Nahdee, and the other was Beattie Greenbird's forebear, the so-called Shawnee nephew of Tecumseh who occasionally went by the name of John Bigknife.[74] The Nahdees, for their part, probably were aware that their ancestor was not the only Native who referred to himself as Oshahwahnoo, but they seem to have kept quiet about it in hopes of avoiding a confrontation. The ploy, if one was intended, did not work. When Greenbird saw that Carty was doting on these usurpers from Walpole Island, he openly challenged them. Beattie Greenbird was riled, as were some of his cousins, and their anger rose to such an extent that they were ready to pounce on the very next person foolish enough to broach the topic of Tecumseh's grave.

On 30 June 1926 – only a day after Carty had gone touring with the Nahdees – the Ontario Historical Society met in London, Ontario, where the prominent historian Fred Landon was installed as the soci-ety's new president. Once this formality was out of the way, the exec-utive members turned their attention to the business at hand, which included a resolution in support of a monument to Tecumseh at the site of the battlefield. Like the Nahdees, the Ontario Historical Society was motivated by the Toronto *Globe*'s publicity.[75] During the discus-sion period, a civil servant and historian named Ernest Green tried to neutralize any possible complications arising from the Nahdee expe-dition by pointing out that the "controversy over the place where Tecumseh is buried need not interfere at all with the erection of a me-morial."[76] He considered the battlefield to be the most appropriate place for a monument, as it was there that Tecumseh made his last stand. The location of his grave was of no historical consequence.

Miss Augusta Gilkison, one of the society's more aged members, piped up in apparent agreement, but after a long ramble down memo-ry lane to the Tecumseh Celebration of 1913, she suddenly contradict-ed herself by suggesting that it was still possible to locate Tecumseh's grave. As she recalled, the chief of Moraviantown, meaning Albert To-bias, had claimed to know where Tecumseh was buried – which seems suspicious. The old lady, however, distinctly remembered asking him: "What will you do if you die?"[77] The chief, who chose to ignore the silliness of her question, solemnly vowed to pass the secret on to his son before fate overtook him. After Miss Gilkison had her say, Andrew F. Hunter, the society's secretary, impatiently counteracted the old lady's unwelcome intrusion by arguing that sixteen or seventeen skeletons belonging to Tecumseh had been unearthed over the years.[78] Hunter, who was convinced that any attempt to find and identify the skeleton of Tecumseh was just "about useless," concurred with Green and insisted that the battlefield where Tecumseh fell was the most logical place for his monument.[79] His colleagues agreed, in principle at least. Yet, despite Hunter's best efforts to steer the society clear of the same old pitfall involving Tecumseh's grave, it was impossible to avoid the jealousies bred by the competition for the great chief's monument.

The first indication of dissent came from within the society's very midst, when George F. Macdonald of Windsor presumed on behalf of his fellow citizens from Essex County, "that the memorial to Tecumseh should be in Amherstburg where Tecumseh lived, not where he died."[80] John Dearness, from London, was quick to react. "If Mr Macdonald's argument were carried to its logical conclusion," Dearness replied, "we would have to build the monument in the United States."[81] After Macdonald's bold – but ridiculous – retort that Amherstburg and Moraviantown were "the only places seriously connected with Tecumseh's life," President Landon intervened with some impartial observations. "It is quite clear," he began,

that Tecumseh's fame will be like Homer's in the conflict over places connected with his life. You know that many places contended for the honour of having been the birthplace of Homer. It is rather a healthy sign that there are so many towns asking for the privilege of doing honour to Tecumseh. The resolution is a rather general one. There is no definite movement as yet for the placing of a memorial in any particular place. The purpose of this resolution in the first place was, I think, to express our sympathy with the idea and to advance it in that degree a trifle toward the time when there will be a real movement in this Province for raising a monument to Tecumseh.[82]

Landon's eloquence brought a reflective mood to the meeting, and elevated the proceedings above partisan interests. Yet, while Landon was able to constrain petty jealousies among his colleagues in the Ontario Historical Society, he certainly had no control over the Natives of southwestern Ontario.

Hunter's remark about Tecumseh's many skeletons featured prominently in both of London's daily newspapers, and in due course reached another descendant of Oshahwahnoo, or John Bigknife.[83] Cornelius Shawano of Kettle Point was offended by what he regarded as an attempt to diminish his family's authority in the matter, and so severely that he penned an angry letter to the *London Free Press* expressing his displeasure. In his missive, Cornelius elaborated on the story Beattie

Greenbird told about Tecumseh's secret burial, adding that Tecumseh's nephew had switched their uncle's body with that of another warrior. "This," he argued, "is why a good many Indians claim that they knew where Tecumseh was buried."[84] Furthermore, as Cornelius emphasized, "no one can say that he has found Tecumseh's grave without showing the [medal] which was put in the grave when the great warrior was buried."[85]

A great deal of importance has been attached to this medal, which also constituted the "article" that Greenbird claimed would prove Tecumseh's identity. The Sac chief Black Hawk supposedly saw a medal on Tecumseh's body after the Battle of the Thames. However, John Richardson did not notice it when Tecumseh passed along the British lines prior to the battle. Abraham Holmes, on the other hand, recalled that Tecumseh wore a "brooch" in the morning before the battle, which might have been the medal in question. Presuming that Tecumseh's body was in fact adorned with a medal, then there is also the distinct possibility that it was removed by an American soldier in search of war trophies.[86] In this case, the most likely scenario is that Tecumseh was buried without a medal or insignia of any kind.

Although the medal might not have warranted the importance Cornelius attached to it, the mere suggestion that Tecumseh's bones could still be found was enough to seal the fate of the proposed monument. No member of Parliament was prepared to support any project that bore the slightest hint of controversy, and a controversy is exactly what Cornelius threatened to cause unless the monument to Tecumseh was built over a skeleton of his choosing – and presumably one buried somewhere on the Kettle Point Reserve. By his interference, Cornelius was able to reassert his family's authority. But he also completely frustrated the executive members of the Ontario Historical Society, and everyone else who hoped to avoid the controversy surrounding Tecumseh's burial. Thus, in his attempt to dictate the location, Cornelius not only quashed all interest in a monument on the battlefield, but in the monument itself. And any hope there might have been to revive the project crashed with the stock market in October of 1929. There would be no further thought of Tecumseh … until a gruesome discovery on Walpole Island in 1931.

Albert Tobias was a respected elder of Moraviantown who firmly believed that Tecumseh's grave remained undisturbed near the battlefield. With Tobias's death in February of 1931, the Delaware of Moraviantown lost their best chance to contest Walpole Island's claim to Tecumseh's bones. Courtesy Moravian Archives, Bethlehem, Pennsylvania

Dr Tecumseh K. Holmes, whose family history was closely linked with the Battle of the Thames, was an avid promoter of Chatham's claim to the Tecumseh monument. *Commemorative Biographical Record of the County of Kent, Ontario*

Having commemorated the Battle of the Thames and Tecumseh's death with a suitably inscribed boulder in 1911, a confident Katherine B. Coutts became determined to secure the proposed Tecumseh monument for Thamesville. Courtesy Christine Coutts Clement

HERE ON
OCTOBER 5, 1813
WAS FOUGHT THE
BATTLE OF THE
THAMES,
AND HERE
TECUMSEH
FELL.
ERECTED BY THE CITIZENS
OF THAMESVILLE A.D. 1911.

To "Tecumseh"
Thamesville, Ont.

In 1913, Jasper Jones of the Six Nations Reserve claimed that Tecumseh was buried in what had become the east end of London, Ontario. *Life of Joseph Brant*

Left: The Tecumseh boulder, as originally placed, was situated on the southeast corner of lot 4 in the Gore of Zone Township. It was on this farm that most of the relics from the Battle of the Thames were found. Courtesy Guy St-Denis

In 1926, London's claim to Tecumseh's grave was disputed by members of the Nahdee family from Walpole Island. Convinced that Tecumseh was buried closer to Wardsville, Willie Nahdee (left), his father William Nahdee (centre), and his cousin McKenzie Nahdee (right) investigated a farm on the outskirts of that village. *Centennial Year Review of London, Canada*

Ambitious Warriors

EARLY IN JANUARY OF 1931, an old lady living on the Walpole Island Reserve resigned herself to the disruption of a major housecleaning spree. It had been arranged that Wilson Knaggs and his family would move in with Sarah White, who was bedridden and unable to care for herself. During the ensuing and thorough scouring of his new abode, Knaggs decided to poke around in the attic. There he discovered a burlap bag, and upon looking inside was appalled to find a jumble of human bones.[1] Mrs White was not the least bit surprised. She knew there were bones in her rafters. Her husband had put them there – and they were supposed to be kept a strict secret. But when Knaggs pressed for an explanation, the tired old lady bluntly replied that the bones belonged to Tecumseh.[2]

Sarah White's husband was Chief Joseph White, the same Chief White who reclaimed Tecumseh's bones from Dr Mitchell in 1910. At that time, the skeleton was thought to have been returned to its grave on St Anne's Island.[3] Chief White, however, justifiably feared another expedition from Wallaceburg, and so he hid the bones in various places around his property. He guarded these relics for the next twenty years, until his death in August of 1929 finally relieved him of the vigil.[4] With no clear provision for the continued care of the bones, his invalid wife suddenly found herself in a dilemma. She decided to keep her husband's secret. If someone just happened to find the bones after she was dead and gone, that was their problem. What Mrs White failed to consider, however, was the possibility that this certain someone might rummage around in her attic while she was still alive.

Poor Knaggs had no idea what he should do with the bones, but finally he decided to pass the heavy responsibility on to the Walpole Island Soldiers' Club.[5] He was sure these Native veterans of the First World War would honour and protect the bones – and he was right. But if he thought these former warriors of Walpole Island would keep quiet about the discovery, he was sadly mistaken. The Soldiers' Club wasted no time calling in an officer of the Royal Canadian Mounted Police and a reporter from the *Sarnia Canadian Observer*.[6] The veterans had a plan. The Mountie would legitimize their claim to the discovery of Tecumseh's bones, and the reporter would publicize the veterans' call for a government-funded monument to the great chief. They had it all figured out, or so they thought.

On 16 January 1931, Corporal Thomas Corless and reporter Jack D. Purves met with the Walpole veterans, who provided them with all the details surrounding Knaggs's discovery. Just as the veterans expected, their white guests were skeptical. But the veterans were confident that they could provide the necessary provenance to uphold their claim to Tecumseh's bones. When Corless and Purves suggested an investigation, the veterans agreed without hesitation. Although this investigation was set to take place the very next day, Purves became impatient and broke the news in the *Sarnia Canadian Observer*, "pending authentication," that the Soldiers' Club could "CLAIM DISCOVERY OF BONES OF TECUMSEH ON WALPOLE ISLAND."[7] This misleading headline drew considerable attention, and continued to do so as Corless and Purves drove back to Walpole Island for the investigation. Corless, however, did not get very far into his examination before he began to have serious doubts. "I was not satisfied with the bones," the Mountie reported, "as they appeared to me to be a mixed lot and not human bones and were practically all in small fragments and dust."[8] Just when it began to appear that the discovery of Tecumseh's bones was nothing more than a clumsy hoax, Silas Shobway stepped in to save the day.

Shobway, who was a stepson to Chief White, made the surprising admission that the skeletal bits and pieces found by Knaggs were not Tecumseh's bones. They were merely a decoy, which his stepfather had planted in order to thwart any attempt to steal the real bones of Tecumseh.[9] Shobway elaborated by explaining that Chief White frequently moved the bones in order to keep them safe from whites, other Natives, and even his wife. The only person allowed to know their place of concealment was Shobway, and it was a long time before Chief White identified the man whose bones he so jealously guarded. The chief had thought it best not to say anything, but in August of 1929 he was obliged to break his silence. He was dying, and this sad fact of life prompted him to make a confession. The bones were all that remained of Tecumseh. As Shobway contemplated the great secret that had just been entrusted to him, Chief White stressed the heavy responsibility attending the revelation, which he did by way of a strict injunction: no white man must ever be allowed to know the place where the great chief's bones were sequestered.[10]

Shobway respected his stepfather's wish, which explains why he remained silent as the veterans set themselves up for an embarrassing disappointment. But when doubts were cast regarding the first set of bones, Shobway spoke up in defence of his stepfather's memory. It was later alleged that he broke his promise in order to draw the search for Tecumseh's bones away from his house, where he had an illicit beer-brewing operation in full swing.[11] Whatever the case, when Constable Corless asked to be shown where the real bones were hidden, Shobway led the way to a log in the nearby bush.[12] Underneath was another bag of bones, which soon had Purves rushing back to press.

On 19 January 1931, readers of the *Sarnia Canadian Observer* awoke to the headline: "REAL SKELETON OF TECUMSEH IS FOUND IN SECOND SEARCH."[13] This time Purves had good reason to believe that the second assortment of bones was authentic. According to him, the skeleton was identified "by means of a fracture in the left leg [thigh] bone, as it was known that Tecumseh broke his leg while buffalo hunting in his youth."[14] Just to be on the safe side, the trauma to the thigh bone would have to be verified. It was a bill any qualified physician could fill. Anxious to proceed, Purves and Corless secured the services of Dr Wilfrid B. Rutherford of Sarnia, and on 21 January 1931 they set out for Walpole Island. They were accompanied by two individuals who shared an interest in seeing the bones. One was Norman Gurd, the lawyer who had written the biography of Tecumseh, and the other was Ross W. Gray, the federal member of Parliament for West Lambton County.[15]

Dr Rutherford's examination went along swimmingly, and within a few minutes he assembled a nearly complete skeleton. All he lacked was one kneecap, several ribs, and a few minor bones. Since none of these missing pieces was crucial to the post-mortem, Dr Rutherford was soon able to deliver the results of his examination. The bones were those of a medium-sized male. This was the good news. The fractured leg bone, or rather thigh bone, was actually an arm bone.[16] This was the bad news. The one solid piece of evidence linking the bones to Tecumseh had suddenly disappeared. But Gurd had no intention of accepting bad news, not when he could cast about for an angle.

In a complete reversal from his own opinion of earlier days, that a broken thigh bone was the best evidence of Tecumseh's identity, Gurd tried to reassure a suddenly unnerved Purves by pointing out "there was no definite proof that Tecumseh had broken his hip [thigh]," since that claim was based "only on Indian lore."[17] Incredibly, while Gurd was quick to dismiss the evidence provided by the broken thigh bone because it was "only Indian lore," he had no qualms about using other "Indian lore" to validate these same bones as being those retrieved by Oshahwahnoo – which were said to have belonged to Tecumseh.[18] This inconsistency is especially curious, given Gurd's belief – which he expressed as late as 1923 – that Tecumseh had been buried "not far from the battlefield," and that it was someone else whose remains were removed to St Anne's Island.[19] A definite agenda lurked behind Gurd's double standard, and he made no effort to hide it.

Convinced that the Natives would obediently yield to the authority of government, Gurd wanted to prolong the investigation in hopes that it would reveal useful information about Tecumseh's secret burial.[20] If need be, he was prepared to compromise himself in the process. This method of historical research, however, made it increasingly difficult and ultimately impossible for Gurd to withdraw his support for Walpole Island's claim to Tecumseh's bones.

Purves was only too happy to go along with Gurd, as downplaying the significance of the broken thigh bone also served to sustain interest in the story, which meant more good copy for his newspaper.[21] Like Purves, Gray also had a personal stake in Gurd's scheme. Walpole Island was in his constituency, and it did not matter that Natives were not allowed the franchise. By helping to secure Tecumseh's monument for the reserve, Gray hoped to boost tourism in his riding – as well as his popularity at the polls.[22] But Gray's political instincts remained alert to the potential for controversy and political fallout. After assisting Gurd in taking down the evidence of several Native elders, the cautious member for West Lambton told the veterans that the results of the investigation would be complied and presented to the federal government and, provided the appropriate agency was satisfied that the bones were those of Tecumseh, he would "do all in his power to secure recognition from the authorities."[23] In effect, Gray was protecting his political career by shifting responsibility from himself to his government.

After Gray's announcement, the Walpole Island veterans were left to ponder how they might bolster his efforts on their behalf. They were well aware that he would have to convince the Canadian government that the skeleton really was that of Tecumseh, and a resolution of the Grand General Indian Council of Ontario seemed an appropriate measure by which to strengthen their case. This inter-tribal association possessed little in the way of political clout, but the veterans believed it was influential enough to legitimize Walpole Island's claim to Tecumseh's bones – and any monument that might result from having them. Despite the fact that most of the delegates who attended the Grand General Indian Council were Ojibwa who lived at Georgian Bay, and being from there should have no particular opinion as to the best site for Tecumseh's monument, the veterans were confident of success.[24] After all, Ojibwa was another name for Chippewa, and the Chippewa were among the original Native peoples of Walpole Island.[25] Given this tribal affiliation, the veterans fully expected that any opposition, particularly from the Moraviantown delegates, could be neutralized by swaying the votes of their Ojibwa/Chippewa cousins.

A month later, on 25 February 1931, a special session of the Grand Council was called to order in the Indian Council House on the Sarnia Reserve. Walpole Island sent eight delegates, but only three of the expected Ojibwa from around Georgian Bay went out of their way to attend.[26] The skeleton of Tecumseh, whether real or imagined, was of little concern to Natives living beyond southwestern Ontario. Yet the question carried considerable significance for the Delaware of Moraviantown, whose long association with Tecumseh prompted the dispatch of what turned out to be the next largest delegation. Although the Moraviantown Reserve could only afford the travel expenses for three of its band members, they hoped to find allies once they got to the Sarnia Reserve.[27]

The first order of business was whether or not the set of bones in the possession of the Walpole Island Soldiers' Club really constituted all that remained of Tecumseh. The veterans presented their case, but many of the delegates were unmoved – which a reporter from the Windsor *Border Cities Star* attributed to the "deep seated" impression "that the Indians of Walpole Island were more keen to have a historical shrine to attract tourists than they were to do honor to the memory of the warrior."[28] As support for the veterans wavered, a young man from Walpole Island suddenly let loose with an angry outburst. "You have heard the evidence," John Kiyoshk declared, "and it is clear to all who want to be convinced." Then he shouted: "Silas Shobway, stand up!" Obediently, Shobway did as he was ordered. "Look at Silas Shobway," Kiyoshk demanded:

Look at him in rags and poverty, but an Indian with the blood of the Indians of the past still red in his veins. Had he chosen, he might have sold the
secret of Tecumseh's bones and himself rode here in a Rolls-Royce. Seventy
percent of the men of Walpole Island went to the war. Eleven of them died.
The war veterans of Walpole Island ask you to be fair. Let Tecumseh rest
amongst his people on that Island. The bones are those of the great warrior.
The man who brought them [to St Anne's Island], Shawano [Oshahwah-
noo], was second in command at the battle of the Thames when Tecumseh
was killed. He rests there. Let Tecumseh rest with him.[29]

As the reporter from the *Border Cities Star* later recalled, the effect
of these dramatics was electric and "applause rent the air."[30] Outside,
a chilling winter wind blew across the St Clair River from Michigan,
but the atmosphere inside the council house quickly became overheat-
ed. It got so hot that the windows had to be raised several times in
order to cool things down. Kiyoshk had ignited a great debate, and the
"Indians were in a ferment."[31]

Eventually, the time came to put the question to a vote and, to no
one's surprise, it was a delegate from Walpole Island who moved to
recognize that the bones "under discussion are the skeleton of the great
warrior Tecumseh, as was killed in the year 1813 during the battle of
[the Thames]."[32] The motion was promptly seconded by another delegate from Walpole Island. But the council's first vice-president called
for an amendment to the motion. Emerson Snake had a particular interest in seeing the matter laid over until June. Being a Delaware from
Moraviantown and a descendant of Timothy Snake, who was widely
regarded as one of the guardians of Tecumseh's secret burial, Snake –
not surprisingly – wanted a postponement in order to allow a full investigation.[33] He justified the necessity of a delay based on the mass of
conflicting testimony.

Embarrassingly, the first of this conflicting testimony was voiced by
a Chippewa from Walpole Island. His name was Willie Nahdee. Speaking on behalf of his father, who was by then deceased, Willie recounted the 1926 expedition to Wardsville in search of Tecumseh's grave.[34]
Unfortunately, Willie did not state for the record that Chief John
Nahdee was also known as Oshahwahnoo. His failure to stress this important point probably had something to do with the presence of a
clearly agitated elder. Cornelius Shawano, the Kettle Point Native who
jealously counted Oshahwahnoo as one of his ancestors, was infuriated by what he perceived as yet another attempt to mitigate his family's
authority – this time by the Walpole Island veterans. Defiantly, he

vowed that he would soon be "leading a party to the grave, and ex-
posing the present discovery as a fraud."[35] Despite his best efforts,
Cornelius failed to browbeat the assembly into backing Snake's call for
a postponement of the vote. When the tally was taken, ten delegates
supported the amendment, but the original motion received eleven
votes and so the Grand Council had no choice but to officially recognize the bones on Walpole Island as those of Tecumseh.[36]

By the smallest of margins, the Walpole Island veterans had won
their case, but there was still the matter of a monument – and the delegates who opposed Walpole Island's claim to Tecumseh's bones were
in no mood to be supportive. Included among this number was John
Nahmabin, who was president of the Grand General Indian Council.
Although Nahmabin was also chief of the Sarnia Reserve, which was
predominantly Chippewa, he was not pleased with the behaviour of
the veterans from Walpole Island. Disregarding tribal affiliations, he
made it perfectly clear that he accepted the vote recognizing Tecumseh's bones only as a matter of duty. "Now that we are in the Tecumseh bones business," Nahmabin declared, "I might I suppose suggest
that the monument be erected in the centre of the Sarnia Reserve, where
thousands of tourists will be certain to see it."[37] His remark sent rip-
ples of laughter through the audience, but not everyone was amused.

Emerson Snake angrily protested these additional proceedings by
vowing to pressure the government into erecting a monument on the
battlefield near Moraviantown. When someone, probably from Walpole Island, observed that Moraviantown already had a monument (in
the form of the Tecumseh boulder), Snake retorted: "That's all right ...
we have found two or three Tecumsehs, have we not?"[38] Before Snake
had a chance to calm himself, a delegate from the Sarnia Reserve
moved to have Tecumseh's remains buried on Walpole Island.[39] Snake
desperately tried to block the motion, but his amendment that the decision be left to the government's discretion was defeated. Then one of
the delegates from Walpole Island resolved to petition the government
of Canada to erect "a suitable monument over the remains of this il-
lustrious warrior of 1812 ... on Walpole Island," of course.[40] This time,
a completely disgusted Snake made no effort to counter the move, and
the resolution was carried.

In the best tradition of political intrigue, the Walpole Island veterans had imposed their will on the Grand General Indian Council. They
saw no need for consensus, as even a majority of one could be glossed
over to give the impression of a broader mandate. The veterans, however, overlooked the irreversible damage they had inflicted upon their

plans for a monument by having coerced Native support. There was great resentment toward them, which could only be taken to mean that there had been a great deal of dissension leading up to the vote that recognized the bones discovered on Walpole Island as being those of Tecumseh. Like controversy, dissension did not go over well with the government, particularly when it came time to consider funding requests. And there was no way to keep the dissension attending the special session of the Grand General Indian Council a secret, not when the reporter from the *Border Cities Star* was Arthur C. Carty.[41]

Carty, who had fond memories of the lucrative expedition to Wardsville in 1926, was not about to miss out on a possible repeat performance. To his credit, however, he went to the Sarnia Reserve hoping that the mystery had finally been solved. But all the bickering over Tecumseh's bones soon cured him of his wishful thinking. As Carty later commented in the *Border Cities Star*, "To an observer who is not an Indian, and who has no bias in either direction, but a strong friendliness for Tecumseh and his memory, it seemed as though the element of thoroughness was lacking in the attempts that had been made to identify the remains as those of the Indian warrior."[42] In other words, the veterans from Walpole Island may have won their case, but they failed to prove their point.[43]

The same lack of thoroughness that troubled Carty appears to have also caused Ross Gray to have second thoughts, particularly after the veterans announced that they would stake their claim to Tecumseh's bones with the Grand General Indian Council of Ontario. Perhaps the evidence regarding the bones no longer seemed as convincing as it had when Gray first helped to assemble it. But the member for West Lambton had promised to present the veterans' claim to the government, and he still felt obligated to do so. At the same time, however, Gray felt the need for an exhaustive investigation. Early in February of 1931, he decided to request the assistance of the deputy superintendent general of the Department of Indian Affairs, which he did by means of a letter urging that someone be sent to investigate the bones discovered on Walpole Island. As if to force the department's collaboration, Gray leaked the details of his request to the *Sarnia Canadian Observer*.[44] The deputy superintendent general received Gray's letter a few days later, with some three weeks remaining before the special session of the Grand General Indian Council. But Duncan Campbell Scott was not willing to take action. He had already come to the conclusion that the bones on Walpole Island were not those of Tecumseh, and he had no intention of changing his mind.

Earlier, and immediately after the discovery of the bones in January of 1931, Ira Hammond, the principal of the Central School in Wallaceburg, had mailed a letter to J.B. Harkin, commissioner of the National Parks Branch of the Department of the Interior, asking if he had "anything authentic" regarding Tecumseh's burial.[45] Harkin did not, and so the letter was promptly referred to the Department of Indian Affairs, where it ended up on Scott's desk.[46] Scott just as quickly moved to disavow Hammond of the notion that Tecumseh might have been buried on Walpole Island, or specifically St Anne's Island. "I consider it extremely unlikely," Scott replied, "that the Indian remains mentioned in your letter as having been discovered on Walpole Island are those of Tecumseh. Tecumseh was killed at the battle of Moraviantown [or the Thames] in October, 1813, and the tradition is that he was buried where he fell. All efforts to discover his burial place in that locality have failed."[47] Scott and his secretary used much the same wording in several other communications.[48] This method of disposal worked quite well, until one of the letters went over Scott's head.

At the end of January 1931, Calvert S. Stonehouse, a merchant from Wallaceburg, wrote to Thomas G. Murphy, the minister of the Department of the Interior, who by virtue of his office was also superintendent general of Indian Affairs. In his letter, Stonehouse requested permission to submit designs for Tecumseh's crypt on behalf of a mausoleum company in Wallaceburg.[49] Scott was given the letter and asked to report on the request. Obviously, pat replies would no longer do. It was soon after that Gray's letter arrived, urging an investigation into the bones discovered on Walpole Island.[50] Along with it came an intriguing report outlining the history of Walpole Island's claim to Tecumseh's bones. The author, who signed his name Norman Gurd, placed great emphasis on the tradition of Oshahwahnoo's involvement in safeguarding Tecumseh's remains. At one point Gurd, who supported Gray's urgent request for an investigation, went so far as to remark: "I am impressed, therefore, with the fact that if anyone should know about Tecumseh, Shawano [Oshahwahnoo] should."[51] Scott was equally impressed, but not for the same reason.

Gurd's report convinced Scott that the question of Tecumseh's burial was historical in nature and therefore beyond the jurisdiction of the Department of Indian Affairs. Moreover, as he advised Murphy, "I have no one either competent or with sufficient leisure on my staff to undertake such an investigation."[52] Scott suggested that perhaps someone on the Historic Sites and Monuments Board of Canada or in the archaeological department at the University of Toronto might be willing to take on the challenge. "So far as Mr Stonehouse's suggestion is concerned," Scott added, "it would first have to be decided that the bones are authentic." Then, after "this was established some action by way of creating a monument would naturally follow."[53] Being a poet who made frequent use of Native themes, Scott thought the idea of a monument to Tecumseh had its merits.[54] But Scott the bureaucrat wanted nothing to do with the controversy surrounding the great chief's bones.

Confident that he had spared his department needless expenditures of time and money, Scott reiterated his position to Gray and singled out General Ernest A. Cruikshank of Ottawa as the person most qualified to undertake the historical research. Not only was Cruikshank an avid historian of the War of 1812 and a member of the Historic Sites and Monuments Board, he was also spending the winter in Jamaica.[55] Cruikshank's absence meant that he could not be called upon to conduct an investigation in time for the special session of the Grand General Indian Council to be held on 25 February, which suited Scott, since there was still the possibility that the vote might go against Walpole Island. As far as Scott was concerned, there was nothing more to do but delay action until Cruikshank's return. His boss, however, was not so sure.

In response to Scott's obvious lack of enthusiasm, Murphy decided to send the Stonehouse letter to the National Parks Branch, which also formed part of his portfolio. As it turned out, the deputy commissioner of that department could offer no more assistance than Scott.[56] But, in relaying this disappointing news, Roy A. Gibson, Murphy's deputy minister, helpfully advised that Dr W.H. Collins, director of the National Museum of Canada, had three anthropologists on staff who would be quite willing to co-operate. "Perhaps," Gibson proposed, "you might wish to suggest to Dr Scott that he have one of his officers get in touch with Dr Collins and go into the matter with a view to determining the advisability of making an investigation on the ground."[57] Murphy thought it an excellent idea, and so Scott soon found the letter from Stonehouse back on his desk.[58] This was not exactly the turn of events the deputy superintendent general had envisioned, but at least he was able to refer the matter to someone else.

On 28 February, three days after the veterans of Walpole Island won the vote at the special session of the Grand General Indian Council of Ontario, Scott obligingly sent Collins all the documentation he had regarding the bones discovered on Walpole Island.[59] Collins then turned the file over to Marius Barbeau, an ethnologist with the National Museum who specialized in Native studies. Based on the infor-

mation provided by Scott, particularly Norman Gurd's report, Barbeau dismissed the discovery as the product of local folklore. As he
explained:

When Tecumseh died on the battlefield, he was just one of several leaders
fallen in the American and British armies. Brave as he was, his name had
not yet been singled out by biographers and historians. Few if any people
at the time paid much attention to the place where his body was buried[,]
presumably with that of many others. But as soon as he became known as
a hero at the hand[s] of his biographers and historians, his former friends
and acquaintances began to think of him retrospectively. His deeds were
magnified. He became a legend. His bones began to be found, and this reported find is not the first, nor the most convincing.[60]

Still, Barbeau thought there might be some merit in examining the
bones to satisfy the public's demand for an official decision. Scott was
not the slightest bit interested in the ethnologist's suggestion. He preferred to let Cruikshank decide the question. "General Cruikshank,"
Scott advised Murphy, "is to my mind as well informed on the subject
as any person in the country and I consider that his co-operation
would be invaluable."[61] Given Barbeau's rather mixed report, Murphy finally agreed with his subordinate and once again Scott was able
to put the investigation on hold. But there was no way to defer the
controversy.

In mid-March of 1931, an aged Native from the Muncey Reserve
near London, Ontario, went to a lawyer all "stirred up" over the alleged discovery of Tecumseh's bones on Walpole Island.[62] Eighty-year-
old Jacob Logan related an incident from his childhood, dating back
to *circa* 1860, when he secretly overheard Jacob Pheasant – the com-
patriot of Timothy Snake – tell his grandfather where Tecumseh was
buried.[63] Logan was convinced that he could recall this conversation
sufficiently to point out the grave, within a few metres of it.[64] But he
would only consent to do so if he got some assurance that the grave
would be marked with a monument. When Logan's lawyer offered his
client's services to the Department of Indian Affairs, Scott's secretary
replied by acknowledging that "the statements made by Chief Logan
will be given consideration."[65] This bureaucratic jargon translated into
an indefinite abeyance. In the meantime, however, Logan took his
story to a newspaper reporter, insisting that the bones found on Walpole Island "are not those of Tecumseh, the Indian warrior, but those
of a man who at birth was named after the great chief, a customary

thing after his death in the War of 1812."[66] Logan's disclosure was not the most serious threat to the ambitions of the Walpole Island veterans – but it was not the last, either.[67]

Toward the end of March 1931, the question of Tecumseh's broken thigh, which Norman Gurd and the veterans of Walpole Island had tried to ignore, suddenly came back to haunt them. The conjuror behind this rising spectre of doubt was Philip Adams, the American consul at Sarnia. Having followed the news of the most recent discovery of Tecumseh's bones with great interest, Adams took it upon himself to procure whatever information he could from the State Historical Society of Wisconsin "that might assist Mr Gurd and Mr Gray in definitely determining the authenticity of the finding."[68] Adams was already aware, perhaps through Gurd, that this society preserved the papers of the late historian Lyman C. Draper, who had collected a mass of information regarding American frontier history – much of which pertained to Tecumseh. The American consul was especially interested to know if there was any truth to the old story that Tecumseh had broken a thigh in his youth. The reply out of Madison confirmed that this had indeed been the case.[69]

The fact that Tecumseh had suffered a broken thigh bone ruled out the possibility that the bones discovered on Walpole Island could have belonged to him, as Dr Rutherford had already determined there was no indication of a healed femur. The veterans, however, simply disregarded the verdict of the State Historical Society of Wisconsin, and embarked on a plan to win public support by organizing a public viewing of the skeleton. Two weeks later, the bones were taken to the Anglican parish hall on Walpole Island, and there reverently placed on a Union Jack which distinguished an otherwise ordinary table. It was a Tuesday night, and although most people had to work the next day, over 250 curious individuals made their way to the parish hall in order to satisfy their morbid curiosity.[70] The success of this event convinced the veterans that they still had a good chance to secure government support through the Department of Indian Affairs, since the opposition to their claim regarding Tecumseh's bones appeared to have run its course. They would soon discover otherwise – on both counts.

News of the grisly exhibit on Walpole Island did not sit well with Emerson Snake, the same Delaware from Moraviantown who made such a fuss during the special session of the Grand General Indian Council at Sarnia. And, true to his earlier promise, Snake launched a separate monument drive in late April of 1931.[71] He was determined to see a monument constructed on the battlefield where Tecumseh was killed, and where he was sure the great chief was still buried. Snake based his argument on the evidence of Elias Dolson, an elder from Moraviantown.[72] Dolson, who considered it his duty to speak on behalf of his recently deceased friend, Albert Tobias, repeated the old story of Tecumseh's secret burial. As for the bones found on Walpole Island, Dolson was emphatic: "Tecumseh buried near Moraviantown ... nowhere else."[73] While this evidence did not carry the same weight as that obtained from the State Historical Society of Wisconsin, Dolson's story was no less compelling – especially in the eastern locales of Kent County where it struck a familiar chord. But as determined as Emerson Snake was in trying to force the government's participation in his monument scheme, Duncan Campbell Scott was just as determined to bide his time until Cruikshank's return.

Finally, on 8 May 1931, Scott was able to invite Cruikshank's assistance in determining the authenticity of the bones on Walpole Island.[74] Cruikshank was only too happy to help, and three days later he submitted a substantial report for Scott's consideration. After analysing the circumstances surrounding Tecumseh's death, Cruikshank conceded that Tecumseh's body might have been "carried off into the woods by some of his comrades, where it must have been abandoned or buried."[75] But Tecumseh's exhumation and removal to Walpole Island seemed "extremely improbable," and the bones found there showed no indication of a fractured thigh bone. Cruikshank could not "see that any case has been made out for the identification of these bones as being those of Tecumseh."[76] He did, however, acknowledge the "propriety of erecting some suitable memorial to Tecumseh" on or near the battlefield, and he even volunteered to take up the matter with his fellow members of the Historic Sites and Monuments Board, whose next meeting would take place at the end of May.[77] Scott could not have been more delighted. Thanks to Cruikshank's report, the bothersome bones on Walpole Island were no longer his concern. Better yet, it appeared a near certainty that Tecumseh would get the monument he deserved.[78] After all, the chairman of the Historic Sites and Monuments Board was none other than Ernest Cruikshank.

When Ross Gray learned that the question of a monument to Tecumseh was going to be taken under consideration by the Historic Sites and Monuments Board, he asked for permission to present Walpole Island's claim.[79] His request was granted, but the politician must have been more than a little peeved when Duncan Campbell Scott, who had also been invited, suddenly spoke up in support of Cruikshank's opinion that the best place for Tecumseh's monument was on the battlefield.[80] Up to that point, Scott had given Gray the impression that he was indifferent as to the location of the proposed monument. But just as the veterans of Walpole Island had coerced the special session of the Grand General Indian Council, Cruikshank and Scott worked the Historic Sites and Monuments Board. The board backed Cruikshank's proposal – including his view that the monument should be a "plain and simple thing," which must have seemed appropriate given the lingering economic reverses caused by the Great Depression.[81] Unfortunately, Cruikshank's plans for a stone shaft rising nine metres in the air, adorned with a bronze effigy of Tecumseh, still proved far too rich for the tight budget of the Historic Sites and Monuments Board.[82] The board could do nothing more tangible than officially recognize that Tecumseh warranted "a suitable national memorial."[83]

Despite Gray's failure to influence Cruikshank and his colleagues on the Historic Sites and Monuments Board, Walpole Island's frustrated monument aspirations did bring about one very important result. Tecumseh was designated a person of national historic significance, and it was this posthumous status that would one day entitle him to a monument.[84]

A Monument or Two

WHEN CHATHAM'S MAYOR and city councillors met in regular session at the beginning of June 1931, they found a special guest waiting for them in the person of Emerson Snake. This Native from the Moraviantown Reserve had come looking for support, and he was determined to bring his white audience on side. Pointing to a Union Jack hanging on an adjacent wall, he declared: "Had it not been for [the] great work of Tecumseh, this section might not be in British territory."[1] There was no argument. Snake then proceeded to his second point by noting there was a widespread belief that something should be done to honour the name of the famous Tecumseh. "If his name is so important," Snake postulated, "it should be honored by a suitable memorial."[2] Again, there was no argument.

As Snake took his seat, he assumed there would be no argument that the best place for Tecumseh's monument was on the battlefield. He was right; there was no argument. The council proceeded to adopt a resolution in favour of his proposal to erect a monument to Tecumseh – but "at a suitable place to be designated by the proper authorities."[3] This vague endorsement came as a nasty surprise, and ruined Snake's plans to organize an influential committee of municipalities to further his cause. Snake fully expected that Chatham's city council would be the first civic body to join forces with him. Once he formed this alliance, he hoped to recruit the assistance of other municipalities – first across Kent County and then farther afield. Then, as soon as the Walpole Island Reserve was sufficiently isolated, Snake's committee would pressure the Canadian government to construct a monument according to his specifications.

The ambiguity of the Chatham city council was a major setback. But Snake's confidence was soon restored by many offers of assistance, all of which resulted from the publicity surrounding the appeal he

made for Tecumseh's sake. In August of 1931, several particularly devoted individuals came forward to help Snake establish the Tecumseh
Memorial Committee. They quickly organized and began securing designs and cost estimates for the proposed monument.[4] With some hard
facts in hand, Snake and his committee hoped to turn agreeable councillors into staunch allies. It soon became evident, however, that the
monument they had in mind would require something "in the neighborhood of $20,000."[5]

The committee members were under no illusions that they could
convince any of Ontario's municipalities to join them in raising such a
large fund, especially given the depressed state of the economy at that
time. Yet, they remained hopeful. Much of their optimism stemmed
from the fact that they had no competition from the veterans of Walpole Island, whose own monument ambitions had been stymied by
Duncan Campbell Scott.[6] In a major revision of Snake's original plan,
the Tecumseh Memorial Committee decided to forego the support of
Ontario's municipalities in favour of a more direct approach for government assistance. The person they chose to represent them was
Calvert S. Stonehouse. This was the same Wallaceburg merchant who,
at the end of January 1931, had tried to interest the Department of Indian Affairs in a crypt for Tecumseh on Walpole Island. Perhaps hoping that memorial sales might be better in Moraviantown, Stonehouse
was keen to see the Tecumseh boulder replaced with "a more suitable
monument" to the great chief and in May of 1932 he tried to sell his
idea to the Canadian government. As in the case of his earlier attempt
to drum up business, Stonehouse addressed a letter to Thomas G.
Murphy, the minister of the Department of the Interior and superintendent general of Indian Affairs.[7] But the minister, who initially had
been quite indulgent, no longer had any patience for either Stonehouse
or Tecumseh.

Murphy wasted no time in having the letter from Stonehouse referred to the Historic Sites and Monuments Board.[8] That advisory
body, however, had already deferred the question of a monument to
Tecumseh due to a lack of funds. In replying to Murphy, the board's
secretary advised that "the promoters of the movement should take the
necessary steps in the matter of approaching governments and the public for contributions with this object in view."[9] Yet the Historic Sites
and Monuments Board did not completely close the door on Tecumseh. Fred Landon, the new representative on the board for western Ontario, was asked to investigate the proposal by contacting Stonehouse
to learn more about it.[10] As Landon discovered, Stonehouse and the

Tecumseh Memorial Committee desired a monument similar to the one erected at Springfield, Ohio, to George Rogers Clark, who, along with his Kentuckians, had waged war on the Shawnee settlements in 1780.[11] Although Landon thought the Clark Monument "a very pleasing type," he could not help but feel that Stonehouse and his friends "are not facing the fact that they are the people who must work up this project and bear a good share of the cost if the monument is ever undertaken."[12]

In September of 1932, Murphy informed Stonehouse that the Tecumseh Memorial Committee would have to rely on its own initiative in order to commemorate Tecumseh.[13] In response, one of the committee members, Omar K. Watson, a lawyer from Ridgetown, devised an imaginative solution to their funding problem: an open air pageant celebrating Tecumseh's life. But after writing the script and scouting out a natural theatre on the banks of the Thames River at Moraviantown, Watson put the project on hold.[14] Convinced that the Great Depression had ruined their chances for a successful pageant, Watson and his fellow committee members agreed that a postponement was the best course of action. It proved a fateful decision.

Earlier, in the spring of 1932, the veterans of Walpole Island – having become completely frustrated with the Department of Indian Affairs – had decided to fund a monument themselves. In a circular calling for donations, they also advertised that the unveiling of their monument would take place sometime in September.[15] Suddenly, Snake and the Tecumseh Memorial Committee had competition.

The veterans of Walpole Island were counting on a major contribution from their band council, but the request they submitted was deferred. Not coincidentally, perhaps, it was a decision approved by the Department of Indian Affairs.[16] The proud veterans of Walpole Island, however, refused to surrender. In July of 1932, they optimistically commissioned the Canadian poet Wallace Havelock Robb to write a poem in tribute to Tecumseh, which they fully expected to have read at the monument's dedication ceremony. As it turned out, the recital did not take place in September of 1932, or even September of 1933, and by the summer of 1934 Robb must have wondered if his poem would ever be read.[17] It certainly appeared that the Soldiers' Club had quietly given up. But August of 1934 brought surprising news: work on Tecumseh's monument would begin at once.[18]

The veterans of Walpole Island had discovered unexpected allies in Gar Wood, the famous speedboat racer, and Lee Barrett, vice-president of the Detroit Tourist and Convention Bureau. Together, these gentlemen made significant contributions toward the estimated $2,500 cost of constructing a monument to Tecumseh.[19] It was a magnificent gesture, but there was just one problem. Gar Wood and Lee Barrett were both Americans. So, too, was H. Lee Pocklington, the village president of Algonac, Michigan, who promised to supply the boulders for the monument.[20] While no one begrudged these Americans their citizenship, the idea that three men from Michigan had to be relied upon in order to honour a Canadian hero was nothing short of a national disgrace. The veterans of Walpole Island, however, had no misgivings about accepting the generosity of their American friends, and if the paternalistic and unresponsive Department of Indian Affairs was suitably embarrassed in the process, then so much the better.

The potential for bad press was immediately recognized by Archie Highfield, the Indian agent for Walpole Island. On 9 August 1934, he telegraphed the Department of Indian Affairs advising that the Walpole Island Soldiers' Club and its American friends planned to turn the sod for their Tecumseh monument in a few days' time. Highfield wanted to know if there were "ANY OBJECTIONS[?]"[21] The officious Indian agent soon had his answer: "DEPARTMENT ACCEPTS NO RESPONSIBILITY IN REFERENCE TO TECUMSEH MEMORIAL WALPOLE ISLAND BUT OFFERS NO OBJECTION."[22] This attitude of non-intervention regarding Tecumseh and his monument had become department policy, and it would take more than a couple of well-heeled Americans to alter the tradition so firmly established by the since-retired Duncan Campbell Scott.[23]

The afternoon of 11 August 1934 was bright and sunny on Walpole Island, and despite the hasty organization of the sod-turning ceremony, there was a large attendance from both the Canadian and American sides of the St Clair River – which actually had more to do with Gar Wood than Tecumseh. Having won the Harmsworth Trophy for the eighth time in September of 1933, Wood retained both his title as the world's champion speedboat racer, as well as his ability to draw crowds. The veterans knew their famous guest would steal the show, and that his presence would also guarantee the success of their event.[24]

The ceremony began with the raising of the Union Jack and the Stars and Stripes, followed by renditions of both the Canadian and American national anthems by the Walpole Island Band. The Reverend Mr Draper, of St John's Anglican Church on Walpole Island, opened the program by giving his parish due credit for having donated the land for the monument, after which he called upon Native speakers to welcome their guests.[25] One after another, Harrison B. Williams, chief of the Chippewa, George Isaacs, chief of the Potawatomi, and Peter Altiman, president of the Walpole Island Soldiers' Club extended greetings.[26] Then it was Wood's turn to speak. After a "rousing ovation," the famous American voiced his appreciation for the honour paid to his country's flag. Wood continued to speak in glowing terms of the impressive ceremony, and then suddenly blurted out the shocking disclosure that his wife was a distant relative of William Henry Harrison, Tecumseh's arch-enemy.[27] This little *faux pas* no doubt raised more than a few eyebrows among the veterans and other Natives. But they were not about to hold their famous guest responsible for his wife's regrettable genealogy. It would have been inhospitable, not to mention undiplomatic, given Wood's promise that construction of their monument would begin in the near future.

The next speaker was Colonel Charles S. Woodrow of Sarnia, a prominent lawyer, police magistrate, and outspoken friend of Walpole Island.[28] He was also a lieutenant-colonel in the Lambton Regiment, and so it came as no surprise when he praised the bravery of the Walpole Island veterans during the First World War. But he too caused a stir when he verbalized what every other patriotic Canadian was thinking that day: "I stand here today with a feeling of shame from two points, first, that in the battle in which Tecumseh was killed the British forces fled leaving [their Native] allies to hold the ground and, secondly, that it has been found necessary that a citizen of the United States [meaning Gar Wood] should be the one to provide the foundation for the memorial."[29] Although the colonel tempered his comments by acknowledging the hard economic times, there was no mistaking his criticism of the Canadian government. The Walpole Island veterans refrained from echoing Woodrow's sentiments. With their American friends footing the bill for Tecumseh's monument, the support of the Department of Indian Affairs was no longer an issue. Besides, there was no reason to disrupt the harmony of the day, since Moraviantown's monument proposal appeared to have been postponed indefinitely.

In keeping with this spirit of harmony, Chief Nicholas Plain of the Sarnia Reserve appealed for a greater sense of brotherhood.[30] To anyone familiar with the strained relations between Walpole Island and the Sarnia Reserve which had resulted from the official recognition of Tecumseh's bones, Plain's remarks must have had a conciliatory ring. As such, they served as a prelude to the highly symbolic gesture of reconciliation that followed Plain's speech. It was time to turn the sod, and this honour went to John Nahmabin of the Sarnia Reserve. The same man who only a few years earlier, as president of the Grand General Indian Council of Ontario, had poked fun at the "Tecumseh bones business" now inaugurated the monument he once ridiculed.[31] Afterwards, Nahmabin shared a peace pipe with the veterans, signifying an end to the hard feelings.

Encouraged by their success, the veterans of Walpole Island enthusiastically planned to lay the cornerstone of their monument at the end of August. In looking for other dignitaries to round out their guest list, they decided to invite the British consul at Detroit. Leslie C. Hughes-Hallet, hardly knowing what to make of the invitation, and somewhat bothered by the American involvement, considered it his duty to alert the Canadian Legation at Washington: "I do not know whether the affair has been brought to your notice or not. In the latter event, I felt it might be of some interest to you in case you should consider it desirable for the Canadian Government to notice the affair officially. It is receiving considerable local publicity and some comment has been made on the fact that it has been left for Americans to dispose fittingly of the remains of their great Indian opponent in 1812."[32] The consul's letter eventually made its way to the Department of External Affairs in Ottawa, and then to the Department of Indian Affairs – where its demand for immediate attention shattered the calm of official routine. Harold W. McGill, the new deputy superintendent general, did not appreciate the imposition. Through his secretary, he replied to the Department of External Affairs by referring to Cruikshank's report and reiterating that the Department of Indian Affairs would not accept responsibility in the matter, either "officially or otherwise."[33] McGill was not about to reward the annoying behaviour of the Walpole Island veterans.

Blissfully unaware of the upset they had caused in Ottawa, the veterans continued making plans for their next gala event.[34] But finding a famous celebrity to open for them proved difficult. Gar Wood was unable to attend, and all they saw of Ontario's premier, Mitchell Hepburn, was his letter of congratulation.[35] In the end, it appeared that the veterans would have to settle for Ross Gray and Norman Gurd, both of whom still professed an interest in their proposed monument. But Gray the politician and Gurd the historian were hardly crowd pleasers, so the veterans accepted the offer made by Village President Pocklington to bring along Algonac's Home Coming Queen and her Court of Beauties. The veterans may have regretted their decision when Pocklington arrived for the ceremony and gleefully declared: "These are my official representatives for the day!"[36]

Fortunately for Norman Gurd and Ross Gray, their stints did not include Algonac's "official representatives." Gurd was given the honour of laying the cornerstone. After tapping the stone with his trowel and declaring it "well and truly laid," he was formally adopted into the Chippewa tribe in recognition of his support for Walpole Island's claim to Tecumseh's bones. His Native name, appropriately enough, was "Shawanee."[37] Gray's services were also acknowledged when he was invited to address the assembly. This honour was bestowed mainly because he was the only representative of the federal government who would have anything to do with the veterans. Indeed, Gray's continued participation is a matter of some curiosity, since he had ample evidence that the bones so revered by the veterans were not authentic.

In late January of 1931, well in advance of the Native vote to recognize Tecumseh's bones, and at the same time that Gray was beginning to think that an exhaustive government-sponsored investigation might be in order, he received information regarding Oshahwahnoo – the Chippewa chief from St Anne's Island (one of the islands comprising the Walpole Island Reserve). Oshahwahnoo it was shown, had also been known as John Nahdee.[38] Initially, Oshahwahnoo's other name was not considered to be of any particular consequence. But during the special session of the Grand General Indian Council, Gray heard Willie Nahdee describe how his ancestor, John Nahdee, had buried Tecumseh near Wardsville. Gray must have thought it strange that the veterans could claim that Oshahwahnoo had buried Tecumseh's bones on St Anne's Island, when his Nahdee descendant insisted they were in a grave near Wardsville. Obviously, there was something amiss, but Gray ignored the Nahdee testimony. Instead, he went along with Gurd – just as he had done on an earlier occasion. His reason for doing so is not clear, unlike Gurd's willingness to compromise himself for the sake of extending the investigation into Tecumseh's bones. Tourism probably was still a factor for Gray, although it appears that the member for West Lambton had also become caught up in the international aspect of the proposed monument. It was a point he emphasized during the ceremony to lay the cornerstone. Marvelling at the lasting peace enjoyed by Canada and the United States, Gray declared his hope "that the day will soon come when other nations of the world will profit by the example we have given them, and realize that they also can do as we have done."[39]

The veterans were well pleased with Gray's expressions of goodwill toward their American friends – the same friends who promised to adorn their monument with a statue of Tecumseh.[40] While the veterans should have known better than to place much faith in white promises, the Americans had already come through for them by providing the foundation for the monument. Just as reassuring was a scale model of the statue, which was displayed during the cornerstone laying ceremony.[41] Surely, the Americans would not disappoint their Native friends on Walpole Island.

Soon after the cornerstone was laid, masons began constructing the cairn in preparation for the much-anticipated statue. The veterans hoped to have it delivered in time for the anniversary of Tecumseh's death on 5 October, but early in September they were forced to launch another fundraising campaign.[42] As big-hearted as their American friends had been, the veterans discovered that there were very definite limits to the generosity they could expect from across the border. Of course, everyone blamed the hard times, but more likely Wood and his friends had come to their senses. Why should they pay for a monument to an enemy of the United States – and in a foreign country, no less? If Canadians were not willing to contribute to the cost of honouring their own hero, then the Americans could find other ways to spend their money. Gar Wood had race boats to build. And if Lee Barrett were going to have a statue of Tecumseh sculpted, it would be unveiled in downtown Detroit – not downtown Walpole Island. As for Lee Pocklington, when he realized how much more expensive it was to ship boulders across the St Clair River, as opposed to Algonac's Home Coming beauties, he discreetly limited his offer of stone to only one load.[43]

Unfortunately for the veterans, their fundraising campaign failed, and they had no choice but to suspend work on the monument.[44] Patiently, they waited for the depression to end so they could solicit the money necessary to finish the job. But rather than peace and prosperity, the depression was replaced by war and rationing. In those final months of 1939, the veterans had no reason to think their monument would ever be finished. But then came a curious twist.

In response to the war effort, formerly reticent government officials suddenly became receptive to the idea of a monument to Tecumseh. There was considerable propaganda value in honouring one of Canada's greatest heroes, especially one of Tecumseh's stature. Without questioning this marked change in attitude, the veterans decided to take advantage of the opportunity to finish their monument – even if it meant letting the Americans off the hook for the promised statue of Tecumseh.[45]

With assistance from the County of Lambton and the Department of Indian Affairs, the scaled-down monument was finally completed in the summer of 1941. Early in August, the veterans announced their plans for a ceremonial interment of the bones in their possession, which would form the last act in a grand pageant depicting Tecumseh's life.[46] This news brought an angry outburst from several Delaware veterans at Moraviantown, who told the familiar old story that Tecumseh was buried near the battlefield, and that his remains had never been disturbed. But the real source of their outrage had more to do with the pageant than Tecumseh's bones. To the Delaware veterans, who still hoped to perform a pageant of their own, it looked as though Walpole Island had stolen Omar Watson's idea and their best chance to fund a monument to Tecumseh. Instead of making a direct accusation, however, the Moraviantown veterans blasted their counterparts on Walpole Island for disgracing the British flag with their false claims to Tecumseh.[47] In mid-August of 1941, with only a week remaining until their unveiling ceremony, the Walpole Island veterans decided they could not afford the bad press coming out of Moraviantown. They secured the services of a lawyer, and that lawyer was Norman Gurd.

The veterans of Walpole Island could not have found better counsel. Not only was Gurd an expert on Tecumseh, he also had a hand in preparing the script for their pageant.[48] And he was not about to let anything interfere with the success of the Walpole Island extravaganza. In laying the veterans' case before the public, Gurd began with a few basic facts. The Natives at Moraviantown "were Delaware Indians," he told a reporter from the *Windsor Star*, while the Moravian missionaries caring for them were pacifists, "refusing to fight for either side [British or American]."[49] Therefore, as Gurd concluded, none of the Delaware could have taken part in the War of 1812 or engaged in the Battle of the Thames, and neither they nor their descendants could have any knowledge of Tecumseh's burial. Gurd presented a strong argument against Moraviantown, and a biased interpretation of its history.

While some of the Delaware at Moraviantown adhered to the strict moral code of the Moravian missionaries, there were also those Delaware who persisted in their ancient traditions, and still other Delaware who vacillated between the two belief systems. They certainly were not of one mind, and according to Christian Frederick Denke, one of the Moravian missionaries at Fairfield in 1813, of the forty-six Delaware who died between 1813 and 1814, six were slain in battle.[50] So, despite Gurd's claim to the contrary, there could very well have been Delaware warriors in the Battle of the Thames. They might not have known anything about Tecumseh's burial, but it was not because they were all pacifists.

To the descendants of these Delaware warriors, Gurd's remarks were interpreted as a charge of cowardice. But being unaware of Denke's vital statistics, and knowing their heritage included Moravian pacifism, they were not certain how they should respond to Gurd's insult.[51] A meeting was quickly called to order, and one particularly outraged elder soon had the full support of the assembly. "We have been challenged as cowards and I will not stand for that," Christopher Stonefish assured his listeners. "If there are people who think we are cowards," he angrily declared, "I will soon change their minds if they come to me."[52] Stonefish continued to vent his fury over this "piece of business" for some time, and, before he finished, he urged the younger generation to "get busy" and find Tecumseh's grave.[53]

While the Delaware at Moraviantown rattled their sabres, the veterans of Walpole Island went ahead with preparations for the combined open air pageant and re-interment ceremony. On 23 August 1941, they put their plans into action. At mid-day, Tecumseh's bones were taken to the Anglican church for public viewing. Several thousand people reportedly filed past the skeleton. Then came a series of addresses at the monument. Gar Wood and Lee Barrett were conspicuous by their absence, but Lee Pocklington managed to put in an appearance – this time without his "official representatives." The guest of honour, however, was Secretary T.R.L. MacInnes of the Department of Indian Affairs. Although MacInnes was not the head of that department, the veterans received him very graciously – because it was the Native thing to do, and also because he clearly embodied official recognition of their claim to Tecumseh's bones by the Department of Indian Affairs.[54] MacInnes, however, made it abundantly clear that he did not "wish to be involved in any rivalry existing between Indians in respect to Tecumseh."[55] Instead, he likened the "friendly competition" between Natives as striking proof of Tecumseh's greatness. The secretary's attempt at impartiality was commendable, but the veterans of Walpole Island preferred their own interpretation.

Later that day, as afternoon turned to evening, an all-Native cast performed Gurd's pageant to a large audience. There were four scenes: Tecumseh's meeting with Brock; a re-enactment of Tecumseh's death at the Battle of the Thames; Oshahwahnoo's vigil over Tecumseh's grave; and the last one, which involved the actual re-interment of Tecumseh's bones. The final scene was also the most dramatic. Four Native "braves" in traditional garb entered the church, and emerged a short time later with a small chest.[56] By the flickering light of torches, the pallbearers made their way to the monument. There they halted. Suddenly, the three and a half metre high cairn was illuminated with floodlights, which was the pallbearers' signal to proceed up a ramp. At the top of the monument, and with heads bowed, they listened to the recital of an Anglican burial service. Then they slowly began to lower the chest down a shaft. A detachment of soldiers fired a salute, and then a bugler sounded the mournful strains of the last post.[57] Tecumseh's bones had finally been laid to rest, or so it appeared.

The spectacle staged by the Walpole Island Soldiers' Club had the desired effect. Regardless of the controversy still surrounding the identity of the skeleton, most Canadians wanted to believe that Tecumseh had been honoured with the last rites he so richly deserved. It seemed an especially appropriate gesture during those dark days of the Second World War. At a time when Canadians looked to the exploits of past heroes to help boost their morale, the honour paid Tecumseh by the Soldiers' Club served as a valuable contribution to the war effort. And no matter how much the Delaware of Moraviantown scoffed, at least Walpole Island had succeeded in producing a skeleton ... as well as a pageant.[58]

Moraviantown had been pre-empted, which led Chief Barney Logan to candidly admit: "we do not pretend to claim that we know where Tecumseh's bones are."[59] This utterance promptly placed him at odds with Christopher Stonefish, who was still upset by Gurd's perceived charge of cowardice against Delaware manhood. Since Stonefish was a respected elder, Logan felt embarrassed enough to go along with his suggestion that regular meetings be held to consider means by which Moraviantown could get its own monument.[60] Nothing came of the meetings and when Stonefish died in February of 1942, they were quietly discontinued.[61] It was no use. The Delaware had no bones, and their plans for a pageant had been upstaged. But, as they would eventually come to realize, they did possess one very important advantage over Walpole Island. It was a provincial highway in need of repair.

In March of 1955, Ontario's Department of Highways announced plans to reduce the number of curves in the Number Two Highway. The project was slated to begin the following summer, and one of the major alterations involved the dangerous sweep of the road around the Tecumseh boulder.[62] News of the impending roadwork renewed interest in the legend concerning the vigil over Tecumseh's grave. When a curious reporter from the *Windsor Star* traced the story back to Nellis Pheasant of Moraviantown, he found the great-great-grandson of

Jacob Pheasant quite receptive. Nellis was not the least bit shy in relating how his ancestor had watched over Tecumseh's burial place during the construction of the nearby railway.[63] After listening intently,
the observant reporter quickly drew a modern parallel. "Perhaps when
construction crews start to soften [the] sharp curves of Highway 2 near
Fairfield Village this year," he observed, "Tecumseh's old friends will
still watch from the shades."[64] And if not, then Mrs Charles Brunner
certainly planned to keep an eye on things.

In addition to reviving interest in Tecumseh's burial, the proposed
improvements to the highway raised concern among Thamesville's citizens that the new line of road might somehow "crowd" the boulder.[65]
As one of these concerned citizens, Mrs Brunner saw an opportunity
to exploit the situation in order to honour Tecumseh's memory with a
proper monument. She knew exactly how to proceed, and before long
she had a letter in the mail to a prominent Canadian historian.[66]

Fred Landon supported the idea of a monument to Tecumseh, just
as he had during the meeting of the Ontario Historical Society he
chaired back in 1926.[67] At that time, the chief topic of discussion had
been a resolution favouring the battlefield as the most appropriate site
for the monument. Landon personally deemed it to be the best choice.[68]
But his fellow executive members were hardly unanimous, and so Landon had opted for a general expression of support until such "time
when there will be a real movement in this Province for raising a monument to Tecumseh."[69] Landon could not have imagined that almost
thirty years would pass before this "real movement" was undertaken,
and that he would be the one to lead it.

Unlike some people, Landon did not change his mind about the best
site for Tecumseh's monument. And his conviction was reinforced as
early as May of 1932 when he attended his first meeting of the Historic
Sites and Monuments Board, which was still chaired by Ernest Cruikshank. It was likely during these proceedings that Landon became familiar with Cruikshank's report on the bones held by the Soldiers'
Club at Walpole Island, and the chairman's opinion that the battlefield
was the most appropriate place for Tecumseh's monument.[70] Landon,
who was in complete agreement with Cruikshank's views, no doubt
found it heartening that Tecumseh had been designated a person of national historic significance.[71] It appeared that Tecumseh would soon have
the monument he deserved, in a location that Landon thought best,
and without having to involve the Ontario Historical Society. But the
"plain and simple" monument that Cruikshank envisioned, a stone
shaft of nine metres in height, proved too expensive for the cash-

strapped Historic Sites and Monuments Board. The proposal was put on hold, and although this was considered only a temporary measure, it soon became apparent that the continuing economic depression and the outbreak of the Second World War would leave Cruikshank's plans in limbo for years to come.[72] In the meantime, Landon had busied himself with a career that included the duties of chief librarian at the University of Western Ontario, the teaching load of an associate professor in history in that same institution, and the prolific crafting of Canadian and American history. He had little time to think about a monument for Tecumseh. Even after his retirement in 1950, Landon continued to be a very busy man – partly because he had agreed to become chairman of the Historic Sites and Monuments Board.[73]

Yet, with his new appointment, Landon suddenly found himself in a position to push for a long-overdue monument to Tecumseh. And what a position. Not only did Landon have the prior approval of the Historic Sites and Monuments Board for such a monument, the economy was in its post-war boom, and the raging controversy surrounding Tecumseh's bones had been largely forgotten. Still, despite these favourable circumstances, the Historic Sites and Monuments Board was already preoccupied with a backlog of projects. As a result, the matter of Tecumseh's monument was deferred from one year to the next.[74] Then came the spring of 1955. With the arrival of Mrs Brunner's letter and news of the roadwork at the Tecumseh boulder, Landon was prodded into taking action. "My own thought at this time," he explained, "is that in the next two or three years we might place one of our standard cut stone monuments with a tablet larger than the standard ... or, better still, if we could erect a monument of cut stone, somewhat larger than regular size, we would have solved this rather troublesome question."[75]

Initially, Landon thought the monument to the French explorer La Salle, erected at Lachine, Quebec, in 1937, would serve as a model for Tecumseh's monument.[76] Standing seven metres high and bearing a bronze effigy of La Salle, which could just as easily depict Tecumseh, the design of this cut stone obelisk was much along the same lines as the monument Cruikshank had envisioned. Landon, however, soon became discouraged when he learned that the La Salle Monument had also carried a pricetag of $5,000.[77] In terms of 1955 dollars, a similar undertaking would require twice as much money, which was simply out of the question. Landon knew the Historic Sites and Monuments Board could ill afford a $10,000 monument, and so he decided not to suggest "anything so extensive."[78] But there was an alternative.

While a La Salle–like monument was definitely too expensive, a smaller version might be cost effective and therefore feasible. Landon decided to investigate the possibility, which he did whenever time would permit.[79] Finally, on 21 January 1957, Landon typed up his proposal for a monument to Tecumseh. In his letter to Jean Lesage, then minister of Northern Affairs and National Resources, whose portfolio included the Historic Sites and Monuments Board, Landon suggested a standard three-metre high monument of cut stone, the standard bronze tablet and, if possible, an additional plaque with Tecumseh's portrait.[80] Although Landon did not raise the issue of cost, he had an idea this lesser monument would require something just under $2,000.[81] It was an amount he thought could be justified if Lesage balked at the expense. But Lesage reacted favourably and never mentioned the money. Instead, he informed Landon that he was having the "exact site" of Tecumseh's death verified, and that his officials were in the process of designing a monument. As enthusiastic as he was, Lesage also stressed the need for secrecy. "The final enquiries, the drafting by you of the inscription and the preparation and approval of plans for the construction of this monument may take some little time yet," and Lesage did not want any complications.[82] It soon became evident, however, that complications were impossible to avoid.

Landon got right to work on the wording for the inscription, which he tabled at the next meeting of the Historic Sites and Monuments Board in June of 1957.[83] The project was underway and Landon was convinced that Tecumseh would finally have his monument. It was only a matter of time. Unfortunately for the old academic, his own time was quickly running out. Early in 1958, ill health forced Landon to announce his resignation from the Historic Sites and Monuments Board.[84] The genial professor remained keenly interested in the progress of Tecumseh's monument, but he was content to let others fuss over the details. After much fussing, the final version of the inscription was agreed upon in May of 1959.[85] There was still work to be done regarding Tecumseh's portrait, but that was not the concern of the Historic Sites and Monuments Board.

The task of designing the plaque bearing Tecumseh's portrait was assigned to the National Parks Branch historians, and a great deal of their time was spent in trying to determine his most accurate likeness. It proved a difficult and time consuming exercise, but eventually the Parks historians made up their minds and in September of 1960 a handsome plaque featuring Tecumseh's effigy was cast.[86] The Parks historians were also responsible for approving the site of the monument,

or the "exact site" of Tecumseh's death as Lesage had termed it. Cruikshank and his colleagues had decided in favour of the battlefield back
in 1931, by which they meant the small park where the Tecumseh
boulder had been placed.[87] Since this park was only a short distance
from lot four in the Gore of Zone Township, which had already been
established as the actual site of the Battle of the Thames, Landon
agreed that it was the best place for a monument.[88] The Parks historians were not so sure, having convinced themselves that the battle was
"an intermittent running engagement, covering two or three miles."[89]
In the end, however, they agreed with Landon – not because they
thought the park was the most historically accurate site, but because it
was public property and therefore free of cost.

As arrangements were being made with the Ontario Department of
Highways, the design of the monument went ahead.[90] Originally, Landon had suggested a traditional style of monument, but Jack Herbert
favoured "something a little more inspiring than most of our tomb-
stones."[91] As chief of the National Historic Sites Division, it was Herbert's responsibility to oversee the design of the monument. He turned
the project over to Gordon L. Scott, the chief of the Engineering Services Division, who delegated Otis Bishopric, a technical officer, who
then assigned the project to a young landscape architect with the National Parks Branch by the name of Roman Fodchuk.[92] After giving it
some thought, Fodchuk concluded that the monument should capture
the essence of Tecumseh's colourful life, which would require a complete departure from the traditional style of monument. Bishopric
agreed, and Fodchuk was given the freedom to explore the possibili-
ties. He began by trying to get a "feel" for Tecumseh.

Fodchuk discovered that Tecumseh's father was a member of the Shawnee nation's panther clan, and that his mother hailed from the turtle
clan. These totems, combined with the symbol of the shooting star associated with Tecumseh's birth, gave Fodchuk an idea for a distinctive
monument.[93] On six panels of sand-sculptured concrete, and in an
abstract form imitating Native petroglyphs, the image of a turtle and
panther converging into a shooting star would symbolize Tecumseh's
birth in suitably mythological fashion. A sidebar of decorative stone ag-
gregate would carry both the standard historic sites textual plaque and
the effigy of Tecumseh. By limiting the dimensions of the monument to
one metre high by two metres long, the project would be kept to a
human scale, and within budget.[94] The Tecumseh boulder, which had
been relocated to the park in 1924, would be incorporated into the
new memorial. In mid-April of 1961, Fodchuk submitted his design,

and his skillful blending of modern and traditional elements met with approval from both his superiors and the Historic Sites and Monuments Board.[95] Construction began in autumn, and by the end of March 1962 motorists on the Number Two Highway could see workmen putting the finishing touches on the Tecumseh Monument.[96]

Although the date of the official unveiling ceremony had not yet been announced, everything appeared to be in order. But before long, an observant newspaper reporter noticed a problem. While the Tecumseh boulder proclaimed "HERE TECUMSEH FELL," the plaque on the new monument indicated that Tecumseh was killed "about one half mile" to the south.[97] Neither inscription was accurate; however, the one chiselled into the boulder provided by the citizens of Thamesville came much closer to the truth. Mrs Coutts may have been forced to compromise on the original location of the boulder, which had since been moved to the park, but at least she knew that Tecumseh had made his last stand on the north side of the river.[98] According to the text on the new monument, however, Tecumseh was killed far beyond the other side of the Thames, which at the time of the Battle of the Thames was deep in the wilds of what is now Orford Township and well out of harm's way. The members of the Historic Sites and Monuments Board were mistaken, and quite badly so.[99] A similar embarrassment was only narrowly averted by the Parks historians.

Fortunately for the reputation of the National Parks Branch, the unveiling of the Tecumseh Monument was continually delayed over the course of 1962.[100] By mid-October of that year, John Coleman, director of the National Parks Division, suggested to Walter Dinsdale, the new minister of Northern Affairs and National Resources, that the unveiling might just as well be put off for another year.[101] That way it would coincide with the 150th anniversary of Tecumseh's death. Dinsdale agreed, no doubt thinking that this arrangement would at least provide his staff with plenty of time to work out the details of the unveiling ceremony.[102] He had no way of knowing that much of their time over the next year would be consumed in modifying the monument – all thanks to a politically-empowered Native.

Early in December of 1962, Carl M. Lewis of Toronto happened upon a very engaging newspaper article. In it, Dinsdale was quoted as saying: "I think it is important that a start be made to identify the various streams of Canadian cultural development by works of art that will be on permanent public display in appropriate locations throughout Canada."[103] This was all very well, but what really caught Lewis's eye was Dinsdale's announcement that his ministry would "begin with monuments to Canada's first inhabitants."[104] As one of the three chiefs of the National Indian Council of Canada (today's Assembly of First Nations), Lewis – or "Sachem Lewis" as he liked to style himself – had a vested interest in the way his ancestors were portrayed by the government. He also held a strong conviction as to which Native should be the first recipient of this new honour. Lewis immediately wrote a letter to Dinsdale suggesting a statue of Tecumseh.[105] Lewis did not bother to provide an explanation, as he saw no need to make a case for the great chief. But there was one thing he wanted to make abundantly clear: "You could at least make it equal in size to that of Champlain, at Orillia Park."[106] Lewis expected immediate compliance, but it soon became apparent that all he was going to get was the runaround.

Lewis was disappointed when he learned that Dinsdale had no specific plans to honour Canada's Natives.[107] Being a decent sort, however, Dinsdale did his best to let Lewis down as gently as possible.[108] After informing the sachem that a monument to Tecumseh had already been constructed, which he described in glowing terms, Dinsdale asserted that there would be no statue to go along with it. It simply was not the practice of the Historic Sites and Monuments Board to erect "statues on the grand scale such as the one to Champlain in Orillia Park."[109] That monument, Dinsdale explained, was constructed by a local group and subsequently transferred to the government for maintenance. The minister, thinking he had made his point, concluded by thanking Lewis for his interest and inviting him to attend the unveiling ceremony.[110] But Dinsdale's diplomacy did not have the desired effect. Lewis interpreted the minister's reply as one more example of the government's paternalistic attitude toward Native Canadians. The sachem would not be fooled by a nicely-worded brush-off, and he was not about to take "no" for an answer.

A few days before Christmas, Lewis sent Dinsdale an angry follow-up letter. This time, he was insistent that there should be a statue of Tecumseh.[111] In the process, he criticized the newly-completed monument by expressing his displeasure with Tecumseh's portrayal in the uniform of a British officer. "This is untrue to historical fact," Lewis contended. "History relates that after his final caucus with General Proctor [sic], he removes his British uniform in disgust and clothed himself same as his men, as a warrior. And so he died."[112] Anticipating that Dinsdale would be suitably horrified by the prospect of such a glaring mistake, Lewis tried to exercise some leverage by letting it be known that he intended to make an issue of the unifrom. "On be-half of the Indians of Canada, I must protest the further purveying of an untruth by your department," the sachem blustered.[113] Dinsdale took the threat seriously. But, as Lewis would discover, the minister of the Department of Northern Affairs and National Resources was not easily intimidated.

Dinsdale simply referred the question of Tecumseh's attire to the National Parks Branch historians, who hastily launched an investigation.[114] They began by trying to find evidence in support of the old stories that Tecumseh had been allowed to hold the rank of a brigadier-general in the British army. It proved a futile exercise, and in January of 1963 they concluded that there was no truth to the old stories involving General Tecumseh.[115] It seemed highly unlikely, therefore, that he could have cast off a uniform that he had never worn. As far as the Parks historians were concerned, the story Lewis had tried to impress upon Dinsdale was a myth, and one that originated in the United States during the mid-nineteenth century when "the rise of romanticism in American literature had elevated Tecumseh almost to the status of a national hero."[116] The Americans might have been at the root of the problem, but the Canadian government was also to blame. As John Coleman, the director of the National Parks Division explained, the mistake regarding Tecumseh's attire resulted from a calculated risk, which was one of many that "had to be taken because of an insufficient number of historical research staff."[117]

Having spread the guilt around, Coleman tried to make light of the embarrassing situation by admitting that "the colour of our faces gives us some claim to be considered blood-brothers of Tecumseh."[118] Coleman and the Parks historians had placed too much faith in Lossing's famous portrait of Tecumseh, in which the great chief is shown wearing the coat of a brigadier-general in the British army.[119] In an attempt to rectify the mistake, Coleman advised that Tecumseh be portrayed in a deerskin jacket – which meant the bronze effigy would have to be recast. This gesture would at least allow the government to "correct an injustice to the man."[120] As Coleman elaborated, "from what we now know of Tecumseh's personality and character – and particularly his motives – it appears that he would have been the last person to compromise with the white man by donning the latter's symbol of authority."[121] Tecumseh could be restored to his rightful place in history, and all it would require was a change of clothes. Dinsdale agreed that a new effigy of Tecumseh was in order. It was the only solution to the problem, and it was just the type of good deed that appealed to his sense of decency. It was also a means of dealing with Sachem Lewis.

At the end of January 1963, Dinsdale met with Lewis and discussed the sachem's ideas concerning the Tecumseh Monument. The meeting went well, and the two men parted on good terms. While Lewis failed to pressure Dinsdale into providing a statue, he was able to exact a major concession when the minister acknowledged that the bronze effigy would have to be recast. Lewis must have felt empowered, especially when Dinsdale obsequiously gave him full credit for correcting a misconception of history. In a follow-up letter, Dinsdale put his government's appreciation in writing: "I asked my officers to research this question thoroughly. They are of the opinion that you were absolutely right on this point."[122] Actually, these officers – the Parks historians – considered Lewis to be absolutely wrong, since they had concluded that Tecumseh had never worn the uniform of a British brigadier-general. This opinion was expressed in the draft letter they prepared for the minister's signature, but Dinsdale revised the letter in favour of the sachem.[123] The minister did not want Lewis to go away angry; he just wanted him to go away.

Dinsdale must have thought himself quite the diplomat. The sachem's demands for a statue had been denied, and in a manner that did not compromise, but actually improved, the Tecumseh Monument. It was just a matter of making the alterations to Tecumseh's outfit, and once this was accomplished Dinsdale could look forward to the unveiling ceremony in October. The minister's well-laid plans, however, were soon upset by a sachem of another kind.[124]

In February of 1963, John Diefenbaker, the then Conservative prime minister of Canada, called a general election for 8 April 1963. After the votes were counted, the Conservatives found themselves relegated to the Opposition.[125] It was bad news for Dinsdale and his plans for the unveiling of the Tecumseh Monument. But for Lewis, the Tory downfall meant he could revamp his proposal for a statue to Tecumseh, which he did with renewed confidence. Not only was Lewis himself a Liberal, he was an active supporter of the party.[126] The election could not have come at a better time and, toward the end of May, Lewis took advantage of the situation by trying to sell his idea to Donald S. Macdonald, the Liberal member for Rosedale in Toronto. "The main objective," Lewis stressed, "is the prompt assignment to an artist," so that the statue would be ready to unveil in time for the 150th anniversary of Tecumseh's death.[127] In his letter, Lewis enclosed the latest Dow Jones report showing the large profits derived from the government's lease of Native hunting lands, "part of which could be devoted to this simple but lasting tribute to an Indian who made Canada possible – and for whom no tribute of consequence has ever been made."[128] Lewis closed, trusting that Macdonald would use his "good offices" in expediting the request. For Macdonald, this meant handing the letter over to John N. Turner, the parliamentary secretary to Arthur Laing, who was Dinsdale's replacement as minister of Northern Affairs and National Resources.[129]

Turner investigated, and within a few days a reply was sent to Lewis. There would be no statue. As Turner explained, his department was unaware of any prior commitment to "change the nature of the Tecumseh commemoration," which was not surprising "since such a change would involve a recommendation by the Historic Sites and Monuments Board of Canada to the Minister."[130] Realizing that he would fare no better with the Liberals than he had with the Conservatives, Lewis angrily reverted to his Native self. In replying, he picked up on Turner's reference to the Historic Sites and Monuments Board, which the sachem denounced for having failed to recognize the mistake in Tecumseh's effigy. "It would appear too," Lewis continued, "that they are unaware of the wishes of the Indian people desiring a statue more in keeping with the importance of Tecumseh."[131] Lewis was building a case, which he abruptly revealed by suggesting the appointment of "an Indian, such as myself," to the Historic Sites and Monuments Board.[132]

The idea of a Native appointment to the Historic Sites and Monuments Board was a novel one, and Arthur Laing thought about it ... but then thought better of it. The minister wanted to increase the board's prestige "among Canada's leading history minded citizens."[133] Furthermore, he firmly believed "the Board must be able to give objective and sound historical advice and appointments should follow that guide-line."[134] A Native appointee, even a Liberal one, did not strike Laing as being quite the right approach. Once again, it fell to Turner to deliver the bad news, which he did by advising Lewis that Dinsdale would take his suggestion into account when considering the future composition of the Historic Sites and Monuments Board.[135] It was another brush-off, and this time Lewis had no choice but to take "no" for an answer.

About a week before Lewis received Turner's letter, Dr James J. Talman, Landon's replacement as chief librarian at the University of Western Ontario and one of the Ontario delegates to the Historic Sites and Monuments Board, received a curious letter. It was from the board's assistant secretary, Maxwell Sutherland, who expressed embarrassment at not having "kept in close touch" with Fred Landon regarding plans to unveil the Tecumseh Monument. "If his interest in this subject is still high," Sutherland wrote, "do you agree that we should write him and bring him up to date?"[136] Talman was perplexed, as he was under the impression that the monument had already been unveiled. After all, photographs of it had been handed around at one of the board's earlier meetings. Still, Talman agreed "that Professor Landon should certainly be kept in the picture."[137] Talman even volunteered to drive the old academic down to the ceremony. As Landon's protégé, successor, and good friend, he was only too happy to help.[138] Little did the ever-gracious Talman realize, he was setting himself up to be something considerably more than Landon's chauffeur.

The following September, Talman received another letter from Sutherland, this time assuming that he would act as chairman for the unveiling ceremony. A surprised Talman could hardly refuse and, fortunately for him, Sutherland and a colleague from the board did most of the leg work.[139] A fairly impressive slate of dignitaries was organized, and on 5 October 1963 they assembled at the Tecumseh Monument. Approximately 200 people showed up to witness the event, which was no where near the throng of 8,000 that had attended the Tecumseh Celebration in 1913.[140] Much of the attraction fifty years earlier had to do with the lavish entertainment provided, which included militia manoeuvres, a marching band, and a fall fair. All the Historic Sites and Monuments Board could offer was a monument that had already been on public display for a year-and-a-half, and a tea party on the nearby "Indian" reserve. It was a good thing that the fifth of October fell on a Saturday, and that it was a magnificent autumn day.

The first dignitary Talman introduced was Arthur Laing, the minister of Northern Affairs and National Resources.[141] He attended because the Historic Sites and Monuments Board formed part of his portfolio, and so there was an implicit obligation to give him the honour of unveiling the monument. Of course, the minister had a few words to say, or rather a few too many. He began by praising Tecumseh for his persistence in fighting against injustice. Then he went on to give a detailed recital of Tecumseh's war record. Finally, he concluded by observing that "Tecumseh dreamed of a restored country, yet he fought against odds that he knew were too heavy."[142] Perhaps the minister thought it best not to give the Natives too many autonomous ideas. If so, the next speaker certainly did not share the same sense of restraint.

John C. Munro, the parliamentary secretary to the Department of Citizenship and Immigration, attended the ceremony in place of his minister, Guy Favreau, whose portfolio included Indian Affairs.[143] Like Laing before him, Munro spoke at length about Tecumseh and emphasized his fame as a great statesman and warrior by remarking that he "fought for self-government and union of Indians."[144] It was rather a bold statement, since the idea of Native self-government was still a troubling prospect for most Canadians in 1963. But for Chairman Talman, a far greater concern must have been the remaining speaker's prospects for something more to say about Tecumseh. Sachem Lewis, however, had no trouble improvising a speech.

Rather than grousing about the government's refusal to erect a statue of Tecumseh, Lewis took his cue from the other dignitaries, who had just praised Tecumseh for standing up to the whites (specifically the American variety). Without beating around the bush, Lewis got right to the point and promptly proposed greater parliamentary rights for Native people. As he saw it, "the early obstacle of language, transport and communication no longer exists for Indians."[145] Therefore, he insisted, Natives should be allowed a parliamentary representation "in ratio with the original 65 seats given to the French at Quebec and similarly with senate seats."[146] Nor did he think that this new arrangement with Native peoples should affect their "existing treaty rights or other claims."[147] Lewis then went one step further, and suggested that the design for the proposed new Canadian flag – which was then becoming quite a contentious issue – "should have as its background, the darker Indian red."[148] He thought it only fair, since "Indians in Canada have led in highest per capita enlistment among other races in war service."[149]

The implications of Native political empowerment failed to register with the docile white audience, which stood transfixed – not by the sight of Tecumseh's Monument, but rather by the thought of refreshments at Moraviantown. As soon as the ceremony concluded, and without so much as a disparaging remark uttered in the sachem's direction, the crowd quickly dispersed as people jumped in their cars and drove off to the reserve. Unfortunately for the two Historic Sites and Monuments Board members, who had driven all the way down from Ottawa, it never occurred to them that they should ask for directions. As Maxwell Sutherland later explained: "Being innocents abroad, so to speak, Mr Roberts and I took a wrong turn at the intersection of the Nth concession of Y and the umpteenth concession of Z; and to make a long story short never got to the reception."[150]

The bureaucrats missed a nice tea party on the reservation, but then again so did the old academic whose efforts were largely responsible for initiating the monument's construction in the first place.[151] Although Fred Landon was unable to attend the ceremony, he must have found considerable gratification in knowing that Tecumseh's contribution to Canada had finally been officially recognized.[152]

Several thousand people travelled to Walpole Island on 25 August 1941 to see Tecumseh's alleged bones before they were sealed inside a stone cairn. Chief Sampson Sands, president of the Soldiers' Club (left), and Tom Isaacs (right) are pictured admiring a casket made especially for the occasion. Courtesy *Windsor Daily Star*, 7 August 1941

In his capacity as chairman of the Historic Sites and Monuments Board of Canada, Fred Landon used his influence to ensure the construction of a monument to Tecumseh. Courtesy University of Western Ontario Archives/*London Free Press*, 30 June 1950

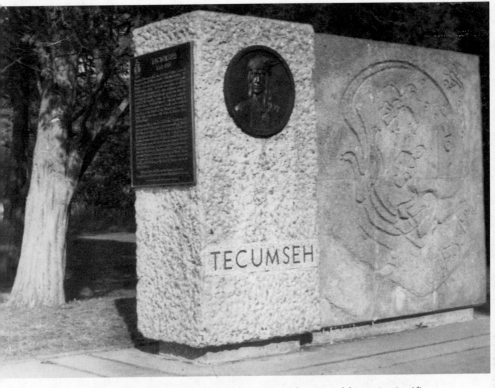

In 1931, Tecumseh was designated a person of national historic significance by the Historic Sites and Monuments Board of Canada. The 150th anniversary of his death at the Battle of the Thames was commemorated with the unveiling of this monument on 5 October 1963. Courtesy Guy St-Denis

Left: The cairn on Walpole Island, constructed by the Soldiers' Club and containing the bones its members believed to be Tecumseh's, faces the St Clair River and the Michigan shore. Courtesy *Windsor Star*, 1 June 1963

Conclusion

THE UNVEILING OF TECUMSEH'S MONUMENT was a far cry from the celebration held in his honour fifty years earlier.[1] For one thing, the monument was old news. Then there was the entertainment, which left much to be desired. And, of course, there was no skeleton – not that anybody really expected one. The quest for Tecumseh's bones had come to be widely regarded as nothing more than a wild goose chase. Yet, there were still a few hopeless romantics who continued to lend credence to the story about Tecumseh's clandestine burial, like the old curator at the Fairfield Museum who repeated time and again that it was a secret "no white man can ever know."[2]

Admittedly, the idea of a secret burial does hold a certain appeal. We would all like to believe that Tecumseh's body was whisked away by his loyal warriors, that it was spared the horrible mutilations inflicted on other Native remains by the vengeful Kentuckians, and that the sanctity of its burial was preserved from one generation to the next. Unfortunately, none of the surviving evidence supports such a sequence of events.

Among the various Native claims regarding Tecumseh's secret burial, only those of Ockawandah, Jacob Pheasant, Timothy Snake, and Oshahwahnoo (John Nahdee) merit consideration. Each of these Natives was reputed to have been a member of Tecumseh's burial party. As such, one would expect their accounts regarding the location of his grave to agree with one another – more or less. But they could hardly have been more divergent. Ockawandah gave directions to a shallow grave near the battlefield; Jacob Pheasant claimed that the grave was located a short distance to the north, near the railway; Timothy Snake spoke of both these graves, plus one more in a nearby farmer's field; and Oshahwahnoo supposedly kept vigil over a grave in a distant delta.[3] Discrepancies such as these constitute a serious challenge to the Native

evidence, and a consideration of historical context only serves to further weaken the case for a secret burial.

To begin with, Tecumseh could not have been laid to rest in the grave
near the battlefield for the simple reason that it was too close to the
American camp.[4] Surely, the wary Kentuckians would have detected any
Native attempt to effect a secret burial in their immediate vicinity. A similar lack of privacy rules out the burial near the Moravian mission. When
the Americans advanced on Fairfield after the Battle of the Thames, the
Delaware inhabitants fled into the adjacent woods.[5] Given the presence
of these refugees, a secret burial in that stretch of wilderness would have
been all but impossible. The forest immediately north of the battlefield
was a feasible enough place to bury Tecumseh without anyone knowing
about it. Not only was it relatively deserted, the Americans did not venture into it for fear of a Native ambush.[6] This situation would have allowed Tecumseh's burial party ample time to accomplish their task –
provided they were able to retrieve his body. However, a number of Native sources agree that Tecumseh's death precipitated an instant retreat
among his nearest warriors.[7] Oshahwahnoo, for one, frankly admitted
that he and his comrades were so panic stricken "that each individual
sought his own personal safety, & could think of nothing else."[8]

In addition to ruling out the possibility of a secret burial, Oshahwahnoo's account also implies that Tecumseh's body was left on the
battlefield, where it would have been subjected to mutilation by the
Americans.[9] But Harrison's failure to positively identify Tecumseh among
the Native dead offered the opportunity for other, less honest, Natives
to deny that such an outrage had ever occurred.[10] Understandably, Tecumseh's warriors resented American reports that their beloved chief's
body had been abused, and so they reacted by inventing the tale of a
secret burial.[11] The claim proved just as effective as the deed itself. On
those rare occasions when Tecumseh's self-styled warriors found themselves pressured into pointing out his grave, they either refused to divulge the secret or they resorted to deception.

Like the Natives, Tecumseh's white admirers also desired a dignified
end for the great chief, and several of the more dedicated among them
enthusiastically took up his cause. Of this number, only Albert Greenwood and Matthew Fisher claimed to know the precise location of
Tecumseh's grave. But, as was the case with each of their Native counterparts, neither Greenwood nor Fisher possessed reliable information.

Greenwood argued that the grave was located near the battlefield,
which he based on Joseph Johnson's story of Tecumseh's burial.[12] Johnson, it will be remembered, was supposed to have fought alongside

Tecumseh, and his alleged participation in the Battle of the Thames was used to explain how he came to be involved in the secret burial. But the militia, including Johnson's regiment, was not deployed by General Procter, and it seems doubtful that Johnson – considering his war record – would have volunteered his services.[13] Granted, he does appear to have had some earlier association with Tecumseh, which became evident when he was seen conversing with the great chief just prior to the battle.[14] Based on this familiarity, Johnson was able to convince most of his neighbours, directly or indirectly, that he was one of Tecumseh's pallbearers. There were skeptics, however, who understandably dismissed Johnson as an "infernal liar."[15] After all, the story that began with a burial under a toppled tree soon began to exhibit outlandish variations and, despite the fact that Johnson was not necessarily to blame in every instance, it was his credibility that suffered.[16] The most dramatic enhancement can be linked to Abigail Smith, the schoolgirl who fundamentally altered the story when she imagined that Tecumseh was buried in the bed of a stream.[17] While none of the early accounts – especially those attributed to Joseph Johnson – include such an elaborate interment, Abigail's fabrication was readily accepted and adapted by other Tecumseh enthusiasts. Albert Greenwood was particularly energetic in this regard, as is evident from his vague and confusing description of Tecumseh's burial.[18] Fortunately for Greenwood, his interpretation was never questioned.

As for Matthew Fisher, his claim that Tecumseh was buried on St Anne's Island was derived from his uncle, whose informant was Oshahwahnoo, the Chippewa chief who was also well known on the Walpole Island Reserve as John Nahdee. According to John Fisher, Oshahwahnoo retrieved Tecumseh's bones from the battlefield for fear they would be ploughed up.[19] Of course, Oshahwahnoo had effectively denied any involvement in Tecumseh's burial, but this admission was never made public.[20] So, when Greenwood disputed Tecumseh's burial on St Anne's Island, Matthew Fisher and his colleagues did not think twice about digging up the grave thought by them to contain the great chief's bones. They were convinced that the skeleton they unearthed would prove Fisher's claim. Before they realized the full extent of their folly, however, the Natives reclaimed the skeleton and sequestered it.[21] Curiously, by the time these same relics resurfaced in 1931, Fisher's peculiar argument – that possession somehow constituted proof – was widely accepted, and even the former skeptic Norman Gurd was willing to vouch for the skeleton's identity. Ignoring the important evidence of a broken thigh bone, and dismissing the objections of Oshahwahnoo's Nahdee descendants, Gurd instead chose to accept that the bones were those of Tecumseh.[22] Moreover, he used his authority as Tecumseh's biographer to further the interests of Walpole Island. In a similarly high-handed fashion, the Walpole Island Soldiers' Club blocked an investigation into the matter during a special session of the Grand General Indian Council of Ontario.[23] Eventually, the veterans succeeded in having a cairn erected in Tecumseh's honour, but their victory proved pyrrhic when the officially sanctioned monument was placed near the site of his death.

Clearly, both the Native and white evidence regarding Tecumseh's burial is invented, which makes it likely that Tecumseh's body remained on the battlefield. This certainly was the judgment of several captured British officers. Soon after the Battle of the Thames was decided in favour of the Americans, and before any of the Native dead were abused, these prisoners were taken to identify the remains of a Native warrior. They all agreed that it was Tecumseh.[24] Undoubtedly, the British officers would have known Tecumseh when they saw him, and, unlike the Native warriors, they had no reason to lie about it. By the time Harrison viewed this same body, which was late in the afternoon of the next day, it was so badly mutilated and swollen that he failed to recognize it as Tecumseh.[25] For this reason, he did not announce the great chief's death in his official dispatch. Still, in the absence of any report that Native remains had gone missing, and based on the evidence provided by the British officers, it would appear that the disfigured corpse was in fact that of Tecumseh.

Tecumseh and his closest warriors were likely buried where they fell, and despite subsequent attempts at desecration, their graves probably remained undisturbed.[26] Hidden between the large and small swamps, the scene of Tecumseh's last stand would have been difficult to find – even for a land surveyor trained to notice geographic anomalies, such as trees blazed with the images of various animals. When Mahlon Burwell conducted his survey of Zone Township in 1821, he did not observe anything unusual about the innumerable trees he encountered. He did, however, sense his proximity to the battlefield, which he took the time to record in his survey notes. Actually, Burwell fell wide of the mark by two lots, as evidenced by a map he prepared for the Surveyor General's Office.[27] Still, it was almost as though he intended to draw attention to the possibility of preserving the place of Tecumseh's death. No such provision was made, however, and the lots comprising the battlefield were destined for settlement. All that remained was for some unsuspecting farmer to plough up Tecumseh's bones.

That farmer was James Dickson, the same farmer who discovered the blazed walnut trees just beyond the small swamp.[28] Although Timothy

Snake and Jacob Pheasant remonstrated when Dickson began felling these trees, they had nothing to say when he questioned them about the significance of the various animals depicted in the carvings. Dickson, who had little patience for this coy behaviour, continued to clear his land. After Snake's death in 1869, Pheasant revealed the meaning behind the carvings. According to him, they marked the place where Tecumseh was killed.[29] Thinking the great chief might be buried nearby, Dickson was frustrated by Pheasant's steadfast refusal to point out Tecumseh's grave. The elder, not wishing to deceive Dickson, was forced to decline for the simple reason that he was unable to comply. None of Tecumseh's warriors could possibly have known the exact location of their leader's grave, since not one of them had lingered long enough to witness his interment. All they knew was that Tecumseh must have been buried somewhere in the immediate vicinity of the place where he was killed, and it was this locale they commemorated with their carvings on the nearby trees. Dickson, having dismissed the Native interest in his property, failed to see a connection with Tecumseh when he subsequently unearthed six skeletons where the blazed trees once stood. Given the "abundance" of human and horse skeletons he encountered elsewhere on his farm, he was not impressed by these most recent discoveries.[30] However, if Tecumseh was buried where he fell, and if the carvings on the walnut trees marked the place where he was killed, then one of the skeletons Dickson ploughed up was that of Tecumseh.[31]

Dickson had no particular interest in these additional skeletons, but he did keep the skull and larger bones of the one he fancied to be a Native warrior. This was the same skull he gave to Daniel Wilson in 1876.[32] But according to the professor, it was a Wyandot skull and therefore could not have belonged to Tecumseh. Wilson did not enquire about the disposal of the other skeletons – or if he did, the response was not included in his report.[33] Thankfully, this gap in the historical record is bridged by Dr Jacob Smith, the physician from Ridgetown with the extremely low opinion of Tecumseh. In countering the United Canadians' claim that they had discovered Tecumseh's grave, Smith unwittingly provided a valuable clue as to the fate of the great chief's bones. As the doctor recalled, whenever Dickson uncovered human remains, he simply reburied them "in some spot where they would not likely be disturbed again."[34]

Assuming that Tecumseh's bones still lie where Dickson buried them, it is not unreasonable to expect that they will come to light again.[35] When that chance discovery is made, there will be no medal and no scarlet sash. Nothing will be found to establish Tecumseh's identity – nothing but a "fully knitted" thigh bone, that is …

A Chronology of the Mystery

This chronology is designed to make it easier to situate the events that comprise the search for Tecumseh's bones and efforts to erect a monument in his honour. Entries in the specific column had a direct impact on the search for his grave and the building of a monument. Those in the general column had an indirect impact.

GENERAL		SPECIFIC
The Battle of the Thames is fought on 5 October. The Americans defeat the British and Natives in the valley of the lower Thames River, near what is now the southwestern Ontario village of Thamesville.	1813	Tecumseh is killed during the battle while leading his warriors. The American general, William Henry Harrison, fails to identify Tecumseh's corpse, giving rise to the mystery surrounding its burial.
Mahlon Burwell undertakes the survey of Zone Township in February, and places a number of elaborate stakes along what later becomes the Base Line Road near the battlefield.	1821	

GENERAL   SPECIFIC

It is generally believed among the   1830   In July, the American Indian
inhabitants of the lower Thames   agent, James B. Gardiner, is
Valley that Tecumseh lies buried   shown Tecumseh's grave near the
near the battlefield, and that a   battlefield. Gardiner pays tribute
wooden post marks his grave.   to Tecumseh with a poem.

Richard M. Johnson capitalizes   1837
on his reputation as Tecumseh's
killer to win the vice-presidency
of the United States.

Unsuccessful rebellions in Upper
and Lower Canada lead to
border tensions, as Canadian
rebels and their American
supporters launch raids against
Canadian targets.

                                        1840   John Richardson, who served
                                                with the British during the Battle
                                                of the Thames, makes an unsuc-
                                                cessful effort in April to locate
                                                Tecumseh's grave.

The American presidential elec-   In June, a "Yankee fellow"
tion of this year inspires remem-   attempts to retrieve Tecumseh's
brances of Tecumseh.   bones for a political rally in
                                                honour of presidential candidate
                                                William Henry Harrison.

The monument to Sir Isaac Brock
on Queenston Heights is severely
damaged by a bomb blast early
in the morning of 17 April. The
culprit is Benjamin Lett, a disaf-
fected Canadian with American
sympathies.

GENERAL		SPECIFIC
At the end of July, upwards of 10,000 people gather on Queenston Heights to support plans to rebuild Brock's Monument.	1840 cont'd	The plans to honour Sir Isaac Brock with a monument inspire a similar undertaking in memory of Tecumseh.
	1841	In April, an anonymous admirer of Tecumseh proposes a monument to the great chief. The citizens of Amherstburg respond with a subscription drive. A branch of their committee is established in Montreal.
Peter Paul Lacroix, a surveyor, promotes a new road connecting Windsor and Chatham.		As Amherstburg's subscription drive wanes in September, Lacroix tries to have the money collected for a monument redirected toward his new road, which he has named in honour of Tecumseh.
Responsible government, a form of limited self-government, is granted to Britain's North American colonies, giving rise to fears of French-Canadian political domination among the English-speaking merchant classes of Montreal.	1846	
A settler named James Dickson receives a government grant of lot 4 in the Gore of Zone Township, which encompasses the site of the battlefield where Tecumseh was killed.		
		An attempt is made to revive Amherstburg's monument scheme in September. Lacroix intercedes by supporting Chatham as a better site for Tecumseh's monument.

GENERAL		SPECIFIC
Britain's abolition of preferential duties on Canadian lumber and wheat intensifies the onset of a severe economic depression toward the end of the year.	1847	The hard times make it difficult to justify the expense involved in having a monument erected to Tecumseh.
	1848	James Holmes of Montreal, a supporter of Amherstburg's monument proposal and one of the members of a committee raising funds for that purpose, decides to use the money entrusted to him for a monument to Tecumseh on Île Sainte-Hélène in the St Lawrence River. Holmes is inspired by his brother's participation in the events leading up to the Battle of the Thames in 1813.
In Montreal, English-speaking merchant classes, disenchanted with British free trade practices and the implementation of responsible government, move to preserve their financial and political status by promoting political union with the United States. The result is the Annexation Association of Montreal.	1849	James Holmes loses interest in promoting a monument to Tecumseh as his brother, Benjamin Holmes, becomes a leading proponent of annexation to the United States.
Fundraising for the reconstruction of Brock's Monument, which has been on-going for several years, complicates similar efforts for a monument to Tecumseh.		An attempt to revive the Tecumseh Monument scheme in Amherstburg fails.
After three years of construction and another three years devoted to landscaping, the new Brock Monument is dedicated in October.	1859	

GENERAL		SPECIFIC
	1864	Oshahwahnoo, a Chippewa chief from St Anne's Island, which forms part of the Walpole Island Reserve at the mouth of the St Clair River, supposedly retrieves Tecumseh's bones from a grave near the battlefield and buries them near his home.
The York Pioneer and Historical Society is established to preserve the history of Toronto and its hinterland.	1869	
Following a highly successful excursion to Queenston Heights in 1870, during which the York Pioneers praised Sir Isaac Brock, another outing to his monument takes place at the end of July.	1871	A good portion of the York Pioneers's program is dedicated to remembrances of Tecumseh, and the framing of a resolution to mark the place of his death with an obelisk.
The United Canadian Association, an amalgamation of historical and patriotic organizations, is established in June.	1872	
		The York Pioneers, having failed to erect their proposed obelisk in time for an anticipated unveiling in June, reschedule for August of 1873.
	1873	When only a fraction of the estimated $20,000 needed to construct an obelisk is raised, the York Pioneers give up on the idea of marking the place of Tecumseh's death.

GENERAL		SPECIFIC
Richard Oates, a millstone manufacturer from Toronto, and a York Pioneer, becomes president of the United Canadian Association in July.	1875	Oates has a particular interest in seeing Tecumseh honoured with a monument.
On 25 June, General George A. Custer and his entire cavalry are killed at the Battle of the Little Bighorn.	1876	
		In July and August, Oates and several fellow United Canadians conduct expeditions in search of Tecumseh's bones, which they propose to reinter at Brock's Monument. They follow a map provided by Chief George H.M. Johnson of the Six Nations Reserve, which is based on the information of a Shawnee elder. The United Canadians also take the opportunity to investigate a report that Tecumseh was buried on a nearby farm. Word of the discovery results in a controversy regarding the authenticity of the bones, which includes an accusation that the United Canadians desecrated the grave of a Moravian missionary. Daniel Wilson, a professor from the University of Toronto, conducts an investigation and concludes that the bones are not those of Tecumseh.

GENERAL | SPECIFIC

1877 In January, a physician from Bothwell makes plans to raise money for a monument to Tecumseh by having Native singers from Moraviantown perform traditional concerts. Dr Graham's attempt at fundraising is interrupted by a physician from Ridgetown who questions the propriety of erecting a monument to a savage. Dr Smith's racist remarks are influenced by the annihilation of Custer and his cavalry at the Battle of the Little Bighorn in 1876. Once the controversy subsides, Graham proceeds with his Native concerts, which fail a short time later.

The Montreal *Witness* launches a literary contest aimed at young people across Canada.

1889 Abigail Smith, from Harwich Township, near Chatham, Ontario, enters the contest. Her submission is an essay in which she recounts Joseph Brenton's participation in Tecumseh's burial in the bed of a stream. Her story wins the provincial literary prize for Ontario.

1890 In August, Albert Greenwood, who became interested in Tecumseh's death and burial through stories he heard as a boy, pays a nocturnal visit to the battlefield and determines – to his satisfaction – the location of the great chief's grave.

GENERAL   SPECIFIC

1893   In December, Thomas Gowman,
        a carpenter from Melbourne,
        Ontario, offers the pubic a fan-
        tastic account of Tecumseh's bur-
        ial based on the veiled story of
        Joseph Johnson, who claimed to
        have been a member of the great
        chief's burial party.

1894   Gowman's contribution puts him
        at odds with Nelles F. Timothy,
        a Delaware from the Caradoc
        Reserve near London, Ontario.
        Starting in January, Timothy
        effectively disputes Gowman,
        and the old carpenter's attempt
        at revisionist history is soon
        forgotten.

1898   Sarah Ann Laird shares the story
        of her father-in-law, George
        Laird, who she claims participat-
        ed in Tecumseh's burial. Mrs
        Laird's story also includes a
        streambed burial.

1901   Thomas Sulman, the mayor of
        Chatham, Ontario, decides that
        his city should have a monument
        to Tecumseh. Sulman is inspired
        by the statue of Chief Joseph
        Brant in Brantford, and by the
        support of the Macaulay Club,
        a local literary society. The
        Macaulays try to secure a monu-
        ment by arguing against the
        importance of the battlefield as
        the best site for such a memorial.

GENERAL

SPECIFIC

The London, Ontario, conference of the Methodist Church
assembles at Goderich, Ontario,
in June. One of the topics discussed is the adequacy of the
liquor licensing laws.

1907

Albert Tobias, the lay delegate
from Moraviantown, takes
exception with the liquor licensing laws as they pertain to the
distribution of whisky among
Native peoples. To emphasize
the inherent difficulty in learning
the identity of white suppliers,
Tobias compares Native secrecy
surrounding the illicit trade with
the secret of Tecumseh's burial.
Tobias's remarks renew interest
in Tecumseh, and prompt
William K. Merrifield of
Chatham to publicly endorse
Joseph Johnson's story of Tecumseh's burial – which is corroborated by the accounts of Joseph
Brenton and George Laird, as
told by Abigail Smith and Sarah
Ann Laird.

1908

In reacting to Mrs Augusta D.
Richardson's attempts to have a
monument to Tecumseh erected
in Chatham, Albert Greenwood
disputes her account of the great
chief's burial in the Thames
River and offers to point out the
real grave if a monument is constructed in the vicinity of the
battlefield.

GENERAL   SPECIFIC

1909   Evelyn Johnson, formerly of the
Six Nations Reserve near Brantford, Ontario, attempts to interest the London, Ontario, branch
of the Canadian Club in sponsor-
ing the erection of a monument
to Tecumseh. In the process, she
gives London's mayor the mistak-
en impression that his city is to
be the site of the monument.
Enthused by the mayor's interest,
Miss Johnson endorses London,
which prompts an outcry from
the citizens of Thamesville – the
village nearest the battlefield.
Despite Miss Johnson's efforts to
distance herself and her monument proposal from controversy,
Albert Greenwood complicates
matters by offering Chatham
his assistance.

1910   In February, Matthew Fisher, a
farmer near Wallaceburg, takes
exception with Greenwood's
offer to assist Chatham in securing a monument to Tecumseh,
and informs the Wallaceburg
Board of Trade that the great
chief's bones were removed from
the battlefield and buried on St
Anne's Island, one of the delta
tracts comprising the Walpole
Island Reserve. The source of
Fisher's story is a deceased uncle,
who supposedly heard the story
directly from the Native elder
who effected the reinterment.

GENERAL   SPECIFIC

In April, the Wallaceburg, Ontario, board of trade devotes the better part of a regular meeting to the surprising news that the community it represents holds the strongest claim to Tecumseh's monument.	1910 cont'd	Fisher encourages the board of trade to press Wallaceburg's case for Tecumseh's monument, which brings a heated response from Greenwood. Fisher reacts by organizing an expedition to St Anne's Island in search of Tecumseh's grave. His success in exhuming a skeleton is marred by controversy and the confiscation of the bones by Chief Joseph White.

In June, Alexander C. Sussex of Bothwell, Ontario, claims that Tecumseh was buried in the bed of Cornwall's Creek, which flows behind the battlefield.

William Leonhardt, a farmer from near Wallaceburg, initiates a correspondence with Greenwood in October, and works on the latter's behalf to undermine confidence in Matthew Fisher's claim that Tecumseh was buried on St Anne's Island.

1911   In May, Dr Mitchell tries to restore Wallaceburg's claim to a monument with the testimony of Mrs Olive Hubble, who recalls that Oshahwahnoo of St Anne's Island pointed out Tecumseh's grave to her.

The citizens of Thamesville place a boulder on the battlefield in September, commemorating both the Battle of the Thames and Tecumseh.

GENERAL   SPECIFIC

The publication of Norman   1912
Gurd's *Story of Tecumseh* is
announced in February, and is
favourably reviewed the following month.

A "working woman" in
Chatham inaugurates a Tecumseh
monument fund for that city in
March. An attempt to secure
financial assistance from the Kent
County Council fails.

In April, Mrs Katherine B. Coutts
announces Thamesville's determination to secure a monument to
Tecumseh. Albert Greenwood
responds by offering Thamesville
a full exposé of Tecumseh's
burial.

The Old Boys donate $1,500
toward the cost of building a
monument to Tecumseh in
Chatham.

The Chatham Old Boys host
a reunion in July.

In October, the annual militia   Edwin Beattie, the Indian agent
manoeuvres are held near   for Moraviantown, attends the
Chatham, Ontario.   militia manoeuvres and leaves
                                          with an idea to commemorate
                                          Tecumseh.

In March, Mrs Coutts is elected   1913   In May, Mrs Coutts and her
president of Thamesville's newly-   fellow association members are
formed Tecumseh Memorial   disappointed in their attempt to
Association.   secure funding from the federal
                                          government for a Tecumseh
                                          monument. Chatham is blamed
                                          for having ruined Thamesville's
                                          chances by making its own bid
                                          for the money.

GENERAL		SPECIFIC
	1913 cont'd	Early in September, Albert Greenwood, feigning exception with Norman Gurd's *Story of Tecumseh*, credits Joseph Johnson as the source of his information, and provides a vague description of Tecumseh's burial. He stops short of giving directions to the great chief's grave.
		Toward the middle of September, Mrs Coutts commandeers several delegates of the Ontario Historical Society who were in Chatham attending their annual convention. Although Mrs Coutts fails to secure their support for a monument to Tecumseh in Thamesville, she is relieved to learn that Chatham is likewise disappointed.
		The Tecumseh Celebration takes place on 16 October at the site of the battlefield. By incorporating the annual militia manoeuvres and the Moraviantown fall fair, Edwin Beattie organizes an event that attracts considerable attention and success.
		In December, while researching the life of Joseph Brant, Mrs Margaret Brown of Brantford happens upon a story that Tecumseh was buried on the outskirts of London, Ontario.
The First World War begins in August.	1914	The outbreak of war eliminates any hope of reviving interest in the proposed monument to Tecumseh.

GENERAL		SPECIFIC
	1915	Judge Ermatinger attempts to persuade American officials that the statue of the *Dying Tecumseh* should be transferred from Washington, D.C., to St Thomas, Ontario. The judge ceases his efforts in 1919.
Alterations are made to the Longwoods Road at the battlefield in order to move it back from the Thames River.	1921	Redundant highway property is designated a memorial park in honour of Tecumseh.
	1924	The Tecumseh boulder is relocated to the memorial park from its original location on John McDowell's farm.
London, Ontario, celebrates the centennial of its founding.	1926	By May, Mrs Brown's biography of Joseph Brant is finally published. Included is the claim that Tecumseh was buried in the east end of London, Ontario, which causes a sensation in that city.
		Arthur C. Carty, a newspaper stringer and publicist, proposes the construction of a monument to Tecumseh as part of London's centennial celebration.
In May and June, the Toronto *Globe* supports an attempt to construct a monument to Tecumseh at the battlefield where he was killed.		Toward the end of June, members of the Nahdee family from the Walpole Island Reserve announce their plans to undertake a search for Tecumseh's grave, which they claim is located near Wardsville, Ontario. They credit the Toronto *Globe's* publicity for their sudden interest in Tecumseh's grave.

1926
cont'd

Prior to their expedition, the Nahdees are disputed by Beattie Greenbird from the Kettle Point Reserve north of Sarnia, Ontario, who claims that his ancestors secretly buried Tecumseh.

On 29 June, the Nahdees set out on their expedition, but fail to find Tecumseh's grave.

The Ontario Historical Society meets in London, Ontario, on 30 June in order to install its new president, the prominent historian Fred Landon. Afterwards, the executive discusses the possibility of supporting the proposal to construct a monument to Tecumseh on the battlefield. After one of the members observes that sixteen or seventeen skeletons reputedly belonging to Tecumseh had been discovered over the years, the executive agrees that the best approach is to avoid the controversy surrounding the place of the great chief's burial. Instead, it expresses sympathy with the idea of a monument, but withholds its support until a definite movement is undertaken to construct the said monument.

Cornelius Shawano, another Native from the Kettle Point Reserve, reacts angrily to the remark about Tecumseh's numerous skeletons, and emphasizes the importance of a medal in

GENERAL	SPECIFIC
	1926 cont'd · positively identifying the right skeleton. Cornelius's interference quashes all interest in the proposal to erect a monument to Tecumseh.
Chief Joseph White dies in August. Chief White was one of the Natives from the Walpole Island Reserve who, in 1910, confiscated the bones exhumed from the grave on St Anne's Island.	**1929**
The stock market crash of October results in a worldwide economic depression that lasts until the outbreak of the Second World War in 1939.	The poor state of the economy further discourages the proposal to erect a monument to Tecumseh, regardless of the proposed location.
	1931 · The bones confiscated by Chief White are discovered in January, investigated, and found to be lacking the important evidence of a broken thigh bone.
	Norman Gurd ignores the evidence of a broken thigh bone and tries to prolong the investigation by involving the Department of Indian Affairs. The Walpole Island Soldiers' Club attempts to influence the government's decision regarding the authenticity of the bones by calling a special session of the Grand General Indian Council of Ontario. On 25 February, despite conflicting testimony, they succeed in having a resolution passed in support of their claim to Tecumseh's bones.

GENERAL	SPECIFIC

	1931 cont'd	Duncan Campbell Scott, the deputy superintendent general of the Department of Indian Affairs, is convinced that the bones discovered on Walpole Island are not those of Tecumseh and opts to let General Ernest A. Cruikshank, an avid historian of the War of 1812 and a member of the Historic Sites and Monuments Board, decide the question.
		In May, Cruikshank decides against the bones discovered on Walpole Island. However, he acknowledges the propriety of erecting a monument to Tecumseh on the battlefield and takes the matter up with the Historic Sites and Monuments Board of Canada. This body is unable to pursue the project due to budgetary constraints.
On 30 May, Tecumseh is designated a person of national historic significance by the Historic Sites and Monuments Board of Canada.		
		Emerson Snake of Moraviantown counters the Walpole Island veterans by promoting a monument to Tecumseh on the battlefield. Although Snake fails to organize a committee of Ontario municipalities to advance his cause, as he had hoped to do, he does gain the assistance of several dedicated supporters who form the Tecumseh Memorial Committee.

GENERAL   SPECIFIC

1932   In the spring of this year, the
Walpole Island veterans decide
to fund their own monument to
Tecumseh. After distributing cir-
culars calling for contributions,
their plans lapse.

By May, Emerson Snake and his
fellow Tecumseh Memorial Committee members determine that
the monument they envision for
Tecumseh will cost upwards of
$20,000. Given the depressed
state of the economy, they decide
to forego an appeal to Ontario's
municipalities for financial aid in
favour of a request to the
Department of Indian Affairs.
The committee's revised plans
unravel when the Department of
Indian Affairs refers the matter to
the Historic Sites and Monuments Board, which had already
declined pursuing the project on
account of insufficient funds.

Gar Wood, the famous American   1933
speedboat racer from Algonac,
Michigan, wins the Harmsworth
Trophy for the eighth time in
September.

1934   The Walpole Island veterans
revive their monument scheme in
August. The source of their optimism is Gar Wood and his promise of financial assistance. Wood
attends a sod-turning ceremony
on Walpole Island, and his
celebrity helps to attract a large
attendance. At the end of August,
the veterans host a cornerstone
laying ceremony. Work on their
monument is suspended soon
after due to a lack of funding.

GENERAL		SPECIFIC
Canada enters the Second World War in September.	1939	The outbreak of war hinders the completion of the monument to Tecumseh on Walpole Island.
	1941	With the assistance of the Department of Indian Affairs and the Lambton County Council, the Walpole Island veterans are able to complete the construction of a scaled-down version of their monument.
		Despite opposition from Moraviantown, the Walpole Island veterans unveil their monument at the end of August. It forms part of a pageant in honour of Tecumseh's life, and one in which the last act is a ceremonial interment of the great chief's bones.
At the end of May, Fred Landon of London, librarian and associate professor of history at the University of Western Ontario, becomes chairman of the Historic Sites and Monuments Board of Canada.	1950	
In March, the Ontario Department of Highways announces plans to reduce the number of dangerous curves in the Number Two Highway.	1955	The proposed roadwork raises concerns in Thamesville for Tecumseh's boulder, and prompts Mrs Charles Brunner to contact Fred Landon with the idea of a new monument to Tecumseh. By June, Landon favours a monument similar to the one erected in Lachine, Quebec, in commemoration of the French explorer La Salle. Landon soon abandons this idea as being too expensive.

GENERAL   SPECIFIC

	1955 However, he begins to think in cont'd terms of a smaller, cost-effective version of the La Salle Monument.
	1957 In January, Landon presents his proposal for a Tecumseh monument to Jean Lesage, the federal minister whose portfolio includes the Historic Sites and Monuments Board. Lesage approves Landon's proposal and instructs his staff to begin work in selecting a site and designing a monument. Landon is responsible for drafting the monument's inscription, which he completes soon after.
Ill health forces Landon to resign from the Historic Sites and Monuments Board in February.	1958
	1959 In May, the Historic Sites and Monuments Board agrees on the final version of Landon's inscription for the Tecumseh monument.
	1960 A plaque bearing Tecumseh's effigy is cast according to a design submitted by the National Parks Branch historians, who also decide that the park of redundant highway property is the most appropriate place for the new monument.

GENERAL	SPECIFIC

1961

Roman Fodchuk, a landscape architect with the National Parks Branch, designs a modern monument that incorporates representations of Native petroglyphs to symbolize Tecumseh's birth.

1962

By the end of March, the finishing touches are made to Tecumseh's Monument, but the official unveiling is delayed until October of 1963, and the 150th anniversary of Tecumseh's death.

In December, Walter Dinsdale, the minister of Northern Affairs and National Resources, announces that Canada's cultural development will be commemorated in a series of monuments beginning with the country's first inhabitants.

Carl M. Lewis of Toronto, one of the three chiefs of the National Indian Council of Canada, suggests that Dinsdale begin his program with a statue of Tecumseh. When Dinsdale replies that there will be no statue, an angry Lewis points out a mistake in the effigy of the great chief displayed on the monument.

1963

In January, Dinsdale agrees with the Parks historians that Tecumseh's effigy should be recast.

The Conservative government of Canada is defeated in the federal election held in April. Walter Dinsdale is replaced by Arthur Laing, the new Liberal minister of Northern Affairs and National Resources.

Lewis takes advantage of the change in government by trying to persuade Laing to commission a statue of Tecumseh. Lewis, however, has no better luck with the Liberals than he did with the Conservatives.

On 5 October 1963, 150 years after his death at the Battle of the Thames, Tecumseh is finally honoured with a monument near the place of his death.

Acknowledgments

The mystery of Tecumseh's bones has become something of a joke. It is a sad but true fact, especially in southwestern Ontario where the mere mention of the great chief's name is likely to prompt the casual observation "Oh, I know where Tecumseh's buried ..." Unfailingly, the disclosure involves some unlikely place meant to be funny, such as under a porch, behind a barn, down a well, and so forth. I should know, as I have received many such directions. Fortunately for me, my search for Tecumseh's bones has also generated a great deal of genuine interest and helpful assistance.

Accordingly, I wish to thank Christopher Aldred, Fairfield Museum, near Bothwell, Ontario; Frederick L. Arbogast, Newark, New Jersey; G. Eugene Archer, Southfield, Michigan; Dr Frederick H. Armstrong, London, Ontario; the late Shirley Bain, Thamesville, Ontario; Grace Baker, London, Ontario; Dr Margaret A. Banks, London, Ontario; Daniel H. Benn, Chatham, Ontario; Laura Benson, Wallaceburg and District Historical Society, Wallaceburg, Ontario; Mark Bowden and Barbara Louie, both of the Burton Historical Collection, Detroit Public Library, Detroit, Michigan; the late Les Bronson, formerly of London, Ontario; Greg Brown, Jack Choules, and Jim Suderman, all of the Archives of Ontario, Toronto, Ontario; Valerie Buckie, Park House Museum, Amherstburg, Ontario; Elise Chodat, Departmental Library, Indian and Northern Affairs Canada, Hull, Quebec; Christine Coutts Clement, Etobicoke, Ontario; Diana Coates, Anglican Diocese of Huron Archives, London, Ontario; Jill Costill, Indiana State Library, Indianapolis, Indiana; Glen Curnoe, Elizabeth Spicer, and Mary Velaitis, all formerly of the London Room, London Public Library, London, Ontario; the late Robertson Davies, formerly of Massey College, University of Toronto, Toronto, Ontario; Allan Day, Ontario Ministry of Natural Resources, Peterborough, Ontario; Edward Day, Chatham, Ontario; Brian Doidge, Ontario Corn Producers' Association, Ridgetown, Ontario; Amedee Emery, Pain Court, Ontario; Margo Fenoglio, Clinton Public Library, Clinton, Indiana; Jean Filby, Thamesville, Ontario; Angela Files, Brantford, Ontario; Bob Garcia, Fort Malden National Historic Site, Amherstburg, Ontario; Alice Gibb, London, Ontario; George Gurney, National Museum of Art, Washington, D.C.; Stephen Harding, London, Ontario; Cindy Hein and her staff, Rockville Public Library, Rockville, Indiana; Heather Home, Queen's University Archives, Kingston, Ontario; Dean Jacobs, Walpole Island, Ontario; Debbie Kennedy, Kent County Library, Thamesville, Ontario; Patricia Kennedy, Timothy Dubé, Anne Goddard, Jean-François Lozier, April Miller, and Kate O'Rourke, all of the National Archives of Canada, Ottawa, Ontario; Leonard Kroon, Gore of Chatham Township, Ontario; the late Clarke Leverton and his wife Eleanor, Camden Township, Ontario; John Leverton, Exeter, Ontario; Hon. Donald S. Macdonald, Toronto, Ontario; Jean MacGregor, Ottawa Public Library, Ottawa, Ontario; Helen Maddock and Anne Ashton, both of the Lambton Room, Lambton County Library, Wyoming, Ontario; Alan Mann, Wallaceburg, Ontario; Karen Marrero, University of Windsor Archives, Windsor, Ontario; Richard Martineau, Don Boisvenue, Colin Old, and Michelle Pilon, all of the Canadian Inventory of Historic Building, Hull, Quebec; Marion Matt, Bothwell, Ontario; Arthur McClelland, London Room, London Public Library, London, Ontario; Lorne McDowell, Gore of Zone Township, Ontario; Barbara McMahon, Camp Verde, Texas; David McNab, Toronto, Ontario; Rev. James Miller, Port Lambton, Ontario; Lloyd Mitton, Chatham, Ontario; Lauren Munn, London, Ontario; David Murphy, Sharon Engel, and Laurraine Pastorius, all of the Interlibrary Loans Department, Weldon Library, University of Western Ontario, London, Ontario; Patricia K. Neal, Ontario Historical Society, Toronto, Ontario; Arnold Nethercott, London, Ontario; Trudy Nicks, Royal Ontario Museum, Toronto, Ontario; Alan Noon, Plant Sciences, University of Western Ontario, London, Ontario; Robert J. Pearce, London Museum of Archaeology, London, Ontario; Rose Ann Perricone, Algonac, Michigan; Art Price, Toronto, Ontario; Lynne Prunskus, Brock University Archives, St Catherines, Ontario; Kewal Rai, Foreign and Commonwealth Office, London, England; Chris Raible, Creemore, Ontario; Theresa Regnier, University of Western Ontario Archives, London, Ontario; Kelly Riley, Muncey, Ontario; Linda Sabathy-Judd, London, Ontario; Emery Shawanoo, Kettle Point, Ontario; Edna Smith, Bothwell, Ontario; Dr David Spencer, Faculty of Information and Media Studies, University of Western Ontario, London, Ontario; Apollonia L. Steele, Special Collections, University of Calgary Library, Calgary, Alberta; Darryl Stonefish, Moraviantown, Ontario; Glenn Stott, Arkona, Ontario; Sharon Tibbotts, Royal Armouries, London, England; Janet Coutts Tieman, Port Credit, Ontario; Rev. Peter Townsend, Grace Anglican Church, Brantford, Ontario; Rob Turner, London, Ontario; Beth Van Oudenhove, Chatham, Ontario; the late Bert Wees, Chatham, Ontario; and Walter Zimmerman, Weldon Library, University of Western Ontario, London, Ontario.

Special thanks are in order for the three gentlemen I have come to regard as my very own community of scholars: Dr Douglas Leighton of London, Ontario, a professor of history at Huron University College, whose stirring lectures in Native studies were a great inspiration to me; Dr John Sugden of Arnside in Cumbria, England, the acclaimed biographer of Tecumseh, whose sincere enthusiasm for my morbid project convinced me that it was in fact worthwhile; and

Dr Michael Friedrichs, of Augsburg, Germany, a dedicated student of the extensive literature on Tecumseh, whose expert assistance allowed me to place Tecumseh's bones in their proper context.

Daniel J. Brock of London, Ontario, also warrants particular notice, as he agreed to read my manuscript – a sizeable task under the best of circumstances, and one that must have been especially taxing for a high school teacher in the middle of his school year.

Captain Michael Mellish of St Peter Port, on the Channel Island of Guernsey, kindly provided me with some very useful information which he inherited as a collateral descendant of Sir Isaac Brock. My introduction to Captain Mellish was arranged by Gillian Lenfestey of Guernsey's St Pierre du Bois Parish who, along with her husband Hugh, has been an enthusiastic and generous supporter of my historical endeavours.

I am very pleased to have McGill-Queen's University Press as my publisher. Kyla Madden, acquisitions editor, Joan McGilvray, co-ordinating editor, and David Schwinghamer, copy editor, helped make this project both an interesting and a rewarding experience.

Ultimately, my greatest obligation is to Dr Didier Flament of Pahoa, Hawaii. Although he could not have cared less about Tecumseh, or his bones for that matter, Didier always insisted that I should persevere in my undertaking – no matter how much aggravation it caused me. Were it not for his unrelenting brand of encouragement, this book might never have materialized out of the mystery that inspired it.

Notes

ABBREVIATIONS

AMC   Archives of the Moravian Church
AO   Archives of Ontario
CIHB Canadian Inventory of Historic Building
HSMB Historic Sites and Monuments Board
ISL   Indiana State Library
KCLR Kent County Land Registry
LAC   Library and Archives Canada
LCLR Lambton County Land Registry
LR   Lambton Room
MNR   Ministry of Natural Resources
PHM   Park House Museum
TNA   The National Archives (UK)
UTA   University of Toronto Archives
UWOA University of Western Ontario Archives
WHS   Wisconsin Historical Society

INTRODUCTION

1 TNA, Court Martial Proceedings of Major-General Henry Procter, 258. The brigade-major to the Forty-first Regiment of Foot was Captain John Hall.
2 Ibid., 259.
3 Ibid.
4 Hitsman, *Incredible War of 1812*, 67–76; Cruikshank, *Queenston Heights*, 15. In the case of Michilimackinac, it was Captain Charles Roberts who was directly responsible for leading the expedition against the American post. However, he acted within the spirit of Brock's orders. See Turner, *British Generals in the War of 1812*, 70; Hyatt, "Defence of Upper Canada in 1812," 66–7.

5 Sugden, *Tecumseh: A Life*, 325; Turner, *British Generals in the War of 1812*, 41, 93.

6 Sugden, *Tecumseh: A Life*, 325. Procter was promoted to brigadier-general for his success at the Battle of the River Raisin on 22 January 1813. He was promoted to major-general in June of the same year. See ibid., 324; Hyatt, "Proctor, Henry," 617.

7 On 7 November 1811, Harrison's forces defeated the Shawnee and their allies at the Battle of Tippecanoe. Prophetstown was destroyed the following day. See Edmunds, *Tecumseh and the Quest for Indian Leadership*, 153–9.

8 Ibid., 114. The Treaty of Fort Wayne, negotiated in 1809 between the United States and the friendly chiefs of the Miami, Potawatomi, and Delaware, transferred over 12,140 square kilometres of Native land to the Americans. It also vindicated Tecumseh's arguments for a strong confederacy to safeguard Native homelands against American encroachment. After the Treaty of Fort Wayne, Tecumseh was able to assume a greater leadership role in the confederacy and recruit a larger Native following. See ibid., 122, 124–5, 136, 146–9.

9 Sugden, *Tecumseh: A Life*, 321–3. At the time of Procter's foray, Tecumseh was lying ill near the ruins of Prophetstown. See ibid., 319.

10 Ibid., 324, 327–39.

11 Ibid., 345–9. For an interesting first-hand account of British operations on the western frontier of Upper Canada preceding the battles of Lake Erie and the Thames, see Casselman, *Richardson's War of 1812*, 132–88. As a seventeen-year-old Canadian volunteer, John Richardson served with Procter's Forty-first Regiment of Foot until its defeat at the Battle of the Thames in October of 1813.

12 Cruikshank, "Contest for the Command of Lake Erie in 1812–13," 96–102; Sugden, *Tecumseh's Last Stand*, 51–2.

13 Sugden, *Tecumseh's Last Stand*, 40, 47–8. The distance between Amherstburg and Chatham was calculated according to the old route along the Detroit River, the shore of Lake St Clair, and the southern bank of the Thames River.

14 Ibid., 45–6, 57–8.

15 Ibid., 67, 69–70, 72–3. It was also on 29 September that Harrison's forces occupied Sandwich. See ibid., 71. At the time of the British retreat up the Thames River in October of 1813, Louis Trudelle lived near Jeanette's Creek, where he owned lots 4, 5, and 6 in what is now the first concession of Tilbury East Township. See KCLR, Abstract Books, Tilbury East Township, con. 1, lots 4–6. See also Hamil, *Valley of the Lower Thames*, 24, 38, 65, 170.

16 Sugden, *Tecumseh's Last Stand*, 73.

17 Ibid., 72–3. Regarding Procter's secretive nature, see ibid., 51–2. Sandy Antal defends Procter's secret instructions as a way of avoiding Native apprehension. He also argues that the general had never before seen the

Thames Valley, and so his reconnaissance was justified. John Sugden sees no excuse for either Procter's secretiveness or his failure to have reconnoitered the Thames Valley. See Antal, *A Wampum Denied*, 301; Sugden, *Tecumseh's Last Stand*, 185.

18 Sugden, *Tecumseh's Last Stand*, 72–3, 76–7. Warburton was Procter's second-in-command. Matthew Dolsen's farm was on the opposite, or north, side of the Thames River. The British troops crossed the stream by means of scows. See ibid., 77. Dolsen operated a tavern and trading post from his property (lot 19, concession 1, Dover East Township). He died in August of 1813. See Hamil, *Valley of the Lower Thames*, 349–50; KCLR, Abstract Books, Dover East Township, con. 1, lot 19; Sabathy-Judd, *Moravians in Upper Canada*, 503.

19 Sugden, *Tecumseh's Last Stand*, 76–7. See also TNA, Court Martial Proceedings of Major-General Henry Procter, 245, 364.

20 Sugden, *Tecumseh's Last Stand*, 77, 81. Mrs Procter and her children arrived at the Moravian mission on 29 September. She immediately demanded the use of a house, and continued to impose upon the Moravians until early in the morning of 5 October – the day of the battle. See Sabathy-Judd, *Moravians in Upper Canada*, 504, 512.

21 Sugden, *Tecumseh's Last Stand*, 84. The ensign, Benjamin Holmes, was captured while attempting to retrieve an ammunition wagon abandoned near Belle River. See TNA, Court Martial Proceedings of Major-General Henry Procter, 136, 243, 246. John Richardson mistakenly recalled that Holmes taken prisoner in the evening of 4 October while swimming his horse across McGregor's Creek at Chatham. In fact, this incident occurred in the morning of the third at Jeanette's Creek as Holmes tried to swim his horse to the north side of the Thames River. See Casselman, *Richardson's War of 1812*, 208; TNA, Court Martial Proceedings of Major-General Henry Procter, 218.

22 Sugden, *Tecumseh's Last Stand*, 84–5. See also Sugden, *Tecumseh: A Life*, 364–5. According to Sandy Antal, the failure to fortify Chatham was a direct result of repeated mishaps in transporting entrenching tools upriver. See Antal, *A Wampum Denied*, 324.

23 Sugden, *Tecumseh: A Life*, 364–5; Sugden, *Tecumseh's Last Stand*, 84. On 3 October, Tecumseh had approximately 1,200 warriors. By the time of the Battle of the Thames, only about 500 remained. See Sugden, *Tecumseh's Last Stand*, 88.

24 Sugden, *Tecumseh's Last Stand*, 86.

25 Ibid., 86–7.

26 Ibid., 89, 91. Lemuel Sherman's farm was located on what is now lot 15, concession B, Camden Township, Kent County, which is southeast of Thamesville. See KCLR, Abstract Books, Camden Township, con. B, lot 15. See also Hamil, *Valley of the Lower Thames*, 305. Procter spent the night with his wife and family. Early the next morning, he sent them upriver to Delaware by canoe. See Sugden, *Tecumseh's Last Stand*, 91. See also Antal,

A *Wampum Denied*, 327; Sabathy-Judd, *Moravians in Upper Canada*, 512.

27 Sugden, *Tecumseh's Last Stand*, 105–7.

28 Ibid., 107, 112–14, 121. The distance between the British lines varied from about ninety to only several metres apart. A small number of dragoons were posted beyond the reserve line. See ibid., 123. According to Robert Breckinridge McAfee, an American who participated in the Battle of the Thames, the large swamp ran "nearly parallel with the river about 2 miles, the distance between them becoming less as you proceed up the river." See McAfee, *History of the Late War in the Western Country*, 388.

29 Sugden, *Tecumseh's Last Stand*, 124; Thomas Verchères de Boucherville, a French Canadian who was present at the battle, recalled that "the day was dark and disagreeable, the wind blowing a gale with frequent showers of cold rain." See Quaife, *War on the Detroit*, 146.

30 Sugden, *Tecumseh's Last Stand*, 122. In addition to being cold and wet, the British soldiers were also tired and hungry. See ibid., 91–2; Antal, *A Wampum Denied*, 338.

31 Sugden, *Tecumseh's Last Stand*, 106–7, 122–3. Perhaps Procter did not think he had time to construct an abatis. He certainly did not anticipate that Harrison would launch a cavalry charge through the woods. See TNA, Court Martial Proceedings of Major-General Henry Procter, 376.

32 Sugden, *Tecumseh's Last Stand*, 124–5. According to Harrison, "the measure was not sanctioned by anything that I had seen or heard of but I was fully convinced that it would succeed." See Esarey, *Messages and Letters of William Henry Harrison*, 2:562.

33 Sugden, *Tecumseh's Last Stand*, 125–6.

34 TNA, Court Martial Proceedings of Major-General Henry Procter, 259.

35 Sugden, *Tecumseh's Last Stand*, 126.

36 TNA, Court Martial Proceedings of Major-General Henry Procter, 260.

37 Ibid. Procter was court-martialled at the end of the war and held responsible for the many tactical errors attending the retreat of his regiment. He was sentenced to suffer a suspension in rank and pay for six months, as well as a humiliating public reprimand. See ibid., 323–7.

38 Sugden, *Tecumseh's Last Stand*, 125, 129–31. In antiquated military terms, the "forlorn hope" refers to those soldiers ordered to launch a particularly dangerous or desperate attack.

39 Ibid., 131, 176.

40 Ibid., 133, 176. Years later, one of Tecumseh's warriors recalled the panic that suddenly seized them, and how "each individual sought his own personal safety, [and] could think of nothing else." See WHS, Draper Manuscript Collection, Tecumseh Papers, ser. YY, vol. 7, no. 65, Jamieson to Draper, 13 March 1882. This warrior was Oshahwahnoo, who resided on the St Anne's Island portion of the Walpole Island Reserve in southwestern Ontario.

41 Sugden, *Tecumseh's Last Stand*, 130. James Fraser of the Indian Department estimated that the Americans were driven back about two kilometres,
   or almost to the outskirts of modern Thamesville, which distance seems
   highly unlikely.
42 Ibid., 132.
43 Allen, *His Majesty's Indian Allies*, 146; Sugden, *Tecumseh's Last Stand*,
   190.
44 Sugden, *Tecumseh's Last Stand*, 174–5.
45 Ibid., 169, 174. These outrages were a natural reaction on the part of the
   Kentuckians, who had suffered similar abuses at the hands of their Native
   enemies.
46 Esarey, *Messages and Letters of William Henry Harrison*, 2:557–65.
   Although Harrison suspected that Tecumseh was dead, a report that he
   was taken wounded from the field cautioned the American general. See
   ibid., 2:752.

CHAPTER ONE

1 *Toronto Patriot*, 23 June 1840, p. 2, col. 1. Although this article refers to
   the Yankee fellow as having been an engineer from Detroit by the name of
   Moore, the Detroit city directory for 1837 indicates that his name was in
   fact Thomas Moores. See MacCabe, *Directory of the City of Detroit ...
   for 1837*, 66. Regarding Probett's British Hotel, see Hamil, *Valley of the
   Lower Thames*, 274.
2 *Toronto Patriot*, 23 June 1840, p. 2, col. 1.
3 Ibid.
4 Ibid.
5 During Andrew Jackson's term (1829–37), presidential power contested
   congressional authority. In response to this perceived constitutional threat,
   anti-Jackson forces united in the 1830s to form the Whig Party (named
   after the English political party which had sought to check the power of
   the king). In addition to promoting states' rights, the Whigs advocated a
   national economic policy based on internal transportation improvements.
   The Whig Party disintegrated in the mid-1850s over internal divisions
   regarding slavery and national expansion, and was succeeded by the
   Republican Party.
6 Gunderson, *Log-Cabin Campaign*, 119.
7 *Montreal Gazette*, 30 June 1840, p. 2, col. 2. John Richardson, a Canadian literary figure of the nineteenth century, left a vivid account of the convention. Yet, he did not recall a display of bones. See Richardson, *Eight
   Years in Canada*, 133–47.
8 Sugden, *Tecumseh's Last Stand*, 137. See also Sprague, "Death of Tecumseh and the Rise of Rumpsey Dumpsey," 457–8. When none of the vice-
   presidential candidates received a majority during the election of 1836, the

Senate exercised its prerogative early in 1837 and elected Johnson. See Meyer, *Life and Times of Colonel Richard M. Johnson*, 425–9.

9 The Battle of the Thames, "it has been estimated, helped create one president, one vice president, three state governors of Kentucky, three lieutenant-governors, four United States senators, and a score of congressmen." See Sugden, *Tecumseh: A Life*, 396. See also Stagg, *Mr Madison's War*, 330. Sugden devotes an entire chapter to the identity of Tecumseh's killer. He narrows the field by sorting through numerous eyewitness accounts, and by weighing each claim based on the strength of its objectivity or the weakness of its partiality. See Sugden, *Tecumseh's Last Stand*, 136–81.

10 Sugden, *Tecumseh's Last Stand*, 152. See also Meyer, *Life and Times of Colonel Richard M. Johnson*, 393–429.

11 Witherell, "Reminiscences of the North-West," 315. At least one other version of this statement is known to exist: "They say it was Tecumseh I shot. I care not, *and I know not*; I would have shot the best Indian that ever breathed, under such circumstances, without inquiring his name, or asking the ages of his children." See *Kentucky Gazette*, 6 August 1840, p. 2, col. 5.

12 The ensign was Henry N. Smith. See *Toronto Patriot*, 23 June 1840, p. 2, col. 1.

13 *Montreal Gazette*, 30 June 1840, p. 2, col. 2. The bones dug up by the Yankee fellow, apparently from several Native graves, would suggest that he raided the cemetery near the site of Fairfield, the original Moravian mission on the Thames River. However, a search of the missionary's diary for New Fairfield failed to reveal any reaction to violated Moravian graves.

14 John Richardson served in the Forty-first Regiment of Foot as a gentleman volunteer. He later pursued a literary career, drawing on his experiences to write an account of the War of 1812, which was published in 1842. See Casselman, *Richardson's War of 1812*, xvi. Richardson also wrote a poem about Tecumseh. He set aside the last remaining printed copy so it could be placed in the proposed monument to Tecumseh. See *Western Herald*, 16 July 1841, p. 1, col. 2; PHM, Committee for Superintending the Erection of a Monument to Tecumseh, Minute Book, Kevill and Grasett to Richardson, 11 August 1841, 7–8; ibid., Richardson to Kevill and Grasett, 20 August 1841, 8–11; ibid., 29 November 1841, 15–16; ibid., Kevill and Grasett to Richardson, 4 December 1841, 21–2. A copy of Richardson's poem can be found in his newspaper. See *New Era*, 22 July 1842, 5–6; ibid., 29 July 1842, 3–6; ibid., 12 August 1842, 3–6; ibid., 19 August 1842, 3–8. See also ibid., 24 June 1842, p. 2, col. 2; ibid., 19 August 1842, p. 1, col. 1.

15 Richardson, *Eight Years in Canada*, 129–30.

16 Ibid., 129. Richardson's failure to recognize the battlefield suggests that it was well camouflaged by the surrounding forest, which also explains why Moores, the Yankee fellow, required guides to find it.

17 *Columbus Sentinel*, 3 January 1832, p. 1, col. 2. John Sugden identifies the

"citizen of Ohio" as James B. Gardner. See Sugden, *Tecumseh's Last Stand*, 216–17. According to Carl Klopfenstein, James B. Gardiner was appointed a special agent and commissioner in 1831 to negotiate the removal of the Natives from Ohio. See Klopfenstein, "Removal of the Indians from Ohio," 85, 89. See also Harvey, *History of the Shawnee Indians*, 190–233. I am indebted to John Sugden for this information. Gardiner appears to have inspired subsequent descriptions of the post. In 1841, Jean-Baptiste Maçon, a gentleman from Montreal, observed that the remains of Tecumseh were buried "with nothing to mark the spot but a small post painted [vermilion]." See *Western Herald*, 25 August 1841, p. 2, col. 1. Maçon, who appears to have had associations with Amherstburg, claimed that he visited the grave "many a time." Seven years later, in 1848, Shaw-an-abb, a Native living on the Walpole Island Reserve, informed John Richardson that Tecumseh was buried under a tree stump, which was hewn on four sides with characters representing the number of enemies he had dispatched with his tomahawk. See [Richardson], "Trip to Walpole Island and Port Sarnia," 18.

18 One of the earliest Native narratives regarding the secret burial of Tecumseh can be traced to Black Hawk, a Sac chief who was fond of boasting that he had fought alongside Tecumseh at the Battle of the Thames. Black Hawk claimed that he and several other warriors retrieved Tecumseh's body under the cover of darkness. See *Army and Navy Chronicle*, 8 November 1838, p. 296, cols 1–2. Black Hawk's presence at the Battle of the Thames, however, is debatable. See Sugden, *Tecumseh's Last Stand*, 116–17, 155–6.

19 Black Hawk, for example, claimed that it was a Potawatomi chief and not Tecumseh who was mutilated by the Kentuckians. In John Sugden's estimation, this and subsequent Native narratives promoting Tecumseh's secret burial were "designed either to torpedo the exaltation of those Kentuckians who had exhibited portions of Tecumseh's skin or to exonerate the Indians from the odium of permitting their leader to suffer the indignities of desecration." See Sugden, *Tecumseh's Last Stand*, 156.

20 In July of 1830, the mound was "still a foot or more above the level of the surrounding earth." By that time the post was lying beside the grave, "having rolled down." See *Columbus Sentinel*, 3 January 1832, p. 1, col. 2. Later that same year, Benjamin B. Thatcher paraphrased Gardiner's description of Tecumseh's supposed grave. In the process, Thatcher appears to have confused Gardiner's reference to a nearby large black oak tree, which had fallen down, with the hewn post that he claimed had "rolled down." See Thatcher, *Indian Biography*, 225.

21 *Columbus Sentinel*, 3 January 1832, p. 1, col. 2. An earlier version of the same poem was published in Upper Canada at the beginning of December 1831. See *Canadian Emigrant*, 1 December 1831, p. 1, col. 2.

22 MNR, Instructions to Land Surveyors, Book 4 (1820–33), no. 355, Ridout to Burwell, 27 February 1821, 60–3; MNR, Report and Field Notes/Diaries,

Field Book, "Field-Notes: Taken on the Survey of the Township of Zone in the Years 1821 & 1822," by M[ahlon] Burwell, no. [741], 23. Burwell's baseline now forms part of the Base Line Road. Burwell was forced to temporarily suspend his survey on account of complications involving the Moravian tract. See MNR, Letters Written, Book 25 (1820–22), Ridout to Burwell, 2 July 1821, 207. Burwell completed his work the following year.

23 MNR, Report and Field Notes/Diaries, Field Book, "Field-Notes: Taken on the Survey of the Township of Zone in the Years 1821 & 1822," by M[ahlon] Burwell, no. [741], 23. Unlike Burwell, who was only interested in the location of the battlefield, Benjamin Springer went so far as to plot the exact location of Tecumseh's death. In 1845, Springer was instructed to survey the route of the plank road through Zone Township and its gore – the wedge-shaped tract of land – below the township's baseline (hence the Gore of Zone). At the end of his survey, Springer "took the necessary bearings and distances" in order to mark "the precise spot on which Tecumseh, the celebrated Indian warrior fell, in the late American War." According to Springer, Tecumseh was killed in what is now the front half of lot 4 facing the Longwoods Road, and on the northwest side of a "narrow but deep swamp." See MNR, Report and Field Notes/Diaries, "Diary of the Survey of the Plank Road and Gore of Crown Lands in the Township of Zone, in the Western District, 1845," by B[enjamin] Springer, no. 740, [9]; ibid., "Field Book of the Plank Road and Gore of Crown Lands in the Township of Zone ...," by B[enjamin] Springer, no. 737, 18. See also MNR, Township Plans, "Plan of the Plank Road through the Township of Zone ...," by B[enjamin] Springer, 23 July 1845, D-26, no. B24. How Springer was able to ascertain that this was the place of Tecumseh's death is unknown, although he might have based his measurements on a stand of walnut trees blazed with Native carvings representing various animals. These carvings were said to indicate the location of Tecumseh's last stand. See Grant, *Picturesque Canada*, 2:535. Whatever the source of his information, Springer's map is the earliest record to link the battlefield with lot 4, Gore of Zone Township. The location of Tecumseh's death, relative to the British and Native positions during the Battle of the Thames, is also noted on a contemporary military map dating from the time of the War of 1812. See Sugden, *Tecumseh's Last Stand*, [118]; Sugden, *Tecumseh: A Life*, bet. 338–9. Interestingly, Benjamin Springer was trained to be a surveyor by Mahlon Burwell. See *Free Press*, 27 February 1877, p. 4, col. 5; *London Evening Free Press*, 1 June 1968, sec. 3, p. 9M, col. 1.

24 The location of Burwell's "centre Picket" is indicated on a plan of his survey in Zone Township. See MNR, Township Plans, "Township of Zone," by M[ahlon] Burwell, 4 February 1823, D-26, no. 35. For a less cluttered version of this map, see ibid., "Map Shewing the Boundaries and Extent of the Reservation for the Moravian Indians in the Townships of Zone and Orford," by M[ahlon] Burwell, 18 June 1830, D-26, no. Q20. In south-

western Ontario, a concession is a range of land divided into lots and separated by roads. It is also a division within a rural district known as a
township.

25 Burwell did raise some fairly elaborate pickets. During his survey of Zone
in 1821, he planted large posts to mark the northwestern and southwestern angles of the township. He described one of them as being made of
black ash, "9 Inches in Diameter, Squared & marked properly with 8 Piles
driven round the same, & all the standing Trees marked circularly about it
for witnesses to the Distance of 50 Links [10 metres]." See MNR, Report
and Field Notes/Diaries, Field Book, "Field-Notes: Taken on the Survey of
the Township of Zone in the Years 1821 & 1822," by M[ahlon] Burwell,
no. [741], 9. For the description of the other post, see ibid., 20. Neither of
these posts was positioned near the battlefield, or discernible from the
Longwoods Road.

26 Daniel R. Dunihue, Gardiner's travelling companion, left a rough map
showing the position of Tecumseh's grave in relation to the battlefield. See
ISL, Journal of Daniel R. Dunihue, 1830, 3. Dunihue's map indicates that
Tecumseh's grave was located beyond the northeastern edge of the battlefield and near the Longwoods Road, which would seem to place it near the
site of Burwell's "centre Picket." Dunihue remarked that he "never saw a
grave of the same age look so new – it may be that the Indians dress it up
every few years." See ibid., 4. This "new" appearance is another indication
that Tecumseh's burial post probably was one of Burwell's "centre Pickets," which had been planted less than a decade earlier.

27 Ibid., 2. At the time of the Battle of the Thames, Thomas Shaw was a
young man who appears to have lived with his father some twelve kilometres downriver from the battlefield and adjacent to modern Kent Bridge.
The senior Shaw, whose first name was William, was a militia officer and
magistrate who received a grant of lot 2, concession 1, Camden Township
in 1803. See KCLR, Abstract Books, Camden Township, con. 1, lot 2. See
also LAC, Upper Canada Land Petitions, Shaw to Russell, 11 March 1797,
S2 (1796–97), no. 140; ibid., Shaw to Maitland, 17 July 1821, S13
(1821–24), no. 38. Thomas Shaw was born in Detroit in 1792, which
would have made him thirty-eight years old at the time of Gardiner's visit
in 1830. According to his tombstone in the Sherman Cemetery near
Thamesville, he died in 1865 (probably on lot 17, concession B, Camden
Township). See *Thamesville Herald*, 14 August 1924, p. 1, col. 6; LAC,
1861 Census, Camden Township, Kent County, Canada West, dis. 1, p. 1,
no. 8; Sherman Cemetery, tombstone of Thomas Shaw. Regarding the relationship between Gardiner and Dunihue, see "Dunihue Correspondence of
1832," 408. I am indebted to John Sugden for the Dunihue reference.

28 Dunihue further noted that the "only growth upon it [the mound] consists
of some briers, two or three white-ash shrubs, a young wild goose-berry
bush, and weeds." See ISL, Journal of Daniel R. Dunihue, 1830, 4.

29 Ibid.

30 Burial posts were reserved for prominent members of tribal society. See
Axtell, *European and the Indian*, 113. Erminie Wheeler Voegelin questioned the use of burial posts by Tecumseh's tribe, the Shawnee, and
linked it instead with the Delaware or possibly the Potawatomi. It must
be remembered, however, that the representatives of many tribes fought
alongside Tecumseh at the Battle of the Thames, including both Delaware
and Potawatomi. Of course, it does not necessarily follow that a burial
post was ever erected in Tecumseh's honour. See Voegelin, *Mortuary
Customs of the Shawnee*, 266–8.

31 Like other tour guides before him, Shaw was paid to show Dunihue and
Gardiner around the battlefield. See ISL, Journal of Daniel R. Dunihue,
1830, 2. Although Dunihue had formed a bad opinion of Shaw, based
upon his reputation for having plundered the dead after the Battle of the
Thames, everything Shaw had to say about Tecumseh's grave was accepted
by the American gentleman.

32 *Western Herald*, 28 April 1841, p. 3, col. 1. The reference to Tecumseh
as a Native version of Napoleon was a common analogy.

33 Ibid. See also ibid., 17 June 1841, p. 3, col. 1.

34 LAC, Upper Canada State Papers, Thorburn to Harrison, 17 April 1840,
58–61; *Toronto Patriot*, 21 April 1840, p. 2, col. 7; *British Colonist*,
22 April 1840, p. 2, col. 7; ibid., p. 3, col. 4; Tupper, *Life and Correspondence of Major-General Sir Isaac Brock*, 28–47. See also *British Colonist*,
29 April 1840, p. 3, col. 5. Completed in 1827, the column honoured
Major-General Sir Isaac Brock, who was killed at the Battle of Queenston
Heights on 13 October 1812. See *Farmers's Journal*, 3 January 1827, p. 3,
col. 2.

35 *British Colonist*, 29 April 1840, p. 3, col. 5. Lett was a Canadian with
American sympathies, and a participant in a series of raids against Upper
Canada following the failed Rebellions of 1837. Known collectively as the
Patriot War, these incursions were directed by the Hunters' Lodges. The
leadership of this vast secret revolutionary society planned to liberate the
Canadas from British rule, and thereby accomplish what earlier insurrec-
tions from within the province had failed to achieve. See MacDonald,
"Lett, Benjamin," 501–2; Kinchen, *Rise and Fall of the Patriot Hunters*,
5–7, 11.

36 *Toronto Patriot*, 2 June 1840, p. 2, col. 2. See also LAC, Provincial Secretary, Canada West, vol. 29, Thorburn to Harrison, 18 April 1840,
13752–6; ibid., 16 May 1840, 13698–703. Later, in 1844, John H. DeWitt
and a man named Wheeler were also implicated. See *Niagara Chronicle*,
10 April 1844, p. 2, col. 5. See also ibid., p. 1, col. 2; ibid., p. 2, col. 3.
The identity of the culprit was finally revealed in 1859. Early in January of
that year, James Mackenzie, editor of the *Allen County Democrat* in Lima,
Ohio, provided a detailed account of Lett's destruction of Brock's monument. Lett, who died in December of 1858, was well known to Macken-

zie's father, William Lyon Mackenzie. The senior Mackenzie was a driving force behind the Rebellions of 1837 in Upper Canada. See *Allen County Democrat*, 5 January 1859, p. 1, col. 6. I am grateful to Chris Raible for directing me to James Mackenzie's biographical sketch of Benjamin Lett.

37 Late in 1837, disillusioned reform politicians and republican sympathizers in Upper Canada (now Ontario) rebelled against the authority and patronage of the Family Compact, or conservative network of government officials. The rebellions were quickly suppressed, but escaped rebels and their American friends continued to harass the British colony with border raids launched from the United States. The increasing involvement of American citizens strained relations between Great Britain and the United States. See Craig, *Upper Canada: The Formative Years*, 226–51, 257–9.

38 *Toronto Patriot*, 23 June 1840, p. 2, col. 1.

39 Ibid., 17 July 1840, p. 2, col. 5. A Martello tower is a small circular fort. Notable Canadian examples can be found at Fort Henry near Kingston, Ontario. "John Bull" also suggested that no American be allowed to participate in the rebuilding of the monument.

40 *British Colonist*, 5 August 1840, p. 2, col. 5; ibid., 12 August 1840, p. 1, col. 1; *Toronto Patriot*, 28 July 1840, p. 2, col. 2; ibid., 7 August 1840, p. 2, col. 1; ibid., 11 August 1840, p. 2, col. 1.

41 *Western Herald*, 2 June 1841, p. 3, col. 3; ibid., p. 2, col. 2; ibid., p. 3, col. 4; ibid., 17 June 1841, p. 3, col. 1. A minute book recording the committee's activities is preserved in Amherstburg. See PHM, Committee for Superintending the Erection of a Monument to Tecumseh, Minute Book. I am grateful to Barbara McMahon for a copy of this record.

42 *Western Herald*, 25 August 1841, p. 2, col. 1. This explanation originated with a supporter from Montreal.

43 Ibid., 17 June 1841, p. 3, col. 2.

44 *Chatham Journal*, 4 September 1841, p. 3, col. 1.

45 *Western Herald*, 8 September 1841, p. 1, col. 5.

46 *St Catharines Journal*, 26 August 1841, p. 4, col. 2.

47 The Panic of 1837 was brought about by excessive speculation and expansion in North America, as well as the retraction of the British money market. See Craig, *Upper Canada: The Formative Years*, 242. The economic situation did not improve much by January of 1842, when the agent of the Tecumseh Monument Committee at Ancaster (near Hamilton, Ontario) complained that "more would be done here but for the hard times amongst us." See PHM, Committee for Superintending the Erection of a Monument to Tecumseh, Minute Book, Chep to Treasurer, 20 January 1842, 32.

48 *Western Herald*, 25 November 1841, p. 2, col. 5.

49 Cobourg and Bytown (Ottawa) were among the few places where money was pledged to the Tecumseh monument. See *Montreal Gazette*, 1 September 1841, p. 3, col. 1; *Western Herald*, 8 January 1842, p. 3, col. 1. A meeting was also held in Kingston, but apparently without success. See

Chronicle and Gazette, 31 July 1841, p. 3, col. 4; ibid., 25 August 1841, p. 3, col. 2.

50 *Western Herald,* 25 August 1841, p. 2, col. 1. See also ibid., p. 3, col. 1. As the editor further observed: "The erection of a monument to this savage warrior will have an electric effect among the untutored Indians, and bind them still closer than ever, with the country whose sons have performed so great an act of justice to the memory of one of their departed chiefs." See ibid., 9 June 1841, p. 3, col. 2.

51 *Chatham Gleaner,* 22 September 1846, p. 2, col. 3.

52 Ibid. See also AO, Western District Court of Quarter Sessions, Minute Book, vol. 2, 13 October 1840, 263. The Tecumseh Road replaced an earlier route undermined by the high waters of Lake St Clair. See *Chatham Journal,* 29 January 1842, p. 3, col. 2. Lacroix claimed that it was the name he chose for the highway (as opposed to the destruction of Brock's Monument) that awakened patriotic feelings in Amherstburg and renewed interest in Tecumseh. See *Chatham Gleaner,* 22 September 1846, p. 2, col. 3.

53 *Chatham Gleaner,* 22 September 1846, p. 2, col. 3.

54 Ibid. The Board of Works was established in 1841 to improve British North American transportation. See Owram, "'Management by Enthusiasm,'" 171–2. The Tecumseh Road formed a link in the Main Province Road, the provincial highway though Canada West (modern southern Ontario).

55 A committee of management was made responsible for overseeing operations, while two subcommittees were formed for specific tasks. One concentrated its efforts on selecting a site for the monument; the other was charged with furnishing a design and cost estimates. See *Western Herald,* 2 December 1841, p. 3, col. 3.

56 *Montreal Transcript,* 25 January 1842, p. 2, col. 4. The two regiments were the Seventy-first and the Seventh Hussars.

57 *Chatham Gleaner,* 22 September 1846, p. 2, col. 3.

58 Moreover, a portion of the nearly £200 deposited in the Montreal Provident Savings Bank came from Amherstburg. See *Western Herald,* 2 December 1841, p. 3, col. 3.

59 James Holmes is better remembered as the registrar of Montreal's Trinity House. Established in 1849, and named after its ancient British counterpart, Trinity House was responsible for improving and regulating shipping on the upper St Lawrence River. See Appleton, *Usque ad Mare,* 22. James Holmes died in Montreal on 25 April 1860. See *Montreal Daily Transcript,* 28 April 1860, p. 2, col. 6.

60 Ste. Croix, "Holmes, Benjamin," 396–7; Sugden, *Tecumseh's Last Stand,* 69. James Holmes never achieved the prominence of his brother Benjamin, which perhaps explains why their relationship is obscured. Fortunately, Benjamin Holmes's obituary identifies him as a brother to James Holmes. See *Montreal Gazette,* 24 May 1865, p. 2, col. 1.

61 Sugden, *Tecumseh's Last Stand*, 84; TNA, Court Martial Proceedings of Major-General Henry Procter, 136.

62 LAC, Indian Affairs, Red Series, Correspondence Concerning Tecumseh's Grave, Holmes to Gore, 23 March 1848.

63 Ibid. Île Sainte-Hélène is better known today as the site of Expo '67.

64 Ibid. See also ibid., Denny to Holmes, 18 March 1848.

65 Ibid., Holloway to Military Secretary, 11 April 1848.

66 Ibid., 24 April 1848; ibid., 13 June 1848; ibid., Byham to Burgoyne, 12 May 1848.

67 Brymner, "Monument to Tecumseh," 117.

68 Careless, *Union of the Canadas*, 114. Britain had been moving toward free trade since the early 1840s. See ibid., 15–17, 77–8, 108–10, 122.

69 Ibid., 3–4, 9–11, 111–12, 115, 120.

70 Ibid., 127–9.

71 *Circular of the Annexation Association of Montreal*, 20–5. Benjamin Holmes was first vice-president of this organization. See ibid., 31.

72 James Holmes was decidedly opposed to the idea of annexation, which he made known by signing his name to a written protest against the movement. See *Montreal Transcript*, 20 October 1849, p. 2, col. 4.

73 *Niagara Chronicle*, 10 April 1849, p. 3, col. 2. The committee members renewed their efforts by trying to account for the money previously donated. How successful they were in this regard is not known – nor is it clear what became of the funds after the project failed. The donations were supposed to have been deposited in the Montreal Provident Savings Bank, but there is also the possibility that all or part of the money was entrusted to the Bank of Upper Canada – and then lost when that financial institution failed in 1866. See *Western Herald*, 2 December 1841, p. 3, col. 3; WHS, Draper Manuscript Collection, Tecumseh Papers, ser. YY, vol. 6, no. 110, Falls to Draper, 6 February 1885; Baskerville, *Bank of Upper Canada*, cxlv.

74 *Niagara Chronicle*, 10 April 1849, p. 3, col. 2.

75 *Weekly Spectator*, 20 October 1859, p. 2, col. 4. The sum of £11,986 included incidentals such as the enclosure at the base of the monument, landscaping, etc. The cost of the column itself was £6,421. See Canada, Legislative Assembly, *Journal*, 9 June 1856, 586–9.

76 PHM, Committee for Superintending the Erection of a Monument to Tecumseh, Minute Book, Robert Dickson et al. to [Tecumseh Monument Committee], 1 August 1841, 5–6.

77 The cornerstone was laid on 13 October 1853. See *British Colonist*, 14 October 1853, p. 2, col. 6.

78 *Globe*, 14 October 1859, p. 2, col. 6.

CHAPTER TWO

1 Killan, *Preserving Ontario's Heritage*, 9. The York Pioneer and Historical Society was "organized for the purpose of gathering and preserving

information as to the historical incidents connected with the settlement of the Town of York (now Toronto), as well as of its early settlers." See *Evening Globe*, 17 August 1870, p. 4, col. 1.

2 *Evening Globe*, 1 August 1870, p. 3, col. 1. The Pioneer who suggested the excursion to Brock's Monument was Richard H. Oates.

3 Ibid., 17 August 1870, p. 4, col. 1.

4 It was estimated that "there could not have been less than 700 or 800 persons on the grounds during the afternoon." See *Globe*, 1 August 1871, p. 4, col. 3.

5 *History of Toronto and County of York*, 123–4. This source credits Oates with having been the founder of the York Pioneers.

6 *Globe*, 1 August 1870, p. 4, col. 3. See also AO, Attorney General, Oates File, "Copies of Resolutions," 21 August 1871. Kerby was the editor of the *Niagara News*. See LAC, 1871 Census, Niagara, Ontario, Centre Ward, dis. 20, sub. dis. C, p. 2, no. 7.

7 Early in June of 1872, Oates was forced to report that, "on account of the condition of the funds of the society," it was impossible to erect the monument. Nor was it even possible to lay the cornerstone. See *Mail*, 5 June 1872, p. 4, col. 7.

8 AO, Attorney General, Oates File, petition, 27 June 1872.

9 *Mail*, 19 August 1872, p. 4, col. 1. See also AO, Attorney General, Oates File, petition, 27 June 1872. For the estimated cost of the monument, see *Mail*, 26 July 1876, p. 1, col. 9.

10 Killan, *Preserving Ontario's History*, 8. The mission of the United Canadians was "to gather and diffuse a knowledge of Canadian history; to encourage a Canadian national sentiment, a pride in our country; confidence in its future, its powers and resources." See *Mail*, 19 August 1872, p. 4, col. 1. Yet, the United Canadians were essentially Ontarian in their outlook – much like the members of the Canada First movement. See Killan, *Preserving Ontario's History*, 10, 13.

11 On 4 June 1872, in Toronto's stately St Lawrence Hall, Oates and a number of other delegates representing various "Canadian Societies" met to consider their amalgamation and the formation of the United Canadian Association. A good deal of the meeting was spent discussing the progress of the proposed monument to Tecumseh, which was Oates's first indication that his fellow United Canadians shared his interest in honouring Tecumseh. See *Mail*, 5 June 1872, p. 4, col. 7; *Globe*, 6 June 1872, p. 1, col. 7.

12 *Mail*, 8 June 1876, p. 1, col. 9. Regarding Oates's election as president of the United Canadians, see ibid., 27 July 1875, p. 4, col. 7.

13 The United Canadians were so impressed with Oates's proposal that they immediately appointed a special committee to obtain the government of Ontario's permission to bury Tecumseh's bones at Brock's Monument. See AO, Attorney General, Oates File, resolution, 19 June 1876.

14 AO, Attorney General, Oates File, report, 14 September 1876, 1–2. Brown was from Niagara Township, Clement was from the village of Niagara,

and Oates was from Toronto. The committee also consisted of two other members: Joseph T. Kerby, of Niagara, and Thomas McCrae, of Chatham. Kerby and McCrae did not participate in the expedition. See *Mail*, 8 June 1876, p. 1, col. 9.

15 AO, Attorney General, Oates File, report, 14 September 1876, 2. Johnson admitted to having drawn the map himself. See *Globe*, 29 September 1876, p. 3, col. 3. This map is now preserved in the Archives of Ontario. See AO, Attorney General, Oates File, *Daily Pocket Diary for 1855* (New York, New York: n.p., 1855).

16 Ockawandah was supposed to have made these trips up until the time of his death in about 1865. See AO, Attorney General, Oates File, report, 14 September 1876, 3–4. According to the 1851 census (enumerated in 1852), "Okawenda" lived with his wife and three children on a farm in Tuscarora Township in Brant County. Although Johnson claimed that Ockawandah lived at the Grand River until his death in 1865, he is not listed in the 1861 census for Tuscarora Township. Furthermore, the 1851 census records that Ockawandah was born in the "State of New York" in 1798. If Ockawandah participated in the Battle of the Thames in October of 1813, he must have been a very youthful warrior. Of course, there is also the possibility that Ockawandah was somewhat older than the age recorded by the census enumerator. See LAC, 1851 Census, Tuscarora Township, Brant County, Canada West, p. 61, no. 36; ibid., Agricultural Census, p. 79, no. 28.

17 AO, Attorney General, Oates File, report, 14 September 1876, 2. Nelles did not identify the Native who pointed out the grave, but another source indicates that it was Timothy Snake. See *Canadian Home Journal*, semi-weekly ed., 3 October 1876, p. 2, col. 1. Snake died on 9 December 1869. See AMC, New Fairfield Mission, Diary, 1869, box 167, folder 4, p. 47. According to Albert Tobias, whose family lived near Snake and were well acquainted with him, his Native name was Chief Tollosh. See *Annual Report of the Ontario Historical Society, 1913*, 55.

18 AO, Attorney General, Oates File, report, 14 September 1876, 2–3. The map provided by Nelles was enclosed in a letter he addressed to Johnson. See ibid., Nelles to Johnson, 5 September 1876.

19 Ibid, report, 14 September 1876, 2, 4, 6.

20 Ibid., 5–6. Chief Frederick Jacobs of Moraviantown was also present. See ibid., 9.

21 Ibid., 2–3. The outline of the log house was found on lot 5 in the Gore of Zone Township. William Watts was the owner of both lot 5 and lot 6. His father, Edward Watts, settled on these properties in 1837 and later purchased them in 1849. See *Commemorative Biographical Record of the County of Kent*, 535–6; AO, Zone Township Papers, Crown Lands Sale to Edward Watts, 11 April 1849, no. 8649, p. 2090. Lot 4 was owned by James Dickson. In 1878, Dickson sold his farm to William Watts. See KCLR, Abstract Books, Zone Township, gore con., lot 4; AO, Kent County Copy-

book of Deeds, Register E, Dickson to Watts, 28 September 1878, no. 1954.

22 AO, Attorney General, Oates File, report, 14 September 1876, 5; *Globe*, 29 September 1876, p. 3, col. 3.

23 AO, Attorney General, Oates File, report, 14 September 1876, 5.

24 Ibid., 5–6.

25 Ibid., 6.

26 Ibid.

27 *Canadian Home Journal*, semi-weekly ed., 14 July 1876, p. 3, col. 1. Regarding the white opposition, see *Sarnia Observer*, 28 July 1876, p. 1, col. 7.

28 *Mail*, 15 July 1876, p. 4, col. 4.

29 *Evening Telegram*, 10 July 1876, p. 4, col. 3. Robertson, who went on to become one of Toronto's leading philanthropists, had a great interest in local history.

30 Founded in 1870, the Grand General Indian Council of Ontario was the first inter-tribal association in Canada. The goals of the Grand Council were the "general advancement of Indian people in education, morals, sobriety and general welfare and the efficient management of band monetary funds by the government." See Lueger, "History of Indian Associations in Canada," 71–2. By 1876, membership in the Grand Council was predominantly Ojibwa. See ibid., 72.

31 *Mail*, 15 July 1876, p. 4, col. 4. The Saugeen Reserve is located on Lake Huron, at the base of Ontario's Bruce Peninsula.

32 Ibid. See also LAC, Indian Affairs, Red Series, Correspondence Concerning Tecumseh's Grave, Chase and Jacobs to the governor-general of Canada and the government of Ontario, 12 July 1876.

33 LAC, Indian Affairs, Red Series, Correspondence Concerning Tecumseh's Grave, McLean to Cascaden, 21 August 1902.

34 AO, Attorney General, Oates File, memo, 8 July 1876.

35 *Mail*, 15 July 1876, p. 4, col. 4.

36 The same United Canadians participated in the second expedition. See AO, Attorney General, Oates File, report, 14 September 1876, 7; *Globe*, 29 September 1876, p. 3, col. 3. The United Canadians arrived at Thamesville in the evening of 29 August. See *Mail*, 12 September 1876, p. 1, col. 9.

37 AO, Attorney General, Oates File, report, 14 September 1876, 7.

38 Ibid., 7–8.

39 Ibid., 10. See also ibid., statement of John Smoke Johnson, September 1876. Johnson was a chief and speaker of the Six Nations. He was regarded as that community's "grand old man." See Leighton, "Johnson, John," 453.

40 AO, Attorney General, Oates File, report, 14 September 1876, 8; LAC, 1871 Census 1871, Orford Township (Moraviantown), Kent County, Ontario, dis. 3, sub. dis. B, div. 4, p. 53, no. 186.

41 AO, Attorney General, Oates File, report, 14 September 1876, 8. Logan told the United Canadians that his father had also known where Tecumseh

was buried, and pointed in the direction of the grave they had just
unearthed.

42 Ibid., 8–9. Brown was a farmer from Niagara Township, Lincoln County,
Ontario.

43 Ibid., 9–10.

44 *Canadian Home Journal*, semi-weekly ed., 1 September 1876, p. 4, cols 1,
3. See also *Globe*, weekly ed., 8 September 1876, p. 5, col. 2.

45 *Mail*, 1 September 1876, p. 1, col. 8. It was also suggested that the scalping knife was nothing more than a gardener's pruning knife. See *Daily Witness*, 2 September 1876, p. 1, col. 6.

46 The editor of the *Mail* was right in stating that *Gulielmus* is the Latin form
of William. But according to Sharon Tibbotts of the Royal Armouries
(H.M. Tower of London), a *W* rather than a *G* was used in King William
III's cipher. In Tibbotts to St-Denis, 16 May 1995.

47 *Canadian Home Journal*, semi-weekly ed., 5 September 1876, p. 4, col. 5.
The farmer referred to as Mr Dixon was in fact James Dickson. He was
the owner of the next farm lot to the west, which was number 4 in the
Gore of Zone Township.

48 Ibid. See also ibid., p. 4, col. 1.

49 *Mail*, 9 September 1876, p. 2, col. 5.

50 Ibid., 12 September 1876, p. 1, col. 9.

51 Ibid. Timothy Snake, it will be remembered, died in 1869. See AMC, New
Fairfield Mission, Diary, 1869, box 167, folder 4, p. 47.

52 *Mail*, 12 September 1876, p. 1, col. 9. David Zeisberger, a clergyman of the
Moravian Church (Unitas Fratrum), founded the Fairfield mission in 1792.
He also established its cemetery, "Hutberg," during that same year. See
Gray, *Wilderness Christians*, 95–6. According to Linda Sabathy-Judd, *Hut-
berg* is a German compound noun consisting of *heüten* (meaning to watch
over) and *berg* (meaning mountain) implying, as Elma E. Gray suggests in
Wilderness Christians, "the little hill under the Watch of the Lord." See
ibid., 96. Hutberg is located on lot B, North of the Longwoods Road, Zone
Township. It is in a farmer's field opposite the Fairfield Museum.

53 *Mail*, 12 September 1876, p. 1, col. 9.

54 AO, Attorney General, Oates File, report, 14 September 1876, 5.

55 *Mail*, 12 September 1876, p. 1, col. 9.

56 Ibid.

57 Ibid.

58 Ibid.

59 Ibid.

60 Ironically, the "singular" mound suggests that the grave held the remains
of a prominent Native communicant to the Moravian Church, rather than
a missionary.

61 The day before the Clergyman's letter was published, the *Nation* deemed
that the United Canadians' discovery "ranked higher than most antiquarian
achievements in this country." See *Nation*, 8 September 1876, p. 1, col. 2.

62 Ibid., 15 September 1876, p. 1, col. 3.

63 AO, Attorney General, Oates File, report, 14 September 1876, 1. The meeting took place a few days earlier on 11 September.

64 In 1876, burials in Ontario were protected by the Cemetery Companies Act and the Municipal Act. See Ontario, revised statutes of Ontario, c. 170, s. 30; ibid., c. 174, s. 19.

65 Evans, *Sir Oliver Mowat*, 75; Romney, "Mowat, Sir Oliver," 729.

66 AO, Attorney General, Oates File, memo, 8 July 1876. Mowat "was commonly referred to, not as Premier or Prime Minister, but as the Attorney General, from the ministry of which he took charge during the whole long period in which he was at the head of the [provincial] Government." See Langton, *Sir Daniel Wilson*, 84.

67 AO, Attorney General, Oates File, report, 14 September 1876, 1–10; *Globe*, 29 September 1876, p. 3, col. 3.

68 Berger, "Wilson, Sir Daniel," 1109–14. Wilson later served as president of the University of Toronto from 1887 to 1892. For another biography of Wilson, see *Globe*, weekly ed., 3 March 1876, p. 5, col. 3.

69 *Globe*, 29 September 1876, p. 3, col. 3. In archaeological terms, *in situ* refers to artifacts and human remains discovered in their original and undisturbed positions.

70 Ibid.

71 Ibid. A rod is an old unit of measurement, and equals five metres.

72 AO, Attorney General, Oates File, report, 14 September 1876, 3; *Globe*, 29 September 1876, p. 3, col. 3. Ockawandah appears to have merely indicated that the grave would be found along a fence to the west of the log house.

73 According to Carl Berger, "Wilson's early interests in cranial types and measurement grew into an obsession, largely in response to the controversy over whether the various races of people had separate origins (polygenesis) or had developed from a single creation (monogenesis)." Wilson argued in favour of the latter. See Berger, "Wilson, Sir Daniel," 1110. Among the several articles Wilson contributed to the *Canadian Journal* (published by the Canadian Institute), one advocates the formation of a "Canadian Collection of Ancient Crania." See W[ilson], "Hints for the Formation of a Canadian Collection of Ancient Crania," 345–7.

74 In contemplating his trip to Tecumseh's supposed grave, Wilson noted in his diary that he hoped "to secure some [skeletal] specimens for my ethnological department in the Museum; and for the rest, must do my best, in this wild-goose quest, for the final rest-ing place of the good chief Tecumseh!" See UTA, Langton Papers, Journal of Daniel Wilson, 15 September 1876, 35.

75 *Globe*, 29 September 1876, p. 3, col. 3. The farmer was James Dickson, and the skull he presented to Wilson was intended as a donation for the "museum of the University of Toronto." See ibid. Wilson judged it "a good Wyandot skull." See UTA, Langton Papers, Journal of Daniel Wilson,

27 September 1876, 35. This skull was likely lost in the fire which raced through the University College on 14 February 1890. See Averill and Keith, "Daniel Wilson and the University of Toronto," 186–7. Curiously, another skull thought to belong to Tecumseh was lost under similar circumstances when a fire destroyed the buildings of the Medical Faculty of McGill University, in Montreal, Quebec, on 16 April 1907. See Hetherington, "Tecumseh," 147. Norman Gurd, a lawyer from Sarnia, Ontario, and one of Tecumseh's biographers, made inquiries regarding the McGill skull – but he found the results less than conclusive. Apparently, the skull was "presented to the [Museum of the McGill Medical College] by a student from Western Ontario, [but] no record having been made of his name or residence, it was said that he had received this skull from an old schoolmaster." See LR, Gurd Papers, letterbook, Gurd to Patullo, 17 June 1918, 308; ibid., Hetherington to Gurd, 29 May 1909. See also *Sarnia Canadian Observer*, daily ed., 29 June 1918, p. 1, col. 6.

76 *Globe*, 29 September 1876, p. 3, col. 3. The burial ground near Florence probably was located on the former Bear Creek Reserve, which the Canadian government "sold by mistake" some thirty years earlier. This tract of 2,071 hectares included a seasonal camp of the Chippewa from the Walpole Island Reserve, as well as their "burying grounds." See LAC, Indian Affairs, Western Superintendency, Sarnia Agency, F. Talfourd Correspondence, Prince to Hogg, 16 November 1849, 108; ibid., J.B. Clench Correspondence, Springer to Clench, 15 October 1845, 123; *Indian Treaties and Surrenders*, 1:50.

77 *Globe*, 29 September 1876, p. 3, col. 3. Wilson identified the skeleton as that of a "Potowattomie." See UTA, Langton Papers, Journal of Daniel Wilson, 27 September 1876, 35.

78 *Globe*, 29 September 1876, p. 3, col. 3.

79 Ibid. Wilson probably meant the ethnological museum in the University College at the University of Toronto.

80 Ibid. After the United Canadians returned from their second expedition, the box containing the bones was left with the mayor of Niagara for safekeeping. At some point, the box was sealed. The other gentlemen who participated in the examination were Dr William T. Aikins, a surgeon; Dr James H. Richardson, a physician and surgeon; Dr James Thorburn, a physician (who attended at Oates's request); and Robert Ramsay Wright, a professor of Natural History in University College. Oates was also in attendance.

81 As Wilson and the other learned gentlemen soon realized: "So far from constituting 'the greater portion of the skeleton,' [the bones] included only an imperfect skull, three bones of the pelvis, one humerus, one radius, one femur, one tibia, a clavicle and a single rib." See *Canadian Home Journal*, semi-weekly ed., 3 October 1876, p. 4, col. 5.

82 As Wilson reported to Mowat: "There are indeed two ossa innominata, with a sacrum, but not only are the two bones both of the left side, and

therefore necessary parts of distinct skeletons; but the three medical gentlemen and Professor Ramsay Wright concurred in pronouncing one *os
innominatum*, with the sacrum, to belong to a female skeleton. The tibia is
that of a person of small size. The clavicle is also small, poorly developed,
and probably that of a female, while the femur must have pertained to a
child little more than seven years of age. Of the other bones, the radius
and rib are certainly not human bones; but probably of a deer and a dog."
See *Globe*, 29 September 1876, p. 3, col. 3.

83 Ibid. As Wilson later concluded in his journal, "It certainly is not Tecum-
seh's skeleton, for it is nobody's!" See UTA, Langton Papers, Journal of
Daniel Wilson, 27 September 1876, 36. See also Langton, *Sir Daniel
Wilson*, 93.

84 *Canadian Home Journal*, semi-weekly ed., 3 October 1876, p. 4, col. 5.

85 On 14 February 1890, a fire destroyed University College at the University
of Toronto, including Wilson's museum and, presumably, the skeleton he
acquired in 1876. See Averill and Keith, "Daniel Wilson and the University
of Toronto," 186–7.

86 *Globe*, 29 September 1876, p. 3, col. 3.

87 Of course, Wilson's remark was a slap against Dr Graham's lazy anatomical
observation. See ibid. The *Canadian Home Journal* was not the least bit
sympathetic toward Graham. "If Dr Graham, of Bothwell, was present at
the discovery, as we understand he was, how could he have committed the
ridiculous blunder of assuming that the bones were Tecumseh's? A mere
tyro in anatomy might have detected the fraud – if a fraud was intended, –
but that a medical man of ten or twelve years' standing should be unable to
distinguish the thigh bone of a child seven years old from that of a man, or
a dog's rib from a man's, is something we cannot comprehend." See *Canadian Home Journal*, semi-weekly ed., 3 October 1876, p. 4, col. 1.

88 The *Globe* published Wilson's entire report three days later. See *Globe*, 29
September 1876, p. 3, col. 3. For the editorial commentary, see ibid., p. 2,
col. 1. The St Thomas *Canadian Home Journal* published the report in two
installments, beginning on 3 October 1876. See *Canadian Home Journal*,
semi-weekly ed., 3 October 1876, p. 4, col. 5; ibid., 6 October 1876, semi-
weekly ed., p. 2, col. 4.

89 Ontario's two leading dailies, both of which were published in Toronto,
exhibited particular unkindness toward the United Canadians. To the Conservative *Mail*, their logic seemed backward, as it was "for the incredulous to
prove an *alibi*." The Liberal *Globe* followed up by noting that the "devoutest
antiquarian ... was able to make anything mean anything." See *Mail*, 28 September 1876, p. 2, col. 3; *Globe*, 29 September 1876, p. 2, col. 1.

90 *Canadian Home Journal*, semi-weekly ed., 3 October 1876, p. 4, col. 5.

91 Ibid., p. 4, col. 1.

92 *Mail*, 28 September 1876, p. 2, col. 3. In a rather more reserved editorial,
the Toronto *Globe* agreed that Tecumseh's grave would never be found.
See *Globe*, weekly ed., 6 October 1876, p. 3, col. 3.

93 At the time of his death in 1881, Oates was eulogized for his efforts in "stimulating interest in the preservation of the relics and memorials of the early days of Toronto and neighbourhood." His embarrassing involvement with Tecumseh's bones was conveniently overlooked. See *Globe*, 2 March 1881, p. 1, col. 6. See also *Toronto Daily Mail*, 2 March 1881, p. 3, col. 5.

94 That the white population of Ontario required Tecumseh's remains before they could pay proper respect to his memory is obvious from the opinion of the *Hamilton Times*: "At present the actual burial place of the great Chief is a mystery, and no one can pay his memory the respect that is due from every Canadian – a respect best shown by giving his remains a public funeral and interring them in a most historic spot in Ontario, side by side with those of Gen. Brock." See *Sarnia Observer*, 28 July 1876, p. 1, col. 7.

95 *Mail*, 25 September 1876, p. 3, col. 3.

96 Specifically, Johnson endured physical violence in order to rid the Six Nations of an illicit liquor and timber trade. See Hale, "Chief George H.M. Johnson – Onwanonsyshon," 138–9; Leighton, "Johnson, George Henry Martin," 451–3.

97 Keller, *Pauline*, 10. George H. Johnson was the father of E. Pauline Johnson, the Canadian poetess of "The Song My Paddle Sings" fame.

98 In a private letter he wrote soon after, Blue observed: "The United Canadian Association claim that they have solved the question, and last week they passed through town with half a dozen of the great chiefs' bones, as they say. I think they are mistaken." See UWOA, Coyne Papers, Blue to Coyne, 5 September 1876. Blue was equally dubious when he learned of a subsequent discovery of Tecumseh's bones in 1910. See *Globe*, 13 June 1910, p. 11, col. 4.

99 UWOA, Coyne Papers, Blue to Coyne, 5 September 1876.

100 Blue became the principal editor of the *Canadian Home Journal* in 1876. See Miller, *Vignettes of Early St Thomas*, 326.

101 Blue was born and raised in Orford Township, Kent County, not far from Moraviantown and the site of the Battle of the Thames. See Morgan, *Canadian Men and Women of the Time*, 93.

CHAPTER THREE

1 *St Thomas Journal*, 19 January 1877, p. 5, col. 1. See also *London Free Press*, 17 January 1877, p. 3, col. 3. The *St Thomas Journal* was the former *Canadian Home Journal*.

2 Ibid. Despite their prior opposition to the removal of Tecumseh's bones, the east Kenters did not object when the United Canadians came to their assistance with a subscription drive. See *Free Press*, 22 June 1877, p. 4, col. 2.

3 *St Thomas Journal*, 26 January 1877, p. 1, col. 4. The editor of the *St Thomas Journal* was Archibald Blue, who had a particular interest in Dr Smith's earlier efforts to refute the bones discovered by the United Canadians.

4 Ibid.

5 Ibid.

6 For a biography of Dr Smith, see *Illustrated Historical Atlas of Essex and Kent*, 63.

7 *St Thomas Journal*, 2 February 1877, p. 4, col. 4.

8 Ibid.

9 Ibid.

10 Ibid.

11 Ibid.

12 Autos probably confused the assault on the Cheyenne village at Sand Creek in 1864, which was led by Colonel John M. Chivington, with Custer's attack on a Cheyenne village in Oklahoma four years later.

13 J.A.W. defended Tecumseh and his race in two separate letters. See *St Thomas Journal*, 6 February 1877, p. 1, col. 4; ibid., 6 March 1877, p. 1, col. 3.

14 Ibid., 9 February 1877, p. 4, col. 3.

15 For a biography of Oronhyatekha (baptized Peter Martin), see: Comeau-Vasilopolous, "Oronhyatekha," 791–5.

16 *St Thomas Journal*, 16 February 1877, p. 5, col. 2.

17 Ibid.

18 Although Wendell Phillips is better known for his abolitionist activities, he also advocated the rights of other minorities in the United States. He was especially fond of Native Americans and deplored their victimization at the hands of his countrymen. See Bartlett, *Wendell Phillips: Brahmin Radical*, 380–1. Oronhyatekha probably drew much of his information from an open letter addressed to General William Tecumseh Sherman, which Phillips published after Custer's defeat at the Battle of the Little Bighorn in June of 1876. See *London Advertiser*, 22 July 1876, p. 2, col. 2.

19 *St Thomas Journal*, 16 February 1877, p. 5, col. 3.

20 Ibid., 20 February 1877, p. 5, col. 3.

21 Ibid.

22 Ibid.

23 In the early 1790s, relations between the United States and Great Britain deteriorated as American expansion into the Northwest Territory met with increased Native resistance. Wishing to accommodate their Native allies, while at the same time securing Upper Canada's border, the British suggested the creation of a Native state encompassing the area bounded by the Mississippi River to the west, the Ohio River to the south, and the Great Lakes to the north. Simcoe fully supported the concept of an independent Native state, but the Americans rejected any suggestion that they relinquish their interest in such a vast, fertile region. In modern terms, the proposed Native state would have encompassed Illinois, Indiana, Ohio, Michigan, Wisconsin, and portions of Pennsylvania, New York, and Minnesota. See Danglade, "John Graves Simcoe and the United States," 102–4; Goltz, "Tecumseh," 37–40. The establishment of a Native barrier state

was also unsuccessfully demanded by the British delegates during negotiations to end the War of 1812. See Sugden, *Tecumseh's Last Stand*, 208–9.

24 Comeau-Vasilopolous, "Oronhyatekha," 792, 794–5. The Independent Order of Foresters, an all-male fraternal order, invested membership dues in order to provide life insurance, disability benefits, and even pension plans.

25 In his sole letter to the *St Thomas Journal*, Oronhyatekha did not mention the proposed monument to Tecumseh. Having browbeat E.D.H. into a quick submission, the Native doctor turned his attention to managing the affairs of the Independent Order of Foresters. See *St Thomas Journal*, 16 February 1877, p. 5, col. 3.

26 Ibid., 23 February 1877, p. 1, col. 3. As Smith observed, "I don't care where the savage comes from – be he white, black or copper colored."

27 Ibid.

28 Autos and J.A.W. persisted against Smith until early in March of 1877. See ibid., 2 February 1877, p. 4, col. 4; ibid., 13 February 1877, p. 1, col. 3; ibid., 27 February 1877, p. 1, col. 3; ibid., 2 March 1877, p. 1, col. 5.

29 Dr Graham was recognized as having organized the troupe of Native singers. See *Transcript*, 28 June 1877, p. 3, col. 1. However, John C. Dent, the prominent editor of the Toronto *Globe*, claimed it was an article he wrote on Tecumseh that "originated the scheme." See WHS, Draper Manuscript Collection, "Brandt" Papers, ser. F, vol. 1, no. 103, Dent to Draper, 28 May 1877. For Dent's article, see *Globe*, weekly ed., 2 February 1877, 1. This sketch was later included in Dent's *Canadian Portrait Gallery* series. See Dent, *Canadian Portrait Gallery*, 2:144–57.

30 Dr Graham's attempt to exploit the Natives of Moraviantown was by no means the first. A few years earlier, in 1875, the missionaries at New Fairfield reported that "a white man got a number of Indians to form themselves into a band of players, and after considerable practising, they went about performing Indian dances, and exhibiting old Indian customs, interspersing their performances with secular, and, alas! also with sacred songs." See Hartmann, "Report of the Mission at New Fairfield," 1874–75, Appendix A, 9.

31 *Daily Advertiser*, 21 May 1877, p. 1, col. 4.

32 According to the Moravian missionaries at New Fairfield, the "plan was, first to try this continent, and then go over to England. But, oh! how the matter failed! Although considerable noise was made about the affair, it would not even pay the very expenses connected with the troupe. And just think – to raise $20,000 by it for the monument!" See Hartmann, "Report of the Mission at New Fairfield," 1876, Appendix B, 13. Dr Graham's Delaware singers performed at the Theatre Comique, where they shared the stage with such popular acts as "Prof. James Lawrence's ballet and golden statue troupe in living historical pictures," as well as "Sam Baylis with his Lilliputian wonders." See *Detroit Free Press*, 27 May 1877, p. 1, col. 8; ibid., 31 May 1877, p. 1, col. 4.

33 *Transcript*, 28 June 1877, p. 3, col. 1. Peter E. Flanders, a Pro[f]. of
   Music," had a small farm in Caradoc Township, Middlesex County,
   between Mount Brydges and Strathroy, Ontario. See UWOA, Caradoc
   Township Assessment Rolls, 1877, div. 2, no. 644.

34 *Free Press*, 22 June 1877, p. 4, col. 2. Dr Graham, it will be remembered,
   was a member of the United Canadian Association.

35 In 1856, for example, a group of Walpole Island Natives were taken to
   England, where they performed at the Panopticon in London's Leicester
   Square with great success. See *Illustrated London News*, 12 July 1856, 41.
   Unfortunately for Graham, the expense of a trans-Atlantic voyage preclud-
   ed the possibility of presenting his singers to English audiences.

36 Dr Graham soon after moved to St Catharines, Ontario. See *Gazetteer and
   Business Directory of Lincoln and Welland Counties, for 1879*, 123.

37 Melbourne is located thirty-four kilometres from London, Ontario.
   Thomas Gowman is listed in the Melbourne section of the 1893 London,
   Ontario directory. See *London City and Middlesex County Directory,
   1893*, 491.

38 There is some disagreement regarding the year of the Gowman family's
   immigration. Omar K. Watson, a lawyer from Ridgetown, Ontario, reck-
   oned it to be 1833. See UWOA, Goulet Papers, Notes and Accounts on the
   Death of Tecumseh, Watson to Gemmill, 30 November 1920. However, a
   close reading of Gowman's manuscript, which begins with a brief genealogy, suggests that the family arrived at Louisville in 1834. See AO, Gowman
   Papers, "Pioneer Life in Upper Canada," 1:3–11. The location of the Gowman farm is not known, except that it was somewhere near Louisville.
   Thomas's father (Samuel) rented the property, which explains why he is
   not listed in the local land registry. See ibid., 1:13; ibid., 2:301. Further
   compounding this question is a paucity of assessment rolls, census returns,
   and other official records – which foiled the author's attempt to link the
   Gowman family with a specific farm.

39 In reference to the allegations that Tecumseh's body had been flayed by
   vengeful Kentuckians, the *Advertiser* countered with Pheasant's story "that
   six Shawnee braves stole to the battle ground under cover of night,
   removed the body of Tecumseh, and gave reverential burial to the remains
   of their chieftain in the depths of a forest a short distance northward." See
   Daily Advertiser, 6 September 1876, p. 2, col. 3. This article first appeared
   in the *Advertiser* on 22 October 1872.

40 Ibid., 14 September 1876, p. 1, col. 4. Gowman mistakenly recalled the
   year as having been 1837. In fact, the incident occurred in 1840. Neither
   Pheasant nor Snake were suspected of complicity at the time. While Gowman does not name Jacob Pheasant's companion, there is no doubt that it
   was Timothy Snake. See *Toronto Patriot*, 23 June 1840, p. 2, col. 1.

41 *Daily Advertiser*, 14 September 1876, p. 1, col. 4. Tecumseh might have
   worn a sash as a type of belt, but John Richardson, who served on the side
   of the British and saw Tecumseh just prior to the battle, did not mention it
   in his description of the great chief. Later, and perhaps less reliable, wit-

nesses maintained that a sash did form part of Tecumseh's attire. See Sugden, *Tecumseh's Last Stand*, 122, 150, 176.

42 *Daily Advertiser*, 14 September 1876, p. 1, col. 4. Gowman also accused "old Partridge," meaning Jacob Pheasant, of having frequently sold bones which he fraudulently misrepresented as those of Tecumseh. See AO, Gowman Papers, "Pioneer Life in Upper Canada," 2:234. It would appear that much of Gowman's hostility toward these Natives stemmed from a childhood incident in 1836 involving Timothy Snake. "He was not old then," Gowman recalled,

> "and if he had known of Tecumseh's grave, I could have bought the secret for one gallon of whiskey, and that in that day would have cost me nineteen cents. I was but a boy then, but I chanced to let Snake see a very handsome white marble image [or a native stone carving] that I had dug out of the river bank, and he teased me for it for two days; said he wanted it for a keepsake, 'cause it made by his fadders,' and as soon as the old skunk got it he went into Louisville and sold it for 10 cents; then he bought a quart of whiskey and him and old Mittreoss had a glorious drunk; and old Snake and old Partridge [Pheasant] have pretended to sell Tecumseh's bones a good many times, but when they sold a skull bone and an arm bone to a British officer for £5 they found 'a stranger and they took him in;' for when the officer arrived back at Little York [Toronto] the doctors there were mean enough to pronounce it a white man's skull, but, no matter – the boys had the money."

See *Free Press*, 27 January 1894, p. 6, col. 4.

43 *Daily Advertiser*, 25 September 1876, p. 1, col. 6.

44 Ibid., 14 September 1876, p. 1, col. 4.

45 Ibid., 25 September 1876, p. 1, col. 6. As noted in chapter two, a rod is an old unit of measurement, and equals five metres.

46 Ibid. Gowman does not mention Tecumseh's death in this account, but elsewhere he describes how Tecumseh suffered a gunshot wound and "at that moment an [American] officer on horseback dashed up in front of Tecumseh, pointing south with his sword. Tecumseh threw a tomahawk at the back of the officer's head and the officer turned quick around just as the tomahawk reached him; the bit struck between the nose and corner of the right eye and sunk into the head, and he and Tecumseh fell over at the same time." See *Free Press*, 30 December 1893, p. 13, col. 3.

47 *Daily Advertiser*, 25 September 1876, p. 1, col. 6. Kishamanite, or Kishi Manite, is more familiarly known as "Gitche Manitou" and means Great Mystery, but it is commonly interpreted as Great Spirit, which is the meaning that Gowman attached to it. I am grateful to David McNab for his translation and insight.

48 Ibid.

49 Dr Smith died at Ridgetown on 27 November 1885. See AO, Registrar General of Ontario, Death Registrations, 27 November 1885, no. 7820.

50 *Daily Advertiser*, 25 September 1876, p. 1, col. 6.

51 Timothy Snake died in 1869, and Jacob Pheasant died in 1872. See AMC,

New Fairfield Mission, Burial Register, 1870–1903, box 168, folder 4, burial of Timothy Snake, 12 Dec. 1869, p. 178; ibid., burial of Jacob Pheasant, 26 July 1872, 181. There is a discrepancy in Pheasant's death date. The mission diary records that he died in 1871. See AMC, New Fairfield Mission, Diary, 1871, box 167, folder 7, 26 July 1871, p. 38. However, the burial register indicates that he died in 1872. The latter source appears to be correct, as it corresponds more or less with a newspaper reference to Pheasant's death that was originally published in October of 1872. See AMC, New Fairfield Mission, Burial Register, 1870–1903, box 168, folder 4, burial of Jacob Pheasant, 26 July 1872, p. 181; *Daily Advertiser*, 6 September 1876, p. 2, col. 3.

52 AMC, New Fairfield Mission, Burial Register, 1870–1903, box 168, folder 4, burial of Timothy Snake, 12 Dec. 1869, p. 178. To the moralizing chagrin of the missionaries, they discovered that "Timothy" had never married the mother of his children. Despite repeated urgings, Snake refused to marry his wife in a Christian ceremony. On one occasion, when a missionary became rather too pressing and persistent, Snake responded by saying that "he & and the mother of his children were faithful to each other, & that was enough." See AMC, New Fairfield Mission, Report, 1869, box 167, folder 5, pp. 9–10.

53 Timothy Snake's tombstone is located in the cemetery at Moraviantown, Ontario. A picture of this tombstone accompanies one of Les Bronson's articles on Tecumseh. See *London Evening Free Press*, 4 May 1968, sec. 3, p. M9, col. 1. I am grateful to the late Mr Bronson for directing me to this series of articles, which he prepared in commemoration of the bicentenary of Tecumseh's birth. In addition to the fine marble tombstone, Snake's corpse was provided with a "walnut coffin, very much too large," which "was embossed with silver washed ornaments, & adorned with silver washed handles, & a plate, inscribed: 'Timothy Snake. Died Dec. 9, 1869. Aged 80.'" See AMC, New Fairfield Mission, Diary, 1869, box 167, folder 4, p. 49.

54 AMC, New Fairfield Mission, Burial Register, 1870–1903, box 168, folder 4, burial of Timothy Snake, 12 Dec. 1869, p. 178.

55 Ibid., burial of Jacob Pheasant, 26 July 1872, 181. Both Jacob Pheasant and Timothy Snake were described as having been "in the Tecumseh battle." See ibid., Diary, 1867, box 167, folder 2, p. 11.

56 LAC, Indian Affairs, Western Superintendency, Sarnia Agency, J.B. Clench Correspondence, Napier to Clench, 28 August 1849, 460. Jesse Vogler, the Moravian missionary at the time, was considerably annoyed by Native claimants seeking his assistance in obtaining these medals: "Had the Yankees been worried by the Indians in the late war as I have been by those that supposed they ought to have a medal for having been in some small skirmishes, then surely the American troops would not enter Canada again under no consideration." See ibid., Vogler to Clench, 2 May 1848, 444.

57 By his own admission, James Dickson settled on lot 4 in the Gore of Zone

Township in 1846. See *Globe*, 29 September 1876, p. 3, col. 3. See also Grant, *Picturesque Canada*, 2:535. It should be noted that in 1876 James Dickson owned lot 4 in the Gore of Zone Township, which encompasses the site where Tecumseh fell (according to Pheasant and Snake). In 1878, however, Dickson sold his farm to William Watts, who already owned the adjacent lot 5. See KCLR, Abstract Books, Zone Township, gore con., lot 4; AO, Kent County Copybook of Deeds, Register E, Dickson to Watts, 28 September 1878, no. 1954.

58 *Globe*, 29 September 1876, p. 3, col. 3. It is not clear when Dickson discovered the carvings on his trees. However, he does indicate that this particular part of his farm was not completely cleared until sometime after Timothy Snake's death, which occurred in 1869. See ibid. It would appear that Dickson concentrated his efforts elsewhere, and that much of his energy was devoted to draining swampland. When Benson J. Lossing visited the site of the battlefield in October of 1860, he observed that the small swamp had disappeared, "but its place was distinctly marked by deep black mould." The large, or "great," swamp continued to hinder area farmers for at least another three years. But by the time of Wilson's investigation in 1876, the large swamp had also been drained. See Lossing, *Pictorial Field-Book of the War of 1812*, 559, 561; *Canadian Illustrated News*, 15 August 1863, p. 163, col. 1; *Globe*, 29 September 1876, p. 3, col. 3.

59 *Globe*, 29 September 1876, p. 3, col. 3. Similar carvings are described in other accounts of Tecumseh's burial. For example, see Sugden, *Tecumseh's Last Stand*, 153, 216. According to another source, the carvings

> were full of meaning for two aged Shawnees [probably Timothy Snake and Jacob Pheasant] who had fought by Tecumseh's side and had afterwards carved on the walnuts these emblems to mark with deepest veneration the spot where the last hope of so many Indian nations expired. The old settlers relate that often at twilight these Shawnee warriors might have been seen stealing to the place. Remaining there for hours in the darkness, and with a silence unbroken except by the sighing of the night-wind through the aged walnut-trees, they would meditate on the life and death of the last great representative of the Indian race. To the inexpressible grief of these poor Indians, and with a most barbarous disregard of the sanctity of the place, the walnut-trees were hewn down, and the scene of Tecumseh's death has been thought irrecoverably lost.

See Grant, *Picturesque Canada*, 2:535.

60 Among those individuals who accepted the story of Tecumseh's secret burial was Daniel Wilson, who first heard it from James Dickson in September of 1876. See *Globe*, 29 September 1876, p. 3, col. 3.

61 Hugh Holmes settled on the south bank of the Thames River (lot 23, concession 1, Harwich Township), near modern Kent Bridge, *circa* 1795. See *Commemorative Biographical Record of the County of Kent*, 36.

62 Ibid. For Daniel Holmes's militia record, see LAC, Militia and Defence, First Regiment, Kent Militia (1812–14), Pay Lists and Muster Rolls,

Captain Thomas McCrae's Company, 2–24 July 1812, p. 479, no. 16; ibid., 25 July-26 August 1812, p. 488, no. 4; ibid., Loyal Kent Volunteers, Kent Militia (1813–15), Pay Lists and Muster Rolls, Lieutenant John McGregor's Company, 15–24 December 1813, p. 563, no. 3; ibid., 25 January 1813–24 February 1814, p. 586, no. 2; ibid., 25 February-24 March 1814, p. 598, no. 2; ibid., 25 March-24 April 1814, p. 610, no. 7; ibid., 25 April-24 May 1814, p. 615, no. 27; ibid., Captain John McGregor's Company, 25 May-24 June 1814, p. 625, no. 27; ibid., 25 June-24 July 1814, p. 633, no. 20; ibid., 25 July-24 August 1814, p. 643, no. 16; ibid., 25 August-24 September 1814, p. 651, no. 16; ibid., 25 September-24 October 1814, p. 659, no. 10; ibid., 25 October-24 November 1814, p. 667, no. 10; ibid., 25 November-24 December 1814, p. 673, no. 8.

63 Sugden, *Tecumseh's Last Stand*, 68–9.

64 LAC, Upper Canada Land Petitions, Holmes to Maitland, 13 July 1822, H13 (1821–23), no. 114. See also ibid., Upper Canada Sundries, "Return of the Loyal Kent Volunteers on the late Pension List," 4 Dec. 1816, 14036. According to family tradition, Daniel Holmes also fought at the Battle of Lundy's Lane in July of 1814; however, the serious nature of the wound he received at the Battle of the Longwoods would seem to have precluded that possibility. See *Commemorative Biographical Record of the County of Kent*, 36. For information regarding the Battle of the Long-woods, see Poole, "Fight at Battle Hill," 7–61; Sheik, "Return to Battle Hill," 5–22. In 1820, Daniel Holmes assigned his property in Harwich Township to Abraham Holmes in return for "Sufficient Board, Lodging, meat, drink and wearing apparell Suitable to his Station in Life and in Sickness if necessary provide the Said Daniel with medical assistance if it can be procured and at the death of the said Daniel to cause him to be buried in a decent and Christian like manner." Obviously, Daniel Holmes believed his end was near. Yet, he was still living in July of 1822, when he requested a change in the location of a land grant. See AO, Kent County Copybook of Deeds, Register C, Holmes to Holmes, 2 May 1820, no. 148; LAC, Upper Canada Land Petitions, Holmes to Maitland, 13 July 1822, H13 (1821–23), no. 114.

65 For example, Gowman claimed to have heard one extraordinary story during a quilting bee hosted by his mother in the summer of 1838. "Mrs Polly Arnold [the wife of John Arnold] said that the Yankees stopped at their farm when they returned to Detroit, 'and,' said she, 'when they showed me the strips of Indian skin and said they had skinned Tecumseh's thighs to get razor strops, my Dutch [blood] boiled over, and I expect that I said some pretty rash words, for Col. Johnson cautioned me not to excite the [American] soldiers, for they might shoot me.'" Johnson's intervention seems unlikely, since he was still recuperating from the severe wounds he received at the Battle of the Thames. See *Daily Advertiser*, 25 September 1876, p. 1, col. 6.

66 The first person to recognize that Gowman had based the character of

Duncan Holmes on Joseph Johnson appears to have been Omar K. Watson, a lawyer from Ridgetown, Ontario. In about 1920, Watson acquired Gowman's manuscript from the editor of the Ridgetown *Plaindealer*, who in turn received it from one of Gowman's daughters. After providing the Archives of Ontario with typescript copies, Watson published portions of Gowman's work relating to Tecumseh's death, which he cautiously thought "may be accurate." See UWOA, Goulet Papers, Notes and Accounts on the Death of Tecumseh, Watson to Gemmill, 30 November 1920. See also *London Evening Free Press*, 18 November 1933, p. 8, col. 1; ibid., 23 March 1935, p. 13, col. 2; Watson, "Moraviantown," 126–9, 131; Watson, "Thomas Gowman's Reminiscences," 14–15. According to Abraham Holmes, Johnson was known to have "lived most of his life among the [I]ndians." See WHS, Draper Manuscript Collection, Tecumseh Papers, ser. YY, vol. 7, no. 67, Holmes to Draper, 20 April 1882.

67 Joseph Johnson arrived in what is now Howard Township, Kent County, in 1794. In 1803, he purchased twenty hectares of lot 12 in the first, or front, concession from his brother-in-law, Jacob Quant. He later sold this land in 1807 – although he remained in Howard Township, as he still owned other property there. This property, which he purchased in 1804, was across the Thames River from present-day Kent Bridge, Ontario (lot 1, concession 1). He later sold this lot in 1831. In the meantime, however, Johnson purchased lot 18, concession 14, Dawn Township in 1826, which is located approximately nineteen kilometres to the north, on the Big Bear Creek (now the Sydenham River) near modern Florence, Ontario. Johnson appears to have been living at the Big Bear Creek for some time prior to his purchase of land there. See LAC, Upper Canada Land Petitions, Johnston to Russell, 28 June 1797, J4 (1798), no. 42; KCLR, Abstract Books, Howard Township, con. 1, lots 1, 12; ibid., Instruments, Quant to Johnson, 27 May 1803, no. 42; ibid., Johnson to Julien, 12 March 1807, no. 43; ibid., Ribley to Johnson, 30 March 1804, no. 201; ibid., Johnson to Arnold, 18 July 1831, no. 202; LCLR, Abstract Books, Dawn Township, con. 14, lot 18; AO, Kent County Copybook of Deeds, Register C, Fields to Johnson, 13 July 1826, no. 196.

68 The earliest known newspaper account featuring Johnson's story appeared in 1873, and was contributed by Thomas Scudimore, a teacher from Sutherland's Corners (now Cairo), Euphemia Township, Lambton County, Ontario. Scudimore's source was a "Col. Kerby" of Florence, Ontario, who apparently received the story from Johnson himself. This "Col. Kerby" probably was Colonel George P. Kerby, an early settler of Florence. Scudimore's article, originally published in an issue of the *Chatham Banner* (which no longer exists), was reprinted in the *Sarnia Observer*. See *Sarnia Observer*, 17 October 1873, p. 1, col. 9.

69 In this article, Joseph Johnson is mistakenly referred to as Jacob Johnston. See *Chatham Weekly Planet*, 6 September 1883, p. 3, col. 1. See also *Sarnia Observer*, 17 October 1873, p. 1, col. 9. The unidentified contributor

to the *Chatham Planet* was very likely William K. Merrifield, who years later admitted his desire "to find an account, from Canadian sources, of the battle of the Thames and death of Tecumseh, which would appeal to me and our people generally as more in accordance with fact than the usual highly colored and dramatic account of his death by Colonel Johnson, as related in United States histories." See *Hamilton Spectator*, 10 August 1907, sec. 2, p. 13, col. 1. The account in *Picturesque Canada* was written by a Canadian named J. Howard Hunter of Brantford. See Grant, *Picturesque Canada*, 2:534–6; *London Evening Free Press*, 20 April 1968, sec. 3, p. M9. Although the *Chatham Planet* did not identify its contributor, the individual undoubtedly was William K. Merrifield, a resident of Chatham, Ontario, who in later years would occasionally promote Joseph Johnson's claim. Compare the following: *Chatham Weekly Planet*, 6 September 1883, p. 3, col. 1 with *Daily Planet*, 15 October 1898, p. 7, col. 1.

70 *Chatham Weekly Planet*, 6 September 1883, p. 3, col. 1.

71 Ibid.

72 Ibid. Joseph Johnson is mistakenly referred to as Jacob Johnston.

73 In Gowman's story of Tecumseh's death, the wounded chief dispatches an American officer with his tomahawk before his own death – which is very similar to the earliest known version of Joseph Johnson's account of the same event. See and compare the following: *Free Press*, 30 December 1893, p. 13, col. 3; *Sarnia Observer*, 17 October 1873, p. 1, col. 9.

74 LAC, Upper Canada Land Petitions, Johnson to Simcoe, 23 May 1796, J2 (1796), no. 20.

75 It was Rev. Andrew Jamieson, the Anglican missionary to Walpole Island, who informed Draper about Abraham Holmes. See WHS, Draper Manuscript Collection, Tecumseh Papers, ser. YY, vol. 7, no. 65, Jamieson to Draper, 13 March 1882.

76 Ibid., no. 67, Holmes to Draper, 20 April 1882. Abraham Holmes should not be confused with the novelist Abraham S. Holmes of Chatham, whose father, Ninian Holmes, was a Methodist circuit rider. See Lauriston, *Romantic Kent*, 31, 713. I am grateful to Daniel J. Brock for this clarification.

77 Abraham Holmes went to Arnold's Mill early in the morning of 5 October 1813. See WHS, Draper Manuscript Collection, Tecumseh Papers, ser. YY, vol. 7, no, 67, Holmes to Draper, 20 April 1882. It appears that Joseph Johnson later identified Tecumseh as the Native he conversed with at Arnold's Mill. According to Holmes, Johnson was one of his father's neighbours, and he was known to have "lived most of his life among the [I]ndians and spoke the Shawnee language well." See ibid. In a subsequent recital of this story, Dr Holmes claimed that his father went to see Tecumseh with "some of his companions." See *Chatham Daily Planet*, 19 October 1901, p. 5, col. 4.

78 With regard to his militia service, Joseph Johnson appears to have participated as little as possible in the War of 1812. He first served in Captain Thomas McCrae's second company of the First Regiment of Kent Militia,

from 2 July until 11 July 1812, when he was reported absent with leave. He later served in Captain George Jacob's flank company, First Kent Regiment, for a further three days between 16 September and 18 September 1812. See LAC, Militia and Defence, First Regiment, Kent Militia (1812–14), Pay Lists and Muster Rolls, Captain Thomas McCrae's Company, 2–24 July 1812, p. 479, no. 16; ibid., Captain George Jacob's Company, 25 August-24 September 1812, p. 494, no. 75.

79 WHS, Draper Manuscript Collection, Tecumseh Papers, ser. YY, vol. 7, no. 67, Holmes to Draper, 20 April 1882. The day after the battle, young Abraham Holmes visited the battlefield but discovered only two bodies – neither of which he recognized as Tecumseh. See ibid. The lad probably arrived on the battlefield after most of the bodies had already been buried. See Sugden, *Tecumseh's Last Stand*, 215. Abraham Holmes died on 30 January 1890 at the advanced age of ninety-two years. See AO, Registrar General of Ontario, Death Registrations, 30 January 1890, no. 8015. In his letter of 20 April 1882 to Lyman C. Draper, Dr Holmes noted that his father was born 13 May 1797. See WHS, Draper Manuscript Collection, Tecumseh Papers, ser. YY, vol. 7, no. 67, Holmes to Draper, 20 April 1882.

80 It is quite possible that Johnson's story was influenced by Pheasant or Snake, or both.

81 *Free Press*, 25 October 1893, p. 6, col. 3.

82 Ibid., 15 November 1893, p. 3, col. 4.

83 Ibid., 17 November 1893, p. 6, col. 3.

84 Ibid.

85 Ibid., 25 November 1893, p. 8, col. 3; ibid., 9 December 1893, p. 14, col. 1.

86 Ibid. Gowman considered the Shawnee to be among the most inferior of the northern tribes. See AO, Gowman Papers, "Pioneer Life in Upper Canada," 2:238–40. See also *Free Press*, 9 December 1893, p. 14, col. 1.

87 *Free Press*, 30 December 1893, p. 13, col. 3. This installment was preceded by one that appeared a week earlier. See ibid., 23 December 1893, p. 13, col. 4. In Duncan Holmes, Gowman created a character who, like Joseph Johnson, had been a Native captive in his youth. See AO, Gowman Papers, "Pioneer Life in Upper Canada," 1:61–3.

88 For the earlier version, see *Daily Advertiser*, 25 September 1876, p. 1, col. 6.

89 Gowman occasionally served as bailiff for the Seventh Division Court of Middlesex County. In June of 1860, the clerk of the court ordered him to serve a summons. Gowman was later indicted for perjury when it was alleged that he grossly misrepresented the distance he travelled in performing his duty. Eventually, in September of 1860, the Grand Jury of the Court of Quarter Sessions concluded that the evidence against Gowman was too weak to proceed with the indictment. See UWOA, Middlesex County Court of Quarter Sessions, Criminal Court Records, Queen v. Gowman, indictment, September 1860; ibid., Minute Book (1859–66), 19 September 1860. The damage done to Gowman's reputation might explain his use of an alias when relating his stories about Tecumseh.

90 *Free Press*, 30 January 1894, p. 6, col. 2.

91 In the 1891 census, Nelles F. Timothy is listed as a forty-year-old farmer. See LAC, 1891 Census, Caradoc Township, Middlesex County, Ontario, dis. 92, sub. dis. a, div. 4, p. 19, no. 140. The Caradoc Reserve is now known as the Chippewas of the Thames First Nation.

92 *Free Press*, 30 January 1894, p. 6, col. 2. Timothy drew heavily on William Coffin's *1812; The War, and its Moral*, a then standard work on the War of 1812 and one which Timothy acknowledged as a source of his information. In particular, see Coffin, *1812; The War, and its Moral*, 232–8.

93 *Free Press*, 30 January 1894, p. 6, col. 2. Timothy based his assertion that Tecumseh was a Delaware on Charles Mair's statement that the "tribe from which Tecumseh sprung was a branch of the widespread *Lenni Lenapé*, or Delaware race, which had long been settled in the south; and which, for this reason, received the name of the Shawanoes." See Mair, *Tecumseh: A Drama*, 187. While the Delaware and Shawnee were linguistically connected (through the Algonquian language), Tecumseh was not a Delaware.

94 *Free Press*, 27 January 1894, p. 6, col. 4. Gowman referred to himself variously as Peter Pancrees, Pete Pancrees, and Uncle Pete Pancrees. Curiously, Gowman's reply was published three days before Timothy's offending installment appeared in the *Free Press* of 30 January 1894, suggesting that Gowman was either privy to Timothy's claims well in advance of their going to press or, more likely, that the *Free Press* mixed things up.

95 Ibid., 27 January 1894, p. 6, col. 4.

96 Ibid. Among other aspersions, Gowman remarked that if Snake "had known of Tecumseh's grave, I could have bought the secret for one gallon of whiskey, and that in that day would have cost me nineteen cents."

97 Ibid.

98 Ibid., 3 February 1894, p. 14, col. 1.

99 Timothy found Glegg's description of Tecumseh in Tupper, *Life and Correspondence of Major-General Sir Isaac Brock*, 243. Timothy also made use of a biographical sketch on the life of Tecumseh, which Tupper included in his book. See ibid., 389–96. Tupper, who was a nephew of Brock, published an earlier edition of his book in 1835, which also includes the sketch of the Tecumseh's life. See Tupper, *Family Records*, 188–208. As well, Timothy made use of the notes in Charles Mair's *Tecumseh: A Drama*, which he did not bother to acknowledge. See Mair, *Tecumseh: A Drama*, 187–9. It should be noted that Glegg was one of Brock's aides.

100 Timothy's source is quite obviously Mair's *Tecumseh: A Drama*. For example, compare the following: *Free Press*, 3 February 1894, p. 14, col. 1 and ibid., 10 February 1894, p. 13, col. 3 with Charles Mair, *Tecumseh: A Drama*, 57–71. Michael Friedrichs deserves the credit for recognizing that Timothy found much of his information on Tecumseh in Mair's poem.

101 *Free Press*, 3 February 1894, p. 14, col. 1.

102 Ibid., 10 February 1894, p. 13, col. 3.

103 Ibid., 24 February 1894, p. 13, col. 3.

104 Ibid.

105 Ibid. John Sugden, for one, provides ample evidence that Tecumseh did in fact attend a meeting with Harrison at Vincennes in August of 1810. See Sugden, *Tecumseh: A Life*, 198–202. Gowman mistakenly thought that this meeting had taken place on 6 November 1811, the day before the Battle of Tippecanoe. Although Gowman was correct about the date of the battle, which was fought while Tecumseh was absent, the council he refers to was actually the second one between Tecumseh and Harrison, and it was held at Vincennes in August of 1811 – not November of 1811. Once it was concluded, Tecumseh set out for the south in order to recruit Native allies. See ibid., 221–36.

106 *Free Press*, 24 February 1894, p. 13, col. 3.

107 Ibid., 3 March 1894, p. 12, col. 3. In Mair's original version, Tecumseh's parting eloquence reads as follows: "Yes, I am shot. Recall some warriors to bear my body hence. Give no alarm, lest our poor braves lose courage; but make haste – I have not long to live. Yet hear my words! Bury me in the deep and densest forest, and let no white man know where I am laid. Promise this ere you go." See Mair, *Tecumseh: A Drama*, 182. Mair, however, did not let Tecumseh go to his reward after just these few utterances, but rather forced him to continue despairing for his people until he finally expired. Timothy incorporated this passage into his own work as well. See Mair, *Tecumseh: A Drama*, 182–3; *Free Press*, 3 March 1894, p. 12, col. 3.

108 *Free Press*, 3 March 1894, p. 12, col. 3.

109 Ibid., 17 March 1894, p. 12, col. 5. Elsewhere in his response, Timothy demanded to know: "Which is your right name of the two, Pete Pancrees, or Wau-pis-skunk?" Of course, the latter name was a corruption of Duncan Holmes's Native name of Waubishkink.

110 Ibid. In his last letter to the editor of the *Free Press*, Gowman admitted to telling "yarns." See ibid., 24 February 1894, p. 13, col. 3.

111 Ibid., 17 March 1894, p. 12, col. 5.

112 *Glencoe Transcript*, 26 May 1898, p. 8, col. 3.

CHAPTER FOUR

1 *Free Press*, 17 March 1894, p. 12, col. 5.

2 *Chatham Daily Planet*, 23 August 1901, p. 5, col. 3. Sulman was a "wall paper, stationery and fancy goods" merchant. See *Commemorative Biographical Record of the County of Kent*, 69–70.

3 *Chatham Daily Planet*, 23 August 1901, p. 5, col. 3. Sulman no doubt shared the opinion of Thomas Scullard, a Chatham barrister, who argued that "this district, and especially that part of the County of Kent lying adjacent to the River Thames, should have some monument [to Tecumseh],

because it was through this country that the retreat [of the British and Natives] was made." See ibid., 8 October 1901, p. 1, col. 7. Scullard also alluded to Chatham's importance as the site of a skirmish between Tecumseh's warriors and the advancing American army. For more information on this skirmish, see Sugden, *Tecumseh's Last Stand*, 86–7.

4 Sulman was mayor of Chatham in 1901 and 1902. See *Commemorative Biographical Record of the County of Kent*, 69–70. With regard to the Macaulay Club's support for a monument to Tecumseh, see *Chatham Daily Planet*, 4 October 1901, p. 1, col. 4; ibid., 17 October 1901, p. 1, col. 6. The Macaulays planned to erect a bronze statue of Tecumseh on the old military reserve, which is now Tecumseh Park. According to Victor Lauriston, Kent County's most notable historian, the Macaulay Club had its origins in 1883 with a series of weekly debates named in honour of Thomas Babington, first Baron Macaulay, the famous nineteenth-century English Whig politician, essayist, poet, and historian. See Lauriston, *Romantic Kent*, 532. Thaddeus Arnold, of Toronto, was an inspector with the British American Assurance Company. See *Toronto City Directory, 1901*, 273.

5 *Chatham Daily Planet*, 26 October 1901, p. 7, col. 1. See also Sugden, *Tecumseh's Last Stand*, 98–9. Christopher Arnold's Mill was located on lot 3 in the broken front of Howard Township, which was across the river and a short distance upstream from what is now Kent Bridge, Ontario. See Hamil, *Valley of the Lower Thames*, 60.

6 Thaddeus Arnold's father was Frederick Arnold. See *Chatham Daily Planet*, 26 October 1901, p. 7, col. 1.

7 Arnold's article was a by-product of the genealogical research he undertook in order to qualify as a member of the hereditary United Empire Loyalist Association. See ibid., 4 September 1902, p. 1, col. 4. Arnold's article was published in the *Annual Transactions* of the United Empire Loyalist Association for 1903, but it first appeared in the *Chatham Planet* toward the end of October 1901. See Arnold, "Battle of the Thames and Death of Tecumseh," 30–5; *Chatham Daily Planet*, 26 October 1901, p. 7, col. 1.

8 *Chatham Daily Planet*, 26 October 1901, p. 7, col. 1.

9 Joseph Johnson is known to have had at least two sons and one daughter. His namesake was identified by Albert Greenwood, whose family lived near Johnson in the Gore of Camden Township. Joseph Johnson junior lived in Camden and eventually retired to Dresden, Ontario, where he died in 1892. See LAC, 1861 Census, Camden Township, Kent County, Ontario, dis. 2, p. 29, no. 21; ibid., 1871 Census, Camden Township, dis. 3, sub. dis. C, div. 2, p. 6, no. 25; ibid., 1881 Census, Dresden, Ontario, dis. 178, sub. dis. J, div. 2, p. 32, no. 174; ibid., 1891 Census, Dresden, Ontario, dis. 47, sub. dis. Dresden, div. 1, p. 21, no. 109; AO, Registrar General of Ontario, Death Registrations, 18 July 1892, no. 7783. Another son was Levi Johnson, who lived in the Gore of Camden Township with a large family. In 1853, Levi Johnson petitioned for land, noting that his father

had "served in the War of 1812–1814, also that at a very early period he was captured by and lived many years among the Indians." See LAC, Upper Canada Land Petitions, Johnson to Administrator of Government of Canada, 28 October 1853, C8, pt. 1 (1855–57), no. 31j. A daughter, Ruth Johnson, married Captain William Caldwell junior of Malden Township near Amherstburg, Ontario, in 1822. See London Roman Catholic Diocese Archives, St John the Baptist Church, Amherstburg, Ontario, parish registers (1802–29), folio 69.

10 Lauriston, *Romantic Kent*, 532. Merrifield was best known as the manufacturer of the "Veteran's Sure Cure," which he named in reference to his military service in the Union army during the American Civil War. See *Vernon's City of Chatham Directory for the Year 1908*, 106. For an interesting account of Merrifield's Civil War experiences, see *London Advertiser*, evening ed., 3 August 1915, p. 2, col. 5.

11 *Chatham Daily Planet*, 3 Mar 1902, p. 3, col. 1.

12 Ibid., 15 October 1901, p. 8, col. 3; ibid., 16 October 1901, p. 1, col. 6.

13 *Free Press*, 4 June 1907, p. 1, col. 7.

14 Ibid.

15 Ibid.

16 *Hamilton Spectator*, 8 June 1907, p. 6, col. 4.

17 Ibid., 27 July 1907, p. 12, col. 1.

18 *Chatham Daily Planet*, 3 August 1907, p. 3, col. 1.

19 Merrifield appears to have been motivated, long after the fact, by Thaddeus Arnold's appropriation of Andrew Fleming's remarks regarding the flaying of Tecumseh's body. According to Merrifield,

> my old friend, T.S. Arnold, did not give me credit for publishing Mr Fleming's statement, as it was to me that he said: 'The Yankees were skinning a stout Indian, and when I asked them what they were doing that for, they replied that they were skinning Tecumseh for razor strops. And when I told them that that was not Tecumseh (as I knew him, he having been at my father's place) they laughed and said the people in Kentucky would not know the difference.' Mr Fleming was a friend of my people; his son is now treasurer of the county of Kent. I feel sure Mr Arnold never spoke to him on the subject; but I lent Mr Arnold my letters.

See *Hamilton Spectator*, 10 August 1907, sec. 2, p. 13, col. 1. Although Merrifield referred to the Fleming story as early as 1898, he was not the first person to go public with it. A school teacher by the name of Thomas Scudimore published Fleming's reminiscences in 1873. See *Daily Planet*, 15 October 1898, p. 7, col. 1; *Sarnia Observer*, 17 October 1873, p. 1, col. 9. In his article, Scudimore suggests that he received some of his information from Andrew Fleming's son, James C. Fleming. See *Chatham Daily News*, 7 April 1923, p. 4, col. 4; see also *Thamesville Herald*, 3 July 1924, p. 3, col. 5. Regarding the Flemings, see *Commemorative Biographical Record of the County of Kent*, 134–5. In sending a copy of his letter to the *Chatham Planet*, Merrifield elaborated on the remarks of E.D. Marshall of Hamilton, who pointed out that Thaddeus Arnold's grandfather could not have known how Tecumseh was killed, as he was not a participant in the Battle of the Thames. Merrifield did not give Marshall credit for this observation. See *Hamilton Spectator*, 2 August 1907, p. 6, col. 2; *Chatham Daily Planet*, 31 August 1907, p. 9, col. 1.

20 *Hamilton Spectator*, 10 August 1907, sec. 2, p. 13, col. 1.

21 *Daily Witness*, 28 September 1889, p. 6, col. 1; see also *Chatham Tri-Weekly Planet*, 4 November 1889, p. 1, col. 4. Although she was described as a school girl, Abigail Smith was born 14 March 1870; thus, she was eighteen years old at the time her essay was published in 1889. See AO, Registrar General of Ontario, Birth and Stillbirth Registrations, 14 March 1870, no. 7044. See also LAC, 1891 Census, Harwich Township, Kent County, Ontario, dis. 79, sub. dis. D, div. 1, p. 35, no. 163. Abigail Smith was a daughter of James Smith.

22 *Daily Witness*, 28 September 1889, p. 6, col. 1. See also *Chatham Tri-Weekly Planet*, 4 November 1889, p. 1, col. 4.

23 *Daily Witness*, 28 September 1889, p. 6, col. 1. See also *Sea, Forest, and Prairie*, 233; *Chatham Tri-Weekly Planet*, 4 November 1889, p. 1, col. 4. Abigail does not specify whether the stream was a creek or the Thames River, which left the question open to interpretation. Soon after, however, she doubted "very much if Tecumseh's bones bleach on the banks of the Thames." See *Daily Witness*, 9 November 1889, p. 6, col. 1.

24 *Daily Witness*, 28 September 1889, p. 6, col. 1; *Chatham Tri-Weekly Planet*, 4 November 1889, p. 1, col. 4. See also *Sea, Forest, and Prairie*, 227–34.

25 Abigail drew inspiration from whatever history books were available to her. One of these books was probably John Frost's *Thrilling Adventures Among the Indians*, in which a surveyor's chance meeting with Tecumseh in Ohio is suspiciously similar to that of Joseph Brenton's in southwestern Ontario. Compare the following: Frost, *Thrilling Adventures Among the Indians*, 187–90 with *Sea, Forest, and Prairie*, 227–9. I am grateful to Michael Friedrichs for alerting me to Abigail's obvious plagiarism.

26 *Daily Witness*, 9 November 1889, p. 6, col. 1. According to Abigail, it was "said by this old Indian [Timothy Snake] that, after the war, he, with four others of the original seven, exhumed the body and reburied it, but he would not disclose the place, although offered a large sum of money to do so." Abigail thought the second burial might have taken place on the lower Ohio River. As for her information regarding the Battle of the Thames, Abigail claimed that her "description of the lay of the land, plan of battle and manner of Tecumseh's death, are strictly accurate" because she "followed the Indian traditions."

27 Regarding the contest rules, see ibid., 2 November 1889, p. 6, col. 1.

28 Consider the following: Merrifield's recital of Johnson's story, dating from 1898, does not include the streambed burial – despite the fact that Abigail Smith's essay describing the preparation of Tecumseh's watery grave had

already been published in an 1889 issue of the *Chatham Planet*, and also in the anthology *Sea, Forest, and Prairie*, which came out in 1893. Merrifield does not appear to have known about the streambed burial until well after Abigail's essay was published, indicating that Johnson's story regarding Tecumseh's burial did not include a stream. See *Daily Planet*, 15 October 1898, p. 7, col. 1; *Chatham Tri-Weekly Planet*, 4 November 1889, p. 1, col. 4; *Sea, Forest, and Prairie*, 233. It is interesting to note that Thomas Gowman did not mention a streambed burial in any of his elaborations on Johnson's story – nor did Albert Tobias in relating Timothy Snake's account of the secret burial. See *Daily Advertiser*, 25 September 1876, p. 1, col. 6; *Free Press*, 30 December 1893, p. 13, col. 3; *Herald*, 18 September 1913, p. 1, col. 3; *Globe*, 12 April 1921, p. 9, col. 5.

29 *Daily Planet*, 12 October 1898, p. 8, col. 4. Mrs Laird's father-in-law, George Laird, died in May of 1879. While his obituary does not refer to Tecumseh's burial, it does describe the capture of an American soldier. See *Bothwell Times*, 22 May 1879, p. 3, col. 6. "As soon as the country was free from the American soldiers," Mrs Laird explained, "Tecumseh's band came back, raised their dead chief and carried his body away. No one but the Indians know where, and they are all dead. They kept the secret and kept it well." See *Daily Planet*, 12 October 1898, p. 8, col. 4. It should be noted that Mrs Laird, the former Sarah Ann Ward, was married to John Laird. See *Commemorative Biographical Record of the County of Kent*, 380.

30 The drummer boy was supposedly bribed to commit the crime, and Mrs Laird claimed to have seen the article describing Tecumseh's assassination some five or six years earlier in *Harper's Bazar*. See *Daily Planet*, 12 October 1898, p. 8, col. 4. A search of *Harper's Bazar* failed to produce the article in question.

31 Ibid. William A. Edwards, a regular contributor of historical articles to the *London Free Press* in the 1920s and 1930s, blamed General Procter's wife for Tecumseh's death and the defeat of the British at the Battle of the Thames. According to Edwards, Mrs Procter's scorned advances toward Tecumseh were discovered during the British retreat. She reacted by laying blame with the chief. Procter took his revenge at the Battle of the Thames, where he deserted Tecumseh to his fate and at the expense of British military honour. Although Edwards credits this ridiculous story to a "venerable chief of the Oneidas," it was likely a fiction of his own creation. For the article and its reprint, see *London Evening Free Press*, 28 April 1928, p. 8, col. 1; ibid., 21 February 1931, p. 8, col. 5.

32 George Laird served in Captain George Jacob's Third Company of the First Regiment of Kent Militia from 2 July 1812 until 8 July 1812, when he was absent with leave, and then from 18 August 1812 until 3 September 1812, when he was discharged. He later served in Captain John Dolsen's Company from 20 January 1813 until 24 January 1813. Although Laird's name does not appear in subsequent militia rolls, Dolsen later attested that Laird had served in his company until 24 April 1813.

See LAC, Militia and Defence, First Regiment, Kent Militia (1812–14), Pay Lists and Muster Rolls, Captain George Jacob's Company, 2–24 July 1812, p. 481, no. 15; ibid., 25 July-24 August 1812, p. 489, no. 35; ibid., 25 August-24 September 1812, p. 493, no. 49; ibid., Captain John Dolsen's Company, 20–24 January 1813, p. 463, no. 35; ibid., Upper Canada Land Petitions, Laird to Maitland, 26 August 1825, L14 (1825), certificate of militia service, no. 94a. While it is doubtful that Laird participated in the Battle of the Thames, he might have assisted the retreating British as a citizen volunteer – although this, too, seems doubtful.

33 *Hamilton Spectator*, daily ed., 10 August 1907, sec. 2, p. 13, col. 1; *Daily Planet*, 12 October 1898, p. 8, col. 4.

34 After petitioning for a grant of land in August of 1825, Laird received the east half of lot 1, concession 6, Dawn Township, now the Gore of Camden Township. In 1829, however, he purchased the east half of lot 14 in the 13th concession and the west half of lot 14 in the 14th concession of Dawn. This relocation placed him within a few lots of Joseph Johnson. Prior to his move to Dawn Township, Laird resided in Raleigh Township. See LAC, Upper Canada Land Petitions, Laird to Maitland, 26 August 1825, L14 (1825), no. 94; AO, Land Record Index, Alphabetical Listing, 6834; LCLR, Abstract Books, Dawn Township, con. 13, lot 14; ibid., con. 14, lot 14.

35 Information regarding Wentworth J. Laird's employment with the *Chatham Planet* can be found in his obituary. See *Chatham Tri-Weekly Planet*, 4 November 1889, p. 1, col. 4. For the reprint of Abigail's essay, see *Daily Planet*, 15 December 1898, p. 8, col. 4.

36 When Professor Wilson conducted his investigation of the United Canadians' discovery in 1876, he questioned George Laird as to what he knew about Tecumseh's burial. Laird had little to say, except that he had concealed Procter's wife and daughter in a canoe under some bushes along the riverbank. Wilson, who somehow mistook Laird for a Native, considered his statement of service during the Battle of the Thames as "improbable." See *Globe*, 29 September 1876, p. 3, col. 3. Earlier, in October of 1875, during a ceremony held in Chatham to honour the surviving militiamen of Kent County, Laird made no mention of either Tecumseh or Mrs Procter. However, he did claim to have participated in the "battles of Maumee [January 1813] and Fort [Meigs] [May 1813]," which seems possible – even if his militia record does not exactly correspond with his recollections. See *Chatham Tri-Weekly Planet*, 11 October 1875, p. 2, col. 1; LAC, Militia and Defence, First Regiment, Kent Militia (1812–14), Pay Lists and Muster Rolls, Captain George Jacob's Company, 2–24 July 1812, p. 481, no. 15; ibid., 25 July-24 August 1812, p. 489, no. 35; ibid., 25 August-24 September 1812, p. 493, no. 49; ibid., Captain John Dolsen's Company, 20–24 January 1813, p. 463, no. 35. Laird's name does not appear in subsequent militia rolls, although Dolsen later attested that he served in his company until 24 April 1813. See LAC, Upper Canada Land Petitions, Laird to Maitland, 26 August 1825, L14 (1825), certificate of militia service, no. 94a.

37 It would appear that the stories told by Abigail Smith and Sarah Ann Laird prompted Merrifield to revise Johnson's story. See *Hamilton Spectator*, 10 August 1907, sec. 2, p. 13, col. 1. Merrifield repeated this exercise in the *Chatham Planet* a short time later. See *Chatham Daily Planet*, 31 August 1907, p. 9, col. 1.

38 *Hamilton Spectator*, daily ed., 10 August 1907, sec. 2, p. 13, col. 1

39 *Chatham Daily Planet*, 23 October 1907, p. 8, col. 4. Augusta D. Richardson was married to Charles W. Richardson, a farmer and "stock raiser" of Howard Township, who had been a newspaper editor and publisher in his younger days. Mrs Richardson was a former school teacher and a member of the Canadian Society of Authors. See *Commemorative Biographical Record of the County of Kent*, 256–8.

40 *Globe*, Saturday Magazine Section, 4 January 1908, p. 3, col. 1.

41 Ibid. Mrs Richardson was convinced that Colonel Richard M. Johnson was Tecumseh's killer. The source of her information was a descendant of Dr John Croley Richardson (not to be confused with the Canadian author Major John Richardson). According to this descendant, Dr Richardson was not far from Colonel Johnson at the Battle of the Thames. At one point in the action, as Dr Richardson was reloading his gun, Johnson called out in rather wordy fashion: "Doctor, observe that black devil. How desperately he is fighting. Hand me your gun. I can see him better than you, and can hit him from where I sit." Richardson complied and, watching intently, witnessed Johnson aim deliberately, fire, "and Tecumseh (as it was afterwards discovered to be) fell." Although Dr Richardson was convinced that Johnson had killed Tecumseh, he acknowledged that "some other shot simultaneously fired with that of Col. Johnson might have killed him, and that Col. Johnson believed and had expressed the same opinion several times in his hearing." See ibid. While Dr Richardson's story cannot be verified, his participation in the Battle of the Thames can be confirmed. See Young, *Battle of the Thames*, 256. As for Gottlieb Tobias, he was Albert Tobias's father. Mrs Richardson's conversation with the senior Tobias must have taken place sometime prior to his death, which occurred in November of 1904. See *Bothwell Times*, 1 December 1904, p. 8, col. 2.

42 *Globe*, Saturday Magazine Section, 4 January 1908, p. 3, col. 1. Snake's fear of ghosts would not necessarily have constrained him from misleading the occasional white into believing that some old grave or collection of bones belonged to his putative uncle. As for Tobias's remark that the government offered Snake "heaps of money to tell where Tecumseh was buried," the author was unable to find evidence that such an incentive was ever offered. With regard to the places Tobias mentioned, Turin was a small village not far to the south of Moraviantown, while "T'emsville" refers to Thamesville, Ontario.

43 Ibid. There is evidence to corroborate Mrs Richardson's claim that a fire had raced through the battlefield. In 1830, an American visitor observed that the undergrowth of the battlefield had "been scorched by some recent,

casual fire running thro the woods." See ISL, Journal of Daniel R. Dunihue, 1830, 2–3. Mrs Richardson may have learned of the fire from Gottlieb Tobias.

44 *Globe*, Saturday Magazine Section, 4 January 1908, p. 3, col. 1.

45 Ibid., 2 May 1908, p. 4, col. 4.

46 Ibid.

47 Ibid. Greenwood wrote from Elmhurst, California.

48 Ibid. Of course, Greenwood was referring to the impressive Brock Monument on Queenston Heights. Also, it would appear that Greenwood gave the Canadian government far more credit for knowing what had happened to Tecumseh's body than it deserved.

49 Ibid.

50 Ibid.

51 Perhaps if Greenwood's letter had been reprinted in the Chatham *Planet*, as was the case with Mrs Richardson's article, it might have met with greater interest from those individuals in southwestern Ontario who desired a monument to Tecumseh. For Mrs Richardson's reprinted article, see *Planet*, 11 January 1908, p. 8, col. 2.

52 Ibid., 4 February 1909, p. 1, col. 3.

53 Ibid. Evelyn Johnson was born 22 September 1856. Although she was christened Helen Charlotte Eliza Johnson, she went by the name Evelyn Johnson. See Johnston, *Buckskin and Broadcloth*, 47.

54 *Planet*, 23 July 1909, p. 1, col. 3. Miss Johnson's subscription was deposited with Walter Wright, a prominent hat manufacturer and treasurer of the Canadian Club in London, Ontario. See Brant Historical Society, Johnson Papers, Wright to Johnson, 15 September 1910. Wright subsequently held that the monument should be erected at the forks of the Thames in London. See *London Advertiser*, 12 July 1909, p. 1, col. 3.

55 Johnston, *Buckskin and Broadcloth*, 22–4, 47. Sibling rivalry probably also played a part in Evelyn Johnson's determination to see a monument raised in Tecumseh's honour. A telling incident occurred years later, in 1922, when it was suggested that the money Evelyn intended for the Tecumseh monument might be used to defray the cost of a memorial to her famous sister in Vancouver's Stanley Park. Evelyn was not the least bit interested, and let it be known in no uncertain terms. See UWOA, Johnson Papers, Wright to Johnson, 20 March 1922; ibid., Johnson to Wright, 4 April 1922.

56 *Herald*, 15 July 1909, p. 1, col. 6.

57 *Free Press*, 23 July 1909, p. 4, col. 3.

58 Ibid.

59 *Planet*, 24 July 1909, p. 1, col. 3.

60 Ibid., 17 August 1909, p. 1, col. 1.

61 *Chatham Daily News*, 4 January 1910, p. 5, col. 3; ibid., 24 January 1910, p. 1, col. 1.

62 Ibid., 24 January 1910, p. 1, col. 1. The story Greenwood often repeated

about Joseph Johnson's refusal to reveal the place of Tecumseh's burial involved Sir Edmund Walker Head, who was governor general of British North America from 1854 to 1861. See *Globe*, Saturday Magazine Section, 2 May 1908, p. 4, col. 4; *Herald*, 26 August 1909, p. 1, col. 4; *Chatham Daily News*, 28 April 1910, p. 1, col. 3. The author was unable to find any evidence of this incident.

63 *Wallaceburg News*, 14 April 1910, p. 3, col. 3.

64 Ibid.

65 In support of his uncle, Fisher claimed that the aide-de-camp "seemed to delight" in relating his experiences at the Battle of the Thames where he boasted having been "next in command to Tecumseh." See ibid.

66 Ibid. According to Fisher, his uncle replaced the stake with a cross.

67 St Anne's Island was considered an ideal place for Tecumseh's burial, as it was remote and superstitious Natives thought it to be haunted. The occasional spontaneous combustion of swamp gases reinforced this belief. See Mann, *History of Wallaceburg and Vicinity*, 66. It was later claimed that Tecumseh's bones were buried at Tilbury and/or Wardsville before they were removed to St Anne's Island. See, for example, *Sarnia Canadian Observer*, 19 January 1931, p. 1, col. 3; Mann, *History of Wallaceburg and Vicinity*, 66.

68 The tracts comprising Walpole Island were populated by Chippewa, Potawatomi, and Ottawa peoples. See *Sarnia Observer*, 22 July 1864, p. 1, col. 6. Regarding the Fisher farm, see *Wallaceburg News*, 14 April 1910, p. 3, col. 3. This farm, consisting of lot 5 in the first concession of the Gore of Chatham Township, was settled by Charles Fisher *circa* 1809. See LAC, Upper Canada Land Petitions, Fisher to Smith, 22 May 1820, F12 (1820), no. 159. John Fisher grew up on the family farm, which eventually passed to his brother, James. Although John moved to the nearby forks of the Sydenham River, now the centre of Wallaceburg, Ontario, he continued to be a regular visitor to the old homestead. John Fisher died in 1907. For his obituary, see *Wallaceburg News*, 23 May 1907, p. 9, col. 3. Matthew Fisher was a son of James Fisher and was born at the home farm in 1845. For his obituary, see ibid., 10 January 1929, p. 2, col. 3.

69 John Fisher's father was Charles Fisher, a discharged sergeant from the Queen's Rangers. In his petition for land, Charles Fisher states that he was "married to a Woman of the Shawnese Nation of Indians, by whom he has seven children." See LAC, Upper Canada Land Petitions, Fisher to Smith, 22 May 1820, F12 (1820), no. 159.

70 *Wallaceburg News*, 14 April 1910, p. 3, col. 3.

71 This report was picked up by the *London Free Press*, and it was through this newspaper that Greenwood learned of Fisher's presentation to the Wallaceburg Board of Trade. See *London Free Press*, 18 April 1910, p. 4, col. 3; *Evening Free Press*, 27 April 1910, p. 4, col. 3.

72 *Evening Free Press*, 27 April 1910, p. 4, col. 3. According to John Sugden, the British force at the Battle of the Thames amounted to 450 men, which

was augmented by 500 Native warriors under Tecumseh. The Americans numbered 3,000, including their own Native allies. See Sugden, *Tecumseh's Last Stand*, 108–10.

73 *Evening Free Press*, 27 April 1910, p. 4, col. 3.

74 Ibid.

75 *Wallaceburg News*, 12 May 1910, p. 7, col. 3.

76 Ibid. The news of Greenwood's support for Chatham no doubt came in the form of a short article Fisher saw in the *Chatham Daily News*. See *Chatham Daily News*, 4 January 1910, p. 5, col. 3. The "important discovery" concerning Tecumseh's grave very likely was the grave itself. According to the late Frank Mann, who was Wallaceburg's well-known historian for many years, he was a teenaged boy in 1910 when he learned of the grave on St Anne's Island. He and a friend, James Fisher, were told about it by an elderly member of Matthew Fisher's family, who was simply identified as "Grandfather Fisher." With this information, the two teenaged boys were soon on their way to investigate the grave, which they found marked by a "wooden cross and staff." As Mann further related, word of their find prompted Dr Mitchell and a group of local men to mount their expedition in search of Tecumseh's bones. Although the boys were not in fact responsible for instigating the St Anne's exhumation, they might very well have provided Matthew Fisher with his first solid evidence of the grave's existence and thus the "important discovery." See Mann, *History of Wallaceburg and Vicinity*, 67.

77 *Wallaceburg News*, 14 April 1910, p. 3, col. 3.

78 Ibid., 12 May 1910, p. 7, col. 3.

79 Ibid. Greenwood insisted that the name of the aide-de-camp, or "old Indian" as he called him, was "as familiar to Mr Fisher as to myself." Yet, Greenwood did not identify the Native in question. See *Evening Free Press*, 27 April 1910, p. 4, col. 3.

80 *Wallaceburg News*, 12 May 1910, p. 7, col. 3.

81 As John Sugden observes, Sha-wah-wan-noo or Oshahwahnoo was "probably a fairly young warrior of no great status in 1813." Also according to Sugden, Oshahwahnoo was erroneously named by Benson J. Lossing as Tecumseh's second-in-command at the Battle of the Thames. The source of Lossing's information might have been Chief George H.M. Johnson of the Six Nations Reserve near Brantford, Ontario. The claim that Oshahwahnoo was Tecumseh's aide-de-camp appears to have originated with John Richardson, who visited Walpole Island in 1848. Richardson probably relied on some ill-informed local resident for this description, as Oshahwahnoo did not refer to himself as Tecumseh's aide-de-camp. See Sugden, *Tecumseh's Last Stand*, 218, 256; Lossing, *Pictorial Field-Book of the War of 1812*, 551; [Richardson], "Trip to Walpole Island and Port Sarnia," 17–18. Richardson's account was later reprinted in book form. See Colquhoun, *Tecumseh and Richardson*.

82 Rev. Andrew Jamieson, the Anglican missionary to Walpole Island, reported that "Ooshawunoo" died on 23 September 1870. See LAC, Indian Affairs, Deputy Superintendent General's Correspondence (1869–70), no. J124, Jamieson to Spragge, 27 September 1870, 485–6.

83 The date of the expedition to St Anne's Island was 2 June 1910. See *Wallaceburg News*, 2 June 1910, p. 1, col. 1. According to a subsequent newspaper report, it was raining when the launch reached St Anne's Island. See ibid., 9 June 1910, p. 5, col. 3. The members from the board of trade were Dr George Mitchell, John Gibb, and Hy Smith. They were accompanied by Will Colwell, Roy Taylor, John Taylor, Isaac Arnold, and a Mr Johnson. At St Anne's Island, they were met by Matthew Fisher, George Arnold, a man named St Pierre, Joseph Fisher, Byron Fisher, Lightning Dodge (the Walpole Island police constable), William Sands, Edward Jackson, Elliott Jackson, Peter Henry, Dan Chawme, and several boys. See ibid., 2 June 1910, p. 1, col. 1. According to another source, Charles Chubb also participated. See *Planet*, 3 June 1910, p. 6, col. 4.

84 *Wallaceburg News*, 9 June 1910, p. 5, col. 3. The flag was an early version of the Red Ensign. See ibid., 14 April 1910, p. 3, col. 3.

85 Ibid., 2 June 1910, p. 1, col. 1. See also ibid., 9 June 1910, p. 5, col. 3. According to the *Wallaceburg News*, "a small box, oak or pine, 12 inches wide, 2½ feet long and 8 inches deep was found. The box was partially decomposed, but was plainly [discernible]." See ibid., 2 June 1910, p. 1, col. 1.

86 Ibid. 9 June 1910, p. 5, col. 3. See also ibid., 2 June 1910, p. 1, col. 1. Dr Mitchell was equally prominent in Wallaceburg, where he lived until his death in 1914. For his obituary, see ibid., 8 October 1914, p. 5, col. 1.

87 Ibid., 9 June 1910, p. 5, col. 3. See also ibid., 2 June 1910, p. 1, col. 1.

CHAPTER FIVE

1 *Chatham Daily News*, 4 June 1910, p. 1, col. 5. See also *Wallaceburg News*, 9 June 1910, p. 5, col. 3. The *Wallaceburg News* was published on a weekly basis, which explains the delay in its coverage of Dr Mitchell's report to the board of trade.

2 *Globe*, 6 June 1910, p. 1, col. 7. Joseph White was a Chippewa chief. He was accompanied to Dr Mitchell's house by Johnston Peters and William Sands. See *Border Cities Star*, 26 February 1931, sec. 2, p. 5, col. 1. The doctor tried to dissuade the chief by expressing his concern for the security of the skeleton, but Chief White assured him that the remains "would be guarded with every care, and would be forthcoming when the authorities wanted them." See *Globe*, 6 June 1910, p. 1, col. 7.

3 *Advance*, 9 June 1910, p. 8, col. 3. Scullard described the exhumation as "a shocking piece of bad taste."

4 *Chatham Daily News*, 6 June 1910, p. 1, col. 1.

5 The Chatham *Planet* predicted that the indignation of many historical

societies should "be somewhat appeased by the news that the bones have been given over to the Indians to be replaced in their former resting place." See *Planet*, 6 June 1910, p. 1, col. 6.

6 Dundas claimed to have the evidence, but declined to produce it. See *Chatham Daily News*, 6 June 1910, p. 1, col. 1.

7 Ibid. Gurd was noncommittal regarding the place of Tecumseh's burial, as evidenced in his subsequent biography of the chief. See Gurd, *Story of Tecumseh*, 176–7, 183–4. He was also undecided as to the best place for Tecumseh's monument. In March of 1910, he favoured London, Ontario. But by August of 1912, well after the collapse of the Wallaceburg monument scheme, he threw his support behind Chatham. See *Planet*, 23 March 1910, p. 1, col. 1; ibid., 9 August 1912, p. 1, col. 3. Gurd maintained a keen interest in local Native affairs until his death in 1943, at the age of seventy-two. See *Sarnia Canadian Observer*, 16 July 1943, p. 1, col. 1. For additional information on Norman Gurd, see *Commemorative Biographical Record of the County of Lambton*, 485–7.

8 *Evening Free Press*, 9 June 1910, p. 4, col. 4.

9 Ibid.

10 Ibid.

11 According to Tobias, Tecumseh "was buried temporarily by his comrades, and a few days after the battle three Shawnee warriors came back to reinter their dead chief and relative. One of these same three men lies in our own cemetery, and from him I have gained my knowledge and particulars of the interment of the great chief. This same Shawnee Indian whose bones are in our graveyard often would give graphic accounts of the Battle of Moraviantown, but was ever and always consistently true and loyal to the solemn covenant which he and the other two made, viz.: 'Never to tell or show where the grave is.'" See ibid. Tobias later identified Timothy Snake as the source of his information. See *Herald*, 18 September 1913, p. 1, col. 3; *Globe*, 12 April 1921, p. 9, col. 5. It will be remembered that Albert Tobias's father, Gottlieb Tobias, also cited Snake as his informant. See *Globe*, Saturday Magazine Section, 4 January 1908, p. 3, col. 1.

12 *Herald*, 16 June 1910, p. 1, col. 5. Davies, whose son went on to become a Canadian writer of great renown, was equally suspicious of discoveries made near the battlefield. "From time to time," Robertson Davies later recalled, "skeletons would appear in fields in that area which enthusiasts were certain must be the bones of Tecumseh. I remember my father's scepticism when one of these skeletons included a brass collar button which he felt was unlikely to be part of Tecumseh's war equipment." In Davies to St-Denis, 2 August 1995.

13 *Planet*, 15 June 1910, p. 1, col. 1. Albert Greenwood made his last visit to what he believed was Tecumseh's grave in 1894. See LR, Gurd Papers, Greenwood to Leonhardt, 9 February 1911.

14 *Herald*, 14 July 1910, p. 1, col. 6.

15 Greenwood remembered that a Native by the name of Tobias was pointed out to him as one of Tecumseh's burial party. But in his haste to refute

Wallaceburg's claim, Greenwood probably mistook Albert Tobias for his father, Gottlieb Tobias – neither of whom professed to know the exact location of Tecumseh's grave. Albert and Gottlieb Tobias got their information from Timothy Snake. Whether or not Greenwood was aware of this fact, he still made good use of the Tobias name. See ibid. He later dismissed the possibility of any Tobias involvement in Tecumseh's burial. See LR, Gurd Papers, Greenwood to Leonhardt, 12 September 1912.

16 Leonhardt lived on a farm north of Wallaceburg, at Thornyhurst, Ontario.

17 LR, Gurd Papers, Leonhardt to Boyce, 20 December 1910.

18 Leonhardt thought the incident in the dark bend occurred about twenty-eight years earlier, or *circa* 1882. However, Oshahwahnoo was already dead by that time, having died in 1870. Perhaps Oshahwahnoo's tradition was carried on by other Natives. See ibid. See also LAC, Indian Affairs, Deputy Superintendent General's Correspondence (1869–70), no. J124, Jamieson to Spragge, 27 September 1870, 485–6. The letter Leonhardt sent to Greenwood regarding the unusual occurrence in the dark bend does not appear to have survived. However, for Greenwood's reply, see LR, Gurd Papers, Greenwood to Leonhardt, 15 October 1910.

19 LR, Gurd Papers, Greenwood to Leonhardt, 15 October 1910.

20 Ibid. Greenwood hoped to hear from Leonhardt, provided he was "independent, willing to know the truth, and share either the credit or blame."

21 Early in November of 1910, Leonhardt informed Greenwood of his attempt to examine the skeleton exhumed on St Anne's Island. Having learned that the bones were in Chief Joseph White's possession, Leonhardt tried to arrange for a private viewing – but White was unreceptive and replied by saying: "[Tecumseh's] bones are with us. We'll take care of them. Had I known it, they would never have been dug up, and they will be dug up no more. They are safe." See ibid., Leonhardt to Greenwood, 6 November 1910. Leonhardt tried to soften White's stand by inviting him to dinner. The chief enjoyed the meal – but still refused to let Leonhardt see the bones. See ibid., 8 November 1910. For Greenwood's reaction, see ibid., Greenwood to Leonhardt, 10 November 1910.

22 Ibid., Greenwood to Leonhardt, 12 November 1910.

23 Ibid. Fisher admitted to having calculated the year of Tecumseh's supposed reinterment, which he based on the information of an old Native at Munceytown, near London, Ontario. This elder supposedly acquired Tecumseh's "rifle" or musket in "about 1864–65." Fisher, believing that the gun was taken from Tecumseh's grave, concluded that Oshahwahnoo must have retrieved the chief's bones at the same time. See *Wallaceburg News*, 14 April 1910, p. 3, col. 3. Regarding Oshahwahnoo's age, Greenwood claimed his informant was "one who heard him." This may have been the case, but Greenwood also appears to have relied heavily upon information collected by Benson J. Lossing. Compare LR, Gurd Papers, Greenwood to Leonhardt, 12 November 1910 with Lossing, *Pictorial Field-Book of the War of 1812*, 551.

24 LR, Gurd Papers, Leonhardt to Greenwood, 20 December 1910. According

to Leonhardt's reckoning, Oshahwahnoo might have retrieved the bones from the battlefield as early as 1840, in which case he would have been only about seventy years old when he went on his long trek, and quite capable of performing the task. See ibid., 8 November 1910. Greenwood, however, was not convinced. See ibid., Greenwood to Leonhardt, 12 November 1910.

25 Ibid., Greenwood to Leonhardt, 28 December 1910. Later, in March of 1911, Greenwood informed Leonhardt that he had found the "real aid[e] to Tecumseh." See ibid., Greenwood to Leonhardt, 8 March 1911. Although Greenwood did not name the aide-de-camp on this particular occasion, he noted his death date, which corresponds with that of the Potawatomi chief Shabbona. Greenwood's source might very well have been Norman B. Wood's *Lives of Famous Indian Chiefs*, published several years earlier with a biography of Shabbona included. See Wood, *Lives of Famous Indian Chiefs*, 408, 438. Greenwood eventually published the information regarding Shabbona; however, he did not exploit it effectively enough in his attempt to dispute Fisher's claim that Oshahwahnoo was Tecumseh's aide-de-camp at the Battle of the Thames. See *Planet*, 19 April 1911, p. 1, col. 1.

26 LR, Gurd Papers, Greenwood to Leonhardt, 31 January 1911.

27 Greenwood prefaced his addendum with the following statement: "In view of the fact that many stories have been circulated regarding the subject of our correspondence, and that I have told one entirely at variance with all others, I am impressed with the idea that there should be one in Canada who has my reasons and at least a part of the evidence in their support." See ibid., addendum.

28 Ibid., Greenwood to Leonhardt, 31 January 1911.

29 Ibid., addendum. According to Greenwood, the source of Laird's information was Johnson's wife, who "loyally kept his secret nearly forty years; then in a fit of anger because the 'old coot' persisted in going [to the grave] when the nights were getting too cold to sleep outdoors, she told the whole story to a garrulous neighbor." See *London Evening Free Press*, 15 April 1912, p. 4, col. 2. See also LR, Gurd Papers, Greenwood to Leonhardt, 31 January 1911, addendum; *Globe*, 3 September 1913, p. 6, col. 4. This neighbour could have been George Laird. Of course, Laird might have heard the same story directly from Johnson himself. Johnson's wife was Rachel (Hartley) Johnson. See London Roman Catholic Diocese Archives, St John the Baptist Church, Amherstburg, Ontario, parish registers (1802–29), marriage of William Caldwell junior and Ruth Johnson, 19 February 1822, folio 69.

30 LR, Gurd Papers, Greenwood to Leonhardt, 31 January 1911, addendum. For a brief history of Ira Greenwood's life, see *Commemorative Biographical Record of the County of Kent, Ontario*, 151.

31 LR, Gurd Papers, Greenwood to Leonhardt, 31 January 1911, addendum.

32 Ibid.

33 Ibid.

34 *Globe*, 3 September 1913, p. 6, col. 4.

35 William Caldwell junior was a son of Colonel William Caldwell of Amherstburg, and is sometimes confused with his half-brother, Billy Caldwell, who was born of the senior Caldwell's earlier marriage to a native woman. See *Commemorative Biographical Record of the County of Essex*, 121. See also Kulisek, "Caldwell, William," 101–4. According to his will, William Caldwell junior died on 7 February 1873 at Malden Township. See AO, Essex County Surrogate Court, Register Book, vol. F, estate of William Caldwell, 217–19.

36 WHS, Draper Manuscript Collection, Draper's Notes, ser. S, 17:224–5. Caldwell blamed the British for having shot Tecumseh, an accusation that is similar to the assassination story involving a drummer boy, as told by George Laird's daughter-in-law, Sarah Ann Laird. However, in an earlier account of Tecumseh's death dating from 1836, Caldwell thought it was a stray shot from one of Tecumseh's own people that killed him. See *Chatham Journal*, 11 February 1843, p. 2, col. 5; Gourlay, *Banished Briton and Neptunian*, 94.

37 Sugden, *Tecumseh's Last Stand*, 157.

38 *Chatham Journal*, 11 February 1843, p. 2, col. 5.

39 Ibid. When Caldwell gave evidence at Major-General Henry Procter's court martial, he made no reference to his gallant efforts to save Tecumseh. See TNA, Court Martial Proceedings of Major-General Henry Procter, 154–5.

40 *Chatham Journal*, 11 February 1843, p. 2, col. 5.

41 The recipient of Caldwell's earlier account was Robert F. Gourlay, whose recollection of the interview appeared in the *Chatham Journal* in February of 1843. See ibid. As well, Gourlay published the interview in one of his books. See Gourlay, *Banished Briton and Neptunian*, 94.

42 William Caldwell junior married Ruth Johnson on 19 February 1822 in a Catholic ceremony at Amherstburg. See London Roman Catholic Diocese Archives, St John the Baptist Church, Amherstburg, Ontario, parish registers (1802–29), folio 69. Draper was aware of the fact that Caldwell and Johnson were related by marriage. His notes refer to Caldwell's father-in-law as a man named Johnson, who had been a "prisoner with the Shawanoes in years past, [and who] knew Tecumseh well." See WHS, Draper Manuscript Collection, Draper's Notes, ser. S, 17:226. Draper also noted that Caldwell believed Joseph Johnson identified Tecumseh's body in Harrison's company, which seems doubtful.

43 Laird became one of Johnson's neighbours in 1829, after he purchased land near what is now Florence, Ontario. See LCLR, Abstract Books, Dawn Township, con. 13, lot 14; ibid., con. 14, lot 14. Albert Greenwood was born 20 April 1845. See *Rockville Republican*, 11 July 1929, p. 1, col. 2.

44 LR, Gurd Papers, Greenwood to Leonhardt, 31 January 1911, addendum. Greenwood did not elaborate on Mrs Johnson's description of Tecumseh's grave.

45 Ibid. According to Greenwood's wife, when Joseph Johnson junior was a child he boasted of his father's exploits and, on one occasion at least, he did so in the company of a little friend by the name of Albert Greenwood. Mrs Greenwood claimed that Joseph Johnson's son heard his father tell how he helped bury Tecumseh in a water hole on the battlefield. There was a "big swamp elm at one end of the grave and a littler tree at the other that had blowed down and lodged in the crotch of the elm." See ibid., Alice Greenwood to Gurd, 5 August 1931. Despite Mrs Greenwood's recollection, her husband never mentioned a water hole or a swamp elm in any of his correspondence with Leonhardt.

46 It would appear that Greenwood partially revealed this lead in February of 1911, when he told Leonhardt that Joseph Johnson's son described Tecumseh's grave as being "about halfway to the battlefield and a little to the left." Unfortunately, Greenwood never specified the starting place for these directions. See ibid., Greenwood to Leonhardt, 9 February 1911.

47 Ibid., 27 January 1911. Greenwood spent a month in the vicinity of the battlefield, apparently employed as a farm labourer. Such an occupation would explain why his search was made at night, as his daylight hours would have been spent working in the fields. See ibid. Although Greenwood did not specify an exact date, he suggests in a subsequent letter to Leonhardt that his nocturnal visit to the battlefield occurred in August of 1890. See ibid., 15 March 1914.

48 Ibid., 31 January 1911, addendum.

49 Ibid. Greenwood's wife later paraphrased his conversation with the man, who she claimed was the owner of the land and someone well acquainted with her husband. According to Mrs Greenwood, her husband asked this friend if he ever found any depressions or water holes on his property. When Greenwood received an answer in the affirmative, he enquired if one of these water holes had a big swamp elm at one end with a smaller tree lodged in it. Again the answer was yes. Greenwood then asked his friend if he found anything in this particular water hole, whereupon he was told that there was the skeleton of a "big Indian." See ibid., Alice Greenwood to Gurd, 5 August 1931. Greenwood, it must be noted, did not include a water hole or an elm tree in his description of Tecumseh's burial.

50 Ibid., Albert Greenwood to Leonhardt, 31 January 1911, addendum. Greenwood's information corresponds with the earliest known published account of Joseph Johnson's story, according to which Tecumseh was "shot in the thigh and fell, having the bone broken." See *Sarnia Observer*, 17 October 1873, p. 1, col. 9.

51 Greenwood discovered that Anthony Shane (a half-blood serving with Harrison's Native forces) attempted to identify Tecumseh's corpse based on this old wound. See LR, Gurd Papers, Greenwood to Leonhardt, 31 January 1911, addendum. The source of Greenwood's information concerning Tecumseh's hunting accident most likely was Eggleston and Seelye's *Tecumseh and the Shawnee Prophet,* which in turn drew heavily on

Drake's *Life of Tecumseh*. Greenwood probably also borrowed from Benjamin Drake and other authors as well. Compare the following: LR, Gurd Papers, Greenwood to Leonhardt, 31 January 1911, addendum; Lossing, *Pictorial Field-Book of the War of 1812*, 556; Eggleston and Seelye, *Tecumseh and the Shawnee Prophet*, 56; Drake, *Biography and History of the Indians of North America*, bk. 5: 124–5; and Drake, *Life of Tecumseh*, 69, 204. Samuel G. Drake was the author of *Biography and History of the Indians of North America*, while Benjamin Drake wrote *Life of Tecumseh*. The two Drakes were not related, although they were contemporaries. I am grateful to John Sugden for this insight. For more information on the topic of Tecumseh's broken thigh, see Sugden, *Tecumseh's Last Stand*, 220.

52 LR, Gurd Papers, Greenwood to Leonhardt, 9 February 1911; *Globe*, 29 September 1876, p. 3, col. 3. In 1931, Greenwood's wife recalled what she had been told by her husband about the conversation that took place between him and the man who found the skeleton. Greenwood was informed that the skeleton had been put back in its grave, but buried deeper, and that the ground over it was not thereafter disturbed. Mrs Greenwood also added that her husband was shown the grave, and that he "bared his head" out of respect. See LR, Gurd Papers, Alice Greenwood to Gurd, 5 August 1931. Greenwood did not admit to such a display. More troubling, however, is the fact that his wife's recollection does not include the all-important fully-knitted thigh bone.

53 Dr Jacob Smith of Ridgetown, who repudiated the United Canadians' discovery of Tecumseh's bones in 1876, was the source of this information regarding Culp. See *Canadian Home Journal*, semi-weekly ed., 5 September 1876, p. 4, col. 5. Abraham Culp's farm consisted of two part lots, which he purchased in 1855. See AO, Kent County Land Registry Office, Abstract Books, Zone Township, con. 5, lot 1; ibid., con. 5, lot 2. Also, Culp would have been considered an old man in 1890. According to the 1891 census, which was taken six months after Greenwood's supposed discovery of Tecumseh's grave, Culp was sixty-two years old. See LAC, 1891 Census, Zone Township, Kent County, Ontario, dis. 47, sub. dis. J, div. 1, p. 16, no. 73. Albert Greenwood's wife, however, was led to believe that the skeleton was found on the battlefield. It would appear that she was mistaken. See LR, Gurd Papers, Alice Greenwood to Gurd, 5 August 1931.

54 *Planet*, 10 June 1910, p. 1, col. 5. Darby Featherston received a patent to the east half of the west half of lot 1, concession 5 in 1857. Later, in 1878, he purchased the west half of the west half of lot 1, concession 5. Both of Featherston's properties were intersected by Cornwall's Creek. See AO, Kent County Land Registry Office, Abstract Books, Zone Township, con. 5, lot 1. Although Featherston died in February of 1891, prior to the census enumeration of that year, the 1881 census records his age as fifty-one years. Therefore, he would have been looked upon as an old man by the time of Greenwood's late-night visit to the battlefield in 1890. However, no evidence was found to indicate that Featherston discovered a solitary

skeleton like that found by Abraham Culp. See *Thamesville Herald*, 26 February 1891, p. 1, col. 6; LAC, 1881 Census, Zone Township, Kent County, Ontario, dis. 178, sub. dis. D, div. 3, p. 20, no. 93.

55 *Planet*, 10 June 1910, p. 1, col. 5.

56 Sussex might have been silenced by the editor of the Chatham *Planet*, who strongly disagreed with his view that the monument be placed on the old Featherston property, or on the farm where the Battle of the Thames took place. The editor thought Chatham was the best place. See ibid., p. 2, col. 1.

57 Greenwood's mistrust was by no means limited to Gurd, which explains why most people – except Leonhardt – studiously avoided any involvement with the surly old man. Nor did Greenwood completely trust Leonhardt, and with good reason. As Gurd revealed in 1923, Leonhardt had assured him that he would have "something" to share once Greenwood was dead. Gurd believed that Leonhardt was "holding back" this certain "something," which "he is afraid to give me in case I should publish it, and it should come to the ears of Greenwood." See LR, Gurd Papers, letterbook, Gurd to Colquhoun, 12 September 1923, 779. Greenwood, however, outlived Leonhardt by a year. Although Gurd appears to have been denied the information that Leonhardt wanted to share with him, he did manage to acquire Leonhardt's correspondence with Greenwood – probably through Mrs Leonhardt's generosity. The letters now form part of the Norman S. Gurd Papers at the Lambton County Library. Gurd could not have been very impressed with the correspondence, as he made no use of it. For Leonhardt's obituary, see *Wallaceburg News*, 12 July 1928, p. 5, col. 6.

58 LR, Gurd Papers, Greenwood to Leonhardt, 6 February 1911.

59 Ibid.

60 Ibid. Greenwood appears to contradict himself regarding his lack of interest in receiving a reward for his information. A few days after this selfless admission to Leonhardt, he recalled how Kent County (presumably meaning the county council) had not accepted his offer of a map showing the exact location of Tecumseh's grave, or the condition that the monument had to be constructed in the vicinity of the battlefield. "Now confound their scheming souls," he declared, "they will pay to see my cards." See ibid., 9 February 1911.

61 Ibid., 6 February 1911. For Greenwood's reply to Gurd's last letter, see ibid., 27 May 1910. This letter is the only surviving piece of correspondence between these two Tecumseh enthusiasts.

62 Ibid., 6 February 1911.

63 Ibid.

64 Ibid., 9 February 1911.

65 Ibid., Leonhardt to Greenwood, 17 February 1911.

66 Ibid. Earlier, in October of 1910, Greenwood claimed to be working on a biography of Tecumseh. But, unable to interest a publisher and unwilling to pay the cost of publication himself, he eventually gave up the project. See ibid., Greenwood to Leonhardt, 15 October 1910; ibid., 23 April 1912; ibid., 17 May 1912.

67 Ibid., 20 February 1911.

68 Ibid.

69 As Greenwood soon after observed, "At the present time there is but one thing to want for, and that is Gurd's book." See ibid., 8 March 1911.

70 Ibid., Leonhardt to Greenwood, 27 March 1911.

71 Ibid. The Wallaceburg Board of Trade got its information about Tecumseh's broken thigh bone from Rufus Boyce, a farmer in New Mexico. Leonhardt managed to contact Boyce and learned that the source of his information was Anthony Shane's account of Tecumseh's death, as contained in Samuel G. Drake's *Biography and History of the Indians of North America*. See LR, Gurd Papers, Leonhardt to Boyce, 20 December 1910; ibid., Boyce to Leonhardt, 11 January 1911; ibid., 9 April 1911. See also Drake, *Biography and History of the Indians of North America*, bk. 5: 124.

72 LR, Gurd Papers, Greenwood to Leonhardt, 2 April 1911. Greenwood soon changed his mind and shared the important consideration of the broken thigh bone with the Chatham *Planet*. See *Planet*, 19 April 1911, p. 1, col. 1.

73 LR, Gurd Papers, Leonhardt to Greenwood, 25 April 1911. Arguing against the St Anne's Island discovery based on the absence of a broken thigh bone, Leonhardt managed to convince Smith that he and his friends were "on a lost trail, and the whole [damn] thing will go to pot."

74 Ibid., Greenwood to Leonhardt, 27 April 1911.

75 Greenwood sent a portion of his poem to Leonhardt, who was flattered to receive it. See ibid., 2 April 1911; ibid., Leonhardt to Greenwood, 6 April 1911; ibid., 25 April 1911. Poetry continued to be a topic of discussion between the two men. Although Greenwood's poem was never published, Leonhardt was given a copy, which is now on file among the Norman S. Gurd Papers in the Lambton Room of the Lambton County Library at Wyoming, Ontario.

76 *Wallaceburg News*, 1 June 1911, p. 2, col. 3. Olive Hubble was the wife of Byron Hubble. The Hubbles took up residence in Wallaceburg sometime during the American Civil War. See ibid., 19 September 1907, p. 4, col. 3. According to Norman Gurd, Mrs Hubble "beheld an old Indian, prostrate over a grave, muttering incantations and pouring a sort of liquid [probably soup] on the mound of earth." See *Planet*, 12 September 1913, p. 1, col. 7.

77 *Wallaceburg News*, 1 June 1911, p. 2, col. 3.

78 Ibid. The editor of the *Sarnia Observer* mustered just enough interest to dismiss the rivalry for the proposed monument as being nothing more than a childish dispute. See *Sarnia Daily Observer*, 9 June 1911, p. 2, col. 2.

79 Greenwood did, however, participate in a brief war of words with someone identified only as "Wabekenosha." See *Wallaceburg News*, 25 May 1911, p. 6, col. 4; ibid., 1 June 1911, p. 4, col. 6; ibid., 22 June 1911, p. 7, col. 5. Greenwood concluded that the person behind the name "Wabekenosha" was "the heroine of the St Anne's fiasco," namely, Olive Hubble. See LR, Gurd Papers, Greenwood to Leonhardt, 20 May 1911. Greenwood's otherwise complacent attitude was the result of information

he received months earlier from Leonhardt, who investigated Mrs Hubble's story and became convinced that Oshahwahnoo had told her a lie. See ibid., Leonhardt to Greenwood, 4 February 1911; ibid., 5 February 1911. Eventually, Greenwood publicly claimed that "Shawanah either was, or was made a deceiver." See *Wallaceburg News*, 25 May 1911, p. 6, col. 4.

80 Leonhardt worked diligently behind the scenes on Greenwood's behalf. In conversations with the Rev. Simpson A. Brigham, the Anglican minister to Walpole Island (who was also a Native) and David A. Gordon of Wallaceburg, the federal member of Parliament for East Kent, Leonhardt disputed Wallaceburg's claim to the Tecumseh monument. Regarding Rev. Brigham, see LR, Gurd Papers, Leonhardt to Greenwood, 25 April 1911; ibid., 2 May 1911; ibid., 26 May 1911; ibid., 7 June 1911; ibid., Greenwood to Leonhardt, 7 May 1911. For reference to D.A. Gordon, as he is known in Wallaceburg, see ibid., Leonhardt to Greenwood, 6 July 1911.

81 *Herald*, 23 November 1905, p. 1, col. 3. See also Coutts, "Tecumseh Memorial Boulder," 85. The meeting of November 1905 did, however, lead to the formation of the Tecumseh Historical Society of East Kent a few weeks later. The purpose of this organization was to promote Thamesville's claim to the Tecumseh monument, but it proved impossible to sustain interest in the project. See *Herald*, 7 December 1905, p. 5, col. 5; ibid., 14 December 1905, p. 1, col. 3.

82 Coutts, "Tecumseh Memorial Boulder," 85. See also *Herald*, 20 July 1911, p. 1, col. 6. Mrs Coutts was a founding member of Thamesville's Art and Culture Club, which was organized in 1903 and promoted the study of poetry, music, and art. See *Herald*, 29 October 1903, p. 1, col. 4; ibid., 19 November 1903, p. 4, col. 4. Katherine B. Coutts died in 1929. Her husband was John Coutts. See *Thamesville Herald*, 28 February 1929, p. 1, col. 4.

83 The boulder, which was ordered from the J.E. Thatcher and Son granite works of Chatham, Ontario, was set up on John McDowell's Tecumseh Farm (apparently the southeast corner of lot 4, Gore of Zone Township) in September of 1911. See *Herald*, 21 September 1911, p. 1, col. 6. There were plans to erect the boulder on a cement block foundation, with a similarly constructed wall enclosing it. Neither improvement appears to have been accomplished. See ibid., 28 September 1911, p. 9, col. 4; *Globe*, Saturday Magazine Section, 11 November 1911, p. 7, col. 1. As Albert Greenwood later observed, the boulder was too close to the Longwoods Road to accurately mark the spot where Tecumseh fell. He concluded that the Thamesville "people must have put the stone where they did in order that all who pass may see it." See LR, Gurd Papers, Greenwood to Leonhardt, 15 March 1914.

84 *Herald*, 11 April 1912, p. 4, col. 2.

85 Ibid., 12 October 1911, p. 4, col. 2. The changeable Greenwood later admitted that he preferred Chatham's Tecumseh Park as the site of the monument. See LR, Gurd Papers, Greenwood to Leonhardt, 23 April 1912.

86 *Planet*, 22 March 1912, p. 1, col. 7.

87 Ibid. The editor of the Chatham *Planet* was Sydney Stephenson. By 3 April 1912, only $12.65 had been donated to the Tecumseh Monument fund, prompting Stephenson to employ a bit of shame against the children of Chatham. "Four little children from La Porte, Indiana, have sent us ten cents apiece," he reported. "Now that the children from out of town are showing such interest in the fund, it is up to the children of Chatham to uphold the name of the Maple City. Don't let anyone get ahead of you, but send in your ten cent subscriptions." See ibid., 3 April 1912, p. 1, col. 6. Regarding the intervention of the interested adults, see ibid., 6 April 1912, p. 1, col. 5.

88 Ibid., 15 June 1912, p. 7, col. 4.

89 Ibid. The request was referred to the Committee of Finance, where it was laid over until the December session. No further action was taken in the matter, however. The fact that Wallaceburg and Thamesville also shared Chatham's interest in the Tecumseh monument probably contributed to the abeyance. All three municipalities were located in Kent County, which would have made it impossible for the county council to favour one over the other. See *Minutes and Proceedings of the Council of the Corporation of the County of Kent*, June Session 1912, 844, 904; ibid., December Session 1912, 921.

90 For coverage of the Old Boys Reunion, see the Chatham *Planet* for the period 29 June to 4 July 1912.

91 *Planet*, 11 July 1912, p. 2, col. 1; ibid., 3 August 1912, p. 1, col. 7; ibid., 10 August 1912, p. 2, col. 1. Earlier, in June of 1912, Sydney Stephenson, the editor of the Chatham *Planet*, proposed that contributions toward a Tecumseh monument be solicited during the Old Boys Reunion. See ibid., 20 June 1912, p. 2, col. 1. Dr Holmes later reported having secured $1,300 for the monument, suggesting that most of the surplus from the reunion was in fact turned over to the Tecumseh Monument Association. See ibid., 4 October 1913, p. 1, col. 5.

92 Ibid., 7 October 1912, p. 1, col. 5; ibid., 4 November 1912, p. 1, col. 5; ibid., 19 March 1913, p. 1, col. 1.

93 *Herald*, 20 March 1913, p. 1, col. 5.

94 Ibid. Mrs Coutts went so far as to request a donation from Robert L. Borden, the prime minister of Canada. Boldly, she asked: "For how much may we put down your name?" See LAC, Borden Papers, Coutts to [Borden], 20 [?] May 1913, 9863–4; ibid., [Borden] to White, 13 May 1913, 9863.

95 *Herald*, 22 May 1913, p. 1, col. 6. See also *Globe*, 21 May 1913, p. 1, col. 1. Samuel de Champlain was an early seventeenth-century French explorer and governor of New France.

96 *Herald*, 29 May 1913, p. 1, col. 5. As Mrs Coutts later recalled, "The Vice-President [Dr Stewart] went to Ottawa to present our claim, which was refused, the reason (or excuse) given being that Chatham was also putting forth a claim and the Government could not decide between two claimants." See Coutts, "Tecumseh Memorial Boulder," 86.

97 *Planet*, 5 June 1912, p. 1, col. 4; *Globe*, 7 June 1912, p. 11, col. 3.
98 *Annual Report of the Ontario Historical Society, 1913*, 49–50.
99 Ibid., 39.
100 Ibid., 39, 54–6. For another account of the visit to Thamesville, see *Herald*, 18 September 1913, p. 1, col. 3.
101 *Annual Report of the Ontario Historical Society, 1913*, 56. Dearness was not willing to commit his society's support, except in general terms.
102 *Planet*, 26 September 1913, p. 1, col. 1; ibid., 30 September 1913, p. 1, col. 2; ibid., 4 October 1913, p. 1, col. 5. Dr Holmes promoted the scheme in his capacity as president of the Kent Historical Society, which had been organized a year earlier. See ibid., 13 September 1912, p. 1, col. 3.
103 AO, Whitney Papers, Whitney to Terry, 29 March 1912. See also ibid., Terry to Whitney, 25 March 1912. Sir James appears to have been a bit brusque with poor Mrs Terry, probably because of the many requests he had to endure for a memorial to honour the heroes of the War of 1812. Earlier, in March of 1911, Whitney stressed his government's position regarding the heroes memorial. "It is a great mistake to imagine that this Government intends to take on its shoulders the burden of this monument. It intends simply to assist." See ibid., Whitney to Merritt, 13 March 1911. As Mrs Terry discovered, the premier was no more indulgent when it came to a monument for Tecumseh.

CHAPTER SIX

1 *London Evening Free Press*, 18 September 1912, p. 1, col. 4; *Planet*, 25 September 1912, p. 1, col. 3; ibid., 1 October 1912, p. 1, col. 3; ibid., 5 October 1912, p. 1, col. 4; ibid., 10 October 1912, p. 1, col. 5.
2 The date of the sham battle was 28 October 1912. See *Planet*, 29 October 1912, p. 1, col. 1.
3 Edwin Beattie was from Highgate, Ontario, a village to the south of Moraviantown. He received his appointment as Indian agent early in 1912. See *Bothwell Times*, 22 February 1912, p. 1, col. 4.
4 After negotiations with the minister of militia, Beattie's plan was presented to the public in February of 1913. See *Planet*, 14 February 1913, p. 1, col. 1. Arrangements with the Moraviantown fair board followed some time later, and it was agreed that the celebration would be postponed in order for it to coincide with the Moraviantown fall fair. See ibid., 16 October 1913, p. 1, col. 3.
5 AO, Whitney Papers, Beattie to Whitney, 8 September 1913. Beattie requested between $300 and $500 to cover the cost of the artillery and other incidentals. Whitney's cabinet agreed to the lesser amount. See ibid., Secretary to Beattie, 10 September 1913.
6 *Herald*, 23 October 1913, p. 1, col. 4.
7 Ibid. See also *London Evening Free Press*, 17 October 1913, p. 7, col. 1. For a list of the regiments involved, see *London Evening Free Press*, 10 October 1913, p. 16, col. 3.

8 Beattie's claim to having originated the idea of the Tecumseh Celebration was firmly established in February of 1913, when his plans were publicized in the Chatham *Planet*. See *Planet*, 14 February 1913, p. 1, col. 1.

9 *Herald*, 23 October 1913, p. 1, col. 4.

10 *London Evening Free Press*, 17 October 1913, p. 7, col. 1. Dr Holmes also thought the monument should be "noble and magnificent and worthy of the man it would commemorate."

11 Ibid. Evelyn's sister was the famous Canadian poetess E. Pauline Johnson, and her father was the well-respected Chief George H.M. Johnson.

12 *Herald*, 23 October 1913, p. 1, col. 4.

13 Ibid.

14 Ibid. Most of the spectators probably arrived by way of more established routes.

15 Ibid. In accepting the title, Colonel Hodgins was also handed an outfit of beaded buckskin and "a gorgeous head-dress of feathers." See *London Evening Free Press*, 17 October 1913, p. 7, col. 1.

16 *Herald*, 23 October 1913, p. 1, col. 4.

17 *Globe*, 3 September 1913, p. 6, col. 4.

18 The Toronto *Globe* announced the publication of Gurd's *Story of Tecumseh* in mid-February of 1912, and reviewed it the following March. See ibid., 17 February 1912, p. 18, col. 4; ibid., 30 March 1912, p. 18, col. 1. Earlier, Gurd published a series of articles on the life of Tecumseh, which he submitted to the *London Free Press* between April and June of 1911. Gurd's serial was no doubt inspired by the success of a paper he presented to the London and Middlesex Historical Society. See *London Evening Free Press*, 26 April 1911, p. 12, col. 3; ibid., 29 April 1911, p. 10, col. 1; ibid., 5 May 1911, p. 7, col. 1; ibid., 13 May 1911, p. 7, col. 2; ibid., 20 May 1911, p. 9, col. 1; ibid., 27 May 1911, p. 9, col. 1; ibid., 3 June 1911, p. 15, col. 1; ibid., 10 June 1911, p. 9, col. 1; ibid., 17 June 1911, p. 15, col. 1.

19 Gurd, *Story of Tecumseh*, 176–7; *Globe*, 3 September 1913, p. 6, col. 4. Greenwood's objection was a sudden departure from a more tolerant attitude he professed at the end of January 1912, when he wrote: "There is plenty of room in the subject [of Tecumseh] for both Gurd and myself as he is 'along historical lines' and I shall endeavor to show that history is utterly unreliable." See LR, Gurd Papers, Greenwood to Leonhardt, 28 January 1912.

20 Greenwood published this account in 1913. See *Globe*, 3 September 1913, p. 6, col. 4. Greenwood objected to Mrs Richardson's suggestion that Tecumseh might have been buried beneath the Thames River. Therefore, his reference to "running water" probably means a creek. See ibid., Saturday Magazine Section, 4 January 1908, p. 3, col. 1; ibid., 2 May 1908, p. 4, col. 4.

21 John Sugden came to the same conclusion. See Sugden, *Tecumseh's Last Stand*, 216.

22 Greenwood, however, did leave his poem behind. It was never published, and although Leonhardt tried to have it read at the Tecumseh Celebration

in 1913, his efforts came too late. See LR, Gurd Papers, Fraser to Leonhardt, 23 August 1913; ibid., 2 September 1913. It should also be noted that Albert Greenwood died on 4 July 1929 at Rockville, Indiana – which was his wife's hometown. See *Rockville Republican*, 11 July 1929, p. 1, col. 2.

23 LR, Gurd Papers, Greenwood to Leonhardt, 17 May 1912. Greenwood first admitted his belief in spiritualism after Leonhardt raised the topic of a seance. See ibid., Leonhardt to Greenwood, 17 February 1911. See also ibid., Greenwood to Leonhardt, 24 February 1911; ibid., Leonhardt to Greenwood, 6 April 1911; ibid., Greenwood to Leonhardt, 15 January 1912.

24 Ibid., Greenwood to Leonhardt, 17 May 1912.

25 Ibid., 31 January 1911.

26 Ibid., 17 May 1911.

27 Mrs Coutts later acknowledged that "the outbreak of the Great War gave us all other things to think of." See Coutts, "Tecumseh Memorial Boulder," 86. The most pronounced reminder of Tecumseh was Ethel T. Raymond's *Tecumseh: A Chronicle of the last Great Leader of his People*, which was published in 1915 as one of the volumes in the Chronicles of Canada Series.

28 John McDowell discovered the skeleton while digging post holes for a new fence on the south side of the Longwoods Road, nearly opposite the Tecumseh boulder (which was then situated on the southeast corner of lot 4, Gore of Zone Township). See *Thamesville Herald*, 13 June 1918, p. 1, col. 7. See also *Globe*, 12 June 1918, p. 3, col. 4; *Glencoe Transcript*, 13 June 1918, p. 1, col. 6.

29 As Greenwood astutely noted, the skeleton was found in a location that would have been under the direct control of the Americans. Greenwood also thought that the presence of brass buttons was another indication of an American victim of the battle, despite his earlier claim that Tecumseh's buttons were made of this metal. Greenwood also tried to argue – unconvincingly and in obvious support of his earlier allusion to a streambed burial – that "no Indian killed in battle is ever buried in ground that is not covered by water." See *Thamesville Herald*, 27 June 1918, p. 1, col. 3; LR, Gurd Papers, Greenwood to Leonhardt, 31 January 1911, addendum.

30 Between 1915 and 1919, Judge Charles O. Ermatinger tried to persuade American officials that the statue of the *Dying Tecumseh* should be transferred from Washington, D.C., to the Elgin Historical and Scientific Institute in St Thomas, Ontario. The Americans resisted, however, and the *Dying Tecumseh* remains in Washington to this day. It is now displayed in the Smithsonian's National Museum of American Art. See UWOA, Ermatinger Papers, Correspondence *re* Statue of Tecumseh, file 38.

31 The Longwoods Road was designated a provincial highway in 1920. In the summer of the following year, amid great controversy, improvements were commenced on that section of the road running through a portion of John

McDowell's farm (which by then included lots 4, 5, 6, and 7 in the Gore of Zone). These improvements included moving the new Number Two Highway back a short distance from the old line of road, which ran too close to the riverbank. See *Thamesville Herald*, 4 March 1920, p. 1, col. 3; ibid., 15 September 1921, p. 1, col. 2; AO, Kent County Land Registry Office, Abstract Books, Zone Township, gore adjoining Camden, lots 5–7.

32 That portion of redundant highway property near the intersection of the Longwoods Road and Base Line Road was set aside as a memorial park in honour of Tecumseh. See *Thamesville Herald*, 9 June 1921, p. 1, col. 2; Coutts, "Tecumseh Memorial Boulder," 86. See also LAC, Parks Canada, Central Registry Files, Coutts to Harkin, 18 April 1922. Earlier, in March of 1921, the secretary of the Kent Historical Society requested the assistance of the Historic Sites and Monuments Board in erecting a memorial to commemorate the Battle of the Thames. James H. Coyne, a member of the board who was a prominent historian from St Thomas, Ontario, did not think a British defeat was a suitable event to be celebrated. However, he did consider it appropriate to honour Tecumseh with a monument. See ibid., Mustard to Williamson, 16 March 1921; ibid., Coyne to Williamson, 5 May 1921; ibid., Coyne to Harkin, 21 July 1921.

33 According to Mrs Coutts's obituary, "a weakness of the heart" developed from her many speaking engagements. See *Thamesville Herald*, 28 February 1929, p. 1, col. 4. Early in 1924, the incised inscription on the boulder was covered with a bronze tablet. The boulder was also placed on a low granite pediment in its new location and rededicated the following July. See Coutts, "Tecumseh Memorial Boulder," 86–7; *Thamesville Herald*, 24 January 1924, p. 1, col. 5; ibid., 6 March 1924, p. 1, col. 2; ibid., 17 July 1924, p. 1, col. 4; ibid., 31 July 1924, p. 1, col. 6.

34 *London Evening Advertiser*, 15 May 1926, p. 1, col. 4.

35 Brown, *Life of Joseph Brant*, 121.

36 Ibid., 121–4. A few years earlier, in 1908, Mrs Brown's novel, *My Lady of the Snows*, was published in Toronto by William Briggs. She achieved a fair degree of fame as a result of this book.

37 Ibid., 124.

38 Ibid., 125.

39 Ibid., 139. John Dearness was also president of the Ontario Historical Society in 1913, when he and several of his fellow members were taken on a tour of the battlefield by Mrs Coutts. See *Annual Report of the Ontario Historical Society, 1913*, 56.

40 Brown, *Life of Joseph Brant*, 139.

41 Ibid.

42 Ibid., 128. See also Drake, *Life of Tecumseh*, 222. According to Drake, the Prophet "resided in the neighborhood of [Fort] Malden [at Amherstburg] for some time, and finally returned to Ohio: from whence, with a band of Shawanoes, he removed west of the Mississippi, where he resided until the period of his death, which occurred in the year 1834." Actually, the

Prophet died in November of 1836 at what is now Kansas City, Kansas. See Edmunds, *The Shawnee Prophet*, 187.

43 As Jasper explained, his father took an assumed name for fear of American reprisal. He identified his father's property as lot 28, concession 4, Moore Township. Land records confirm that Simon Jones owned a portion of this property during the time in question. See LCLR, Abstract Books, Moore Township, con. 4, lot 28. Jasper made his first visit to his father's Moore Township farm in 1854. See Brown, *Life of Joseph Brant*, 122.

44 Brown, *Life of Joseph Brant*, 123. As Daniel J. Brock observes, Tecumseh could not have been buried alongside the Governor's Road (Dundas Street), as its western extent had not yet been constructed. At the time of the Battle of the Thames, the only road through what later became London was the Commissioners' Road, about four kilometres to the south, and on the opposite side of the Thames River.

45 The epitaph on William Shakespeare's tombstone in Holy Trinity Church, Stratford, England reads as follows: "GOOD FREND FOR JESVS SAKE FORBEARE, TO DIGG THE DYST ENCLOASED HEARE. BLESE BE YE MAN [THAT] SPARES THES STONES, AND CVRST BE HE [THAT] MOVES MY BONES."

46 Brown, *Life of Joseph Brant*, 84. See also ibid., 81–119.

47 Although the title page of this peculiar little book lacks the year of publication, an article in the *London Advertiser* dating from mid-May of 1926 describes Mrs Brown's *Life of Joseph Brant* as having been "recently published." Elsewhere, Mrs Brown acknowledged that she had written the book for the Brant Historical Society, which presumably was also her publisher. See *London Evening Advertiser*, 15 May 1926, p. 1, col. 4; LAC, Indian Affairs, Red Series, Correspondence Concerning Tecumseh's Grave, Brown to Scott, 24 November 1913. Later, during another Tecumseh controversy in 1931, Mrs Brown was challenged when she tried to repeat Jasper Jones's stories about the Prophet and Tecumseh. After her contribution to the Toronto *Globe* was described as "perhaps more ingenious than convincing," Mrs Brown refrained from further involvement in questions regarding the Prophet's relatives and Tecumseh's burial. See *Globe*, 30 January 1931, p. 4, col. 5; ibid., 11 February 1931, p. 4, col. 6. Margaret Brown died in Brantford in 1941. See *Brantford Expositor*, 22 December 1941, p. 6, col. 5.

48 *London Evening Advertiser*, 17 May 1926, p. 1, col. 6. The search referred to was the one conducted by John Dearness in 1913.

49 Ibid.

50 Carty went into business with his uncle, Edmund Carty. See Gibb, "Death or Glory," 215.

51 *Globe*, 22 June 1926, p. 11, col. 2. Half a mile equals approximately 804.5 metres, and ten miles is approximately sixteen kilometres.

52 Ibid. For examples of the *Globe*'s support, see ibid., 12 May 1926, p. 4, col. 2; ibid., 28 June 1926, p. 4, col. 2. Evelyn Johnson was also in favour

of this new scheme. See ibid., 14 May 1926, p. 1, col. 4.

53 With the support of Moraviantown, Roy H. Abraham, then Agricultural Representative of the Department of Indian Affairs at Chatham, tried to arrange funding for a monument to Tecumseh from Native sources. Nothing came of his efforts, although he was still promoting the idea as late as March of 1927. See *Chatham Daily News*, 12 Mar 1927, p. 3, col. 3. See also *Globe*, 21 April 1926, p. 9, col. 4; ibid., 11 May 1926, p. 13, col. 2; ibid., 26 June 1926, p. 1, col. 1; ibid., 21 July 1926, p. 11, col. 4.

54 *Toronto Daily Star*, 30 June 1926, p. 21, col. 1.

55 Ibid. Carty was a stringer for the *Toronto Daily Star*. His identity was revealed by means of his byline.

56 Ibid.

57 Ibid.

58 Ibid. The landmarks Nahdee tried to find also figure prominently in George Laird's story about Tecumseh's burial. According to his daughter-in-law's retelling, "Mr Laird always claimed that the grave of Tecumseh would never be found. He said that after Tecumseh was killed the Indians carried him to a large tree near the bank of the river on the side of a deep ravine at the foot of which a little stream trickled into the Thames." See *Daily Planet*, 12 October 1898, p. 8, col. 4. The similarity between the Laird and Nahdee traditions is striking.

59 *Toronto Daily Star*, 30 June 1926, p. 21, col. 1.

60 Ibid. Actually, the distance from the Walker farm to the Tecumseh boulder was only ten miles, or sixteen kilometres.

61 Ibid.

62 Ibid.

63 Ibid. As Carty calculated: "A few hundred feet to the east the remnants of an old culvert that carried the first of the streams shows that the road fifty years or more ago was fifty feet south of the route last abandoned. At least fifty feet of the face of the cliff is gone within present recollection."

64 See *Toronto Daily Star*, 30 June 1926, p. 21, col. 1; *London Evening Advertiser*, 30 June 1926, p. 1, col. 6; [Carty], "History and Romance in London's Environs," 66.

65 [Carty], "History and Romance in London's Environs," 66.

66 Gibb, "Death or Glory," 227–8. The *Sir John Carling* and its two pilots went down somewhere over the north Atlantic.

67 The Nahdees may have had second thoughts, however. Soon after their expedition, they considered returning to Wardsville with a medicine man who they claimed possessed the power to "see in the dark," and by this means "bring to light the warrior's bones." It does not appear that the Nahdees were able to find a ride back to the Walker farm. See *Globe*, 1 July 1926, p. 9, col. 1.

68 According to Norman Gurd, Oshahwahnoo's "real" name was John Naudee. Rev. Andrew Jamieson, the Anglican missionary to Walpole Island, claimed that "Ooshawunoo" had no other name. Yet, Oshahwahnoo

was recognized in the Anderdon Township land surrender of 1848 as "John Natty." By this surrender, those Chippewa settled near Amherstburg were removed to Walpole Island. Furthermore, in an affidavit dating from 1867, Oshahwahnoo identifies his father as "Nangie," which suggests the derivation of the name Nahdee. See LAC, Indian Affairs, Red Series, Correspondence Concerning Tecumseh's Grave, Gurd to Gray, 29 January 1931; WHS, Draper Manuscript Collection, Tecumseh Papers, ser. YY, vol. 7, no. 68, Jamieson to Draper, 22 April 1882; *Indian Treaties and Surrenders*, 1:238–9; *Memorial of the Chippeway, Pottawatomy, and Ottawa Indians, of Walpole Island!*, 9. In any case, Oshahwahnoo's descendants assumed the surname Nahdee. I am grateful to David McNab for sharing his knowledge of Native names with me.

69 It was not the first time that someone failed to make full use of the Nahdee tradition in order to set the record straight. Prior to the discovery of Tecumseh's grave in 1910, Joseph Sampson from Walpole Island claimed that Chief John Nahdee had taken part in Tecumseh's burial along the Thames River, and that the grave had never been disturbed. Unfortunately for Sampson, he also failed to make the connection between John Nahdee and Oshahwahnoo, and so his revelation went unnoticed as Matthew Fisher and Albert Greenwood battled it out in the press. See *Wallaceburg News*, 12 May 1910, p. 7, col. 1.

70 *London Evening Free Press*, 28 June 1926, p. 2, col. 2. Greenbird was already perturbed by a story in the *London Free Press* about Tecumseh's burial on St Anne's Island. See ibid., 22 May 1926, p. 1, col. 3. Greenbird's letters still exist in manuscript form. See UWOA, Elliott Collection, Historical Files, Tecumseh File, Greenbird to *London Free Press*, 20 May 1926; ibid., 25 June 1926. Greenbird's story is similar to that told by William Caldwell junior, in so much as Tecumseh was shot from behind. See LR, Gurd Papers, Greenbird to Gurd, 8 December 1934; *Chatham Journal*, 11 February 1843, p. 2, col. 5.

71 UWOA, Elliott Collection, Historical Files, Tecumseh File, Greenbird to *London Free Press*, 20 May 1926. Greenbird was adamant that only he and certain of his relatives would be able to "get pretty close to where Tecumseh's grave is." See *London Evening Free Press*, 22 May 1926, p. 1, col. 3.

72 *London Evening Free Press*, 3 November 1948, sec. 2, p. 22, col. 2. In addition to stating his relationship to Oshahwahnoo of Kettle Point, Greenbird repeated his family's version of Tecumseh's death and burial – which he delighted in doing whenever the occasion permitted.

73 By the end of 1934, Greenbird recognized that there were two Oshahwahnoos. See LR, Gurd Papers, Greenbird to Gurd, 8 December 1934.

74 Both elders are listed in the 1861 census, and both are referred to by the name Oshahwahnoo. See LAC, 1861 Census, Walpole Island Reserve,

Lambton County, Ontario, "Chippewa Indians belonging to Walpole Island," p. 58, no. 44; ibid., Sarnia Reserve, Lambton County, Ontario, "Chippeway Indians belonging to Sarnia Band residing in the Township of Bosanquet," p. 47, no. 1. Although Oshahwahnoo of St Anne's Island was Chippewa and Oshahwahnoo of Kettle Point was supposedly Shawnee, their respective languages share an Algonquian origin – which would appear to explain the duplication of their names. Yet, despite the linguistic similarity, English interpretations of their names could vary to a considerable degree. For example, Oshahwahnoo of Kettle Point was referred to as "Shahwuhno" when he died in the autumn of 1861. And when Oshahwahnoo of St Anne's Island died in September of 1870, he was known as "Ooshawunoo." See *Christian Guardian*, 23 April 1862, p. 4, col. 1; LAC, Indian Affairs, Deputy Superintendent General's Correspondence (1869–70), no. J124, Jamieson to Spragge, 27 September 1870, 485–6. For additional information on Oshahwahnoo of Kettle Point, otherwise known as John Bigknife, see *Forest Standard*, 12 April 1995, p. 7, col. 1. I am grateful to John Sugden for the reference to "Shahwuhno" from the *Christian Guardian*, and also to Emery Shawanoo for the article from the *Forest Standard*, which he authored.

75 Ontario Historical Society, *Proceedings of the Annual Meeting and Annual Reports for the Year 1926*, 14–16. Fred Landon was also the librarian at the University of Western Ontario.

76 Ibid., 16.

77 Ibid. Such a boast seems out of character for Tobias.

78 Ibid., 16–17. Hunter exaggerated to a considerable degree. Much of his information pertained to the United Canadians' discovery of Tecumseh's grave in 1876. Hunter assembled this material for his "Bibliography of the Archaeology of Ontario," which had appeared in serial format in the Ontario *Sessional Papers* almost thirty years earlier. See Hunter, "Bibliography of the Archaeology of Ontario," 67–87.

79 Ontario Historical Society, *Proceedings of the Annual Meeting and Annual Reports for the Year 1926*, 17.

80 Ibid. George F. Macdonald was the owner of a department store in Windsor, Ontario.

81 Ibid.

82 Ibid., 18. Landon, however, personally believed that the battlefield was the best place to erect a monument to Tecumseh, since that was where he was killed. See Middleton and Landon, *Province of Ontario*, 1:192.

83 *London Evening Advertiser*, 30 June 1926, p. 1, col. 7; *London Evening Free Press*, 30 June 1926, p. 1, col. 3.

84 *London Evening Free Press*, 31 July 1926, p. 8, col. 5.

85 Ibid. The medal was referred to as a "metal."

86 Sugden, *Tecumseh's Last Stand*, 98, 122, 147, 156.

CHAPTER SEVEN

1 The discovery of the bones took place a week earlier, on or about 10 January 1931. See *Sarnia Canadian Observer*, 17 January 1931, p. 1, col. 2. Although this article claims that Wilson Knaggs discovered the bones, another article published in the same paper only a few days later gives the credit to his wife. See ibid., 19 January 1931, p. 1, col. 3. Adding to this confusion, the Wallaceburg correspondent of the *Chatham News* reported that Mrs White discovered the bones after her husband's death in August of 1929, even though she is described elsewhere as having been bedridden for thirty years. See *Chatham Daily News*, 17 January 1931, p. 2, col. 6. See also *Sarnia Canadian Observer*, 19 January 1931, p. 1, col. 3. It would appear that Wilson Knaggs was in fact responsible for the discovery of the bones.

2 *Sarnia Canadian Observer*, 19 January 1931, p. 1, col. 3.

3 *Planet*, 6 June 1910, p. 1, col. 5.

4 At the time of his death, Chief White was also a preacher of the United Church. See *Wallaceburg News*, 29 August 1929, p. 6, col. 3.

5 *Chatham Daily News*, 17 January 1931, p. 2, col. 6. The representative members of the Walpole Island Soldiers' Club were President Sampson Sands, Secretary Robert Williams, Harrison B. Williams, and Walter Wright. See LAC, Indian Affairs, Red Series, Correspondence Concerning Tecumseh's Grave, Corless to Jennings, 18 January 1931; *Sarnia Canadian Observer*, 22 January 1931, p. 5, col. 5. Harrison B. Williams appears to have been the prime architect of the scheme. See *Sarnia Canadian Observer*, 1 August 1934, p. 3, col. 7.

6 *Sarnia Canadian Observer*, 16 January 1931, p. 1, col. 3.

7 Ibid.

8 LAC, Indian Affairs, Red Series, Correspondence Concerning Tecumseh's Grave, Corless to Jennings, 18 January 1931. Corless considered it very suspicious when he "could not find any teeth."

9 *Sarnia Canadian Observer*, 19 January 1931, p. 1, col. 3.

10 Ibid. Shobway claimed to have moved the real bones in June of 1930, presumably well before Wilson Knaggs and his family arrived to take care of Mrs White.

11 *Windsor Star*, 13 February 1960, sec. 3, p. 11A, col. 7.

12 This fallen tree was not far from Mrs White's house, which in turn was only a short distance from Shobway's house. See *Sarnia Canadian Observer*, 19 January 1931, p. 1, col. 3.

13 Ibid. Purves was delayed in reporting the news, as the second set of bones was discovered on 17 January 1931, which was a Saturday. Since there was no Sunday edition of the *Sarnia Canadian Observer*, he could not go to press with his story until Monday, 19 January 1931.

14 Ibid.

15 Ibid., 21 January 1931, p. 5, col. 4. Gray was a Sarnia lawyer and a member of the Liberal Party. See Lauriston, *Lambton's Hundred Years*, 249.

16 *Sarnia Canadian Observer*, 22 January 1931, p. 5, col. 5. In 1968, Dr Rutherford recalled: "It was my job to identify the bones and arrange them in their proper anatomical positions to form the skeleton. The bones were in various stages of degeneration but the long bones showed their proper outlines etc. We were searching for the scars to the left femur; for it is recorded that Tecumseh suffered a fracture of the left thigh bone when he was thrown from his horse while hunting buffalo in the Ohio Valley where he at one time lived. There was no evidence of there having been a fracture." See LR, Gurd Papers, Rutherford to Smith, undated but in reply to George Smith's letter of 26 February 1968.

17 *Sarnia Canadian Observer*, 22 January 1931, p. 5, col. 5. In Gurd's biography of Tecumseh, published in 1912, the broken thigh bone is considered an important element in the identification of the skeleton. See Gurd, *Story of Tecumseh*, 184. Gurd's remark about "Indian lore" was a vague reference to Anthony Shane's recollection regarding Tecumseh's broken thigh, which John Sugden holds in high regard. See Sugden, *Tecumseh's Last Stand*, 220.

18 In the editorial section of the *Canadian Historical Review*, Gurd was forced to admit that the "skeleton brought to light recently shows no trace of a fracture of the leg," but he went on to add that "the Indians of Walpole Island have made out a case sufficient to warrant an investigation." See "Notes and Comments," 118. Gurd was swayed by the sincerity of the Natives, who he thought "seem honestly to believe these to be the bones [of Tecumseh], and further, they have not hesitated to say that they did not know as to certain points I have pressed them. They do not seem at all to be eager to put the story over regardless of the facts." Based on this perception, Gurd was more inclined to accept the possibility that Tecumseh's bones might have been taken to St Anne's Island, and "that if anyone should know about Tecumseh, Shawano [Oshahwahnoo] should." See LAC, Indian Affairs, Red Series, Correspondence Concerning Tecumseh's Grave, Gurd to Gray, 29 January 1931.

19 In September of 1923, Gurd shared his opinion regarding Tecumseh's place of burial with Ontario's deputy minister of education – and he left no room for doubt: "I believe he was buried not far from the battlefield by his Indians. I do not believe that it was Tecumseh's body which was removed to St Anne's Island." See LR, Gurd Papers, letterbook, Gurd to Colquhoun, 12 September 1923, 778. Obviously, Gurd's opinion changed dramatically between 1923 and 1931.

20 Gurd was convinced that the Native evidence justified Ottawa's intervention: "I believe that anyone representing the Government would find it much easier to obtain evidence than the ordinary investigator." See LAC, Indian Affairs, Red Series, Correspondence Concerning Tecumseh's Grave, Gurd to Gray, 29 January 1931. Furthermore, Gurd was anxious to have the investigation begin, as the evidence "becomes less from year to year." See "Notes and Comments," 118.

21 See, for example, *Sarnia Canadian Observer*, 22 January 1931, p. 5, col. 5.

22 Soon after the bones resurfaced in January of 1931, rumours began to circulate that tourism was the reason behind Walpole Island's interest in a monument. See *Border Cities Star*, 28 February 1931, p. 15, col. 1. Gray's support for a monument honouring Tecumseh on Walpole Island certainly did not hurt his political career. He was returned to Parliament after both the 1935 and the 1940 federal elections. It was only in the election of 1945 that he went down to defeat. See Lauriston, *Lambton's Hundred Years*, 249. It should be noted that Gurd was a fellow Liberal.

23 *Sarnia Canadian Observer*, 22 January 1931, p. 5, col. 5.

24 Lueger, "History of Indian Associations in Canada," 109–11. Apart from Walpole Island, Moraviantown was the only other reserve from southwestern Ontario that participated in the Grand General Indian Council of Ontario on a regular basis.

25 Nindawaabjig, *Walpole Island*, 7.

26 The delegates from Walpole Island were Chief William Peters, Charles R. Jacobs, George Isaacs, F.A. Ermatinger, Andrew Isaacs, Peter Miskokoman, Solomon Kewayosh, and George Shogonsh. See LAC, Indian Affairs, Red Series, Correspondence Concerning Tecumseh's Grave, "Minutes of the Grand General Indian Council of Ontario, held at Sarnia on February 25, 1931," [1]. There were also Ojibwa/Chippewa on the Sarnia and Kettle Point reserves, but those who attended the special session tended to be hostile toward the veterans of Walpole Island.

27 The delegates from Moraviantown consisted of Chief Fred Stonefish, Monroe Pheasant, and Christopher Stonefish. See ibid.

28 *Border Cities Star*, 28 February 1931, p. 15, col. 1.

29 Ibid.

30 Ibid.

31 Ibid.

32 The delegate from Walpole Island was F.A. Ermatinger. See LAC, Indian Affairs, Red Series, Correspondence Concerning Tecumseh's Grave, "Minutes of the Grand General Indian Council of Ontario, held at Sarnia on February 25, 1931," [2].

33 Ibid. The amendment was seconded by a Native from Rama, one of the Ojibwa delegates who the Walpole veterans hoped could be won over to their side. Emerson Snake claimed to be a great-grandson of Timothy Snake. See *Globe*, 11 May 1926, p. 13, col. 2.

34 *Border Cities Star*, 26 February 1931, sec. 2, p. 5, col. 1. The name Nahdee is corrupted in this article to Maudee – although Willie Nahdee no doubt pronounced it correctly. Isaac Nahdee, another descendant of John Nahdee/Oshahwahnoo, found a means by which to reconcile his family's claim with that of the Walpole Island Soldiers' Club. According to him, Tecumseh was first buried near Wardsville, but subsequently reinterred on St Anne's Island. In this way, Isaac Nahdee managed to accommodate both his family and his neighbours. See Mann, *History of Wallaceburg and Vicinity*, 66.

35 *Border Cities Star*, 28 February 1931, p. 15, col. 1.

36 LAC, Indian Affairs, Red Series, Correspondence Concerning Tecumseh's Grave, "Minutes of the Grand General Indian Council of Ontario, held at Sarnia on February 25, 1931," [2].

37 *Border Cities Star*, 26 February 1931, sec. 2, p. 5, col. 1. See also ibid., 28 February 1931, p. 15, col. 1. Despite his contempt, Nahmabin later took it upon himself to suggest a design for the monument. See LAC, Indian Affairs, Red Series, Correspondence Concerning Tecumseh's Grave, Nahmabin to Scott, 2 April 1931.

38 See *Border Cities Star*, 28 February 1931, p. 15, col. 1.

39 LAC, Indian Affairs, Red Series, Correspondence Concerning Tecumseh's Grave, "Minutes of the Grand General Indian Council of Ontario, held at Sarnia on February 25, 1931," [2]. This delegate was Nicholas Plain.

40 Ibid. Chief William Peters was the delegate in this instance.

41 Among Arthur Carty's papers in the University of Western Ontario Archives is the manuscript version of his article covering the proceedings of the Grand General Indian Council. This same piece was published in the Windsor *Border Cities Star*, but Carty was not given credit for it. See UWOA, Carty Papers, Carty News and Publicity Correspondence, 1920–29, file 11–1, typescript copy regarding Grand General Indian Council of Ontario special session, 25 February [1931]; *Border Cities Star*, 26 February 1931, sec. 2, p. 5, col. 1.

42 Although this article does not carry Carty's name, the author is satisfied that Carty was responsible for it. See *Border Cities Star*, 28 February 1931, p. 15, col. 1.

43 Carty would have been hard to convince, given that his uncle had Tecumseh's tombstone in his backyard. In 1968, Ernest J. Suter recalled an incident from many years earlier, when a man in East London, Ontario, showed him a flagstone off his back steps. Upon closer examination, it was found to be crudely engraved in memory of Tecumseh. Suter did not name the man who possessed the recycled tombstone, but in June of 1948 a photographer from the *London Free Press* took pictures of both it and its owner – who he identified as Robert Carty, Arthur Carty's uncle. See *London Free Press*, 23 April 1968, p. 7, col. 1; UWOA, London Free Press Collection of Photographic Negatives, "Tecumseh's Tombstone," 28 June 1948. While the *London Free Press* does not appear to have published the story of Tecumseh's tombstone, Suter remembered being told that it was found in a gravel pit "somewhere west of Thamesville." Curiously, Arthur Carty did not publicize his uncle's relic of the great chief.

44 LAC, Indian Affairs, Red Series, Correspondence Concerning Tecumseh's Grave, Gray to Scott, 3 February 1931. No doubt, this leak was accomplished through Jack Purves, the reporter for the *Sarnia Canadian Observer* and the author of the resulting article. See *Sarnia Canadian Observer*, 5 February 1931, p. 16, col. 5.

45 LAC, Indian Affairs, Red Series, Correspondence Concerning Tecumseh's Grave, Hammond to Harkin, 10 January [1931]. See also ibid., Parks Canada, Central Registry Files, Hammond to Harkin, 10 January 1931.

I am grateful to Alan Mann for information he supplied regarding Ira Hammond.

46 LAC, Parks Canada, Central Registry Files, Williamson to Hammond, 17 January 1931; ibid., Williamson to Scott, 17 January 1931.

47 LAC, Indian Affairs, Red Series, Correspondence Concerning Tecumseh's Grave, Scott to Hammond, 22 January 1931.

48 See ibid., MacKenzie to Gardiner, 23 January 1931; ibid., MacKenzie to Highfield, 26 January 1931; ibid., Scott to Starnes, 29 January 1931.

49 Ibid., Stonehouse to Murphy, 31 January 1931. I wish to thank Alan Mann for the description of Calvert S. Stonehouse.

50 Ibid., Gray to Scott, 3 February 1931.

51 Ibid., Gurd to Gray, 29 January 1931.

52 Ibid., Scott to Buskard, 5 February 1931. As Scott later elaborated in a letter to Gray: "This is really a historical question and would require an examination of all existing material on the subject, and then a sifting of the local evidence." See ibid., Scott to Gray, 10 February 1931.

53 Ibid., Scott to Buskard, 5 February 1931.

54 Later, in July of 1931, Scott supposedly expressed his support for a monument by offering "funds under the control of the Indian Department from which they would be glad to make a substantial donation." Presumably this offer was made conditional on the monument being erected at the battlefield. Apparently, and by way of an afterthought, Scott added that "these funds belong to the Indians, and such a grant must be approved by the Indians." See Ontario Historical Society, *Proceedings of the Annual Meeting and Annual Reports for the Year 1931*, 37.

55 LAC, Indian Affairs, Red Series, Correspondence Concerning Tecumseh's Grave, Scott to Gray, 10 February 1931.

56 Ibid., Williamson to Gibson, 11 February 1931.

57 Ibid., Gibson to Buskard, 16 February 1931.

58 Ibid., [Buskard] to Scott, 19 February 1931.

59 Ibid., Scott to Collins, 28 February 1931.

60 Ibid., Barbeau to Collins, 17 March 1931. The inference here is that Tecumseh was a general in the British army, which was not the case.

61 Ibid., Scott to Murphy, 21 March 1931.

62 The lawyer's name was George N. Weekes. See ibid., Weekes to Superintendent of Indian Affairs, 18 March 1931. Nor was this the first time that Jacob Logan had gotten all "stirred up." In 1912, he offered to assist the Department of Indian Affairs in finding Tecumseh's bones, if the government would agree to construct a monument over his grave. See *London Evening Free Press*, 14 March 1912, p. 12, col. 2; *Planet*, 6 July 1912, p. 1, col. 5; LAC, Indian Affairs, Red Series, Correspondence Concerning Tecumseh's Grave, Logan to Minister of the Interior, 25 March 1912.

63 LAC, Indian Affairs, Red Series, Correspondence Concerning Tecumseh's Grave, Weekes to Superintendent of Indian Affairs, 18 March 1931. Logan identified his grandfather as Abraham Huff. According to the 1851 census

(enumerated in 1852), the families of both Abraham Huff and Henry Logan (Jacob's father) lived on the Muncey Reserve, Caradoc Township, in Middlesex County. This same record indicates that Jacob Logan was born in 1846, and so he would have been about fourteen years old when he overheard Jacob Pheasant's account of Tecumseh's burial. See LAC, 1851 Census, Caradoc Township, Middlesex County, Canada West, p. 131, no. 36; ibid., p. 133, no. 3. Jacob Logan may have been related to William Logan, the Native from Moraviantown who in 1876 assured the United Canadians that they had found the grave of Tecumseh. It should also be noted that Jacob Logan's story resembles that told by Thomas Gowman. Compare the following: *London Evening Free Press*, 25 July 1931, p. 8, col. 3 with *Daily Advertiser*, 25 September 1876, p. 1, col. 6.

64 LAC, Indian Affairs, Red Series, Correspondence Concerning Tecumseh's Grave, Weekes to Superintendent of Indian Affairs, 18 March 1931. A yard, or three feet, equals approximately 2.7 metres. Wilfrid Jury, a curator from the Museum of Indian Archaeology at the University of Western Ontario, found Logan "very confused" when he tried to point out Tecumseh's grave. As Jury later noted, "many of the old land marks were missing; trees had been cut down and the farm divided by fences." Eventually, after several hours, Logan selected a site near the battlefield and announced: "Here … is where they buried him, and you are the first white [man] to know where the grave of Tecumseh is." As honoured as Jury was, he could not help but notice that "[five] or [six] acres would need to be excavated at least [five] feet deep before the truth of this story was known." See London Museum of Archaeology, Jury Papers, "Tecumseh Burial, 1930," 3. When this account was later published, Jury made no reference to his earlier doubts and instead gave his readers the impression that Logan was able to conduct him to the very "spot he claimed to be that in which their beloved leader was buried." See *London Evening Free Press*, 25 July 1931, p. 8, col. 3.

65 LAC, Indian Affairs, Red Series, Correspondence Concerning Tecumseh's Grave, MacInnes to [Weekes], 21 March 1931.

66 *London Evening Advertiser*, 10 March 1931, p. 9, col. 4. Logan claimed that Tecumseh was buried well-equipped, with a tomahawk, war club, musket, bayonet, and even a knife.

67 Although Logan was unable to pinpoint the exact site of Tecumseh's burial, which he thought was close to the battlefield, his assertion that Tecumseh's bones were not on Walpole Island seemed to be validated for a short time in 1933. In the summer of that year, the skeleton of a Native man was discovered on the Pickard farm near Kent Bridge, Ontario, not far downriver from the battlefield where Tecumseh was killed. There was speculation that the bones might be those of Tecumseh – based on a silver armlet bearing the arms of King George III. Kent Bridge appeared to rival Walpole Island's claim to Tecumseh, even though it meant that his burial would necessarily have taken place behind enemy lines. A few days after

the discovery, however, two anthropologists from the University of Toronto examined the skeleton looking for any evidence of Tecumseh's fractured thigh bone. There was none, which led Professor Thomas F. McIlwraith to comment, "Well, that rather washes out Tecumseh, doesn't it?" See London Museum of Archaeology, Jury Papers, "Tecumseh Burial, 1930," 3; *Border Cities Star*, 29 June 1933, p. 17, col. 1; ibid., 5 July 1933, p. 11, col. 1.

68 *Sarnia Canadian Observer*, 25 March 1931, p. 5, col. 4.

69 Gurd received a carbon copy of the letter that was sent to Adams. See LR, Gurd Papers, Nunns to Adams, 28 March 1931.

70 *Sarnia Canadian Observer*, 9 Apr. 1931, p. 16, col. 3. The date of the exhibition was 7 April 1931.

71 *London Evening Advertiser*, 23 April 1931, p. 18, col. 2.

72 Ibid. This article refers to "Mrs Dolson," which is a mistake. The person in question was Elias Dolson. See *Border Cities Star*, 27 February 1931, p. 17, col. 1.

73 *Border Cities Star*, 27 February 1931, p. 17, col. 1. Albert Tobias died on 8 February 1931. See *Chatham Daily News*, 10 February 1931, p. 3, col. 2.

74 LAC, Indian Affairs, Red Series, Correspondence Concerning Tecumseh's Grave, Gurd to Cruikshank, 8 May 1931.

75 Ibid., Cruikshank to Scott, 11 May 1931.

76 Ibid.

77 Ibid. The Historic Sites and Monuments Board, which then operated within the Department of the Interior, was responsible for casting plaques to mark historically significant sites across Canada. The question of a monument to Tecumseh was raised on 30 May 1931. See HSMB, Minute Book, 30 May 1931, 28–9. See also LAC, Parks Canada, Central Registry Files, Cruikshank to Harkin, 12 May 1931; ibid., Harkin to Cruikshank, 16 May 1931.

78 Scott expressed his pleasure in the following terms: "Personally I concur in your view as to the difficulty of identifying the bones in question. I agree, however, with your comment as to the propriety of erecting a suitable memorial and I note that you intend that the proposal should be considered at the next meeting of the [Historic Sites and Monuments] Board." See LAC, Indian Affairs, Red Series, Correspondence Concerning Tecumseh's Grave, Scott to Cruikshank, 15 May 1931.

79 LAC, Parks Canada, Central Registry Files, Gray to Harkin, 14 May 1931. Gray perhaps did not argue Walpole Island's case as forcefully as he might have, since Cruikshank seemed unable to form a clear idea of his intention. Of course, there is also the very real possibility that Cruikshank was biased, as he had already decided that the battlefield was the best place for the monument. See Ontario Historical Society, *Proceedings of the Annual Meeting and Annual Reports for the Year 1931*, 36.

80 LAC, Parks Canada, Central Registry Files, Harkin to Gray, 18 May 1931; ibid., Harkin to Landon, 27 October 1931. For information on Scott's

participation, see Ontario Historical Society, *Proceedings of the Annual Meeting and Annual Reports for the Year 1931*, 37.

81 Ontario Historical Society, *Proceedings of the Annual Meeting and Annual Reports for the Year 1931*, 37.

82 Ibid. See also LAC, Indian Affairs, Red Series, Correspondence Concerning Tecumseh's Grave, Harkin to Scott, 2 July 1931. Later, in 1938, Cruikshank tried to win support for his proposed monument from the Department of Indian Affairs. His plans went awry when the Indian agent for Moraviantown recommended that the monument be placed at the site of Fairfield – the Moravian mission to the Delaware. See LAC, Parks Canada, Central Registry Files, Cruikshank to Williamson, 30 November 1938; ibid., Williamson to McGill, 10 December 1938; ibid., Williamson to Cruikshank, 10 December 1938; ibid., MacInnes to [Williamson], 17 December 1938; ibid., 3 February 1939.

83 HSMB, Minute Book, 30 May 1931, 28–9. The board, however, also suggested that other sources of funding be investigated at the provincial and federal levels of government.

84 Ibid.

CHAPTER EIGHT

1 *Chatham Daily News*, 2 June 1931, p. 3, col. 7.

2 Ibid.

3 Ibid. Mayor Arthur W. Sanderson of Chatham was later quoted as saying, "You can be assured that the city of Chatham is behind the proposal to erect a memorial in honor of Tecumseh." See ibid., 5 June 1931, p. 8, col. 4.

4 Ibid., 18 August 1931, p. 3, col. 1. Snake was appointed chairman of the committee, and Fred Arnold of Kent Bridge was instructed to obtain the necessary designs and estimates.

5 Ibid., 22 October 1931, p. 2, col. 4.

6 Ibid.

7 LAC, Parks Canada, Central Registry Files, Stonehouse to Murphy, 20 May 1932.

8 Ibid., Rowatt to Harkin, 2 June 1932.

9 Ibid., [Secretary?] to Rowatt, 8 June 1932.

10 Ibid., Harkin to Landon, 17 June 1932.

11 Ibid., Stonehouse to Landon, 12 September 1932. The monument to George Rogers Clark at Springfield consists of a full-length metal statue standing two and a half metres in height, and surmounting a rectangular stone base which rises three and a half metres above the ground. This monument should not be confused with the George Rogers Clark Memorial at Vincennes, Indiana.

12 Ibid., Landon to Harkin, 14 September 1932.

13 Ibid., [Murphy] to Stonehouse, 20 September 1932; ibid., 10 June 1932.

14 *Border Cities Star*, 17 August 1934, p. 13, col. 2.

15 LAC, Indian Affairs, Red Series, Correspondence Concerning Tecumseh's Grave, circular entitled "The Tecumseh Monument," enclosed in MacKenzie to Harkin, 27 April 1932.

16 Ibid., Highfield to Department of Indian Affairs, 25 April 1932; ibid., MacKenzie to Highfield, 3 May, 1932.

17 Robb, *Tecumtha*, 2. In addition to being a poet with an interest in Native themes, Robb was a naturalist who wrote numerous articles for various magazines. He is better remembered in eastern Ontario for having established Abbey Dawn, a wildlife sanctuary near Kingston. The reading of Robb's poem did eventually take place in 1941. See *Windsor Daily Star*, 25 August 1941, p. 9, col. 1. For a copy of the poem, see Robb, *Tecumtha*, 195–6.

18 *Sarnia Canadian Observer*, 1 August 1934, p. 3, col. 7. The veterans planned to have the monument completed by the middle of October.

19 Ibid. The Soldiers' Club organized a special international committee to solicit additional funding. Wood signified his intention to build the foundation, while Barrett expressed his willingness to take care of the financial details. This information agrees with a record of the ceremony made by Evelyn Cartwright of Algonac, Michigan. See Algonac/Clay Township Historical Society, Walpole Island Papers, Account of the Tecumseh Monument Cornerstone Laying Ceremony, 31 August 1934. Incidentally, Barrett was wealthy in his own right, and an avid yachtsman as well.

20 *Sarnia Canadian Observer*, 1 August 1934, p. 3, col. 7. In this article, Village President Pocklington is mistakenly referred to as Mayor Mitchell. Pocklington may have been acting on his own, as there is no reference to his offer in the Algonac council minutes for 1934. I am grateful to Rose Ann Perricone, the Algonac city clerk, for her searches on my behalf. Pocklington is credited with having been the "prime mover" in the formation of the international committee established by the Walpole Island Soldiers' Club for the construction of a monument to Tecumseh. See *Globe*, 1 September 1934, p. 15, col. 4.

21 LAC, Indian Affairs, Red Series, Correspondence Concerning Tecumseh's Grave, Highfield to Department of Indian Affairs, 9 August 1934. Earlier, on 2 August, Highfield wrote a letter to the Department of Indian Affairs expressing his concern over plans to start work on the monument using "American money." The rapid pace of developments forced him to make a trip to the telegraph office in Wallaceburg. See ibid., Highfield to Secretary, Department of Indian Affairs, 2 August 1934.

22 Ibid., MacKenzie to Highfield, 10 August 1934.

23 Scott retired in 1932. See Titley, *A Narrow Vision*, 198.

24 The veterans of Walpole Island were well aware of Wood's popularity, which became evident when a multitude of spectators came to watch him race in a nearby stretch of the St Clair River. The Harmsworth Race of 1933 was held on the American side of the river, between Port Lambton, Ontario and Marine City, Michigan. See *Border Cities Star*, 30 August 1933, p. 5, col. 2.

25 *Sarnia Canadian Observer*, 13 August 1934, p. 3, col. 8; *Chatham Daily News*, 13 August 1934, p. 12, col. 1. St John's Church is still a prominent landmark on Walpole Island.

26 Ibid. Chief Williams was credited with having been "largely responsible for the campaign for erection of the monument." See *Sarnia Canadian Observer*, 1 August 1934, p. 3, col. 7.

27 *Sarnia Canadian Observer*, 13 August 1934, p. 3, col. 8.

28 *Lester's Sarnia and Point Edward Directory*, 1931, 301; Lauriston, *Lambton's Hundred Years*, 335.

29 *Sarnia Canadian Observer*, 13 August 1934, p. 3, col. 8. The foundation was part of Wood's contribution to the monument project. See ibid., 1 August 1934, p. 3, col. 7.

30 Ibid., 13 August 1934, p. 3, col. 8. Chief Plain had supported the Walpole Island veterans at the special session of the Grand General Indian Council of Ontario, which was held at Sarnia in February of 1931. See LAC, Indian Affairs, Red Series, Correspondence Concerning Tecumseh's Grave, "Minutes of the Grand General Indian Council of Ontario, held at Sarnia on February 25, 1931," [2].

31 *Border Cities Star*, 28 February 1931, p. 15, col. 1; LAC, Indian Affairs, Red Series, Correspondence Concerning Tecumseh's Grave, "Minutes of the Grand General Indian Council of Ontario, held at Sarnia on February 25, 1931," [1]; *Sarnia Canadian Observer*, 13 August 1934, p. 3, col. 8.

32 LAC, Indian Affairs, Red Series, Correspondence Concerning Tecumseh's Grave, Herridge to Secretary of State, 17 August 1934.

33 Ibid., MacKenzie to Robertson, 27 August 1934.

34 *Sarnia Canadian Observer*, 22 August 1934, p. 3, col. 3. This article also relates that the veterans hoped "to have officials of the federal and provincial governments in attendance as well as representatives of the United States Government."

35 *Border Cities Star*, 31 August 1934, p. 11, col. 1.

36 *Wallaceburg News*, 6 September 1934, p. 5, col. 4. The queen of the St Clair Water Carnival and her court also attended the ceremony. See *Border Cities Star*, 31 August 1934, p. 11, col. 1.

37 *Wallaceburg News*, 6 September 1934, p. 5, col. 4. Gurd's Native name was chosen in recognition of the fact that Tecumseh was a "Shawanee," or Shawnee.

38 Gray probably knew of this dual identity through his association with Gurd, who was aware of it by the end of January 1931. Confirmation followed in mid-February of that same year, when allegations that Oshahwahnoo was from Kettle Point prompted Gray to write Duncan Campbell Scott seeking verification of the chief's place of residence. Scott replied that there was in fact a "Shawanaw" from St Anne's Island, and that he was also known as John Nahdee. See LAC, Indian Affairs, Red Series, Correspondence Concerning Tecumseh's Grave, Gurd to Gray, 29 January 1931; ibid., Gray to Scott, 19 February 1931; ibid., Scott to Gray, 23 February 1931.

39 *Border Cities Star*, 31 August 1934, p. 11, col. 1.

40 The veterans expected Lee Barrett to use his influence with the Detroit Tourist and Convention Bureau. See *Windsor Daily Star*, 7 August 1941, p. 16, col. 1.

41 The sculptors were Corrado J. Parducci and Pierre Birchener. See ibid., p. 11, col. 1.

42 *Sarnia Canadian Observer*, 7 September 1934, p. 1, col. 6.

43 *Windsor Daily Star*, 25 August 1941, p. 9, col. 1.

44 *London Evening Free Press*, 6 October 1934, p. 13, col. 4.

45 *Windsor Daily Star*, 7 August 1941, p. 16, col. 1.

46 Ibid.

47 Ibid., 14 August 1941, p. 15, col. 1. Regarding Watson's idea for a pageant, see *Border Cities Star*, 17 August 1934, p. 13, col. 2.

48 *Windsor Daily Star*, 7 August 1941, p. 16, col. 1.

49 Ibid., 18 August 1941, p. 11, col. 1.

50 Gourlay, *Statistical Account of Upper Canada*, 1:296. For more on the topic of Moravian pacifism, see Sabathy-Judd, *Moravians in Upper Canada*, xxii–xxv.

51 *Windsor Daily Star*, 18 August 1941, p. 11, col. 1. Gurd must have known that he was asking for trouble, which probably explains why he praised Moraviantown for having "flocked to the colors" during the First World War. This bit of flattery did nothing to mollify the angry Delaware. Nor did it help matters when Gurd tactlessly observed that Tecumseh despised their ancestors.

52 Ibid., 26 August 1941, p. 6, col. 7. Stonefish also exclaimed: "I am no coward and no cross-breed! I am a Delaware Indian and proud of it. When the last war broke I was one of the first to go and would go again if they would take me."

53 Ibid. According to Stonefish, all they had to do was find a set of bones with Tecumseh's medal.

54 Ibid., 25 August 1941, p. 9, col. 1. The minister responsible for Indian Affairs was Thomas A. Crerar, who held the Mines and Resources portfolio in Mackenzie King's cabinet. Although Crerar was sympathetic toward Natives, he showed little interest in the issues facing them. See Rea, *T.A. Crerar*, 172–3, 183.

55 *Windsor Daily Star*, 25 August 1941, p. 9, col. 1.

56 Ibid. The chest was made by the Algonac boat builder Chris Smith, of Chris-Craft fame. See *Sarnia Canadian Observer*, 20 February 1931, p. 5, col. 5; ibid., 9 April 1931, p. 16, col. 3.

57 *Windsor Daily Star*, 25 August 1941, p. 9, col. 1. See also *Chatham Daily News*, 25 August 1941, p. 5, col. 2; *Sarnia Canadian Observer*, 25 August 1941, p. 3, col. 8.

58 *Windsor Daily Star*, 26 August 1941, p. 6, col. 7.

59 Ibid, 16 August 1941, sec. 3, p. 6, col. 1.

60 Ibid., 26 August 1941, p. 6, col. 7.

61 *London Daily Free Press*, 28 February 1942, p. 13, col. 6.

62 *Windsor Daily Star*, 25 March 1955, p. 5, col. 3. See also *London Evening Free Press*, 10 March 1955, p. 8, col. 5. This section of the Number Two Highway was the former Longwoods Road.

63 *Windsor Daily Star*, 25 March 1955, p. 5, col. 3. According to Pheasant, when the danger had passed, his ancestor returned home and announced, "they missed my friend's grave."

64 Ibid.

65 Ibid.

66 LAC, Parks Canada, Central Registry Files, Landon to Richardson, 15 November 1956. According to the late Shirley Bain and Jean Filby, both of Thamesville, Mrs Brunner was the former Ada May Hubbell, who descended from some of the earliest settlers in the vicinity of Thamesville. Mrs Brunner was also one of the people responsible for having the Tecumseh boulder placed on the site of the Battle of the Thames in 1911. Jean Filby recalls that Mrs Brunner knew Fred Landon through a common interest they shared in having a plaque cast to commemorate the Sherman barn at Thamesville, which had been used as a military hospital by both British and American forces during the War of 1812. The plaque was unveiled in November of 1954. See *Thamesville Herald*, 25 November 1954, p. 1, col. 1.

67 Ontario Historical Society, *Proceedings of the Annual Meeting and Annual Reports for the Year 1926*, 14.

68 Landon endorsed the battlefield in a history of Ontario he co-authored. See Middleton and Landon, *Province of Ontario*, 1:192.

69 Ontario Historical Society, *Proceedings of the Annual Meeting and Annual Reports for the Year 1926*, 18. A few years later, in 1931, the Society passed a resolution in support of a monument to Tecumseh "at or near the place where he fell." See ibid., 35, 37.

70 Landon was appointed to the Historic Sites and Monuments Board in June of 1931. See UWOA, Landon Papers, Genealogical Papers, Private Correspondence, 1956–60, file 10, Richardson to Landon, 28 March 1956.

71 Tecumseh was designated a person of national historic significance in 1931, and at the same meeting of the Historic Sites and Monuments Board in which Cruikshank presented his monument proposal. See HSMB, Minute Book, 30 May 1931, 28–9. Landon was informed of Tecumseh's designation at Cruikshank's request. See LAC, Parks Canada, Central Registry Files, Harkin to Landon, 27 October 1931.

72 HSMB, Minute Book, 30 May 1931, 29; Ontario Historical Society, *Proceedings of the Annual Meeting and Annual Reports for the Year 1926*, 37; HSMB, Minute Book, 30 May 1932, 16; ibid., 25 May 1933, 15; ibid., 29 May 1939, 17; ibid., 24 May 1944, 34. Cruikshank later scaled back his proposed monument to "an obelisk of cut stone of about sixteen feet in height." See LAC, Parks Canada, Central Registry Files, Cruikshank to Williamson, 30 November 1938. The cost of this lesser monument was estimated to be in the range of about $6,000. See HSMB, Minute Book,

29 May 1939, p. 17; LAC, Parks Canada, Central Registry Files, Williamson to Cruikshank, 10 December 1938.

73 Landon was sixty-nine years old at the time of his retirement. See *London Evening Free Press*, 30 June 1950, sec. 2, p. 17, col. 7. He was elected chairman of the Historic Sites and Monuments Board at the end of May 1950. See *London Free Press*, 1 June 1950, morning ed., p. 1, col. 3. Earlier, in 1946, Landon took on the added responsibilities of Western's first vice-president. See Armstrong, "Fred Landon, 1880–1969," 2. But despite Landon's busy schedule, there were occasions when the question of Tecumseh's monument became the focus of his attention. The most notable example occurred in 1937, when he suggested that the estimates of the Parks Bureau of the Department of Mines and Resources include the cost of a monument to Tecumseh. The suggestion was not acted upon. See LAC, Parks Canada, Central Registry Files, Gibson to Williamson, 7 September 1937; ibid., [Williamson] to Gibson, 4 October 1937; ibid., Gibson to Williamson, 7 October 1937; ibid., Williamson to Murray, 14 October 1937. Generally, however, Landon's attitude toward the monument tended to be negative, in the sense that he had the question deferred several times. See HSMB, Minute Book, 30 May 1932, 16; ibid., 25 May, 1933, 15; ibid., 29 May 1939, 17; ibid., 24 May 1944, 34.

74 HSMB, Minute Book, 30 May 1951, 21; ibid., 27 May 1952, 12; ibid., 26 May 1953, 25; ibid., 7 June 1954, 34.

75 LAC, Parks Canada, Central Registry Files, Landon to Richardson, 10 June 1955. Landon read Mrs Brunner's letter at the 1955 session of the Historic Sites and Monuments Board.

76 LAC, Parks Canada, Central Registry Files, Landon to Richardson, 10 June 1955. In this letter, Landon mentions that he happened upon a picture of the monument to René-Robert Cavelier de La Salle in a booklet of national historic sites and parks. See *Canada's Historic Heritage*, [28].

77 LAC, Indian and Northern Affairs, Tecumseh Memorial File, Hutchison to Côté, 30 January 1957

78 It was the secretary of the Historic Sites and Monuments Board who led Landon to believe that a monument like La Salle's would cost $10,000. See LAC, Parks Canada, Central Registry Files, Richardson to Landon, 26 January 1956; ibid., Landon to Richardson, 1 February 1956.

79 Although Landon was eager to see a monument erected to Tecumseh, he found it difficult to find the time necessary to pursue the project. The secretary of the Historic Sites and Monuments Board had to prod him into taking action. See ibid., Richardson to Landon, 12 April 1956; ibid., 10 May 1956; ibid., Landon to Bryan, 14 May 1956; ibid., Richardson to Landon, 22 May 1956; ibid., 18 September 1956; ibid., Landon to Richardson, 15 November 1956; ibid., Richardson to Landon, 14 December 1956.

80 LAC, Indian and Northern Affairs, Tecumseh Memorial File, Landon to Lesage, 21 January 1957. See also ibid., Hutchison to Côté, 30 January 1957. An example of the standard Historic Sites and Monuments Board

monument can be seen at the Fairfield Museum, not far from the Tecumseh Monument. Jean Lesage was subsequently Liberal premier of Quebec from 1960 to 1966.

81 Ibid., Hutchison to Côté, 30 January 1957.

82 Ibid., Lesage to Landon, 21 February 1957. The caution exercised by Lesage probably was the result of Landon's intimation that there formerly was "a certain amount of jealousy as to where the monument should be placed." See ibid., Landon to Lesage, 21 January 1957.

83 HSMB, Minute Book, 3 June 1957, 50–1. Landon had the first draft of the inscription ready by the end of April. See LAC, Parks Canada, Central Registry Files, Landon to Richardson, 23 April, 1957; ibid., Richardson to Landon, 26 April 1957. See also ibid., Richardson to Landon, 6 March 1957; LAC, Indian and Northern Affairs, Tecumseh Memorial File, Lesage to Landon, 13 March 1957.

84 UWOA, Landon Papers, Scrapbooks, "Mostly Landon," Richardson to Landon, 7 February 1958; *London Evening Free Press*, 25 February 1958, sec. 2, p. 17, col. 7.

85 HSMB, Minute Book, 25 May 1959, 34.

86 The National Parks historians appear to have relied heavily on Lossing's engraving of Tecumseh. See LAC, Indian and Northern Affairs, Tecumseh Memorial File, Hutchison to Côté, 7 March 1957. See also CIHB, Central Registry, Tecumseh File, Smyth to Reid, 10 September 1985. The earlier discovery of another portrait of Tecumseh, which surfaced in 1954, probably complicated their efforts to a considerable degree. This second portrait is now thought to be of Paukeesaa, Tecumseh's son. See Sugden, *Tecumseh: A Life*, 403–4.

87 LAC, Indian and Northern Affairs, Tecumseh Memorial File, Lesage to Landon, 21 February 1957. HSMB, Minute Book, 30 May 1931, 29.

88 LAC, Indian and Northern Affairs, Tecumseh Memorial File, Landon to Lesage, 21 January 1957. Although the battle no doubt carried over to lot 5, and perhaps some distance beyond, most of the military artifacts and human remains were discovered on lot 4. The significance of lot 4 is cited in at least two published sources. See Gurd, *Story of Tecumseh*, 183; Coutts, "Thamesville and the Battle of the Thames," 23. An unpublished source is Benjamin Springer's survey map dating from 1845, which indicates that the place where Tecumseh was killed was on lot 4, Gore of Zone Township. Springer might have based his plan on the blazed walnut trees, which James Dickson had not yet chopped down. See Grant, *Picturesque Canada*, 2:535. Landon learned of this map in March of 1957, after National Parks historians discovered it referenced in *Picturesque Canada*. See LAC, Parks Canada, Central Registry Files, Richardson to Deputy Minister, Department of Lands and Forests, 31 January 1957; ibid., Beatty to Richardson, 7 February 1957; ibid., Richardson to Beatty, 7 March 1957; ibid., Beatty to Richardson, 15 March 1957; ibid., Landon to Richardson, 17 March 1957.

89 CIHB, Central Registry, Tecumseh File, Bennett to Apted, 27 November

244 Notes to page 129

1972. How the National Parks historians came to this conclusion is unknown. Granted, the action along the British line may have extended back as far as lot 7 or perhaps even a bit farther, but not likely two or three miles.

90 It was Landon who negotiated with the Ontario Department of Highways on behalf of the Historic Sites and Monuments Board. See LAC, Parks Canada, Central Registry Files, Richardson to Landon, 22 March 1957; ibid., Landon to Richardson, 27 March 1957; ibid., Landon to Richardson, 13 April 1957; ibid., 17 April 1957. For information on the monument's early progress, see ibid., [Côté] to Hutchison, 21 February 1957; ibid., Scott to Hutchison, 28 February 1957; ibid., Robinson to Scott, 11 March 1957.

91 Ibid., Herbert to Scott, 29 December 1959. John Coleman, the director of the National Parks Division, shared Herbert's opinion. See ibid., Coleman to Côté, 5 May 1961. Roman Fodchuk recalls that the Tecumseh Monument "was the beginning of a new approach to some of the future commemorative designs." In Fodchuk to St-Denis, 24 August 2002. However, there is evidence to suggest that officials in the Department of Northern Affairs and National Resources were thinking along more modern lines as early as 1957. See LAC, Indian and Northern Affairs, Tecumseh Memorial File, Hutchison to Côté, 7 March 1957. Furthermore, by the time the Tecumseh Monument was unveiled in 1963, several other monuments of a modern design had already been completed. See ibid., Côté to Turner, 27 June 1963.

92 Fodchuk to St-Denis, 24 August 2002. Fodchuk was assisted by Arthur Price, a sculptor of Cyrville, Ontario, who was commissioned to execute the sand-sculptured panels and provide other services. See LAC, Parks Canada, Central Registry Files, contract between Arthur Price and the Queen, 6 September 1961; ibid., Oswald to Richardson, 23 April 1957; ibid., 13 May 1957; *London Evening Free Press*, 7 October 1963, p. 9, col. 4; LAC, Indian and Northern Affairs, Tecumseh Memorial File, press release, 3 October 1963.

93 LAC, Indian and Northern Affairs, Tecumseh Memorial File, Fodchuk to Scott, 19 April 1961. Fodchuk found his information regarding the clan totems of Tecumseh's parents in Ethel T. Raymond's *Tecumseh*. This same book provided Fodchuk with an explanation regarding the shooting star, which Tecumseh supposedly saw during a dream quest, and which was claimed to have been the inspiration behind his name. See Raymond, *Tecumseh*, 2–3, 24–6. According to John Sugden, however, Tecumseh's name was in reference to his clan, and in "tribal mythology the spiritual patron of Tecumseh's clan was a celestial panther, a brilliant starry creature that jumped across the skies." See Sugden, *Tecumseh: A Life*, 23.

94 LAC, Indian and Northern Affairs, Tecumseh Memorial File, Fodchuk to Scott, 19 April 1961; Fodchuk, "Perspective of Memorial, Tecumseh Memorial," 17 April 1961 in Fodchuk to St-Denis, 17 September 2002.

See also LAC, Parks Canada, Central Registry Files, Fodchuk, "Site Layout, Tecumseh Memorial," 17 July 1961; ibid., "Staking Plan & Construction Details, Tecumseh Memorial," 17 July 1961; ibid., "Construction Details, Tecumseh Memorial," 17 July 1961. The estimated cost of Fodchuk's design was $3,700. Although this sum was almost twice the amount Landon thought acceptable, the Department of Northern Affairs and National Resources thought it was reasonable enough. The final cost of the Tecumseh Monument was approximately $5,000, which did not bother the officers of the department since they felt they had received good value for their money. See LAC, Indian and Northern Affairs, Tecumseh Memorial File, Hutchison to Côté, 30 January 1957; ibid., Fodchuk to Scott, 19 April 1961; ibid., Coleman to [Robertson], 29 January 1963.

95 LAC, Indian and Northern Affairs, Fodchuk to Scott, 19 April 1961.

96 The contract for the construction of the monument was awarded to a London, Ontario, company at the end of September 1961. See LAC, Parks Canada, Central Registry Files, articles of agreement between the Queen and Bernardo Marble, Terrazzo and Tile Company, 29 September 1961. Work on the monument was underway by the last week of October, 1961. See LAC, Indian and Northern Affairs, Tecumseh Memorial File, Coleman to Côté, 25 October 1961. See also *Chatham Daily News*, 30 March 1962, p. 13, col. 7.

97 *Windsor Star*, 3 May 1962, sec. 2, p. 7, col. 6. The reporter who noticed the problem was Brair McKinnon.

98 Strictly speaking, the boulder should have been set up somewhere toward the middle of John McDowell's farm, lot 4 north of the Longwoods Road. However, McDowell "assigned to it an obscure corner bordering the Longwoods Road." See Coutts, "Tecumseh Memorial Boulder," 85.

99 This glaring mistake was the result of editorial revision. Landon was responsible for the original inscription which claimed that "the place of his [Tecumseh's] death is about one half mile southwest of this monument." See LAC, Parks Canada, Central Registry File, Landon to Richardson, 23 April 1957; HSMB, Minute Book, 3 June 1957, 50–1. Initially, Landon thought the site where Tecumseh was killed was in a northwesterly direction from the park dedicated to him. Landon discovered his reckoning to be a mistake, as "the highway is so winding, following somewhat the course of the river Thames, that one finds difficulty in knowing where north or any other point of the compass lies." See LAC, Parks Canada, Central Registry File, Landon to Richardson, 10 May 1957. The historians Donald Creighton and Arthur Lower fell victim to this complication of geography when they subsequently revised the wording of the inscription by omitting the all-important "west" from "southwest." See HSMB, Minute Book, 25 May 1959, 34. Mistake or no mistake, the wording was allowed to stand until 1979, when it was finally corrected with the much safer reference that Tecumseh "was killed near here." See HSMB, Minute Book, 21–25 May 1979, 52.

100 Originally, it was planned that the monument would be unveiled in the autumn of 1961, but Walter Dinsdale, the minister of Northern Affairs and National Resources, postponed the ceremony until the spring of 1962. It was just as well, since the contractor encountered problems with the concrete work. See LAC, Indian and Northern Affairs, Tecumseh Memorial File, Côté to Coleman, 2 November 1961; ibid., Coleman to Côté, 23 February 1962. For details of the contractor's problems, see LAC, Parks Canada, Central Registry Files, Bernardo to [Persson], 9 December 1961; ibid., Persson to Scott, 14 December 1961; ibid., Persson to Bernardo, 20 December 1961.

101 Administrative delays and seasonal weather concerns contributed to the delays. See LAC, Indian and Northern Affairs, Tecumseh Memorial File, Coleman to [Robertson], 15 October 1962; ibid., Dinsdale to McBain, 17 October 1962. Dinsdale was a Conservative who became minister of Northern Affairs and National Resources after John Diefenbaker's election in June of 1957.

102 Ibid., Dinsdale to McBain, 17 October 1962.

103 *Ottawa Citizen*, 8 December 1962, p. 16, col. 5. Lewis was a Chippewa from Muncey, near London, Ontario. See Greene, *Who's Who in Canada*, 1962–63, 1507.

104 *Ottawa Citizen*, 8 December 1962, p. 16, col. 5.

105 LAC, Indian and Northern Affairs, Tecumseh Memorial File, Lewis to Dinsdale, 8 December 1962.

106 Ibid. The Champlain Monument had also inspired the veterans of Walpole Island. See *Sarnia Canadian Observer*, 1 August 1934, p. 3, col. 7. Samuel de Champlain was a French explorer and governor of New France in the early part of the seventeenth century.

107 Dinsdale admitted as much in his press release: "Sites and designs have not been determined." See *Ottawa Citizen*, 8 December 1962, p. 16, col. 5.

108 Perhaps the strongest evidence of Dinsdale's charitable nature is his affiliation with the Salvation Army. See Greene, *Who's Who in Canada*, 1962–63, 29–30.

109 LAC, Indian and Northern Affairs, Tecumseh Memorial File, Dinsdale to Lewis, 18 December 1962. While the federal government did not instigate the construction of the monument to Champlain at Orillia, it did provide funding for the project in the amount of $7,500. See *Globe*, 21 May 1913, p. 1, col. 1.

110 LAC, Indian and Northern Affairs, Tecumseh Memorial File, Dinsdale to Lewis, 18 December 1962.

111 Ibid., Lewis to Dinsdale, 22 December 1962.

112 Ibid.

113 Ibid.

114 Ibid., Coleman to Côté, 9 January 1963. This was not the first problem encountered with the effigy. Soon after it was cast, J.D. Herbert, chief of the National Historic Sites Division, Department of Northern Affairs and

National Resources, observed that the medal worn by Tecumseh portrayed a rather effeminate-looking George III. The foundry succeeded in altering the effigy so that the king looked "a little more masculine." See LAC, Parks Canada, Central Registry Files, Herbert to Sleep, 16 June 1960; ibid., Sleep to Herbert, 22 June 1960; ibid., 19 September 1960.

115 LAC, Indian and Northern Affairs, Tecumseh Memorial File, Coleman to Côté, 9 January 1963. According to Benson J. Lossing, however, Tecumseh did wear a British brigadier-general's coat on at least one occasion. See Lossing, *Pictorial Field-Book of the War of 1812*, 288. The Parks historians were influenced by eyewitness accounts that described Tecumseh in Native attire just prior to the Battle of the Thames. See LAC, Parks Canada, Central Registry Files, Sutherland to Chief, 18 June 1963.

116 LAC, Indian and Northern Affairs, Tecumseh Memorial File, Coleman to Côté, 9 January 1963. As Coleman explained, Tecumseh "came to epitomize all that was noble in the American Indian, the defender of aboriginal virtue against the insensate progressiveness of the white man. In addition to being endowed with a multitude of personal and military virtues he was portrayed as being mustered into the British Army as a general officer, only to throw off his uniform in disgust."

117 Ibid.

118 Ibid.

119 Ibid., Coleman to Côté, 9 January 1963; Lossing, *Pictorial Field-Book of the War of 1812*, 189, 288.

120 LAC, Indian and Northern Affairs, Tecumseh Memorial File, Coleman to Côté, 9 January 1963. The Parks historians made particular use of John Richardson's description of Tecumseh, which recalled his appearance just prior to the Battle of the Thames. See LAC, Parks Canada, Central Registry Files, Sutherland to Chief, 18 June 1963; Casselman, *Richardson's War of 1812*, 212. Although a report of the necessary changes was finished by mid-June of 1963, it was not until mid-August that the bronze effigy was removed and sent for recasting. See LAC, Parks Canada, Central Registry Files, Sutherland to Chief, 18 June 1963; ibid., Imrie to Sleep, 8 August 1963; ibid., Herbert to Chief, Engineering Services Division, 12 August 1963; ibid., Sleep to Herbert, 16 August 1963.

121 LAC, Indian and Northern Affairs, Tecumseh Memorial File, Coleman to Côté, 9 January 1963.

122 Ibid., Dinsdale to Lewis, 30 January 1963.

123 For the draft letter, see ibid., Dinsdale to Lewis, 28 January 1963. For a copy of the letter Dinsdale sent to Lewis, see ibid., 30 January 1963. For the Parks historians' objection, see ibid., Coleman to [Robertson], 7 February 1963. Earlier, Coleman reported that "the American author of the latest biography of Tecumseh has taken some pains to demolish the brigadier-general myth." This American author was Glenn Tucker, whose *Tecumseh: Vision of Glory* was published in 1956. See ibid., Coleman to Côté, 9 January 1963; Tucker, *Tecumseh: Vision of Glory*, 259–60.

124 In mid-August of 1963, the plaque featuring Tecumseh's effigy was quietly removed and promptly melted down. A new plaque was speedily commissioned, and this time Tecumseh came back more appropriately attired. See CIHB, Central Registry, Tecumseh File, Bennett to Apted, 27 November 1972; ibid., Smyth to Reid, 10 September 1985.

125 Diefenbaker, *One Canada*, 3:174, 189.

126 Greene, *Who's Who in Canada*, 1962–63, 1507; Macdonald to St-Denis, 31 December 2002. Lewis had also been a Liberal candidate in the 1959 provincial election. His campaign proved unsuccessful.

127 LAC, Indian and Northern Affairs, Tecumseh Memorial File, 24 May 1963. Donald S. Macdonald rose to prominence in the government of Pierre Trudeau.

128 Ibid.

129 John N. Turner went on to become prime minister of Canada in 1984.

130 Ibid., Turner to Lewis, 30 May 1963.

131 Ibid., Lewis to Turner, 5 June 1963.

132 Ibid.

133 Ibid., Laing to Turner, 13 June 1963.

134 Ibid.

135 Ibid., Turner to Lewis, 13 June 1963.

136 UWOA, Talman Papers, Sutherland for Herbert to Talman, 6 June 1963.

137 Ibid., Talman to Herbert, 12 June 1963. Talman was appointed a member of the Historic Sites and Monuments Board in 1961. See Stevenson, "James John Talman," 15.

138 Stevenson, "James John Talman," 5.

139 UWOA, Talman Papers, Sutherland to Talman, 9 September 1963. Normally, some local group would be asked to sponsor the unveiling ceremony, with the understanding that their chief officer would act as chairman of the event. In the case of the Tecumseh monument, however, the Historic Sites and Monuments Board assumed that Talman would be willing to take on the responsibility. Besides being the board member who represented the area, Talman had already performed admirably in this capacity on an earlier occasion. See Long, "Historic Sites and Monuments Board," 6–7; UWOA, Talman Papers, Sutherland to Talman, 9 September 1963. Sutherland and his colleague spent several days preparing for the unveiling ceremony. Their duties included making arrangements for a public address system, a platform, chairs, bunting for the monument, and publicity. In Sutherland to St-Denis, 4 August 2002.

140 *London Evening Free Press*, 7 October 1963, p. 9, col. 4; *Herald*, 23 October 1913, p. 1, col. 4.

141 According to the order of ceremony, John C. Munro, representing the Ministry of Citizenship and Immigration, was supposed to precede Laing. However, newspaper coverage of the event suggests that this arrangement was reversed. See LAC, Indian and Northern Affairs, Tecumseh Memorial File, "Unveiling of Tecumseh Monument, October 5, Order of Ceremony;

LAC, Parks Canada, Central Registry Files, Sutherland to Talman, 27 September 1963; *London Evening Free Press*, 7 October 1963, p. 9, col. 4; *Windsor Star*, 7 October 1963, early final ed., p. 5, col. 4.

142 *Windsor Star*, 7 October 1963, early final ed., p. 5, col. 4.

143 LAC, Indian and Northern Affairs, Tecumseh Memorial File, Dumont to Robertson, 23 September 1963.

144 *Windsor Star*, 7 October 1963, early final ed., p. 5, col. 4.

145 *London Evening Free Press*, 7 October 1963, p. 9, col. 4. The federal franchise was extended to Natives in 1960.

146 Ibid.

147 Ibid.

148 Ibid.

149 Ibid.

150 UWOA, Talman Papers, Sutherland to Talman, 16 October 1963.

151 Ibid., Talman to Sutherland, 18 October 1963.

152 Landon remained in London, Ontario, on the day the monument was unveiled. It would appear that he did not feel up to the long car ride. See UWOA, Landon Papers, Diaries, 1963, 5–6 October 1963.

CONCLUSION

1 In 1913, over 8,000 people assembled to hear dignitaries pay tribute to Tecumseh. In 1963, barely 200 spectators watched as a monument near the battlefield was finally unveiled in his honour. See *Herald*, 23 October 1913, p. 1, col. 4; *London Evening Free Press*, 7 October 1963, p. 9, col. 4.

2 The curator probably heard the story of the secret burial from Big White Owl, or Jasper Hill, a Delaware from Moraviantown who frequently told how "a few of Tecumseh's loyal aides and warriors came back, under the cover of night, to recover and bury the body of their great chief in a grave that has remained 'secret' even to this day." See *Globe and Mail*, 9 July 1965, p. 6, col. 3.

3 AO, Attorney General, Oates File, report, 14 September 1876, 3–4; *Daily Advertiser*, 6 September 1876, p. 2, col. 3; *Canadian Home Journal*, semi-weekly ed., 3 October 1876, p. 2, col. 1; *London Evening Free Press*, 28 June 1924, p. 8, col. 1; *Globe*, 29 September 1876, p. 3, col. 3; *Wallaceburg News*, 14 April 1910, p. 3, col. 3; ibid., 12 May 1910, p. 7, col. 3.

4 The grave discovered by the United Canadians was on lot 5, near the fence separating that lot from the adjacent lot 4. See AO, Attorney General, Oates File, report, 14 September 1876, 2–3. For George H.M. Johnson's map showing the location of the grave, see ibid., *Daily Pocket Diary for 1855* (New York, New York: n.p., 1855). James Dickson owned lot 4, while William Watts owned lot 5.

5 Sabathy-Judd, *Moravians in Upper Canada*, 504, 513.

6 The Kentuckians learned their lesson at the Battle of Fort Meigs early in May of 1813, when Lieutenant Colonel William Dudley's command

pursued Native snipers deep into the forest – only to be ambushed and slaughtered. See Antal, *A Wampum Denied*, 223–5.

7 For example, see Sugden, *Tecumseh's Last Stand*, 133, 152, 155, 159, 167. William Caldwell junior, who fought with the Natives, made the unconvincing claim that they "retired by degrees as the Americans advanced." See ibid., 131.

8 Oshahwahnoo is not referred to by name, but there can be no mistaking his identity. See WHS, Draper Manuscript Collection, Tecumseh Papers, ser. YY, vol. 7, no. 65, Jamieson to Draper, 13 March 1882. In another letter, Rev. Andrew Jamieson, the Anglican missionary to Walpole Island, identifies Oshahwahnoo as one of the Natives who fled the field "precipitately" when Tecumseh was killed. See ibid., no. 70, Jamieson to Draper, 2 May 1882.

9 Oshahwahnoo acknowledged that Tecumseh's body was mutilated by repeating the story of a fellow Native, Shaw-an-abb. See [Richardson], "Trip to Walpole Island and Port Sarnia," 18.

10 By the time Harrison viewed the body in the afternoon of 6 October, it was badly mutilated. See Sugden, *Tecumseh's Last Stand*, 169.

11 The most prominent of these warriors was Black Hawk, who was also one of the earliest proponents of the secret burial story. See ibid., 155–6. A good deal of Harrison's reticence probably had to do with Andrew Clark's claim that Tecumseh had been killed and taken "off the ground." See ibid., 153. Clark claimed to have served Tecumseh as an aide and interpreter. See ibid., 154.

12 *Globe*, 3 September 1913, p. 6, col. 4.

13 Sugden, *Tecumseh's Last Stand*, 68–9. As noted elsewhere, Joseph Johnson's militia service during the War of 1812 was brief. He served in Captain Thomas McCrae's second company of the First Regiment of Kent Militia, from 2 July until 11 July 1812, when he was reported absent with leave. He then served in Captain George Jacob's flank company, First Kent Regiment, for a further three days between 16 September and 18 September, 1812. See LAC, Militia and Defence, First Regiment, Kent Militia (1812–14), Pay Lists and Muster Rolls, Captain Thomas McCrae's Company, 2–24 July 1812, p. 479, no. 16; ibid., Captain George Jacob's Company, 25 August-24 September 1812, p. 494, no. 75.

14 Abraham Holmes, for one, recalled seeing Johnson and Tecumseh engaged in conversation at Arnold's Mill on the day of the battle. See WHS, Draper Manuscript Collection, Tecumseh Papers, ser. YY, vol. 7, no. 67, Holmes to Draper, 20 April 1882.

15 LR, Gurd Papers, Greenwood to Leonhardt, 31 January 1911. Thaddeus Arnold, who dismissed Johnson's story in the press, was perhaps the greatest of these skeptics. See *Chatham Daily Planet*, 26 October 1901, p. 7, col. 1.

16 The story told by William Caldwell junior regarding Tecumseh's assassination was of this order. See *Chatham Journal*, 11 February 1843, p. 2, col. 5.

17 *Chatham Tri-Weekly Planet*, 4 November 1889, p. 1, col. 4.

18 *Globe*, 3 September 1913, p. 6, col. 4.

19 *Wallaceburg News*, 14 April 1910, p. 3, col. 3.

20 It was to Rev. Andrew Jamieson that Oshahwahnoo made his admission regarding Tecumseh's burial. Jamieson later supplied this information to the American historian Lyman C. Draper. See WHS, Draper Manuscript Collection, Tecumseh Papers, ser. YY, vol. 7, no. 65, Jamieson to Draper, 13 March 1882; ibid., Jamieson to Draper, 2 May 1882. Additionally, when Oshahwahnoo provided John Richardson with an account of Tecumseh's death and burial in 1848, it was not his own recollection but rather that of "Shaw-an-abb" – which further suggests that Oshahwahnoo did not participate in Tecumseh's burial. See [Richardson], "Trip to Walpole Island and Port Sarnia," 17.

21 *Wallaceburg News*, 1 June 1911, p. 2, col. 3.

22 As late as 1923, Gurd doubted the story that Tecumseh's bones had been buried on St Anne's Island. But he changed his mind by the time of their rediscovery on Walpole Island in 1931. See LR, Gurd Papers, letterbook, Gurd to Colquhoun, 12 September 1923, 778; LAC, Indian Affairs, Red Series, Correspondence Concerning Tecumseh's Grave, Gurd to Gray, 29 January 1931.

23 *Border Cities Star*, 26 February 1931, sec. 2, p. 5, col. 1; ibid., 28 February 1931, p. 15, col. 1.

24 Sugden, *Tecumseh's Last Stand*, 135, 174–5. The worst of these mutilations appear to have been inflicted the next morning, 6 October 1813. See ibid., 156.

25 Ibid., 169.

26 According to David Sherman, he and his father assisted several other settlers in burying the dead after the Battle of the Thames. While Sherman mentions a pit into which the bodies were thrown, Daniel Dunihue found evidence of a number of individual graves. James Dickson, the first owner of the farm encompassing the battlefield, did not indicate whether the six skeletons he discovered near the blazed walnut trees beyond the small swamp were found in one grave, several individual graves, or some combination of the two. See Coutts, "Thamesville and the Battle of the Thames," 24; ISL, Journal of Daniel R. Dunihue, 3; *Globe*, 29 September 1876, p. 3, col. 3.

27 MNR, Township Plans, "Township of Zone," by M[ahlon] Burwell, 4 February 1823, D-26, no. 35.

28 Dickson recalled an eagle, horse, turtle, and other animals. Perhaps the turtle was symbolic of Tecumseh's mother's clan. If there was a panther to represent his father's clan, Dickson failed to recognize it as such. See *Globe*, 29 September 1876, p. 3, col. 3. Dickson told Wilson that he occupied lot 4, Gore of Zone Township in 1846. This statement is substantiated by a surveyor's report, which indicates that the site of the battlefield was still unoccupied as late as the autumn of 1845. See AO, Zone

Township Papers, Return of the Areas of the Lots in the Gore of the Township of Zone, October 1845, 2083.

29 *Globe*, 29 September 1876, p. 3, col. 3; Grant, *Picturesque Canada*, 2:535.

30 Dickson also found numerous relics such as "iron tomahawks, horse shoes, scalping knives, lead shot, &tc." See *Globe*, 29 September 1876, p. 3, col. 3.

31 According to Thaddeus Arnold, Joseph Johnson took Frederick Arnold to "the spot between two beech [walnut] trees on which there were markings, which Johnston [*sic*] claimed signified that the Shawanee chief was buried there." See *Chatham Daily Planet*, 26 October 1901, p. 7, col. 1.

32 *Globe*, 29 September 1876, p. 3, col. 3. This skull likely went up in flames with much of the University of Toronto in 1890. See Averill and Keith, "Daniel Wilson and the University of Toronto," 186–7.

33 *Globe*, 29 September 1876, p. 3, col. 3. Presumably, the six skeletons discovered by Dickson were placed in one grave.

34 *Canadian Home Journal*, semi-weekly ed., 5 September 1876, p. 4, col. 5.

35 Dickson might very well have reburied the six skeletons, including Tecumseh's bones, somewhere on the perimeter of lot 4 in the Gore of Zone Township.

Bibliography

MANUSCRIPTS

CANADA
Archives of Ontario, Toronto, Ontario (AO)
Attorney General of Ontario, Central Registry (RG 4–32)
   Criminal and Civil Files
      R.H. Oates File (E 2187), 1876
Essex County Surrogate Court (RG 22-311)
   Register F, 1867–76
Thomas Gowman Papers (MU 2330)
   "Pioneer Life in Upper Canada"
Kent County Land Registry (RG 61-24)
   Abstract Books
      Zone Township
   Copybooks of Deeds
      Register C, 1818–27
      Register E, 1874–78
Ontario Land Record Index, c. 1780–1920
   Alphabetical Listing
Registrar General of Ontario (RG 80-2/8)
   Birth and Stillbirth Registrations, 1870
   Death Registrations, 1885, 1890, 1892
Township Papers (RG 1-58)
   Zone Township, 1845, 1849
Western District Court of Quarter Sessions (RG 22-108)
   Minute Book (vol. 167), 1834–46
James P. Whitney Papers (F 5)
   Correspondence, 1911–12

Brant Historical Society, Brantford, Ontario
Evelyn Johnson Papers

Canadian Inventory of Historic Building, Hull, Quebec (CIHB)
Central Registry
  Tecumseh File (C8400/930)

Historic Sites and Monuments Board of Canada, Hull, Quebec (HSMB)
Minute Books, 1931–33, 1939, 1944, 1951–55, 1957,
  1959, 1979

Kent County Land Registry, Chatham, Ontario (KCLR)
Abstract Books
  Camden Township
  Chatham Township
  Dover East Township
  Howard Township
  Tilbury East Township
  Zone Township
Instruments
  Howard Township, 1803–04, 1807, 1831

Lambton County Land Registry, Sarnia, Ontario (LCLR)
Abstract Books
  Dawn Township
  Moore Township

Lambton Room, Lambton County Library, Wyoming, Ontario (LR)
Norman S. Gurd Papers

Library and Archives Canada, Ottawa, Ontario (LAC)
National Archives:
Robert Laird Borden Papers (MG 26, H1a)
  Correspondence (ser. OC, vol. 26), 1893–1921
Census Returns (RG 31, C1)
  Camden Township, Kent County, Ontario, 1861, 1871
  Caradoc Township, Middlesex County, Canada West/Ontario, 1851, 1891
  Dresden, Ontario, 1881, 1891
  Harwich Township, Kent County, Ontario, 1891
  Niagara, Ontario, 1871
  Orford Township (Moraviantown), Kent County, Ontario, 1871
  Sarnia Reserve, Lambton County, Ontario, 1861
  Tuscarora Township, Brant County, Canada West, 1851
  Zone Township, Kent County, Ontario, 1881, 1891
Civil Secretary's Correspondence (RG 5, A1)
  Upper Canada Sundries (vol. 30), 1816

Department of Indian Affairs (RG 10)
  Deputy Superintendent General
      Correspondence (vol. 355), 1869–70
  Red Series
      Correspondence Concerning the Location of the Grave of Tecumseh
          (vol. 1993, file 6828), 1876–1934
      Western Superintendency, Sarnia Agency
          J.B. Clench Correspondence (vols 439–40), 1842–54
          F. Talfourd Correspondence (vol. 450), 1855–64
Indian and Northern Affairs Canada (RG 22)
  Tecumseh Memorial File
      Correspondence (vol. 1393), 1957–65
Militia and Defence, Pre-Confederation Records (RG 9)
  Adjutant General, Upper Canada
      First Regiment, Kent Militia, Pay Lists and Muster Rolls (vol. 32),
          1812–14
          Captain John Dolsen's Company
          Captain George Jacob's Company
          Captain Thomas McCrae's Company
      Loyal Kent Volunteers, Kent Militia, Pay Lists and Muster Rolls (vol. 32),
          1813–15
          Captain John McGregor's Company
          Lieutenant John McGregor's Company
Parks Canada (RG 84)
  Central Registry Files
      Historic Sites, Western Ontario
          Battle of Thames, Chief Tecumseh (vol. 1345, file HS9-12-3), 1921–63
Provincial Secretary, Canada West (RG 5, C1)
  Correspondence (vol. 29), 1840
Upper Canada/Canada Land Committee (RG 1, L3)
  Petitions, 1796–97, 1820–25, 1855–57
Upper Canada State Papers (RG 1, E3)
  Correspondence (vol. 90), 1840

London Museum of Archaeology, London, Ontario
Wilfrid Jury Papers

London Roman Catholic Diocese Archives, London, Ontario
St John the Baptist Church, Amherstburg, Ontario
  Parish Registers, 1802–29

Ministry of Natural Resources, Peterborough, Ontario (MNR)
Department of Lands and Forests
  Instructions to Land Surveyors
      Book 4, 1820–33

Letters Written
  Book 25, 1820–22
Report and Field Notes/Diaries
  Zone Township, 1821–22, 1845
Township Plans
  Zone Township, 1823, 1830, 1845

Park House Museum, Amherstburg, Ontario (PHM)
Committee for Superintending the Erection of a Monument to Tecumseh
  Minute Book, 1841

University of Toronto Archives, Toronto, Ontario (UTA)
Langton Papers
  Journal of Daniel Wilson, 1876

University of Western Ontario Archives, London, Ontario (UWOA)
Talman Regional Collection:
Caradoc Township Assessment Rolls, 1877
Arthur C. Carty Papers
James H. Coyne Papers
W.E. Elliott Collection
Ermatinger Papers
Louis Goulet Papers
Evelyn H.C. Johnson Papers
Fred Landon Papers
London Free Press Collection of Photographic Negatives
Middlesex County Court of Quarter Sessions
  Criminal Court Records, 1860
  Minute Book, 1859–66
James J. Talman Papers

ENGLAND
The National Archives, Kew, Richmond, Surrey (TNA)
Public Record Office:
War Office
  Judge Advocate General (WO 71)
    Court Martial Proceedings of Major-General Henry Procter,
      1814–15 (WO 71/243)

UNITED STATES
Algonac/Clay Township Historical Society, Algonac, Michigan
Walpole Island Papers
  Account of the Tecumseh Monument Cornerstone Laying Ceremony, 1934

Archives of the Moravian Church, Bethlehem, Pennsylvania (AMC)
New Fairfield Mission
   Burial Register, 1870–1903
   Diaries, 1867, 1869, 1871
   Report, 1869

Indiana State Library, Indianapolis, Indiana (ISL)
Manuscript Section:
Journal of Daniel R. Dunihue, 1830

Wisconsin Historical Society, Madison, Wisconsin (WHS)
Library – Archives:
Draper Manuscript Collection
   Joseph "Brandt" Papers (ser. F)
   Draper's Notes (ser. S)
   Tecumseh Papers (ser. YY)

ARTICLES, BOOKS, AND THESES

Allen, Robert S. *His Majesty's Indian Allies: British Indian Policy in The Defence of Canada, 1774–1815.* Toronto, Ontario: Dundurn Press, 1992
Annual Report of the Ontario Historical Society, 1913. Toronto, Ontario: Ontario Historical Society, 1913
Antal, Sandy. *A Wampum Denied: Procter's War of 1812.* Carleton Library Series, vol. 191. Ottawa, Ontario: Carleton University Press, 1997
Appleton, Thomas E. *Usque ad Mare: A History of the Canadian Coast Guard and Marine Services.* Ottawa, Ontario: Department of Transport, 1968
Armstrong, Frederick H. "Fred Landon, 1880–1969." *Ontario History* 62, no. 1 (March 1970): 1–4
Arnold, T[haddeus] S. "Battle of the Thames and Death of Tecumseh." United Empire Loyalists' Association of Ontario *Annual Transactions* 4 (1901–02): 30–5
Averill, Harold and Gerald Keith. "Daniel Wilson and the University of Toronto." In *Thinking with Both Hands: Sir Daniel Wilson in the Old World and the New*: 139–210. Edited by Marinell Ash and colleagues. Toronto, Ontario: University of Toronto Press, 1999
Axtell, James. *The European and the Indian.* New York, New York: Oxford University Press, 1981
Bartlett, Irving. *Wendell Phillips: Brahmin Radical.* Boston, Massachusetts: Beacon Press, 1961; reprint ed., Wesport, Connecticut: Greenwood Press, 1973
Baskerville, Peter, ed. *The Bank of Upper Canada: A Collection of Documents.* Toronto, Ontario: Champlain Society/Ontario Heritage Foundation, 1987
Berger, Carl. "Wilson, Sir Daniel." In *Dictionary of Canadian Biography* 12: 1109–14

Brown, Margaret A. *Life of Joseph Brant, Comprising in Part the Origin and History of the Iroquois or Six Nation Indians.* Brantford[?], Ontario: [Brant Historical Society, 1926]

Brymner, Douglas. "Monument to Tecumseh." *Canadiana* 2, no.6 (June 1890): 115–18

Canada's Historic Heritage: National Historic Parks and Sites in Canada. Ottawa, Ontario: Queen's Printer, 1952

Careless, J[ames] M.S. *The Union of the Canadas: The Growth of Canadian Institutions, 1841–1857.* The Canadian Centenary Series, no. 10. Toronto, Ontario: McClelland and Stewart, 1967

[Carty, Arthur C.] "History and Romance in London's Environs: The Burial Place of Tecumseh at Last Revealed." In *The Centennial Year Review of London, Canada:* 66. Edited by Edmund J. Carty and Arthur C. Carty. London, Ontario: Hayden Press, 1926

Casselman, Alexander, ed. *Richardson's War of 1812.* Toronto, Ontario: Historical Publishing Company, 1902

Circular of the Annexation Association of Montreal. Montreal, Quebec: James Potts, Herald Office, 1849; reprint ed., *The Annexation Manifesto of 1849.* Montreal, Quebec: D. English and Company, 1881

Coffin, William. *1812; The War, and Its Moral.* Montreal [Canada East]: John Lovell, 1864

Colquhoun, A[rthur] H.U. *Tecumseh and Richardson: The Story of a Trip to Walpole Island and Port Sarnia.* Toronto, Ontario: Ontario Book Company, 1924

Comeau-Vasilopolous, Gale M. "Oronhyatekha." In *Dictionary of Canadian Biography* 13: 791–5

Commemorative Biographical Record of the County of Essex, Ontario. Toronto, Ontario: J.H. Beers and Company, 1905

Commemorative Biographical Record of the County of Kent, Ontario. Toronto, Ontario: J.H. Beers and Company, 1904

Commemorative Biographical Record of the County of Lambton, Ontario. Toronto, Ontario: J.H. Beers and Company, 1906

Coutts, Katherine B. "The Tecumseh Memorial Boulder." Kent Historical Society *Papers and Addresses* 6 (1924): 85–7

– "Thamesville and the Battle of the Thames." Ontario Historical Society *Papers and Records* 9 (1910): 20–5

Craig, Gerald M. *Upper Canada: The Formative Years, 1784–1841.* The Canadian Centenary Series, no. 7. Toronto, Ontario: McClelland and Stewart, 1963

Cruikshank, Ernest A. "The Contest for the Command of Lake Erie in 1812–13." In *The Defended Border: Upper Canada and the War of 1812:* 84–104. Edited by Morris Zaslow and Wesley B. Turner. Toronto, Ontario: Macmillan Company of Canada, 1964

– *Queenston Heights.* Welland, Ontario: Lundy's Lane Historical Society, 1890

Danglade, James Kirby. "John Graves Simcoe and the United States,

1775–1796: A Study in Anglo-American Frontier Diplomacy." Ph.D. dissertation, Ball State University, Muncie Indiana, 1972

Dent, John Charles. *The Canadian Portrait Gallery.* 4 vols. Toronto, Ontario: John B. Magurn, 1880

Diefenbaker, John G. *One Canada: Memoirs of the Right Honourable John G. Diefenbaker.* 3 vols. Toronto, Ontario: Macmillan of Canada, 1977

Drake, Benjamin. *Life of Tecumseh, and of his Brother the Prophet.* Cincinnati, Ohio: E. Morgan and Company, 1841

Drake, Samuel G. *Biography and History of the Indians of North America.* 10th ed. Boston, Massachusetts: Benjamin B. Mussey and Company, 1848

"Dunihue Correspondence of 1832." *Indiana Magazine of History* 35 (1939): 408–26

Edmunds, R. David. *The Shawnee Prophet.* Lincoln, Nebraska: University of Nebraska Press, 1983

– *Tecumseh and the Quest for Indian Leadership,* ed. Oscar Handlin, Library of American Biography. Boston, Massachusetts: Little, Brown and Company, 1984

Eggleston, Edward and Seelye, Lillie Eggleston. *Tecumseh and the Shawnee Prophet.* New York, New York: Dodd, Mead and Company, 1878

Esarey, Logan, ed. *Messages and Letters of William Henry Harrison.* 2 vols. Indianapolis, Indiana: Indiana Historical Commission, 1922; reprint ed., New York, New York: Arno Press, 1975

Evans, A. Margaret. *Sir Oliver Mowat.* Ontario Historical Studies Series. Toronto, Ontario: University of Toronto Press, 1992

Frost, John. *Thrilling Adventures among the Indians.* Philadelphia, Pennsylvania: J.W. Bradley, 1849

Gazetteer and Business Directory of Lincoln and Welland Counties, for 1879. Brantford, Ontario: William W. Evans, 1878

Gibb, Alice. "Death or Glory: The 1927 London-to-London Flight." In *Simcoe's Choice: Celebrating London's Bicentennial, 1793–1993:* 215–31. Edited by Guy St-Denis. Toronto, Ontario: Dundurn Press, 1992

Goltz, Herbert C.W. "Tecumseh, the Prophet and the Rise of the Northwest Indian Confederation." Ph.D. thesis, University of Western Ontario, London, Ontario, 1973

Gourlay, Robert F. *The Banished Briton and Neptunian: Being a Record of the Life, Writings, Principles, and Projects of Robert Gourlay, Esq., Now Robert Fleming Gourlay.* Boston, Massachusetts: Samuel N. Dickinson, 1843

– *Statistical Account of Upper Canada.* 2 vols. London, England: Simpkin and Marshall, 1822

Grant, George Munro, ed. *Picturesque Canada; The Country as It Was and Is.* 2 vols. Toronto, Ontario: Belden Brothers, 1883

Gray, Elma E. *Wilderness Christians.* Toronto, Ontario: Macmillan Company of Canada, 1956

Greene, B.M., ed. *Who's Who in Canada, 1962–63.* Toronto, Ontario: International Press Limited, 1962

Gunderson, Robert Gray. *The Log-Cabin Campaign*. Lexington, Kentucky: University of Kentucky Press, 1957

Gurd, Norman S. *The Story of Tecumseh*. Canadian Heroes Series, no. 2. Toronto, Ontario: William Briggs, 1912

Hale, Horatio. "Chief George H.M. Johnson – Onwanonsyshon." *Magazine of American History* 13, no. 2 (February 1885): 131–42

Hamil, Fred Coyne. *Valley of the Lower Thames*. Toronto, Ontario: University of Toronto Press, 1951

Hartmann, A[dolphus] et al. "Report of the Mission at New Fairfield, Canada, from July 1st, 1874, to July 1st, 1875." In *Proceedings of the Ninety-Ninth General Meeting and Eighty-Eighth Anniversary of the Society of the United Brethren for Propagating the Gospel among the Heathen, Held at Bethlehem, August 26th, 1875*. Bethlehem, Pennsylvania: Moravian Publication Office, 1875: Appendix A

– "Report of the Mission at New Fairfield, Canada, 1876." In *Proceedings of the One Hundred and First General Meeting and Ninetieth Anniversary of the Society of the United Brethren for Propagating the Gospel among the Heathen, Held at Bethlehem, August 30th, 1877*. Bethlehem, Pennsylvania: Moravian Publication Office, 1877: Appendix B

Harvey, Henry. *History of the Shawnee Indians*. Cincinnati, Ohio: Ephraim Morgan and Sons, 1855; reprint ed., New York, New York: Kraus Reprint Company, 1971

Hetherington, Lynn. "Tecumseh." *The University Magazine* 8 (February 1909): 135–47

History of Toronto and County of York, Ontario. Toronto, Ontario: C. Blackett Robinson, 1885

Hitsman, J. Mackay. *The Incredible War of 1812*. Toronto, Ontario: University of Toronto Press, 1965

Hunter, A[ndrew] F. "Bibliography of the Archaeology of Ontario." In Ontario *Sessional Papers*, Annual Archaeological Report (appended to the report of the Minister of Education) 30, pt. 1, no. 1 (1897–98): 67–87

Hyatt, A.M.J. "The Defence of Upper Canada in 1812." M.A. thesis, Carleton University, Ottawa, Ontario, 1961

– "Procter, Henry." In *Dictionary of Canadian Biography* 6: 616–18

Illustrated Historical Atlas of the Counties of Essex and Kent. Toronto, Ontario: H. Belden and Company, 1880–81; reprinted., London, Ontario: Edward Phelps and Ross Cumming, 1973

Indian Treaties and Surrenders. 3 vols. Ottawa, Ontario: Brown Chamberlin, Queen's Printer, 1891

Johnston, Sheila M.F. *Buckskin and Broadcloth: A Celebration of E. Pauline Johnson, Tekahionwake, 1861–1913*. Toronto, Ontario: Natural Heritage, 1997

Keller, Betty. *Pauline*. Vancouver, British Columbia and Toronto, Ontario: Douglas & McIntyre, 1981

Killan, Gerald. *Preserving Ontario's Heritage: A History of the Ontario Historical Society*. Toronto, Ontario: Ontario Historical Society, 1976

Kinchen, Oscar A. *The Rise and Fall of the Patriot Hunters*. New York, New York: Bookman Associates, 1956

Klopfenstein, Carl Grover. "The Removal of the Indians from Ohio, 1820–1843." Ph.D. dissertation, [Case] Western Reserve University, Cleveland, Ohio, 1955

Kulisek, L.L. "Caldwell, William." In *Dictionary of Canadian Biography* 6: 101–4

Langton, H[ugh] H. *Sir Daniel Wilson: A Memoir*. Toronto, Ontario: Thomas Nelson and Sons, 1929

Lauriston, Victor. *Lambton's Hundred Years, 1849–1949*. Sarnia, Ontario: Haines Frontier Printing Company, [1949]

– *Romantic Kent: More than Three Centuries of History, 1626–1952*. Chatham, Ontario: County of Kent and City of Chatham, 1952

Leighton, Douglas. "Johnson, George Henry Martin." In *Dictionary of Canadian Biography* 11: 451–3

– "Johnson, John." In *Dictionary of Canadian Biography* 11: 453–4

Lester's Sarnia and Point Edward Directory, 1931. Sarnia, Ontario: Earl A. Lester, 1931

London City and Middlesex County Directory, 1893. Toronto, Ontario: Might Directory Company, 1893

Long, M.H. "The Historic Sites and Monuments Board of Canada." In Canadian Historical Association *Report of the Annual Meeting ... for 1954*: 1–11. Edited by George F.G. Stanley.   Ottawa, Ontario: Canadian Historical Association, 1954

Lossing, Benson J. *The Pictorial Field-Book of the War of 1812*. New York, New York: Harper and Brothers, 1869

Lueger, Richard R.H. "A History of Indian Associations in Canada, 1870–1970." M.A. thesis, Carleton University, Ottawa, Ontario, 1977

MacCabe, Julius P. Bolivar. *Directory of the City of Detroit, with its Environs, and Register of Michigan, for the Year 1837*. Detroit, Michigan: William Harsha, 1837; reprint ed., Detroit, Michigan: R.L. Polk and Company, 1937

MacDonald, Allan J. "Lett, Benjamin." In *Dictionary of Canadian Biography* 8: 501–2

Mair, Charles. *Tecumseh: A Drama*. Toronto, Ontario: Hunter, Rose and Company, 1886

Mann, Frank. *A History of Wallaceburg and Vicinity, 1804 to the Present*. [Wallaceburg, Ontario: Standard Press], 1968

McAfee, Robert B. *History of the Late War in the Western Country*. Lexington, Kentucky: Worsley and Smith, 1816; reprint ed., Ann Arbor, Michigan: University Microfilms, 1966

Memorial of the Chippeway, Pottawatomy, and Ottawa Indians, of Walpole Island! Sarnia, Ontario: Canadian Book and Job Office, 1869

Meyer, Leland Winfield. *The Life and Times of Colonel Richard M. Johnson of Kentucky*. Studies in History, Economics and Public Law, no. 359. [New York, New York: Columbia University Press, 1932]; reprint ed., New York, New York: AMS Press, 1967

Middleton, Jesse E. and Landon, Fred. *The Province of Ontario – A History, 1615–1927*. 5 vols. Toronto, Ontario: Dominion Publishing Company, 1927

Miller, Warren Cron, ed. *Vignettes of Early St Thomas*. St Thomas, Ontario: Sutherland Press, 1967

Minutes and Proceedings of the Council of the Corporation of the County of Kent. Chatham, Ontario: Daily News Print, 1912

Morgan, Henry James. *The Canadian Men and Women of the Time*. 1st ed. Toronto, Ontario: William Briggs, 1898

Nindawaabjig. *Walpole Island: The Soul of Indian Territory*. Walpole Island, Ontario: Nindawaabjig, 1987

"Notes and Comments." Canadian Historical Review 12, no. 2 (June 1931): 117–18

Ontario Historical Society, *Proceedings of the Annual Meeting and Annual Reports for the Year 1926*. Toronto, Ontario: Ontario Historical Society, 1926

– *Proceedings of the Annual Meeting and Annual Reports for the Year 1931*. Toronto, Ontario: Ontario Historical Society, 1931

Owram, Doug. "'Management by Enthusiasm': The First Board of Works of the Province of Canada, 1841–1846." *Ontario History* 70, no. 3 (September 1978): 171–88

Poole, J[ohn] I[rving]. "The Fight at Battle Hill." London and Middlesex Historical Society *Transactions* 4 (1913): 7–61

Quaife, Milo Milton, ed. *War on the Detroit: The Chronicles of Thomas Verchères de Boucherville and The Capitulation by an Ohio Volunteer*. The Lakeside Classics, no. 38. Chicago, Illinois: The Lakeside Press, 1940

Raymond, Ethel T. *Tecumseh: A Chronicle of the last Great Leader of his People*. Chronicles of Canada Series, no. 17. Toronto, Ontario: Glasgow, Brook and Company, 1915

Rea, J[ames] E. *T.A. Crerar: A Political Life*. Montreal, Quebec and Kingston, Ontario: McGill-Queen's University Press, 1997

[Richardson, John]. "A Trip to Walpole Island and Port Sarnia." *The Literary Garland* 7, no. 1 (January 1849): 3–26

– *Eight Years in Canada*. Montreal, Canada East: H.H. Cunningham, 1847

Robb, Wallace Havelock. *Tecumtha: Shawnee Chieftain – Astral Avatar*. Kingston, Ontario: Abbey Dawn Press, 1958

Romney, Paul. "Mowat, Sir Oliver." In *Dictionary of Canadian Biography* 13: 724–42

Sabathy-Judd, Linda, trans. and ed. *Moravians in Upper Canada: The Diary of the Indian Mission of Fairfield on the Thames, 1792–1813*. Toronto, Ontario: The Champlain Society, 1999

Sea, Forest, and Prairie: Being Stories of Life and Adventure in Canada Past and Present, by Boys and Girls in Canada's Schools. Montreal, Quebec: John Dougall and Son, Witness Office, 1893

Sheik, Joe. "A Return to Battle Hill: Re-Interpreting the Battle of the Longwoods." *London and Middlesex Historian* 19 (autumn 1992): 5–22

Sprague, Stuart S. "The Death of Tecumseh and the Rise of Rumpsey Dumpsey: The Making of a Vice President." *The Filson Club History Quarterly* 59, no. 4 (October 1985): 455–61

Stagg, [John] C.A. *Mr Madison's War: Politics, Diplomacy, and Warfare in the Early American Republic, 1783–1830.* Princeton, New Jersey: Princeton University Press, 1983

Ste. Croix, Lorne. "Holmes, Benjamin." In *Dictionary of Canadian Biography* 9: 396–7

Stevenson, Hugh A. "James John Talman: Historian and Librarian." In *Aspects of Nineteenth-Century Ontario:* 3-18. Edited by F.H. Armstrong, H.A. Stevenson, and J.D. Wilson. Toronto, Ontario: University of Toronto Press, 1974

Sugden, John. *Tecumseh: A Life.* New York, New York: Henry Holt and Company, 1998

– *Tecumseh's Last Stand.* Norman, Oklahoma: University of Oklahoma Press, 1985

Thatcher, Benjamin B. *Indian Biography.* New York, New York: J. and J. Harper, 1832

Titley, E. Brian. *A Narrow Vision: Duncan Campbell Scott and the Administration of Indian Affairs in Canada.* Vancouver, British Columbia: University of British Columbia Press, 1986

Toronto City Directory, 1901. Toronto, Ontario: Might Directories, 1901

Tucker, Glenn. *Tecumseh: Vision of Glory.* New York, New York: Bobbs-Merrill Company, 1956

Tupper, Ferdinand Brock. *Family Records.* [St Peter Port], Guernsey: Stephen Barbet, 1835

– *The Life and Correspondence of Major-General Sir Isaac Brock, K.B.* London, England: Simpkin, Marshall and Company, 1845

Turner, Wesley B. *British Generals in the War of 1812: High Command in the Canadas.* Kingston, Ontario: McGill-Queen's University Press, 1999

Vernon's City of Chatham Directory for the Year 1908. Hamilton, Ontario: Henry Vernon, 1908

Voegelin, Erminie Wheeler. *Mortuary Customs of the Shawnee and Other Eastern Tribes.* Prehistory Research Series, vol. 2, no. 4. Indianapolis, Indiana: Indiana Historical Society, 1944; reprint ed., New York, New York: AMS Press, 1980

Watson, O[mar] K. "Moraviantown." Ontario Historical Society *Papers and Records* 28 (1932): 125–31

– "Thomas Gowman's Reminiscences." *Western Ontario Historical Notes* 3, no. 1 (March 1945): 14–17

W[ilson], D[aniel]. "Hints for the Formation of a Canadian Collection of Ancient Crania." *Canadian Journal* 3 (October 1855): 345–7

Witherell, [Benjamin] F.H. "Death of Tecumseh." *Third Annual Report and Collections of the State Historical Society of Wisconsin* 3 (1857): 312–15

Wood, Norman B. *Lives of Famous Indian Chiefs.* Aurora, Illinois: American Indian Historical Publishing Company, c. 1906

Young, Bennett H. *The Battle of the Thames*. Filson Club Publications, no. 18.
Louisville, Kentucky: John P. Morton and Company, 1903

NEWSPAPERS

Advance (Dutton, Ontario), 1910
Allen County Democrat (Lima, Ohio), 1859
Army and Navy Chronicle (Washington, D.C.), 1838
Border Cities Star (Windsor, Ontario), 1931, 1933–34
Bothwell Times (Bothwell, Ontario), 1879, 1904, 1912
Brantford Expositor (Brantford, Ontario), 1941
British Colonist (Toronto, Upper Canada/Canada West), 1840, 1853
Canadian Emigrant (Sandwich, Upper Canada), 1831
Canadian Home Journal (St Thomas, Ontario), 1876
Canadian Illustrated News (Hamilton, Canada West), 1863
Chatham Daily News (Chatham, Ontario), 1910, 1923, 1927, 1931, 1934,
    1941, 1962
Chatham Daily Planet (Chatham, Ontario), 1901–02, 1907
Chatham Gleaner (Chatham, Ontario), 1846
Chatham Journal (Chatham, Ontario), 1841–43
Chatham Tri-Weekly Planet (Chatham, Ontario), 1875, 1889
Chatham Weekly Planet (Chatham, Ontario), 1871, 1883
Christian Guardian (Toronto, Canada West), 1862
Chronicle and Gazette (Kingston, Canada West), 1841
Columbus Sentinel (Columbus, Ohio), 1832
Daily Advertiser (London, Ontario), 1876–77
Daily Planet (Chatham, Ontario), 1898
Daily Witness (Montreal, Quebec), 1876, 1889
Detroit Free Press (Detroit, Michigan), 1877
Evening Free Press (London, Ontario), 1909–10
Evening Globe (Toronto, Ontario), 1870
Evening Telegram (Toronto, Ontario), 1876
Farmer's Journal (St Catharines, Upper Canada), 1827
Forest Standard (Forest, Ontario), 1995
Free Press (London, Ontario), 1877, 1893–94, 1907, 1909
Glencoe Transcript (Glencoe, Ontario), 1898, 1918
Globe (Toronto, Canada West/Ontario), 1859, 1871, 1876–77, 1881, 1908–13,
    1918, 1926, 1931, 1934
Globe and Mail (Toronto, Ontario), 1965
Hamilton Spectator (Hamilton, Ontario), 1907
Hamilton Times (Hamilton, Ontario), 1910
Herald (Thamesville, Ontario), 1903, 1905, 1909–13
Illustrated London News (London, England), 1856
Kentucky Gazette (Lexington, Kentucky), 1840

London Advertiser (London, Ontario), 1876–77, 1909
London Daily Free Press (London, Ontario), 1942
London Evening Advertiser (London, Ontario), 1915, 1926, 1931
London Evening Free Press (London, Ontario), 1911–13, 1924, 1926, 1928, 1931, 1933–35, 1948, 1950, 1955, 1958, 1963, 1968
London Free Press (London, Ontario), 1877, 1894, 1926, 1950, 1968
Mail (Toronto, Ontario), 1872, 1874–76
Montreal Daily Transcript (Montreal, Canada East), 1860
Montreal Gazette (Montreal, Canada East), 1840–41, 1865
Montreal Transcript (Montreal, Canada East), 1842, 1849
Nation (Toronto, Ontario), 1876
New Era (Brockville, Canada West), 1842
Niagara Chronicle (Niagara, Canada West), 1844, 1849
Ottawa Citizen (Ottawa, Ontario), 1962
Planet (Chatham, Ontario), 1908–13, 1920
Rockville Republican (Rockville, Indiana), 1929
Sarnia Canadian Observer (Sarnia, Ontario), 1918, 1931, 1934, 1941, 1943
Sarnia Daily Observer (Sarnia, Ontario), 1911
Sarnia Observer (Sarnia, Canada West/Ontario), 1864, 1873, 1876,
St Catharines Journal (St Catharines, Canada West), 1841
St Thomas Journal (St Thomas, Ontario), 1877
Thamesville Herald (Thamesville, Ontario), 1891, 1909–10, 1918, 1920–21, 1924, 1929, 1954
Toronto Daily Mail (Toronto, Ontario), 1881
Toronto Daily Star (Toronto, Ontario), 1926
Toronto Patriot (Toronto, Upper Canada), 1840
Transcript (Glencoe, Ontario), 1877
Wallaceburg News (Wallaceburg, Ontario), 1907, 1910–11, 1914, 1928–29, 1934
Weekly Spectator (Hamilton, Canada West), 1859
Western Herald (Sandwich, Canada West), 1841–42
Windsor Daily Star (Windsor, Ontario), 1941, 1955
Windsor Star (Windsor, Ontario), 1960, 1962–64

GOVERNMENT PUBLICATIONS

CANADA
Legislative Assembly
Journal, 1856

ONTARIO
Legislative Assembly
Revised Statutes, 1877
Sessional Papers, 1897–98

Index

123; and Delaware warriors, 123; and Number Two Highway, 126; and Nellis Pheasant, 126; sanctity of, 138; and Fairfield Museum curator, 138; north of battlefield, 139; as invented by Native warriors, 139, 141; near Moravian mission, 139; Native case for, 139; and Abigail Smith, 140; location of, 141; and James Dickson, 142; on St Anne's Island, 209n67; and George Laird, 227n58; and Jacob Logan, 235n64, n66; and Black Hawk, 250n11

Tecumseh's grave: and author's interest in, xvii; and Thomas Moores, 10–11; and James B. Gardiner, 12; and John Richardson, 12; and Thomas Shaw, 13, 178n31; and Yankee fellow, 14; and George H.M. Johnson, 24, 36, 64; and A.J. Nelles, 24; and Richard Oates, 24, 26–7, 30; and Ockawandah, 24–5, 138; and Timothy Snake, 24, 30, 44, 47, 54, 63, 138; and United Canadians, 25, 29, 32; and William Watts, 29; and Robert Marcus, 30; and Daniel Wilson, 33; and Thomas Gowman, 45, 47; and Jasper Hill, 249n2; and Duncan Holmes, 45–6; and Shawnee opportunists, 45; and Jacob Pheasant, 47, 138, 142; and Albert Tobias, 58, 71; and William Merrifield, 59; and Albert Greenwood, 63, 65, 68, 72–4, 76–80, 88–90, 139, 218n60; and Augusta Richardson, 63; and Evelyn Johnson, 64, 88; and Matthew Fisher, 66–9, 139–40; and Wallaceburg Board of Trade, 69, 80; and William Leonhardt, 73–4, 80; and Joseph Johnson, 74; and Joseph Johnson junior, 76; and Olive Hubble, 81; and Oshahwahnoo (of St Anne's Island), 81, 138; and Tecumseh Celebration, 88; and

Edwin Beattie, 90; and John Dearness, 92; and Margaret Brown, 92; and Jasper Jones, 93; and tombstone, 93, 233n43; and burial post, 177n26, 178n30; and McKenzie Nahdee, 94; and Nahdees, 95, 97; and Arthur Carty, 96; London's claim to, 97; and Beattie Greenbird, 97; and Augusta Gilkison, 98; and Andrew Hunter, 99; and Willie Nahdee, 106; and Cornelius Shawano, 100, 107; and Jacob Logan, 111; and Christopher Stonefish, 124; and roadwork near, 125–6; and Nellis Pheasant, 126; near battlefield, 139; and warriors, 139, 142; and Jacob Smith, 142

Tecumseh's monument: promoted for Amherstburg, xvii, 13, 15–18, 20, 180n50; for Montreal, 16–20; and Chatham, 17–18, 56–8, 62–5, 70, 72, 78, 82–5, 221n87, n89, n91; on battlefield, xvi, 22–3, 25–6; 38–9, 43–4, 98–100, 112–117, 119, 123–131, 218n56, n60, 225n32, 229n82, 234n54, 237n3, n82, 241n69; at London, 64–5, 93–4, 208n55; and Wallaceburg, 65–8, 71, 81, 89, 141, 220n80; and Thamesville, 82–5, 87; on Walpole Island, 102, 104–5, 107, 116–25; crypt proposed as, 109, 116; cairn on Walpole Island substituted for, 117–22, 124–5, 141, 232n22, 236n79, 238n21, 239n26, n29; constructed near battlefield, xvi, 130–1, 133, 135–8, 141, 242n73, nn79–80, 244n91, 245n96, 246n100, 249n1, n152

Terry, Mrs D.H., 222n103

Thames, battle of the: and Tecumseh, xvii, 66, 100, 109, 119, 140–1, 247n115, n120; and William Henry Harrison, xvii; and Forty-first Regiment, 3; account of, 7–9,

107; impose their will on Grand Council, 107–8, 110, 114; and Jacob Logan, 112; ignore evidence of a broken thigh bone, 112; and Emerson Snake's committee, 116; decide to fund monument themselves, 117; accept American financial assistance, 118; and Gar Wood, 118–19; praised for bravery during First World War, 119; improve relations with Sarnia Reserve, 120; plan to lay cornerstone, 120; propose slate of dignitaries to attend ceremony, 120, 239n34; annoy Department of Indian Affairs, 120; anticipate statue of Tecumseh, 121–2, 240n40; inspired by Champlain Monument, 246n106; and plans to complete construction of cairn, 122, 238n18; finish cairn, 122; announce plans for ceremonial interment, 122; enlist Norman Gurd's assistance, 123; stage pageant and ceremonial reinterment, 124; hostility toward, 232n26. See also Walpole Island Soldiers' Club

Warburton, Augustus, 6
Wardsville, Ontario, 94, 96, 106, 108, 121
Washaway, 45–6
Washington, D.C., 90
Watson, Omar K.: plans pageant to celebrate Tecumseh, 117, 123, recognizes Duncan Holmes as Joseph Johnson, 196n66
Watts, Edward, 183n21
Watts, William: farm of, 25, 30, 183n21, 194n57, 249n4; bones discovered by, 29
Waubishkink, 52, 54, 56. See also Holmes, Duncan; Johnson, Joseph
Weeks, George N., 234n62
Whig Party (American), 11, 32, 173n5

White, Joseph: retrieves bones, 70, 211n2; resists attempts to view bones, 80, 213n21; hides bones, 101; reveals secret to Silas Shobway, 102–3; death of, 102, 230n4
White, Sarah, 101–2, 230n1
Whitney, James, 85–7, 222n103
Williams, Harrison B., 118, 230n5, 239n26
Williams, Robert, 230n5
Wilson, Daniel: investigates discovery of Tecumseh's bones, 32–6, 38, 45, 77–8, 187n82, 206n36; presented with Native skull, 47, 142, 186n75, 252n32; as president of University of Toronto, 186n68; cranial interests of, 186nn73–4; and George Laird, 206n36
Windsor, Ontario, 17, 99
Wisconsin (State) Historical Society. See State Historical Society of Wisconsin
Wood, Gar, 117–20, 122, 124, 238n19, n24, 239n29
Woodrow, Charles S., 119
Wright, Robert Ramsay, 187n82
Wright, Walter (of London, Ontario), 208n54
Wright, Walter (of Walpole Island, Ontario), 230n5
Wyandot: skull, 142, 186n75

Yankee fellow, 10–15, 44, 174n13, n16. See also Moores, Thomas
York Pioneer and Historical Society: aims of, 181n1
York Pioneers, 22–3, 35, 181n1

Zeisberger, David, 185n52
Zone Township: Upper Canada, 12, 141; Ontario, 129; Gore of, 129